Regional Policy, Economic Growth and Convergence

Juan R. Cuadrado-Roura
Editor

Regional Policy, Economic Growth and Convergence

Lessons from the Spanish Case

Editor
Professor Juan R. Cuadrado-Roura
University of Alcala
Department of Applied Economics
Plaza de la Victoria, 2
28802 Alcalá de Henares - Madrid
Spain
jr.cuadrado@uah.es

ISBN 978-3-642-02177-0   e-ISBN 978-3-642-02178-7
DOI 10.1007/978-3-642-02178-7
Springer Heidelberg Dordrecht London New York

Library of Congress Control Number: 2009930391

© Springer-Verlag Berlin Heidelberg 2010
This work is subject to copyright. All rights are reserved, whether the whole or part of the material is concerned, specifically the rights of translation, reprinting, reuse of illustrations, recitation, broadcasting, reproduction on microfilm or in any other way, and storage in data banks. Duplication of this publication or parts thereof is permitted only under the provisions of the German Copyright Law of September 9, 1965, in its current version, and permission for use must always be obtained from Springer. Violations are liable to prosecution under the German Copyright Law.
The use of general descriptive names, registered names, trademarks, etc. in this publication does not imply, even in the absence of a specific statement, that such names are exempt from the relevant protective laws and regulations and therefore free for general use.

Cover design: WMXDesign GmbH, Heidelberg, Germany

Printed on acid-free paper

Springer is part of Springer Science+Business Media (www.springer.com)

Preface

The analysis of the praxis in regional development policies and the study of changes which have taken place in specific cases are of increasing interest. They contribute to clarifying the problems and restrictions which appeared when those policies were designed, the results achieved and also, the errors or flaws which resulted. All this, together with the in-depth studies about some questions of regional growth, as are the reduction or not of the regional disparities, the structural changes, the evolution of productivity, the role played by the main factors which explain growth, the intra-regional inequalities, or the study of some of those factors, as are infrastructures, human capital formation and the advances in terms of competitiveness, make it possible to obtain some interesting lessons for the future.

The origin of this book has been rather long in time, but in the end it was satisfactorily completed. The aim has been to offer a fresh contribution to the analysis of the relationship between economic growth, regional convergence and the regional policies really applied, departing from different approaches to a specific case study. To that end, a number of contributions have been selected which, although do not cover all the questions which perhaps might be desirable, offer to the interested reader a rich enough panorama about the Spanish experience and policy-makers, academics and interested people from many countries.

I wish to express my gratitude to all the colleagues who accepted to take part in this effort, for their collaboration and their excellent work. Equally, my gratitude to those who in some cases granted permission for including into this book some works that had already been published into Spanish, although logically, they have been reviewed and updated. And, of course, I also want to show my gratitude to Springer Publishing for their decision to publish this book.

I wish that all those who read it can find useful the contributions and suggestions contained in the different chapters. We set as our goal to contribute to the growing effectiveness of regional policies, and in this sense, past experience can contribute to learning and improving their design and implementation.

University of Alcala. Madrid Juan R. Cuadrado-Roura
May, 2009

Contents

Part I The Spanish Experiences of Regional Policies

1 Spain as a Case-Study: Regional Problems and Policies 3
  Juan R. Cuadrado-Roura

2 Regional Economy and Policy in Spain (1960–1975) 19
  Juan R. Cuadrado Roura

3 The Evolution of Spanish Regional Policy (1977–2008) 53
  Tomás Mancha-Navarro and Rubén Garrido-Yserte

Part II Regional Growth, Structural Changes and Convergence

4 Macroeconomic Effects of the European Cohesion Policy
  in the Spanish Economy 85
  Simón Sosvilla-Rivero

5 The Spanish Regional Puzzle: Convergence, Divergence
  and Structural Change 103
  Rubén Garrido-Yserte and Tomás Mancha-Navarro

6 The Sources of Spanish Regional Growth 125
  Matilde Mas, Francisco Pérez, and Javier Quesada

7 Regional Productivity Convergence and Changes in the Productive
  Structure 149
  Juan R. Cuadrado-Roura and Andrés Maroto-Sánchez

8 Infrastructure Investment, Growth, and Regional
  Convergence in Spain 171
  Angel de la Fuente

9 **Public Capital Effects and Regional Spillover in Spain** 187
   Oriol Roca-Sagalés and Hector Sala

10 **Supply and Use of Human Capital in the Spanish Regions** 211
   José Manuel Pastor, Josep Lluis Raymond, José Luis Roig,
   and Lorenzo Serrano

11 **Inequality and Welfare in Intra-Territorial Income Distribution** ... 233
   Luis Ayala, Antonio Jurado, and Francisco Pedraja

12 **The Competiveness of the Spanish Regions** 261
   Ernest Reig-Martínez

13 **Regional Growth and Regional Policies: Lessons from the Spanish Experience** 285
   Juan R. Cuadrado-Roura

Contributors

Ayala, Luis, PhD in Economics from the Complutense University, Madrid. He is currently Associate Professor in Economics at the Rey Juan Carlos University and Deputy Director of the Spanish Institute for Fiscal Studies.

Cuadrado-Roura, Juan R., PhD (Econ), Complutense University, Madrid. Fulltime Professor of Applied Economics and Founder–Director of the IAES, University of Alcalá. Director of "Investigaciones Regionales". He has been President of the European Reg. Science Association and Member of the Council of the RSAI (Reg.Sc.Assoc.International). He has published numerous books and articles, mainly on regional problems, the service sector and the EU economic and social policy.

De la Fuente, Angel, PhD (Econ.), University of Pennsylvania. Senior researcher at the Institute for Economic Analysis (CSIC) in Barcelona. Executive editor of "Revista de Economía Aplicada".

Garrido-Yserte, Rubén, PhD (Econ.), University of Alcalá. Associate Professor of Applied Economics and Director of the Regional and Urban Area, IAES (Institute of Economic and Social Analysis), University of Alcalá, Madrid.

Jurado, Antonio, PhD.(Econ.), University of Extremadura. Associate Professor of Applied Economy, Department of Economics, University of Extremadura, Spain. Main research fields: Public Economics, Poverty, Inequalities.

Mancha-Navarro, Tomás, PhD (Econ.), University of Malaga. Full Professor of Applied Economics and Director of the IAES (Institute of Economic and Social Analysis), University of Alcalá, Madrid. Author of books and articles on Regional policy, Political cycles and Industrial analysis.

Maroto-Sánchez, Andres, PhD (Econ.), University of Alcala, Madrid. Visiting Professor, Autonomous University of Madrid and Researcher of the IAES (Institute of Economic and Social Analysis), University of Alcala. His main research fields are Services Sector Analysis; Productivity and Efficiency; and Competitiveness and Growth.

Mas, Matilde, PhD (Econ.), University of Valencia. Full-time Professor of Economics at the University of Valencia and Senior Researcher at the IVIE. Her specialized fields are Growth, Regional Economics, and Infrastructures. She is author of 38 books and has published more than 50 articles in Spanish and international journals. She is member of the Editorial Board of *Investigaciones Regionales* (Spain).

Pastor-Monsálvez, Jose Manuel, PhD (Econ), University of Valencia. Lecturer at the University of Valencia and Researcher at the IVIE. He has been a visiting scholar at Florida State University (1996–1997) and an external consultant of the World Bank. His research interests include Human Capital, Banking and Regional Economics. Co-author of several books and has published articles in international academic journals.

Pedraja, Francisco M., PhD in Economics by the Complutense University, Madrid. Full-time Professor of Economics and currently Head of the Economics Department at the University of Extremadura.

Pérez, Francisco, PhD (Econ.). Full-time Professor of Economics at the University of Valencia and Research Director at the IVIE. His specialized fields are Growth, Regional Economics, Education and Banking. He is author of 32 books and has published more than 100 articles in Spanish and international journals.

Quesada, Javier, PhD (Econ.) University of Valencia. Full-time Professor of Economics at the University of Valencia and Senior Researcher at IVIE. His specialized fields are ICT, R&D and Innovation policy. He is the co-author of five books and has published more than 40 articles in Spanish and international journals.

Raymond, Josep Lluis, PhD (Econ.), University of Barcelona. Full-time Professor of Economics at the Autnonomous University of Barcelona, Department of Economics. Main fields of interest: Applied econometrics, Labour economics and Economics of education. Recent publications in: *Applied Economics, The Developing Economics and Transportation Research.*

Reig-Martínez, Ernest, PhD (Econ), University of Valencia. Full-time Professor of Applied Economics in the Faculty of Economics of the University of Valencia (Department of Applied Economics II) and Senior Researcher at the IVIE (Valencian Institute of Economic Analysis). His main fields of research are: Regional Economics, Agricultural Policy, and Environmental Efficiency Analysis using nonparametric methods.

Roca-Sagalés, Oriol, PhD (Econ.), Autonomous University of Barcelona. Associate Professor of Applied Economics, Autnomous University of Barcelona. His research interests focus on the link between quality of government and fiscal and political decentralization, and the macroeconomic and distributive effects of fiscal policies. He has recently published his research in the *Journal of Urban Economics*, the *Journal of Policy Modelling*, and *Fiscal Studies*, among others.

Roig, José Luis, MSc. Regional and Urban Planning Studies, London School of Economics. PhD (Econ.) Autonomous University of Barcelona. Lecturer in Economics, Department of Applied Economics, Autonomous University of Barcelona.

Sala, Hector, PhD (Econ.), Autonomous University of Barcelona. Associate Professor at the Department of Applied Economics (Autonomous University of Barcelona). His research interests include the macroeconomic impact of public capital stock, the macroeconomics of the labor market, and the inflation–unemployment tradeoff. He has recently published articles in the *Cambridge Journal of Economics*, *Macroeconomic Dynamics*, the *Scottish Journal of Political Economy*, and *Economic Modelling*, among others.

Serrano, Lorenzo, PhD (Econ.),University of Valencia. Lecturer of Economics at the University of Valencia and Researcher at the IVIE. He has published several books and articles in academic journals on topics such as Human Capital, Economic Growth and Regional Economics.

Sosvilla-Rivero, Simon, MSc in Economics (Autonomous University of Barcelona and London School of Economics); PhD (Econ.), University of Birmingham. He is currently Professor Titular at the Complutense University, Madrid. He has been senior researcher and deputy director at FEDEA and Associate Researcher at the Spanish Ministry of Economy, as well as acting as consultant for the European Commission.

Part I
The Spanish Experiences of Regional Policies

Chapter 1
Spain as a Case-Study: Regional Problems and Policies

Juan R. Cuadrado-Roura

1.1 Introduction

Spain is considered to be a very interesting case-study regarding regional problems, in general, and regional development policies, in particular. This is something which has been acknowledged by the many scholars who have studied this issue who, on the one hand, have always highlighted the convergence of deeply rooted political, sociological, and economic questions in what is now the Spanish State and on the other hand, have pointed out the positive effects of regional policies applied since the end of the eighties up to present date.

As is the case with other European States, Spain's history is a complex one. A large number of events, dates, and decisions have influenced the shape taken by Spain as a State. Although the first great progression towards a unified State took place in the last decades of the fifteenth century, a number of the kingdoms and territories which made it up retained their differences with the rest, either in the form of important legal norms, taxes, language or other questions of the economic and social life of their inhabitants. This situation was maintained during more than two centuries, and although later the effective unification of the country was gradually imposed by the authorities, this did not prevent the survival of a number of differences and claims in some of its territories, as in Catalonia or in the Basque Country.

As a country, Spain does not exhibit the same homogeneity than other States do. This and the historical evolution followed explain, to a large degree, the persistence of the claims for self-government that have appeared in Spain from time to time. The proclamation of the First Republic (on February 1873) meant the writing of a Constitution which transformed Spain into a Federal State, although the restoration

J.R. Cuadrado-Roura
Universidad de Alcalá, Departamento de Economía Aplicada, Pl. Victoria, 2, 28802 - Alcalá de Henares, Madrid, España
e-mail: jr.cuadrado@uah.es

of the Bourbon monarchy laid to rest such idea for decades. However, the claims for self-government were again especially prominent during the Second Republic (1931–1936); during this period, the self-government Charters for Catalonia and the Basque Country were approved, while those for Galicia and Aragón were submitted for their approval practically at the start of Spain's Civil War (July 1936–April 1939). During the years after the Civil War, under Franco's Regime (1939–1975), a clear parenthesis opened, along which the concept itself of "region" was relegated and the claims for the recognition of their differences were persecuted. However, the transitional period towards democracy which began at the end of 1975 put back to center stage the need to solve somehow Spain's "regional question"; this question played a very important role in the elaboration process of the new democratic Constitution.

In effect, the text of the Constitution enacted in 1978 acknowledges the existence of "nationalities" and "regions," which can and must enjoy wide self-government powers within the country. This has promoted during the last 25 years a large devolution process from the Central Administration to the 17 autonomous regional governments, which currently exist today.[1] For many academics and constitutional experts, that which really contains the new Constitution is a federal project. A project, which in opposition to other instances of Federal States, has not been built from something which was already working, but which is the product of a collective political decision whose historical roots go back several centuries.

The decision taken in 1978 in favor of a wide devolution form the Central Administration to the country's "regions" and "nationalities"[2] cannot be understood without taking into account the precedents and conflicts, which have plagued Spain's History during the last few centuries. This process must also be known in order to understand the regional problems which arose in the country and the policies taken in order to solve them.

The studies and analysis included into this book basically refer to the evolution of regional policies since the middle of the seventies up to now. They describe those policies, focusing later on the analysis of the effects and trends observed in Spain in regional convergence, the factors which explain regional growth, the evolution of productivity and the structural changes, the impact of the infrastructures, the role played by Human capital, inequalities and welfare, or the problem of regions' competitiveness. But, as has already been noted, some of the country's regional problems have very far roots which must be taken into account.

---

[1] The cities of Melilla and Ceuta, which have belonged to Spain for centuries, although they are surrounded by the territory of Morocco, have their own self-government statutes too.

[2] That is, towards a State organization which is in a way unique, and which has been called the "State of the Autonomous Regions."

1.2 Spain, a Country with a long History of Regional Self-Government

Unlike that which happens in many European and non European countries, in Spain *regions do exist*, and most of them are not the result of recent political and administrative decisions, but have historical roots which go back a long time. In this sense, it must be remembered that, beginning in the eighth and ninth centuries, Spain's History records the birth of a number of different kingdoms (Asturias, León, Navarre, Castile, ...), as well as the existence of a large number of counties (Urgell, Barcelona, Girona, Aragón, ...) that, after different mergers, not always stable, ended up merged into a single state more than 500 years ago.

1.2.1 The Long "Unification" Process of the Country

The most significant step towards "unification" took place in 1469, thanks to the marriage between Ferdinand II, King of Aragón and Catalonia, and Elizabeth I, Queen of Castile and León, who were latter known as the Catholic Kings. However, one of the most relevant features of this "union" was that, in many questions it was of a more "formal" than "real" nature. Actually, it did not entail the *effective merger* of both kingdoms. On the contrary, in a number of areas (legal, financial and taxation, and the political organization itself) both kingdoms maintained rather significant differences between themselves. Differences which existed also within each kingdom, as the rights, norms, and privileges, which were enjoyed by some territories and cities continued in force. Not even the end of the Reconquest of Southern Spain, which still was in part in the hands of the Moors at the end of XVth century, meant the country's total legal and political unification.

The situation which has been described might be defined as a "flexible union or State," continued clearly during the sixteenth and seventeenth centuries. The Kingdom of Castile, which included the historical regions of León and both Castiles, Andalusia, the Basque provinces, Murcia, the Canary Islands and, since 1512, the former kingdom of Navarre, began a defeudalization and integration process, marked by the creation of the *Audiencias* (as jurisdictional spaces) and by the exclusive representation of the "Royal" or "popular" arm (the urban oligarchies) in the Courts (since 1538). On its part, in the Kingdom of Aragón (which was made up by the Principality of Catalonia and the kingdoms of Aragón, Valencia and Mallorca), regional awareness grew with a somewhat different profile than the former one. The actions which sought to unify this kingdom existed side by side with the survival of some different internal legal norms, as well as with a number of tax and political privileges.

The Habsburg kings (1506–1700) attempted, in general, to respect the charters and privileges enjoyed by each of the historical kingdoms, as they did with the aristocracy, the Church or the cities, depending on each case. Actually, this was the basis of Spanish imperial policy during the sixteenth and seventeenth centuries (Charles I, Philip II,...), whose costs, as well as a large part of its benefits, fell basically on the kingdom of Castile. The attempts to redistribute military expenses among all territories and the Catalonian rebellion in 1640, when its *Diputación* and Courts were opposed to the tax and military charges, which the Conde-Duque Olivares sought to impose[3] with the support of king Philip IV, entail some of the features that continue to explain the differences and attitudes of the different territories which were under the rule of the Habsburg monarchy.

The attempt to really "unify" the country takes place during the reign of the first Bourbon king, Philip V, who through the successive "Decretos de Nueva Planta" (between 1707 and 1716) reduces the tax privileges enjoyed by the kingdom of Aragón, attempts to eliminate the internal custom offices between Aragón and Castile, and orders the abolition of many of the institutions which existed solely in Aragón and Catalonia. However, neither all charters were abolished, nor the taxation system was really unified. Thus, for instance, Navarre's charter (with its own custom offices and currency) or the acceptance of a contribution which took the form of an allotment, which for a time was also accepted for Catalonia. The historical studies make it clear that the former kingdoms were not dismantled as administrative units, but were transformed and became the basis for the Bourbon reorganization of the territorial Administration. Thus, Spain was divided in 11 districts plus Navarre, which made up the historical regions.

During the eighteenth century, the need to promote the whole integration of the country was more deeply felt, and the idea of governing it through "provinces" and not on the basis of the regions and the former kingdoms grew. In this sense, it is illustrative the "Discurso sobre el fomento de la industria popular" (1774), whose author was Campomanes[4], and in which he asked Spain's articulation for the creation of a real national market. However, neither these proposals nor some decisions taken at the time could eliminate the clear conflict between those who were in favor of more centralization and homogeneity in the country and those who claimed for the recognition of the cultural and political differences of the different territories. Thus, in 1812, the Liberals, who defended that the equality of all persons should entail that of all regions and, as a result, the end of some territorial privileges, succeeded in achieving that the text of the Constitution enacted in Cadiz acknowledged the existence of 19 historical regions, raising the need of a better territorial organization and delimitation.

However, only 2 years later, the return of Ferdinand VII and the abolition of the Constitution paralyzed these projects, although it did not mean the total return to the past situation. Actually, the Courts of 1820–1823 (the so-called "Liberal triennium") approved a new organization of the country in 15 historical regions and in

---

[3] Actions included in the *Gran Memorial*, submitted to the king in 1624, which proposed Spain's political and legal unification.

[4] Pedro R. de Campomanes (1723–1802) filled a number of relevant posts. He was Minister of the Treasury, later he chaired different State bodies, and ended up being Chairman of the Courts.

52 provinces, and latter, once the king died in 1833, the Regent María Cristina put Javier de Burgos in charge of designing a *provincial* division, which should prove more definitive.

1.2.2 From the First Federalist Attempt to the Current State of the Autonomies

The remainder of the Spanish nineteenth century was, as it is probably known, a period of frequent political changes and social convulsions. The independence of the American Spanish-speaking colonies represented, without any doubt, a very serious political and economic blow for Spain. Although it took a long time to assimilate its consequences, this event had the positive effect that, although with a large delay, the country began to think about itself and about what should be done in the future. The "regional question," naturally understood as something more than the mere existence of economic inequalities among the country's "regions," continued being one of the issues, which was fiercely debated. Actually, the project for a Federal Constitution of 1873, prepared when the First Republic came into being, included the recognition of the "regional States," and it represented an attempt of solving the claims for self-government, which were still alive in some Peninsular territories, especially in the Basque Country, Navarre and Catalonia.

But the Federal experience and the explosive "cantonalist movements" which it engendered ended provoking that one of the main objectives which the monarchical restoration (1875) set for itself was, once again, the reinforcement of the most centralist positions which favored the elimination of the Basque charters, as well as of other privileges which were still in force. However, this lead to the passing of the so-called *Conciertos Económicos* (Economic Agreements) (1878), which identified the contribution of the Basque provinces to the Central Treasury with a quota, with the provincial government bodies (*diputaciones*) in charge of tax collection. This meant the acceptance of a special tax system, in force in the Basque provinces and in Navarre, which was very advantageous for the companies which operated there and favorable too for the economic growth of the regions concerned. Thus, it is hardly surprising that in Catalonia there were also those who asked for a similar treatment, and that the debate about the political and administrative organization of Spain continued in later years. It is in this context, in which appear the politically nationalist movements of Catalonia and the Basque Country, as well as the claims by Galicia and other areas of the country.

The debate about the regional question or, put in other way, about *how to solve the conflict which Spain could not get rid off in this field*, did not stop with the beginning of the new century. Actually, during the first three decades of the twentieth century the question was always present, although with unequal intensity, while at the same time economic, industrial, and demographic factors, among others, introduced new discrepancy items, which were added to those of a political nature. Unity, as it is thought of in a Centralist State, became more and more difficult, although the military coup of General Primo de Rivera (1923) opened a clear parenthesis during which Centralism and political and economic intervention played central stage until the fall of the monarchy and the proclamation of the Second Republic (April 1931).

During the new Republican period, the historical nationalist claims were again center stage, mainly in Catalonia and in the Basque Country. In Catalonia, the day following the proclamation of the Second Republic took place too the proclamation of the Catalonian Republic, although it was later accepted the proposal of enjoying a Charter of self-government within the Republic Constitution; this Charter was approved in 1932. Equally, in the Basque Country and in Navarre, the idea of having their own join Charter was raised; the resulting text was passed even before than the Republic Constitution, and it gave birth to a joint Basque–Navarre Charter (1932), which later was abandoned by Navarre. Similar self-government claims took place in other Spanish regions, although their approval took place, under very precarious political conditions, during the Spanish Civil War.

The politically fascist-oriented regime imposed by General Franco since April 1939 meant not only the abolition of the Republic Constitution, but also that of all the self-government Charters which had been passed during the Republic. The political system set up by Franco's regime meant the restoration of a highly centralized organization, one in which "regions" had no place as differentiated political entities. The country was governed as a dictatorship in which the *provincias*, at the head of each one was a Representative of the Government, were the only recognized territorial institution. The "*diputaciones provinciales*," (or Provincial Administrations) a figure which had some tradition, were also under the direct or indirect control of the political regime, through the systems for appointing the mayors and the council political representatives.

The process for the transition to Democracy which began at the time of Franco's death (November 1975), awakened and reignited again many of the historical claims for territorial and political pluralism, which have been mentioned above. It is within this context where it must be fitted and understood that which was established by the Spanish Constitution of 1978, whose text gave place to the birth and development of a highly decentralized Spanish State, quasi-federal and in many regards with a distribution of powers and faculties for the regions (or autonomous communities) which is more favorable than that enjoyed by the States in many Federal States.

The new Constitution, besides recognizing the existence of a number of historical *nationalities* (Catalonia, Basque Country and Galicia, basically), which were granted a special treatment, extended to the rest of the country the possibility that the regions which organized themselves as Autonomous Communities could develop a self-government level similar to that enjoyed by the first group. In no time, the 17 autonomous communities which have been set up in Spain[5] were defined,

---

[5] The cities of Ceuta and Melilla too enjoy an Autonomy Charter similar to those of the regions, although adapted to their geographical peculiarities.

which are ruled by Autonomous Charters passed through an Organic Act, a type of norm which requires the favorable vote of the absolute majority of the Lower Chamber of the Spanish Parliament.[6] Any change or expansion of those Charters must be subject to the same procedure.

Really, the Constitution of 1978 represents the attempt to combine two goals which are not easily balanced. On the one hand, it states "the indissoluble unity of the Spanish nation," on the other hand, it recognizes "the right to the autonomy of the nationalities and regions" (art. 2). The development of these principles, which has taken place during the last few years, mean that Spain is today comparable to an advanced Federal State.

1.3 Industrialization and Regional Imbalances

As is evident, that presented in the above section happens in parallel with the growing dynamism and the economic changes taking place in the country, and particularly in some regions, among which Catalonia and the Basque Country ended up leading the industrialization.

In any case, there are two features which must be taken into account. First, that the industrialization process cannot be compared with what happened in other European countries. Second, that since the last years of the nineteenth century appear a number of personalities, the so-called "*regenaracionistas*," who advocated developing inner Spain, the exploitation of the country's own resources (with a special attention paid to agriculture), and the need that the State assumes its responsibilities in order to promote economic growth.[7]

1.3.1 The Country's Growth and Industrialization

In the race for industrialization, Spain did not get off to a very good start. Actually, some Historians have supported the idea of the *failure* of the initiatives aimed at industrializing the country.[8] Besides, such failure took place at the historical point in which it would have been more pertinent and necessary, since the country had

---

[6]The Charters, include not only the name of the corresponding Autonomous Community and its territorial limits, but also the institutions which will rule it, the powers which it aims to achieve, as well as any other issue that affects its political personality, as can happen with the recognition of the use of its own language, beside Spanish.

[7]Mention is made to these "*regeneracionistas*" (regenerationist) ideas in Chap. 2, as they were at the basis of some "territorial policies" proposals at the end of the nineteenth century and the first three decades of the twentieth century.

[8]In this sense, Professor Jordi Nadal published a wide study (which was an extension of another which he had published before in English) under the "*El fracaso de la revolución industrial en España*", (The Failure of Industrial Revolution in Spain), in which he proposes the idea that the

Table 1.1 Yearly accumulated growth rates of industrial production and GDP in Spain and in other European countries

Country	1815–1861		1861–1913		1913–1950	
	IPI	GDP	IPI	GDP	IPI	GDP
Germany (RFA)	2.9[a]	1.6[a]	4.0	2.8	1.5	1.3
France	2.8[b]	1.5[b]	2.4	1.5	1.7	1.0
United Kingdom	2.9	2.5	2.2	1.9	1.9	1.3
Spain	4.7[c]	0.9[c]	2.2	1.3c	1.4	0.3[c]

Source: A. Carreras, "La industrialización Española", in: *España: Economía*, J.L. García Delgado (director), Edit. Espasa Calpe, 1988
IPI Industrial production index; *GDP* Gross domestic product
[a] only the 1850–1861 period; [b] 1820–1861 period; [c] 1831–1861 period, in the case of the IPI, it has been proposed that its growth was of just 2.6% instead of 4.7%

stopped being an Empire and became just a nation. Not withstanding the above, the foreign investment which took place in Spain between 1855 and 1866, with the support of the legislation passed by the Liberals, represented a relatively important starting point for Spanish capitalism. That is why the most recent analyses are not so pessimists regarding the path followed by the Spanish Economy. Of course, nobody disputes that during several decades, Spain was clearly economically behind other Western countries, and that only since 1960 began a much more dynamic industrialization process, which made it possible to begin to close the gap. But, at the same time, it is necessary to talk about the first industrial steps, which put Spain a bit above the level of a typically underdeveloped country.

According to the estimates made, Spain's industrial production index (Table 1.1) grew at a fairly strong rate between 1842 and 1861. During the first three decades of the ninteenth century, Spanish economy had gone through a very negative economic period, and this would justify that later the industrial production indicators were higher, although the GDP grew at a comparatively low level. During the following period (1861–1913), the growth of industry slows down in Spain, although it keeps a level close to those recorded in France and in the United Kingdom, always taking into account the relative levels of their respective manufacturing activities. In the case of Spain, this evolution has been attributed to the fact that none of the large infrastructure projects (mostly the railways) and industrial investments were capable of generating the expectations and profits forecasted. To this must be added, without any doubt, the limits to the production and the traffic imposed by the capacity and size of the domestic market, since the possibilities of the country for winning access to foreign markets were always a very clear burden. Trade relations and investments from other countries into Spain were specially concentrated in the United Kingdom and France, while the Spanish economy held a rather limited relationship with the two countries, which went through the most intensive industrialization processes: Germany and the United States, something which, for instance, did not happen in the case of Italy, whose economy took strongly off since the middle of the nineteenth century.

efforts and initiatives carried out since the beginning of the 19th century ended up in failure, determining that Spain became one of the late comers to Industrial Revolution.

Starting in the second decade of the twentieth century and up to 1935–1936, Spanish industry recorded a significant dynamism, especially in the years before and those immediately after the First World War, in large part thanks to the fact that the country did not take part in it and became a supplier of some minerals and manufactures to the countries in war. Obviously, this process was interrupted during the Spanish Civil War (1936–1939), undergoing later an international isolation period which did not allowed the country to benefit neither from the demand for raw materials and products which the II World War entailed, nor from the strong recovery which took place after the war in Western Europe and the US. The forties and fifties were characterized in Spain by a "autarchy" policy, focused on the domestic market and import – replacing production. Only as a result of the opening to the rest of the world, which began with the Stabilization Plan in 1959, the situation began to change, giving place to a period of a strong economic and industrial expansion.

1.3.2 Territorial Concentration of the Production Activity and Regional Imbalances

The sources available for studying the evolution of production and regional imbalances during the nineteenth century are scarce and they present a rather limited reliability level. Only starting in 1900, and with more certainty since the middle of the fifties of the last century, it has been possible to rely on sources of data with enough regularity (the BBVA series, specifically).

Notwithstanding the above, some estimates have made possible to have an approximate knowledge of the GDP concentration and dispersion indexes between 1800 and 1960. Table 1.2 includes, specifically, the Gini indexes referred to the GDP per km^2 and the GDP per capita, as well as the variation coefficient of the GDP per capita.

The basic data available and the calculations made show that between 1800 and 1900, there was in Spain a practically continuous process of concentration of the production into a small number of regions. The Gini coefficient for the GDP per km^2 demonstrates it, and this trend was maintained between 1900 and 1960. The regions in which that concentration took place are, almost exclusively, Catalonia

Table 1.2 Concentration and dispersion of the GDP per capita in Spain, 1800–1960

Years	Gini indexes GDP per km^2	Variation coefficient GDP p.c.	GDP p.c.
1800	0.1875	0.1853	0.3266
1860	0.2958	0.2127	0.5379
1900	0.3062	0.1677	0.3654
1930	0.3517	0.2210	0.3262
1960	0.4257	0.2079	0.3093

Source: Martín Rodríguez (1992), for the Gini Indexes and Domínguez (2002) for the variation coefficient

(Barcelona province, in particular), the Basque Country (its three provinces), and Madrid. In 1860, the weight of the economically active population engaged in manufacturing in these three regions, and especially in the first two, already was the largest in the country, and during the years 1900–1960 those regions continued in the first places in the ranking based on the GDP per capita. On the contrary, several regions of the center of the country, such as Extremadura, Castile-La Mancha, and Castile y León, appeared in 1860 a very long way behind, both in terms of their income per capita and by the weight of the their economically active population in manufacturing as a proportion of all the economically active population in each region.[9]

As several studies show, the protectionist policy followed for cereals production resulted in the maintenance of a low-productivity traditional agriculture in the central regions of the country. This lead to a progressive loss of their economic importance. On the contrary, regions such as Catalonia, which had already developed a substantial industry for export to Latin America, was progressively oriented towards the domestic market. The textile manufactures experienced a large expansion, competing advantageously with this type of activity which was distributed on the national territory. Equally, it also developed a strong food industry, together with other industries, such as furniture, cork, and paper manufacturing. Starting in 1890, Catalonia developed also hydroelectricity and promoted a strategy of specialization in very diversified metal transformation industries, which turned the region's economy into a basically industrial one already before 1931, when the II Republic was proclaimed.

But mining and industrial development had also other actors in Northern Spain. Asturias had already a hegemonic role in the steel industry by 1864, thanks to the availability of coal. But since 1880, the Basque province of Vizcaya took over this position, thanks to the existence of iron ore and the capitalization which its export to the United Kingdom made possible. During the following years, the Basque Country developed not only a strong iron and steel industry and other for capital goods and metal transformation, but also a chemical industry.

At the same time, most of the remaining regions kept their profile of traditional agricultural regions which, due to the stagnation of their populations and the protectionist policies, maintained their undercapitalized farming estates, with a low productivity and equally low income per head.

During the first three decades of the twentieth century, the trends already mentioned continued, which provoked population movements from the inland regions towards those located on the coast (mainly to the Basque Country, Catalonia and Valencia) and towards central Spain (Madrid). As for the share in the production, that for Andalusia and Galicia kept decreasing, while the fast growth for that of the Basque Country and Catalonia continued. What is now the Comunidad Valenciana also progressed, thanks to a highly productive intensive agriculture and the promotion resulting from a large number of small-and-medium sized industries which manufactured furniture and ancillary products, footwear, metallic

---

[9]Data from the series estimated by Martín Rodríguez (1992) and Domínguez (2002).

transformation, building materials, and other products. The remaining regions were able to hold their ground, or lost positions with regard to their relative weight of their population and their production against the whole of Spain.

Chapter 2 provides data about the regional evolution since 1940 and about the policies applied before and after that date. What must be highlighted out in any case is that, since the Spanish Civil War, the slow recovery of the Spanish economy took place in a context of a *growing concentration of the population and of the production* in very specific areas of the country. The city of Madrid and its province (nowadays the Comunidad de Madrid) attracted significant migratory flows from other Spanish regions, which resulted in an increase of 2.5 points of its population weight (from 5.98% of the Spanish total in 1940 to 8.48% in 1960). Also, its weight in terms of the value of the production increased in almost 3 points (8.58% in 1940 to 11.47% in 1960). The other two regions which increased more their weight in terms of population and production are the Basque Country and Catalonia. In the first case, while its population represented 3.6% of the total of Spain in 1940, it reached 4.47% in 1960, while its production went from 6.5% to 7.91% of the Spanish total. Catalonia, whose weight in the country as a whole was much higher, records increases which are comparatively lower, although very significant: its population increased in 1.7 points when comparing both years, and production went from 20.2% to 22.2%, in 1940 and 1960, respectively.

These advances were offset by the losses suffered in terms of population and production weight by regions such as Andalusia, Castile-La Mancha, Castile y León, Extremadura, and Galicia, in particular, although practically all the remaining regions lost positions, with the exception of some, which succeeded in keeping their relative weight, as was the case of Navarre, or which recorded some progress, as in the Canary Islands.

A logical consequence of the large population movements which took place is that, between both years, the GDP per head of the regions recorded a somewhat convergence process, as is reflected by the variation coefficient of the GDP per head in Table 1.2. Most of the available analysis agree that more than 50% of this convergence process can be explained just by the population movements, which experienced the least developed regions (with population flows towards the main development areas, but also towards other European countries) and, from the opposite point of view, by the increases in population experienced by the most dynamic regions (Madrid, Catalonia and the Basque Country).

As will be seen in the next chapter, the policies with a territorial dimension – but not of a regional nature – applied during the historical period, which we are analyzing (1940–1960), only in a very limited way sought to promote the poorest regions. Actually, the actions carried out by one of the bodies which was in charge of industrializing the country – the Instituto Nacional de Industria – reflect that, with the exception of a limited number of cases, the location of the new factories was more due to criteria linked to some natural resources sited in specific regions and to political criteria, than to the wish to use this tool as a means for promoting regional development. Something similar can be said about the infrastructures or the policy of provincial plans, just for mentioning two more examples. Only part of the so-called colonization policies, which were mainly oriented to promoting farming estates in specially backward regions, could be said that belong to what nowadays is regarded as "regional development policies," as well as the start of specific plans for the provinces of Jaén and Badajoz, although the results were rather limited.

1.3.3 The Strong Promotion to the Economic Development during the Sixties and Early Seventies and the Presence of Regional Policies

Since 1957, Franco's regime, forced by the evolution of the economy and by its own political isolation, sought to increase its openness to the outside world, especially to then called Western economies. Since 1953, the US had already broken the Western blockade imposed to Spain after the Second World War, channeling some economic aid towards the country, which were compensated by the opening of a number of US airbases. But the evolution of an economy, which was basically autarchic, faced growing difficulties in terms of imbalances of the payment account, decrease of the foreign reserve, and inflationary pressures. All this forced the need to apply an Economic Stabilization Plan (1959), in whose preparation took part both the IMF and the OECD, and which meant a very important turning point for the country's economic future.

As a result of the above, a new openness phase begins, with the deregulation and growth of the Spanish economy, which has been the subject of many studies.[10] The Report by the World Bank in 1962 was very critical of many of the policies which had been applied previously and pointed out some priorities for the future. Almost at the same time, the *Comisaría del Plan de Desarrollo* (institution in charge of the Development Plans) was created, attached to the Presidency Department, with the responsibility of designing the first three 4-year plans for the economic and social development, which began to be applied since 1964 following the French model of indicative plans, although with a reinforced role of the State, which was in line with the interventionist political system then in force.

Then began a period of strong economic growth, based on the exploitation of assets which the favorable international situation allowed to incorporate into the production processes. Specifically, the availability of a relatively cheap energy, the access to the technological advances which had taken place, the entry of significant financial flows (foreign investment, tourism and remittances by Spanish emigrants abroad), availability of a large pool of labor and the large expansion of foreign trade. The development plans, with a basically industry focus, promoted the development of the basic industries (steel, chemistry), the growth of construction and of a number of more traditional industries (wood and furniture, iron, textiles and footwear, food) and of others which were going to play a significant role in growth, as car manufacturing. All this takes

---

[10]The above can be seen, among others, in: Fuentes Quintana (1988), Donges (1976), García Delgado and Jiménez (1999), Sardá (1970), Velarde (1969).

place when the economy is undergoing an intense structural evolution, which entails the reduction of the agriculture weight and strong promotion of services, besides the expansion and diversification of the manufactures.

A very clear consequence of this strong economic growth, whose mean value for the period 1964–1973 has been calculated above 5% in real terms, was that Spain closed part of the gap in terms of GDP per head with the average of the Western countries. In 1950 it represented 50% of the level recorded by the UK, when the expansionary period to which we are referring ends, it was already of 70%.

As will be seen in the next chapter, the development plans already included actions which might already be regarded as *regional development policies*, since they are fully in keeping with the meaning of this concept. The awareness that the country recorded strong imbalances among its regions and that during the previous decades, a strong concentration of the production and population had taken place in some areas of the country resulted in the introduction in the three development plans of a chapter in which were defined the actions and tools which should contribute to achieve a more balanced regional development. The most significant policy tool was that of the so-called "*polos de desarrollo*" (development poles), a category which was made up by a number of cities, which generally were located in the country least developed areas (Andalusia, Galicia, Castile y León), or with specific problems (Oviedo, in Asturias, due to its relationship with coal mining), as well as in other places, such as Saragossa (Aragón) and later in Logroño (La Rioja), which due to their geographical location had the potential to become important industrial areas. These actions were based in the grant of aids or incentives to the companies which opened facilities in those "*polos*," in some less important "industrial parks," and in some larger areas, as happened with the Campo de Gibraltar or in Tierra de Campos. In the 3rd Development Plan use began to be made of a figure oriented to the industrial promotion of much wider areas: the "*Grandes Áreas de Expansión Industrial*" (GAEI, Great Areas of Industrial development), whose first example was Galicia (1973), followed later by Andalusia (1976), Extremadura (1978), and Castile y León (1979). Almost at the same time, the INI decided to allocate some assets and its organization to the creation of regional development agencies (the so-called "SODI," *Sociedades de Desarrollo Industrial*, or Agencies for Industrial Promotion), but, as happened with the GAEI, their activities were very influenced by two facts: on the one hand, the political change which began with the death of General Franco (1975) and, on the other hand, by the serious consequences which the international crisis of the seventies (the oil crisis) had on the Spanish economy (Cuadrado, 1988; Cuadrado and Fuentes, 1990).

The assessment of the regional policies applied in the sixties and seventies is made in the next chapter. That is why we are not going to see it here, although it can be already said that the results were very uneven, and that only in a few cases it is possible to affirm that such policies contributed to promote the growth of the more backward regions in the country. In many cases, the policies lacked continuity; in other cases, the selection of the "*polos*" was wrong and, besides, the real participation of the actors –the regions- in the design and application of the actions was nonexistent, or was politically very conditioned.

1.4 A Radical Change in Past Approaches: The State of the Autonomous Regions and a Regional Policy Based on the EU Criteria

Two very significant events mark the turning point with regard to what has been said up to now. First, the *passing in 1978 of the new Spanish Constitution* which, as was mentioned above, meant a very important change in the power distribution and government structure in Spain. A change which opened a large administrative, political, and financial devolution process, in which the State losses weight at the central level in favor of the autonomous regions, which gain it. This will result in the start of the passing process of the Autonomous Charters, the transfer of functions and resources from the Central Administration to the regions, debates about the financing system, etc., which continued up to the end of the eighties and which regarding some aspects is still open. The second significant event is, without a doubt, *the accession of Spain into the European Union in January 1986,* which, besides contributing to a large extent to the expansion of the Spanish economy, implied that the country might benefit from the beginning of the aids of the Community regional policy.

This two important events implied radical changes in the way regional policy was made and applied in Spain.

First, because that policy could have at its disposal a *very large amount of resources* which did not exist before, especially as a result of the promotion of the Community regional policy since 1988. Actually, for the program 1989–1993, the funds earmarked to Spain amounted to €12,206 million (in 2000 values). During the program period 1994–1999, this amount increased more than twofold because besides the structural funds, Spain began to receive also the new Cohesion Fund, which was created in Maastricht for those countries which were supposed to be in a worse situation for gaining entry into the Economic and Monetary Union (the Euro) and which might be worst affected by the commitment to accept a common monetary policy. In total, the amount earmarked for Spain during the period 1994–1999 reached €30,459 million, which in the next program period (2000–2006) became €61,624 million (Mancha, T. and Cuadrado, JR, 2000).

The second change which took place is that the existence of the autonomous communities made possible their *direct participation* in the preparation of the programs submitted to Brussels and which give place to the corresponding final agreements between the European Commission, the Spanish State, and each of the autonomous communities. The above means that the different regions which benefit from the Community aid take also part in the proposals and, to a large extent too, in the final decisions about the regional policy to be applied. In other words, the role of the regional authorities in the process for the preparation and application of the Spanish regional policy has been clearly reinforced.

There is also a third change which must be highlighted, and which has to do with the *discipline* meant for the different levels of the Spanish Administration (Central, regional and local) the need to respect and apply the *EU norms and criteria* in the implementation of the regional policy. On the one hand, Community law has made it necessary to program actions for the medium-long term, which cannot been affected by political changes in the national or regional authorities. On the other hand, it has been necessary to improve the systems for managing the resources and introduce *ex ante* assessment of the results expected, the level of execution *during* the programming period, and the results *finally* achieved. All this has meant, without any doubt, significant qualitative changes which positively contribute to the modernization of the different levels of the Spanish Administration.

In Chap. 3, a detailed analysis of the regional policy implemented by Spain as a Member State of the EU is made, while the impact which the Community funds have had on the Spanish economy is studied in chapter 4.

1.5 Final Note

The purpose of this chapter was to provide a panoramic vision of the regional problems in Spain through a more historical and institutional approach. As was stated at the beginning, Spain's case presents features which differentiate it clearly from other countries. The different paragraphs have sought to shed light on the political, economic, and institutional framework, which constitutes the background of the current situation. A number of ideas can be highlighted. The first, the persistence of the claims for regional self-government which reflects the country's History and which has lead to the institutional structure set by the current Spanish Constitution, which has provoked the development of the so-called "State of the Autonomous Regions." The second, that the regional problems have also had, as was logical, an economic profile which has been marked by the economic differences among the regions, and the attempts to correct them. And, finally, that although there are antecedents, it is since the first half of the sixties of the last century when really began the implementation of this kind of policies, with the goal of correcting the regional imbalances then existing. Those policies have been substantially promoted as a result of Spain's accession into the European Union.

References

Cuadrado-Roura, J. R. (1988). Tendencias económico-regionales antes y después de la crisis en España. *Papeles de Economía Española, 34*, 17–61.
Cuadrado-Roura, J. R., & Fuentes Quintana, E. (1990). El desarrollo económico español y la España desigual de las autonomías. *Papeles de Economía Española, 45*, 2–61.
Domínguez, R. (2002). *La riqueza de las regiones*. Madrid: Alianza Editorial.
Donges, J. B. (1976). *La industrialización de España*. Barcelona: Oikos-Tau.
Fuentes Quintana, E. (1988). Tres decenios de la economía española en perspectiva. In J. L. García Delgado (director) *España. Economía* (pp. 1–75). Madrid: Espasa Calpe.

García Delgado, J. L., & Jiménez, J. C. (1999). El proceso de modernización económica: Perspectiva histórica comparada. In J.L. García Delgado (director) *España, Economía, Ante el siglo XXI* (pp. 7–30).

Mancha, T., & Cuadrado-Roura, J. R. (2000). Política Regional. In L. Gámir (Ed.), *Política Económica de España* (7th ed., pp. 681–727). Madrid: Alianza Editorial.

Martín Rodríguez, M. (1992). Pautas y tendencias de desarrollo económico regional en España: una visión restrospectiva. In J. L. García & D. y A Pedreño (Directors) (Eds.), *Ejes territoriales de desarrollo: España en la Europa de los noventa* (pp. 133–155). Madrid: Economistas.

Sardá, J. (1970). El Banco de Espanña, 1931–1962. In *El Banco de España, una historia económica*, Madrid (pp. 420–479).

Velarde, J. (1969). Lecturas de economia española. Madrid: Gredos.

Chapter 2
Regional Economy and Policy in Spain (1960–1975)

Juan R. Cuadrado-Roura

2.1 Introduction: Objectives and Approach

This chapter considers the main features of "regional policy" in Spain from 1960 to 1975, with a brief description of some of the most significant results. It also describes some background, with reference to several previous policies.

As in other countries, the history of regional policies in Spain is a long one. Some examples can be found during the reign of Carlos III (1759–1788), in the form of attempts to repopulate and develop some parts of Andalusia (Jaen, Cordova and Seville), or to promote the country's economic development by creating public enterprises and new ports. More recently, in the nineteenth century, decisions were made in Spain regarding the centralised design of rail and road networks, with a long-lasting impact on the country's territorial structure. These and other measures applied in the past, however, do not fit into the currently accepted category of "regional policies". Indeed, "regional development policies" have only been described as such in Spain since the early 1960s, although with a singular approach and characteristics.

However, before focusing on the subject of this chapter, it is well worth to mention some aspects of the measures applied during the Primo de Rivera dictatorship (1923–1930), the Second Republic (1931–1936) and the first 20 years of the Franco's regime (1940–1960).

J.R. Cuadrado-Roura
Universidad de Alcalá, Departmento de Economia Aplicada, Pl. Victoria, 2, 28802 - Alcalá de Henares, Madrid, España
e-mail: jr.cuadrado@uah.es

2.2 From the Primo de Rivera Dictatorship to the Early Years of the Franco's Regime

Numerous studies on the Primo de Rivera dictatorship (1923–1930) and the early years of the Franco regime refer to "re-generationist" ideas as part of the ideological background. This political–ideological current, which started in the last part of the nineteenth century, when Spain was experiencing a very delicate economic and political situation, was based on looking inside the country to develop its own resources and productive capacities. "Re-generationism", which included numerous criticisms of the parliamentary system and political parties ("due to their verbalism and inefficacy" and "inoperative government"), advocated the need for Spain to have strong governments in order to develop the country's natural resources and economic possibilities, thus increasing its self-sufficiency.[1] J. Costa, a supporter of re-generationism, was in favour of development of the agricultural sector and the need for a hydraulic policy,[2] but he also claimed that the country's modernisation required an "iron surgeon" capable of suspending democracy for a time, while focussing on applying effective policies. Democracy could be re-established after a period of "regeneration, order and nationwide policies". In the pessimistic context found throughout the country at the end of the nineteenth century, different "re-generationist" authors advocated not only the need to promote the agrarian sector, but also to speed up industrialisation and decisively improve and extend the scope of education.[3]

It is not surprising that these essentially interventionist ideas inspired the government of General Primo de Rivera when he came into power in September, 1923. Later, although confused with "falangista" (fascist) doctrine, the same ideas were also present during the dictatorship of General Franco after the 1936–1939 Civil War.

2.2.1 Territorial Policies in the Primo de Rivera Dictatorship (September, 1923 – January, 1930)

There was no coherent regional development policy at this time. Indeed, for decision-making purposes, the existence of "regions" (previously kingdoms and principalities) was not even recognised. The dictatorship governed from the centre, based on the idea of "more administration and less politics". Action should be visible, covering many parts of the country and different fronts, especially improving the road system, agriculture and the use of water resources. In the first case, the

---

[1] People, such as Lucas Mallada (1841–1921), Macías Picavea (1847–1899) and Joaquín Costa (1846–1911), each in their own style, were outstanding members of this current aimed at political and economic regeneration.

[2] One of the most significant books by Joaquín Costa is *Colectivismo agrario en España*, Madrid, 1911. In the same year, he also published *Política Hidráulica*, Madrid, 1911.

[3] Macías Picavea (1899)

focus was on building and repairing roads, particularly secondary routes. The second involved the development of an irrigation system; in this case, it could be argued that there was at least some attempt to apply a territorial policy.

One of the most outstanding projects during the Primo de Rivera dictatorship was the creation of *Confederaciones Hidrográficas* (river basin authorities). Royal Decree laws dated March 5, 1926, which were promoted by the Count of Guadalhorce, applied an old idea aimed at the integral exploitation of the basins of some of the country's greatest rivers, simultaneously developing electric power production, irrigation, forest repopulation and industrial activities linked to each area's agricultural production, all coordinated by the State and with public funding. This concept, which was supported by a specific development plan for each river basin, had some similarities to the ideas and objectives which inspired the creation of the "Tennessee Valley Authority" in 1933, although President T. W. Roosevelt's proposal was evidently much more ambitious and coherent.

The *Confederación Sindical Hidrográfica del Ebro* (Ebro river basin Authority), the first to be approved in 1926, had been conceived in 1916 by engineer Lorenzo Pardo as an integral action programme in which the river basin represented a single development unit. Subsequently, this scheme spread to other basins, such as the Guadalquivir (September, 1927), the Duero (December the same year) and, a little later, the Segura and Western Pyrenees. Finally, the Tajo river Authority saw the light in 1931, at the beginning of the second Republic.

However, the only basin authority which attained some of its goals was the Ebro, in spite of a clear lack of coordination. New reservoirs were built along the river, irrigation zones were developed, and abandoned or poorly used lands were converted to crop production. Nonetheless, these and other measures applied by some of the new river basin authorities lacked continuity, possibly – as Velarde (1968) suggested – because everything that was done during the Primo de Rivera dictatorship was rejected by principle, but also because of the changes made to water policies by the Second Republic and Franco's new regime. Moreover, action aimed at the long-term could hardly be expected to produce much in just over 4 years, which were largely spent creating new irrigation systems.

2.2.2 The Republic's Water Policy

Neither was the Second Republic (1931–1936) known for its regional development policies as such. There are three issues, however, which were of particular significance in this period: (1) new attempts to develop a coherent irrigation policy; (2) debates and partial application of a broad agrarian reform; and (3) the reappearance of demands for autonomy – and even independence – by Catalonia, the Basque Country and, much later, Galicia.[4]

---

[4]The Statutes of Catalonia and the Basque Country were approved during the Second Republic, and much progress had been made with the Statute of Galicia.

As it has been pointed out, the success of the projects designed for some river basins during the Primo de Rivera dictatorship was rather limited. The republican governments therefore decided to design a much more ambitious plan with nation-wide scope, resulting in the 1932 *Ley de Obras de Puesta en Riego* (Irrigation Scheme Act) and the *Plan Nacional de Obras Hidráulicas* (National Hydraulic Plan) presented to parliament in 1934. According to this Act, this project could not be undertaken by private initiative, which is usually reluctant to become involved in something of this scope, emphasising that, together with basic utilities (irrigation and drainage networks), the chosen areas also required roads, housing and other infrastructures. However, the philosophy of the ambitious *Plan Nacional de Obras Hidráulicas* was based on solving the imbalance found in the Iberian Peninsula with regards to water resources. Indeed, most of the rivers flow towards the Atlantic, while the Mediterranean basin, which is more fertile and has great crop farming possibilities, receives only a quarter of the water. The Plan not only included the development of more irrigation in several regions, but also some major projects which had been contemplated in the past, such as transferring water from the Tajo and Guadiana rivers to Murcia and Alicante, where it was estimated that 238,000 ha of irrigated land could be established. This project, however, progressed little during this period. Unfortunately, most of it was not even started, although it did represent an attempt to establish a well-coordinated, global water policy. Political changes and excessive red tape prevented its application, and then the start of the Civil War (July, 1936) put an end to the country's medium and long-term plans.

The "agrarian reform" issue was the subject of agitated debates during the Second Republic, based on article 47 of the new Constitution, a text which was too ambitious to be enforced without considerable conflict. The *Ley de Bases de la Reforma Agraria* (Bases for Agrarian Reform Act), approved in 1932, included a definition of expropriable land, which depended on the *Instituto de Reforma Agraria* (Institute of Agrarian Reform) and was in turn transferred to the provincial councils which were to assign land to peasant communities, which in turn could choose collective or individual exploitation schemes. In practise, the outcome of the proposed reform was very poor. Just over 12,000 peasants were settled in the 2 years in which the law was applied, far from the 60,000 per year target. Indeed, the reform was practically suspended at the end of 1934, with a new, much laxer text being approved in 1935,[5] although it was practically never applied.

2.2.3 Territorial Development Policies in the First 20 Years of the Franco Regime (1939–1959)

The Civil War (July, 1936 – April, 1939) left the country in a very sorry state. Besides other factors involved in a new dictatorship period, infrastructures – which

---

[5] During the war, expropriations were made in the republican zone, largely of land which had been abandoned when its owners fled to areas controlled by Franco's army.

were never first class – were severely damaged (roads, bridges, power lines and water pipes, etc.). There was a shortage of human resources and many of the country's industrial facilities were practically abandoned or rather damaged. On top of all this, the start of the II World War did nothing to solve the food, raw material and manufactured products shortage in the following years. Additionally, at the end of the Second World War, the allies decided to put in practise an economic and political embargo against Spain, making matters even worse.

In this context, the Franco regime, which was based on an austere and statist ideology, favoured a productive strategy based on the imports substitution strategy, both in industry and agricultural production. The application of this policy gave rise to the creation of a complex network of political-administrative agencies, regulations, controls and economic interventionism which lasted from 1940 to the late fifties, when there was a significant turnaround involving more foreign relations and less economic interventionism. A start had already been made on some changes in 1953, when the country received the first financial and material aid from the US, but economic policy remained basically unaltered until 1957. This process of change culminated in the need to solve the severe disequilibria found in the Spanish economy in mid-1959 (growing inflation, foreign deficit, economic sluggishness, etc.), which gave rise to a Stabilisation Plan supported by the OEEC (now OECD), the IMF and other international agencies. This plan represented the start of a period of greater foreign involvement (trade and international capital investment) and relative deregulation process, which led to the strong economic growth to be discussed later.

There was no coherent regional development policy in Spain in this period (1940–1959). Indeed, the predominant autarchy, centralism and interventionism did help to reduce the country's regional differences, even though there was much emigration from the more backward areas to the more developed Spanish regions (Catalonia, the Basc Country, Madrid, in particular) and to some European countries, as France, Switzerland, Germany and the UK.

Table 2.1 shows the GDP per capita of each region (now Autonomous Regions) in 1940 and 1960. We can see that some of the more underdeveloped areas (such as Andalusia and Extremadura) registered values far below the country average. Several more developed regions, however, increased their per capita GDP although, as their population was increasing due to immigration, the comparative index with the Spanish average is also lower. This does not mean that regional differences diminished. As shown in Table 2.2, in the 1940–1960 period, the weight of three regions, Madrid, Catalonia and the Basque Country, increased considerably both in terms of total population and of their contribution to the country's total production.

As it is reasonable, numerous measures taken at the central level along the first 20 years of the Franco's regime did have a clear regional impact. Initially, most of them focused on repairing the damage caused by the Civil War, although subsequently, thanks to the *Instituto Nacional de Industria* (National Institute of Industry – INI) and the facilities and aid granted to established or new manufacturing companies, the country's industrialisation was also promoted. "Regional" development programmes proper, however, were never considered. From a political perspective, and this was a key aspect of the dictatorship, the country was governed almost absolutely

Table 2.1 Per capita GDP of Spanish autonomous regions. In constant 1995 pesetas. Spain = 100

	1940	1960
Andalusia	71.7	68.8
Aragon	100.4	100.5
Asturias	112.7	100.1
Balearic Islands	163.1	147.8
Canary Islands	102.1	92.8
Cantabria	95.4	99.2
Castilla-La Mancha	61.7	72.1
Castilla y Leon	73.3	77.1
Catalonia	161.8	148.1
Extremadura	55.8	54.0
Galicia	72.7	73.0
Madrid	192.9	180.4
Murcia (Region)	75.8	82.9
Navarre	104.7	106.4
Basque Country	166.7	150.4
La Rioja	114.2	108.3
Valencia (Region)	105.0	99.8

Source: The author, with BBVA series data, Alcaide (2003)

Table 2.2 Variations in the relative weight of the Autonomous Regions as % of population and total production value

	% Population 1940	% Population 1960	% Production value 1940	% Production value 1960
Andalusia	20.0	19.37	15.37	12.74
Aragón	4.05	3.64	4.07	3.76
Asturias	3.30	3.24	3.59	3.36
Balearic Islands	1.56	1.47	2.08	1.77
Canary Islands	2.61	3.08	2.25	2.32
Cantabria	1.52	1.44	1.59	1.72
Castilla-La Mancha	7.45	6.52	4.73	4.60
Castilla y Leon	10.46	9.40	8.36	7.42
Catalonia	11.10	12.83	20.26	22.22
Extremadura	4.75	4.54	2.61	2.28
Galicia	10.04	8.62	6.35	5.52
Madrid	5.98	8.48	8.58	1.47
Murcia (Region)	2.77	2.64	2.14	2.02
Navarre	1.38	1.32	1.52	1.52
Basque Country	3.60	4.47	6.50	7.91
La Rioja	0.84	0.76	0.99	0.87
Valencia (Region)	8.60	8.18	8.71	8.50

Source: The author with BBVA data, Alcaide (2003). Spain = 100

from "the centre". The provincial authorities, handpicked by the government or falsely elected through the so-called "organic democracy" system, have only been performing the control and enforcement functions, ordered and monitored by the central government. The policies applied during these years, then, can only be described as essentially interventionist (González, 1981; Tamames, 1973).

Following is a brief description of the measures applied with regional effects or clear territorial impacts:

2.2.3.1 Reconstruction Works

This policy was basically focused on repairing the most damaged infrastructures during the Civil War: roads, railways, canals, ports and other projects. One of the priorities of the new political regime was to identify solutions for the best use of water, both for agrarian purposes and power production. In this respect, the *Plan General de Obras Hidráulicas* was an essential part of the *Plan General de Obras Públicas* (General Public Works Plan) approved in 1940. It gave rise to significant investment in irrigation, defence and water supply (around 21,170 million pesetas from 1940 to 1960, equivalent to approximately 32 million as of 1995, a rather significant figure at the time). One of the plan's highlights was the construction,[6] between 1940 and 1960, of 1,162 dams over 15 m high, all over Spain, with a water storage capacity of 78,000 Hm.^{3}

Although these projects certainly had a "regional" impact, they were clearly not part of a policy aimed at reducing "regional" imbalances. They focused on regulating the country's use of water and the resource's availability. Indeed, a regional development approach was incompatible with the political and economic dogma of the new political regime, and the construction of dams was, if anything, part of the "*armatoste dirigista que se levantó bajo el pretexto de la reconstrucción económica*"[7] (González, 1981, p. 506). However, it certainly helped to improve the water problem that the country had been suffering for years.

2.2.3.2 Colonisation Policy

This policy's main goal was to increase agrarian production by creating new irrigation systems and infrastructures covering large farming areas. Initially (1939), the State undertook to do the basic works (dams, canals and irrigation ditches), leaving the individuals concerned to convert the land. In 1946, it was decided to favour smaller holdings (described as being of "local interest"), with the State collaborating with councils and colonisation groups. The results were poor, so a new *Ley de Colonización y Distribución de la Propiedad de las Zonas Regables* (Irrigatable Area Property Colonisation and Distribution Act) was passed in 1949. The measures were applied by the *Instituto Nacional de Colonización* (National Institute of Colonisation – INC), which established a general project for selected areas, fixing the prices to be paid for expropriations, the type of crop and the maximum amount which could be reserved for the grower–owners of the areas to

---

[6]Data estimated from Mortes (1963).

[7]"A dirigist apparatus built up to carry out the economic reconstruction of the country".

be turned to irrigated. The tenants were granted an administrative concession enabling them to purchase the property after a certain time. The outcome is shown by the figures in Table 2.3.

Additionally, it must be noted that: (1) the resulting property was always very small (from 4 to 8 ha); (2) the tenants were often people/families from non-adjacent geographical areas; (3) modern production techniques (e.g. use of machinery) were not contemplated; and (4) many of the tenants finally left their assigned land because of low returns. This policy was officially described as an agricultural modernisation programme; as such, it was a complete failure.

2.2.3.3 Industrialisation: The INI

One of the new regime's basic objectives was to "industrialise" the country, based on the autarchic idea of substituting imports. The starting basis of this policy were the industry laws of 1939, which were highly protectionist of existing industry, and the creation of the *Instituto Nacional de Industria* (INI) as a State agency for fostering industrial development.

The INI was responsible for substituting private initiative, if necessary, in the development of basic industries, and also for opening new production fronts, particularly in relation to national defence and economic autarchy. The Institute was funded by the State (up to 1958 by issuing government bonds and subsequently with more transparent budgetary allocations), by credit lines available at the Bank of Spain, by business profits and by banks and savings banks, which were forced to invest part of their resources in shares in the Institute and related companies. Its activities have mainly been focused on the development of basic manufacturing sectors and electric power production. Investments were made in car manufacture (SEAT, the product of an agreement with Fiat), steel (ENSIDESA and Altos Hornos Mediterráneo), shipbuilding (in Bilbao, Galicia, Cadiz and Cartagena), mining (HUNOSA, coal), paper mills (E.N. de Celulosa, in Pontevedra) and machinery (Babcock Wilcox, La Maquinista, etc.).

Table 2.3 Measures taken by *Instituto Nacional de Colonización* and *Instituto de Reformas y Desarrollo Agrario* (Institute of Agrarian Reform and Development) in matters of irrigation

Years	(1)	(2)	(3)	(4)	(5)
1939–1952	9.707	75.132	199.095	27.498	9.707
1952–1956	72.389	120.099	109.888	8.392	82.096
1957–1960	87.947	47.609	81.574	6.873	170.043
1961–1962	54.162	53.788	30.812	3.036	224.206
Totals	224.205	296.628	421.639	45.299	224.206

Source: INE and INC data (R. Tamames, *Estructura Econ. España*, 14th ed., 1982)
(1) Practically irrigatable surface area dominated by INC networks (in ha)
(2) Surface area converted to irrigated land with the support of the Colonisation Act (in ha)
(3) Land occupied by INC (ha)
(4) Tenants installed by INC
(5) Cumulative total hectares converted to irrigation (ha)

2.2.3.4 Two Singular Regional Projects: The Badajoz Plan and the Jaen Plan

In spite of their meagre results, these two projects could accurately be described as regional planning measures.[8] In both cases, the aim was to have an effect in two very underdeveloped provinces, with high unemployment and poverty rates, large landowners and a water shortage. In the case of Badajoz, an initial Ordinance Plan (1948) was followed by the *Plan de obras, colonización e industrialización de la provincia* (Provincial works, colonisation and industrialisation plan) of 1952 (the "Badajoz Plan" proper), aimed at solving three problems. Its main objectives were to improve the rural population's standard of living, compensate for the area's lack of resources and correct the poor use of existing resources. One basic goal was to convert dry land to irrigation (based on colonisation operations), but others were product industrialisation "in situ" and to improve the area's infrastructures (forest repopulation, roads and communications, electrification, etc.). Application of the Plan was not completed by the early sixties, and in 1964, these goals were integrated into development plans.

The Jaen Plan, approved in 1953, established the following objectives: the construction of major hydraulic works and conversion of dry land to irrigation, land preservation and forest repopulation; improved communications; mining research and programmes in favour of industrialisation, seeking private initiative. Indeed, the province's industrialisation, supported by different incentives and grants, largely failed because of the shortage of investment by new firms and their limited competitiveness.[9]

2.2.3.5 Provincial Plans

This policy saw the light in 1957 and was actually a way for the central Government to create minor infrastructures in the country's different provinces and towns. It was never economically significant (1,000 million pesetas in 1957) and its goals were largely political: to provide resources with which to satisfy requests from local and provincial authorities, helping to solve some infrastructure-related problems. To a certain extent, the programme's "technical" management was left to the Provincial Technical Services Commissions, which received the demands from different provincial (*Diputaciones*) and local authorities. These commissions comprised both political and technical officials, in an attempt to harmonise the objectives and interests of both the State and its regions. The "Provincial Plan" programme lasted until 1975.

---

[8] For further information, see Siguán (1963), Fernández (1975), Ortega (1973) and González (1981).

[9] This is recognised, for example, in the texts of the Regional Development part of the Second Development Plan (1968).

2.3 Regional Economy and Policy in 1960–1975

2.3.1 The Stabilisation Plan, The World Bank Report and the New Economic Development Policy

As it has been stated previously, the Spanish economic policy started to change in 1957, when Franco made ministerial changes and the economy became the responsibility of a couple of ministers described as "technocrats". They immediately started to deregulate the existing economic system, by eliminating the multiple exchange system, freezing public wages and salaries, establishing a new credit policy, reorganising the banking system, introducing investment programming, etc. However, economic equilibrium was not accomplished and this led to the *Plan de Estabilización* (Stabilisation Plan) approved in July, 1959 with the support of the OEEC (of which Spain had been a member since 1958) and the International Monetary Fund. Its immediate goals were to stop the inflation process, tore establish the balance of trade, and to deregulate international economic relations, making the peseta a convertible currency and supporting to free economic activity in Spain. Indeed, the Plan was the start of a period of considerable economic expansion in terms of growth and structural transformation of industry and trade, even leading to what was known as the "Spanish economic miracle" (Donges, 1976). The Stabilisation Plan, then, was a turning point in an essential economic reforms project aimed at integrating Spain into an open market system, fostering the efficient use of productive resources and thus ensuring economic development (Fuentes Quintana, 1984, 1988).

These stabilising measures produced a shock in both the economy and the expectations of businesses and other social agents, practically paralysing the economy for a year and a half. However, by the end of 1961, the Spanish economy was showing symptoms of embarking upon a period of growth which was to characterise the entire 1960s and the early 1970s, a period in which there were important structural changes in the productive system and no less important social changes, which certainly helped along the transition to democracy after Franco's death in 1975.

From our perspective, the report on the Spanish economy issued by the World Bank (WB) in 1962 upon the request of the Spanish Minister of Public Finance is of particular interest. It was intended to suggest measures to promote the country's economic development, and included numerous criticisms of the economic policy applied in previous years. It was particularly critical of agrarian policy, both because of its protectionism of cereal crops and its marketing and distribution methods, or the colonisation policy based on intensive irrigation. The WB report emphasised the high cost of this policy, suggesting that more attention should be paid to individual farm reforms, seed enhancement, the use of fertilisers and fostering the use of machinery. It also criticised the dispersion of the projects which had been completed in relation to the resources used, and the results of the

Badajoz and Jaen plans, in view of the limited number of direct beneficiaries relative to their high cost. With regards to road infrastructures, the report suggested the need to act on many fronts: reform of RENFE (the national railway company), preference being given to road transport, recommending promotion of the Mediterranean axis with a huge motorway following the coast from France to the south. It also included some guidelines regarding port and navigation policy.[10] Of course, the report also criticised the interventionist industrial policy applied in the previous 20 years, suggesting a need for a free marketplace and elimination of the regulations which had hindered Spanish growth and prevented the country's productive system from being more competitive.

2.3.2 National Development Planning: Some Keys to Understanding the Role of Regional Factors and Development Policies

The Development Plans established during the period 1964–1975 followed the French "indicative plan" model, although the public sector played a more important role in Spain. The First Development Plan covered the 1964–1967 period; the Second Plan covered 1968–1971, but did not actually start to be applied until 1969, as it was delayed for a year due to economic adjustment and devaluation measures applied to solve the inflation and current account balance disequilibrium problems. The Third Plan was designed for the 1972–1975 period and, formally, there was also a Fourth Plan (1976–1979), which was never applied due to political changes (Franco's death in 1975; start of the democratic transition, culminating with the new 1978 Constitution) and the growing impact of the international economic crisis of the 1970s.

From a global perspective, these Development Plans were basically aimed at fostering the growth of the Spanish economy using a sectoral approach. The issue of "regional development", however, was also included in all Development Plans approved, although with some premises and constraints which are well worth mentioning.

One of the fundamental "keys" for understanding regional policy in Spain after 1960, particularly from 1964 to 1975, is the *political* context. Not only because of the peculiar aspects of the Franco regime, with its evident implications, but also because of two specific, *basically political* issues which conditioned such a policy. The first is that it refused to recognise any kind of "region" per se, because the very existence of regions was politically unacceptable and everything was seen from a "centralist" political and economic perspective. The Central Administration was

---

[10]Criticisms of the report were compiled in a book coordinated by Fuentes Quintana (1963).

the true protagonist of what was known as the "regional development policy", and the political and administrative units involved were *provinces* and/or *boroughs*.[11]

There is also a second essentially *political* issue which needs to be highlighted to understand the regional policy applied from 1964 to 1975/1976. The Plan's Commissariat, which was responsible for promoting and ordering the country's economic development after 1962–1963, was an area of the government dominated by the so-called "technocratic" sector. López Rodó, the minister in charge of the Commissariat, spent several years in a trial of strength with the men of the *Sindicato Vertical* (vertical trade union) (who had always paid some attention to regional problems) and politicians most directly linked to the so-called *Movimiento Nacional* (National Movement).[12] This lengthy confrontation was not helped by the fact that the principal regional policy instrument (the "development poles") was an exclusive competence of the Plan's Commissariat, with no interference from the provincial government's and the local authorities, which were generally closer to *neo-falangist* political sectors.

Focusing on the strict economic field, we find another of the keys which helps to explain the evolution of regional policy from the early 1960s to the mid-1970s. We are referring to the role assigned to "regional policy" in the growth process found in Spain from the early sixties on.

The fundamental aspects of Spanish growth in the sixties have been studied in depth elsewhere. Briefly, the Spanish growth "model" of the time was based, on the one hand, on heavy capital input from Spain's presence in the world economy (foreign investment, emigrants' remittances and income from tourism) and surplus formation and, on the other hand, on the mobilisation of hand labour, as people had been emigrating both abroad, to France, Germany and other central European countries, and to the country's most dynamic regions, especially the Basque Country, Catalonia and Madrid, since the 1950s.

Industry and the growth of tourism were the two main protagonists of this period of expansion. The year-on-year growth rates registered by Spanish industrial production in the sixties were always higher than those of other sectors (agrarian and services), and of decisive importance in the evolution of the Spanish GDP which, in real terms, rose to an annual average rate of over 6.5% in the 1961–1970 period, the highest in western Europe. This industrial expansion, together with tourism and a growing domestic demand, also determined significant growth in a series of service subsectors.

---

[11] There were two basic reasons for this: first, in the Spanish Napoleonic-style administration, the country 'provincial' organisation was a fundamental part of its governance; secondly, we have to remember that the political-administrative system under France had reinforced the provinces against a possible increase in historically based regionalist and nationalist claims.

[12] Indeed, the *Movimiento Nacional*, which arose after the Civil War, comprised most of the country's most retrograde forces: *falangistas*, members of the single Trade Union, members of the military linked to Franco, etc. It was actually a highly complex network based on elementary principles but with internal discrepancies.

Four aspects characterise industrial growth in Spain in this period:

1. Industrial expansion involved much greater *capitalisation* of the sector. Industrial growth was supported by the development of a small number of sectors with a high capital-product ratio (steel, metal, shipbuilding, chemicals and so on)
2. *Foreign direct investments* played a crucial role in some fields; foreign capital consolidated positions in a set of decisive sectors
3. The existing *geographical* concentration of industrial activity increased considerably between 1960 and 1973, as shown by series concerning provincial distribution of income and
4. Finally, the deregulation of imports and subsequent *protectionism* against foreign trade helped to support the industrialisation process

Along the 12 years of intense economic growth (1962–1973), economic policy merely "accompanied" the expansion process, which it helped to finance through official credit agencies, privileged financing circuits, concentrated public investment and low tax pressure, etc.

The question is: what role did "regional policy" really play in this context? The answer is clear: it played a *subsidiary* role and, as was to be expected, lost the unequal battle between *sectoral growth on a nationwide scale*, strongly supported by the authorities, and the more modestly funded *development of depressed areas*. The chosen type of growth gave nearly absolute priority to sectoral expansion, determining its *geographical concentration* (Madrid, Barcelona and surrounding area, and the Basque Country). Only in a few cases were sectoral priorities consistent with regional development goals.

Finally, following are some of the characteristic aspects of *regional policy* at the time, all of which had considerable impact on outcomes.

The first was the *dispersion* and parallel *lack of coordination* of the measures applied on a regional level. Although the Plan's Commissariat controlled the most important regional policy instruments and included many of the measures depending on other ministries and agencies in successive Development Plans, the lack of coordination soon became manifest, reducing their effectiveness.

The second refers to a more fundamental problem: the *division* between *regional policy* and so-called *town planning policy*. They should both be designed according to principles of unity and coordination. This, however, was not the case. They were two practically independent fields in the First and Second Development Plans. It was not until the Third that the issue was approached, although little practical progress was made.

The third important aspect is that regional policy was often aimed at *short or medium-term goals*. In several reports, H. W. Richardson and other Commissariat advisors suggested that a regional development policy only makes sense if it is designed with *long term objectives* in mind, and that the idea is not to seek immediate success, rapidly replacing what were originally long-term instruments. Spanish regional policy provides many examples of cases in which instruments were abandoned (explicitly or tacitly; development poles are again a good point of reference) or replaced much before they could have been expected to mature according to international experience. There was an attempt to correct this in the Third Development Plan (1972–1975), where the regional development strategy was contemplated from a long-term perspective. However, spoilers arose in the form of the oil crisis (1973) and, particularly, the Spanish planning crisis.

2.3.3 Regional Policy in the Three Economic and Social Development Plans

We have seen that the development plans established during the 1964–1975 period followed the French "indicative" model. Without referring to their overall objectives, instruments and outcomes, we will be focusing on their most outstanding "regional policy" features.

2.3.3.1 Regional Development in the First Development Plan, 1964–1967

Formally, regional policy was of considerable importance in the First Development Plan. As drafted, it considered not only some of the suggestions found in the World Bank Report of 1962, but also a concern for the income differences found between Spanish provinces. Specifically, in 1962, two southern provinces (Granada and Jaen) were at only just over 50% of the Spanish per capita GDP, and another (Almeria) was at 60%. The two provinces of Extremadura (Badajoz, 60%; Caceres, 55%) and two in Galicia (Orense and Lugo) were in a similar situation. Furthermore, the per capita GDP in some provinces in Castile and Leon (Soria, Zamora, Valladolid, Palencia, Segovia, Avila) was declining, in spite of part of their population having emigrated to the rest of Spain and Europe.

The law approving the Plan defined the main regional policy goal as "to increase the standard of living in regions or areas with low per capita income", and the text itself included regional development among its four objectives, describing it as one of the basic guidelines of all development policies. A regional development policy was therefore designed according to four lines of action:

1. To establish a limited number of *areas for industrial promotion and development* (poles) in low income areas meeting the conditions for potential development
2. To apply *incentives and programmes* established by agreement with local corporations, to ensure the best possible use of resources and foster local initiatives
3. To promote irrigation policies, concentration of land, association of farms and other measures aimed at increasing agrarian production, and
4. To favour *domestic migratory movements* according to development requirements

Far more attention was paid to the first of these four lines than to the others. The creation of "development poles" and the support given to the creation of industrial estates were key factors in a policy which believed that "industrialisation" was the fastest and most effective means of regional development. The Second Plan established the possibility of creating seven poles, distinguishing between two different types: promotion poles (in places where there was hardly any industry but where there were sufficient human and natural resources to turn them into important industrial sites) and industrial development poles (in cities with some industry, but also with a low income level, considerable emigration and too much reliance on agriculture).

On January 30, 1964, Burgos and Huelva were designated promotion poles, and La Coruña, Seville, Vigo and Zaragoza became industrial development poles. This involved the physical delimitation of areas around these cities where new industries would be established, thanks to the incentives provided to new firms, and existing industries would expand. Specifically, the firms involved could apply for official grants covering up to 20% of their investment in promotion poled and up to 10% in development poles, preferential treatment when applying for bank loans, some fiscal incentives, less onerous asset depreciation terms and advantages when importing equipment and materials, etc.

Together with these "development poles", the authorities were also interested to establish industrial estates in other parts of the country, with benefits equivalent to those obtained by preferential interest industry and preferential treatment when applying for official loans.

The First Plan's regional policy also included some specific plans for three concrete areas: *Campo de Gibraltar* (Andalusia) and *Tierra de Campos* (Castilla y Leon), both indexed in 1966, plus the *Canary Islands*. The first was intended to apply to the entire area, although not all its boroughs were included. It contained steps to reorganise the agrarian sector, incentives for industrial development similar to promotion poles, port improvements, renewal of the fishing fleet and an ambitious social investment programme (housing, healthcare services, schools, sports, etc.). The *Tierra de Campos* Plan covered a large area in the provinces of Palencia, Leon, Zamora and Valladolid. It was basically aimed at rural development and proposed to accelerate conversion to irrigation, foster livestock breeding and fodder production, an agrarian research programme and support for the installation of agro-food industries. Finally, the specific Plan for the Canary Islands focused on the agrarian sector, tourism and fishing and included different infrastructure improvements which were less specifically defined.

The Badajoz and Jaen Plans, created in the fifties, were also included in the First Development Plan as part of the regional policy, although they did not become more active. As with other policies applied elsewhere (tourist areas, preferential agrarian industry areas, etc.), the formal inclusion of these plans did not mean that the Commissariat intended to nurture them as its own.

It is not easy to evaluate the First Plan's impact on regional development. The available statistics present considerable differences and the data cannot be globally analysed. In any event, if we consider the calls for projects from 1964 to 1967, we find a huge difference between the number of firms attracted by the first and the last year, as this number fell from a total of 1,003 to a mere 158. There were also large differences between the approved or presented investment figures and the investment actually made; indeed, as of December 31, 1967, the latter represented only 43% of the original total. Table 2.4 summarises the investments made and jobs created in all the poles during the First Plan. This information, however, is merely orientative, as this policy should be evaluated with reference to longer periods, as we shall see later.

2.3.3.2 The Basic Features of Regional Policy in the Second Plan (1968–1971)

The economic disequilibria leading to the devaluation of the peseta in November, 1967 necessarily required a review of the figures in the draft version of the Second Plan, extending the previous Plan until the start of 1969. In all essential aspects, however, there are few regional policy differences between the two plans. Several aspects, nonetheless, did show some progress:

1. Firstly, the Second Development Plan had access to much better statistics related to each area's problems and situation
2. Secondly, it contemplated the need to change the First Plan's approach, applying a more functional concept of regional issues
3. Although the poles had not long been instated, the possibility of promoting "industrial complexes" was considered, conducting studies of productive sectors and different regions
4. At least in theory, there was an attempt to overcome the First Plan's limited approach to regional policy, contemplating "a global territorial framework of reference", according to which the major lines of the country's spatial organisation in the long term were defined by reorganising the coastal areas, promoting the Ebro and Guadalquivir valleys, decongesting Madrid and connecting the Atlantic to Madrid through Burgos and Valladolid

Table 2.4 Summary of operations in all poles (First Plan) as of 31-12-1967

Firm status	Number of applications	Approved investment (in millions of pesetas)	Jobs
Operating	291	16,942	29,382
Under construction	200	19,657	20,284
In project stage	228	20,030	23,393
Total projects	719	56,629	73,059

Pro memoria:
Total accepted dossiers 1,149
Investment involved (millions of pesetas) 84,708.1
Jobs 106,773
Source: Execution reports. Plan Commissariat

5. For the first time ever, the Plan's text recognised that "the Spanish provinces, considered individually, are too small to be subject to specific programmes", adding that "regional promotion areas must be delimited according to the possibilities of areas of uniform and sufficiently large economic potential"

These changes were more symbolic than real. The regional development policy in the Second Plan was practically identical to the first. Even the idea of decentralising regional measures, more directly involving provincial and local authorities in decision-making and projects, was scarcely applied. Numerous ministries continued to retain full executive and programming powers in their respective fields of responsibility.

As for goals, the Second Plan's regional policy distinguished between the short and long term. In the short term, it was necessary to achieve and maintain an acceptable political and social balance between standards of living in different parts of the country and promote a satisfactory national growth rate (at least 4–5%). In the long run, the two basic goals were the economy's spatial integration and efficiency of location and investment costs, although the Plan failed to describe how these goals could be made compatible.

The text also contained some declarations of intent related to the Second Plan's emphasis on social goals. Regional development was considered to be *fundamental* for income redistribution and reducing migration, by creating jobs in underdeveloped areas. Policies aimed at providing social services (education, healthcare, housing, transport, etc.) were also a *priority*, as were the infrastructures of cities and metropolitan areas.

From the instrumental viewpoint, practically nothing new was introduced by the Second Plan's regional policy, with poles continuing to be focal points. The poles of Zaragoza (1969), Valladolid (1970) and Seville (1970) were completed while the Plan was in force, and they were replaced by Granada, Cordova and Oviedo, respectively. The specific programmes for *Campo de Gibraltar*, *Tierra de Campos* and *the Canary Islands* were also in force, as it was the case of the Badajoz and Jaen Plans, although the latter were much more due to political inertia than to a firm decision to attain their goals.

Table 2.5 shows some basic information about the investment involved in all these plans. In any event, the *Campo de Gibraltar* plan did result in considerable development, largely thanks to the industrial sector. By the end of 1971, when the Plan ended, investments totalled 11,308 million pesetas, representing 3,946 new jobs. According to the Plan, regional policy included measures related to agrarian policy (colonisation, rural ordinance, irrigation, industrialization), industrial policy (creation of industrial estates, decongestion of highly industrialised areas, preferential industrial location areas) and services (tourism, education, transport, housing, urban services, etc.). Most of the projects and control responsibilities, however, depended on different Ministries (Agriculture, Industry, Public Works, Housing, Education and Information and Tourism), so that coordination was difficult and outside the Commissariat's capabilities. Most of these aspects, therefore, were never integrated into regional policy.

Table 2.5 Investment in special regional action plans from 1968 to 1971 (in millions of pesetas)

	Campo de Gibraltar	Tierra de Campos	Canary Island Plan	Badajoz Plan	Jaen Plan
Public investment:					
Programmed	8,258.7	8,279.9	13,124.3	2,917.3	1,376.1
Made[a]	6,786.7	3,343.5	11,833.2	1,538.7	1,039.5
Deviations (b/a. 100)	82.2	40.4	90.2	52.7	75.5

Source: Execution report of Second Plan. Development Plan Commissariat
[a]Data up to 1970 for Badajoz and Jaen Plans

We will later be taking a look at the results of the poles. There were clearly both success stories and failures. Examples of the former are Huelva, Burgos and Zaragoza, with the latter represented by La Coruña, Vigo and Seville.

2.3.3.3 Regional Policy in the Third Plan (1972–1975)

In the Third National Development Plan, regional policy continued the trend of the previous two ones, although there were some changes in the underlying philosophy:

1. The idea of "structuring the territory" became the principle on which all future action should be based, integrating sectoral goals, location policy, urban policies and all measures with a regional impact.
2. The new Plan clearly underlined that regional policy should be seen from a long-term perspective and not based on short-term goals.
3. For the first time, it also considered that regional development policy required selective, but coordinated, measures applicable to some historic regions; hence, the "large area of industrial expansion" idea applied to Galicia.

As Richardson (1976) pointed out, the planning team hoped that combining regional and national development in a global spatial organisation strategy would ensure both fairness and efficiency. One of the goals was therefore to hierarchically articulate each region in large metropolitan areas, counterweight cities, medium sized towns and other urban and district areas. From the State's perspective, the national urban hierarchy and the interregional transport network would connect the different regions, configuring a national economic system which would also include the spatial dimension.

This approach involved coordination between different ministerial departments and required considerable reorganisation of institutional structures. However, these principles and guidelines were clearly more a series of philosophical statements than the basis on which the authorities had actually decided to develop the "new" regional policy, among other reasons, because it was evident that the application of such principles would not only have a significant impact on the organisation of the central and local administration, but also important political consequences.

According to the planners' previsions, the Third Plan's regional development policy should attempt to ensure more balanced national development, which involved discontinuing the system of concentrating industry in poles. Indeed, no new poles were foreseen in the Plan, although Villagarcia and Logroño replaced Vigo and La Coruña after completion of their cycle, and neither did it include "areas for preferential industrial location". Indeed, the Plan referred to Galicia as a "major area of industrial expansion" (known by the initials G.A.E.I.), with more comprehensive regional planning covering the industrial sector, urbanisation and infrastructures and paying special attention to the transport sector.

Together with the steps to be taken in Galicia, the Third Plan included new selective regional programmes for *the Canary Islands* and the *South-east*, similar to those established in prior plans. Indeed, the *Campo de Gibraltar*, *Tierra de Campos*, Jaen and Badajoz Plans were still in force in the 4 years covered by the Third Development Plan.

The outcome of the regional policy 1972–1975 was nowhere near its goals. Two events had a major impact on its enforcement: the onset of the oil crisis, which started to be felt in Spain in the last 4 months of 1974, and Franco's illness and death, which not only created political instability, but also disturbed, and partially paralysed, the normal functioning of the State Administration from mid-1975 onwards. Also in June 1973, a government and administrative reorganisation took place, which included the creation of the Ministry of Planning. This decision did not really increase but reduce the power that the Plan's Commissariat had previously had, as an institution directly linked and dependent of the Presidency of the Government.

With regards to the differences between programmed and actual public investment in selective plans (Table 2.6), non-compliance was high during the Third Plan. The reason can be found in the events described above, leading to the Plan being paralysed in 1974 and 1975. In the existing poles, there was also a clear decline in the number of companies interested in making investments and their total amount. This issue is analysed in more detail below.

Table 2.6 Public investment in selective regional programmes 1972–1975 (in millions of pesetas)

	Campo de Gibraltar (1972–1974)	Tierra de Campos (1972–1974)	Canary Islands Plan	Galicia C.A.E.I.	South-east Plan
Public investment:					
Programmed	7,574.6	7,894.3	42,619.0	60,896.1	46,642.9
Made (1)	3,757.5	4,824.4	27,407.4	40,301.1	34,191.5
Deviations (b/a. 100)	49.6	61.3	64.3	65.2	73.3

Source: Third Plan and Execution Report

2.4 Theory and Practise of Development Poles in Spain

The poles were unquestionably the most outstanding examples of Spanish regional policy in the 1964–1975 period, well worth describing some of their features and results.

The idea of "growth poles" was very popular from the late fifities to the end of the sixties. In many countries, although with heterogeneous formulas, policies aimed at greater balance between regions resorted to the idea of concentrating investments in certain areas, with the assumption that they would have a positive knock-on effect on their surroundings. The idea of regional policy based on selective measures, concentrated in a small area, was also supported by the limited resources available. In Italy, a polarised action strategy was applied from 1957 on, particularly affecting industrial implantation projects associated to the Bari–Taranto–Brindisi area. France had its *metropoles d'equilibre*; in Federal Germany in 1963, the authorities established a support programme for a series of medium-sized and small towns which were to act as poles. Sweden used a growth centre strategy in small, but viable, towns in rural areas. Checoslovakia, Venezuela, Brazil, Greece and many other countries also used the idea of growth centres in their respective regional development policies.

Although based on a similar philosophy, the above examples had relatively little in common. And they were not, as some have claimed, based on the theory put forward by F. Perroux concerning *pôles de croissance,* not even in Spain, where there were considerable connections with the French school of regional studies. Only from a nominal perspective is the practical model consistent with the theory.

The modality of development poles used in the Spanish planning was basically very simple. Although there were two different types, aimed at either promotion or industrial development, they both involved identifying a town with a modicum of conditions for industrialisation and delimiting industrial estate-like areas within or around their borders. Firms interested in them had to present investment proposals – based on public calls for bids – and, if they were approved, the State granted them preferential loans, tax and other incentives and possible grants. Table 2.7 summarises the benefits available to firms according to the group in which their projects were classified. A list of preferential industries and services was established for each pole. Initially, the conditions required (capital and new jobs to be created) were minimal (3 million pesetas investment or 20 jobs), although this was subsequently increased to 40 million pesetas or 100 jobs.

The real practise of the "development poles" shows some characteristics and specific aspects, which must be underlined to evaluate the achievements and limitations of this regional instrument in the Spanish case:

2.4.1 Selection

The largest number of poles in progress at the same time in the three planning periods was seven, although there were several replacements (Table 2.8). The first

2 Regional Economy and Policy in Spain (1960–1975)

Table 2.7 Benefits for each of the different groups

Benefits	Groups			
	A	B	C	D
Free investments depreciation for the first 5 years	Yes	Yes	Yes	Yes
Preference in obtaining official loans when other sources of financing were not available	Yes	Yes	Yes	Yes
Mandatory expropriation	Yes	Yes	Yes	Yes
95 per 100 reductions in fiscal licence tax during the installation period	Yes	Yes	Yes	Yes
Up to 95% reduction in the capital income tax on the returns on loans made by Spanish firms and loans with international agencies or foreign banks, when the funds are used to finance new real investments	95%	95%	50%	No
Up to 95% reduction in the tax on property transfers and documented legal acts, in the terms established in point 3 of article 66 of the rewritten text approved by Decree 1018/1967, of April 6	95%	50%	50%	No
Up to 95% reduction in business transaction tax on sales representing acquisition of equipment for initial installation which is not manufactured in Spain	95%	50%	50%	No
Up to 95% reduction in duties and compensation taxes on equipment not manufactured in Spain	95%	50%	25%	No
95% reduction in local taxes on the establishment or enlargement of industrial plants	Yes	Yes	No	No
Grant[a]	10%	5%	No	No

Source: Order of the Ministry of Development Planning of October 31, 1974
[a]In promotion poles, the total grant could represent up to 20 per 100

Table 2.8 Start and end dates of development poles

Poles	Creation	Completion
Burgos	1-2-1964	31-12-1974
Huelva	1-2-1964	31-12-1974
La Coruña	1-2-1964	31-12-1971
Seville	1-2-1964	31-12-1970
Valladolid	1-2-1964	31-12-1970
Vigo	1-2-1964	31-12-1971
Zaragoza	1-2-1964	31-12-1969
Granada	1-1-1970	31-12-1979
Cordova	1-1-1971	31-12-1980
Oviedo	1-1-1971	31-12-1980
Logroño	1-1-1972	31-12-1981
Villagarcia de Arosa	1-1-1972	31-12-1981

Source: Own elaboration

seven poles were located in provinces which were either in the middle or higher up in the national per capita income rating, a criterion which was also applied later except for Granada and Cordova, which were among the lowest in the country.

The reasons why these locations were selected were actually varied and not always consistent. In most cases, the chosen town or city was on, or close to, an internationally important transport network. The most obvious example is Zaragoza, which is in the centre of the Madrid–Barcelona–Bilbao triangle and on the Ebro axis. The city's conditions were also favourable with regards to size, industrial tradition, available infrastructures and the fact that it was the capital of a region with a very low income level. This case's relative success was certainly thanks to these favourable conditions. Valladolid and Burgos were selected for two fundamental reasons: the fact that they were on the axes connecting Madrid with northern Spain (Bilbao, Santander and Asturias) and the region's underdevelopment. In fact, Burgos was one of the most successful examples, largely because a series of growing industries were attracted from the nearby Basque Country.

The election of Seville, and subsequently Cordova, were also justified by the fact that they are both on the Guadalquivir axis and that Andalusia was one of the least developed areas in Spain. Although it was further away, Huelva was also on the axis, and in theory, it was believed that it would complete a dynamic Seville–Cadiz/Campo de Gibraltar–Huelva industrial triangle. However, the results show that they were each developed separately for very different reasons. Huelva received large investments, as the area was in a position to create a huge chemical complex which grew based on a national and international strategy. Seville and Cordova, however, did not receive much investment and scarcely benefited from their poles.

The choice of Vigo and La Coruña was justified as a means of promoting industrial development in Galicia, one of the country's most backward areas. Both cities met the conditions for growth, particularly Vigo, and they were at the head of the future Galician coastal axis. The subsequent choice of Villagarcia de Arosa was also based on the same premises.

Granada was selected as a pole in 1970 for strictly political reasons, in response to local pressure. It was certainly not because of its location, shortage of infrastructures or practically non-existent industrial tradition. Indeed, the project had few consequences for the city and its surroundings, except for some improvements to the roads, which were greatly delayed, the airport and the installation of some essentially local industries. Finally, there was an attempt to justify Oviedo (from 1971) and Logroño (from 1972) with economic and technical arguments, but they also obeyed political reasons and social pressure. Indeed, Oviedo was suffering serious labour and social problems because of a decline in mining and industry; Logroño and its region were complaining of the industrial and economic competition from Navarre and Alava, thanks to their fiscal advantages and the better infrastructures derived from their particular status.

2.4.2 Duration and Results of the Spanish Pole Policy

International experience shows that regional industrial centres of some importance need around 10 years to develop. If they do not have a significant industrial base beforehand, it could take up to 20. When the First Plan was approved, however, it was thought that their duration would be less than 5 years, which was clearly insufficient, especially if we consider the problems involved in providing the necessary infrastructures, none of which had been programmed beforehand, the time required for firms to make final decisions, the time required for their installation and the time it took to create appropriate conditions with which to attract other related companies by offering beneficial synergies.

The authorities were therefore forced to review their criteria. Zaragoza ceased to have pole status after 5 years, but it was the only case in which the term was not extended. Burgos and Huelva lasted for around 11 years; those created after the end of the Second Plan (Granada, Cordova, Oviedo, Logroño and Villagarcia) for ten, and the rest were extended to a 7-year period. Nonetheless, these extensions did not ensure positive outcomes, largely because there was no parallel acceleration in the provision of infrastructures and official support did not increase. Indeed, from 1972 on, the authorities showed signs of tacitly ceasing to support poles, although there continued to be regular calls for proposals.

The only way in which to avoid generalisation when analysing the results would be to study the poles case by case. For the sake of brevity, however, we will use a global approach, with some comments on specific examples.

Three warnings should be considered with regards to the available data. The first is that the available statistics show considerable differences, as they are published in different documents; we have therefore been forced to select the data which best reflect reality, and even to revise this information. The second is that the data pertaining to the different cases cannot always be compared because of timing differences. Thirdly, some of the variations found in the number of firms presenting proposals appear to be due to the fluctuations registered in the Spanish economy as a whole (in 1967 and 1968, for instance), and this also has to be taken into account when analysing the information.

Indeed, the number of firms applying for benefits through poles varied considerably, both over time and between locations. The record is held by the first (1964), followed by a reduction in the number of firms showing interest. By the end of 1974, Burgos and Zaragoza, in spite of the latter's shorter duration, accumulated the largest number of applications (see Table 2.9).

This number could have fallen for several reasons. Although the system created great expectations, they decreased when it was found that the authorities took a long time to review the proposals and issue a final decision. Furthermore, the time it took to solve firms' installation problems and receive loans and grants also discouraged many new applicants. Finally, their number fell when the conditions to be met regarding investment and new jobs were tightened, although global investment volume was nearly as high as on previous occasions (except those affected by the 1967–1968 recession).

The sectoral distribution of investment in the different poles is highly varied (see Table 2.10). In several cases, there is considerable concentration – Huelva, 67.9% chemicals; Zaragoza, 52.9% paper; Valladolid, 56.1% metal products; La Coruña, 53.5% energy; Vigo, 60% metal products – and this is nearly always explained by the presence of an important company with a major impact on the area's development. The importance of so-called "community services" could be confusing, but this concept includes investments made by the national telephone company, which

Table 2.9 Applicants for installation in poles (as of 31-12-1974)

Calls for applications	Burgos	Huelva	Coruña	Seville	Valladolid	Vigo	Zaragoza	Granada	Cordova	Oviedo	Logroño	Villagarcía	Total
First	236	96	81	173	85	113	217	–	–	–	–	–	1,001
Second	72	46	34	43	42	30	81	–	–	–	–	–	348
Third	78	38	19	45	26	24	87	–	–	–	–	–	317
Fourth	64	37	9	23	26	18	67	–	–	–	–	–	244
Fifth	48	25	14	20	13	8	35	–	–	–	–	–	163
Sixth	39	34	19	51	24	16	31	–	–	–	–	–	214
Seventh	9	8	4	12	3	4	28	–	–	–	–	–	68
Eighth	16	3	6	7	4	8	–	49	–	–	–	–	93
Ninth	17	14	14	–	–	27	–	12	32	69	–	–	185
Tenth	18	17	15	–	–	19	–	7	18	51	45	40	230
Eleventh.	26	23	–	–	–	–	–	16	24	39	14	22	164
Twelfth.	52	40	–	–	–	–	–	8	24	56	23	25	228
Total	675	381	215	374	223	267	546	92	98	215	82	90	3.255

Source: Data from Pole Management Office

Table 2.10 Percentages of different production sectors investing in poles (as of 31-12-1974)

Poles	Sectors											Total
	Food	Textile	Wood	Paper	Chemical	Construction	Basic metal	Metal products	Energy	Teaching	Community services	Catering	
Burgos	8.99	2.84	4.80	2.53	23.76	4.63	–	34.24	–	5.41	12.80	–	100
Huelva	2.42	0.14	3.41	0.53	67.91	0.61	13.19	2.15	6.13	0.28	2.84	0.39	100
La Coruña	14.09	0.38	0.71	0.79	2.75	1.31	13.67	10.25	53.52	2.53	–	–	100
Seville	6.32	5.39	0.26	4.72	12.70	25.75	1.27	18.18	22.71	2.70	–	–	100
Valladolid.	9.02	0.65	–	5.28	21.65	5.66	–	56.17	0.25	1.32	–	–	100
Vigo	5.92	3.72	1.82	2.79	3.98	13.82	1.16	60.02	1.76	3.71	1.30	–	100
Zaragoza	6.88	–	1.89	52.94	3.81	7.19	2.90	17.02	5.32	2.00	–	–	100
Granada	–	0.34	0.44	–	13.36	3.43	–	2.00	16.34	–	64.06	–	100
Cordova	24.58	2.69	0.07	1.27	4.35	2.81	20.11	11.74	4.37	–	28.01	–	100
Oviedo	6.71	–	0.30	6.62	3.30	6.10	8.77	21.51	35.80	2.07	8.82	–	100
Logroño	29.12	25.69	–	6.98	4.85	1.63	–	10.55	–	3.71	17.47	–	100
Villagarcia	21.17	12.99	6.97	–	7.56	–	–	29.19	–	4.52	17.60	–	100
Total	11.35	4.56	1.72	7.03	14.16	6.07	5.09	22.75	12.18	2.35	12.74	–	100

Source: Data from Pole Management Office

in some cases, such as Granada and Cordova, represented a large proportion of the total volume.[13]

In general, the presence of these development areas did not substantially alter local industrial structure, except for Zaragoza and, to a certain extent, Huelva. All the poles housed a large number of local small and medium-sized enterprises (with little participation in the total investment) and a small number of major projects developed by important firms, nearly always with at least some foreign stock capital. Examples are the Explosivos Riotinto group in Huelva, Citroën in Vigo, Renault in Valladolid, Secem in Cordova, Telefónica in Granada, etc. These were certainly the major beneficiaries.

2.5 The Role Reserved for Public Companies and other Policies with a Regional Impact in the 1960–1975 Period

2.5.1 The INI and Regional Problems

As we specified earlier, the INI was created in 1941. Its objectives were closely linked to national reconstruction and the development of new industrial activities, aimed at self-sufficiency and autarchy. In this respect, the INI was always nationally, and not regionally, oriented. Indeed, the location of the public companies created by the INI was based on varied criteria: location of raw materials, existence of a company which the Institute joined, or political reasons which only occasionally coincided with the possible industrialisation of the country's most underdeveloped areas. This was the case during the early history of the INI, and no major changes took place during the Development Plans phase. However, 1959 saw the start of a strategic change in the organisation's orientation which involved applying the principle of subsidiarity in relation to private enterprise. Therefore, in 1964–1975, the INI focused on solving its internal problems and restructuring. Only in the Third Plan was the INI assigned a more active role in industrial restructuring and technological research, albeit subject to the sectoral criteria defined on a nationwide scale.

The information regarding INI plant locations shows that their geographical distribution was not based on criteria linked to regional re-equilibrium goals (Cuadrado-Roura, 1981; González, 1981). On the contrary, the provinces and regions which received most of the investments included some of the most developed in the country as far as their per capita income and industrial development were concerned. This was clearly the case in Madrid, Barcelona and Tarragona, although some more backward provinces also received investments because of location advantages and not a deliberate decision to promote their development, even though they were presented as promotional projects; they include Ciudad Real

---

[13] The telephone monopoly thus made use of the benefits afforded by poles to enlarge their facilities, with considerable tax savings and other advantages.

(Puertollano refinery), Cadiz (shipbuilders) and La Coruña (refinery and shipbuilders). Asturias was privileged in that the INI bought up most of its private coal mining operations and created the Aviles steel plant, as well as other smaller investments. Table 2.11 summarises the location of INI investments by region, with aggregate data up to December, 1976.

The criticism launched against the INI for its limited collaboration with regional development led to the creation of *Sociedades de Desarrollo Regional* (Regional Development Agencies – SODI), with the Institute holding a majority share and contributions from some local corporations and savings banks (Cuadrado-Roura, 1977, 1980). The first was created in Galicia (1972) and its programmed activities were broad-based, although its effective activity was always very limited. Other Agencies of this type were created in 1976 in Andalusia, the Canary Islands and Extremadura and lately in Castile-La Mancha. They all arose, then, towards the end of the period under study, when Spain was immersed in an important economic crisis and a time of major political and institutional change, including the country's division into Autonomous Regions.

2.5.2 Other Regional Development Policies

Dispersion was one of the main characteristics of "regional policy" in Spain during the period being analysed. The Development Plans were intended to coordinate

Table 2.11 INI investments: Distribution of cumulative investment by region (thousands of pesetas 1976)

Regions	Total cumulative investment	Percentage of total
Andalusia	23,193	3.7
Aragón	14,465	2.3
Asturias	157,143	25.1
Balearic Islands	10,134	1.6
Canary Islands	12,489	2.0
Cantabria	4,199	0.7
Castilla y Leon	27,374	4.4
Castilla-La Mancha	30,436	4.9
Catalonia	98,411	15.7
Extremadura	2,636	0.4
Galicia	48,003	7.7
La Rioja	236	0.1
Madrid	29,946	4.8
Navarre	9,361	1.5
Murcia	23,464	3.7
Basque Country	5,489	0.9
Valencia	3,982	0.6
Inv. not attributable to regions	124,451	19.9
Total Spain	625,412	100

Source: Data from INI balance sheets

activities dependent on several ministerial departments, but their real success was rather limited. Positive results were obtained in some cases, but integration and coordination were only formal aspects of others. In quite a few cases, reluctance to change was for political reasons; maintaining an instrument provided the means with which to "work politics" in the provinces. The different policies with a clear regional impact included the follows:

2.5.2.1 Zones of Preferential Industrial Location

This system depended on the Ministry of Industry when it was created (1963). In areas officially designated as such, firms could benefit from nearly all the same advantages as were available from poles (taxes, loans, land expropriation, etc.). These zones were not coordinated with the rest of the regional policy during the first two Development Plans. The Third Plan attempted to integrate them with decongestion estates, industrial estates previously pertaining to poles and special regional plans (*Campo de Gibraltar*, Jaen, Canary Islands, Badajoz). The established zones of preferential industrial location are shown in Table 2.12.

There were also created – at least formally – zones of preferential industrial location for *mining* (Santiago de Compostela, 1973; and part of the provinces of Badajoz, Seville and Huelva, 1974), the *agrarian sector* (consistent with the special plans for Badajoz, Jaen, *Campo de Gibraltar*, the *Canary Islands* and *Tierra de Campos*, plus La Mancha, Caceres, *Valle del Cinca*, several districts in Alava, Burgos, Logroño and Navarre and wine-making areas with designation of origin), and even for *film-making*, approved for Almeria in July, 1969.

2.5.2.2 Industrial Estates

The creation of industrial estates had actually started in 1956, although the concept was not very clear and progress was extraordinarily slow. The first programme (1956–1959) included ten estates representing 369 ha of land, although some of them were not fit for use until 1964/1965. The second programme (1960–1964) comprised 19 estates and a total of 1,300 ha, which also suffered from slow progress

Table 2.12 Zones of preferential industrial location

Name	Valid until
Campo de Gibraltar	Fourth Plan (1975)
Tierra de Campos	Fourth Plan (1975)
Caceres	14-8-1978
Valle del Cinca (Huesca)	21-9-1978
Canary Islands	20-4-1979
Badajoz	31-12-1979
Corrales de Buelna (Santander)	End of Fourth Plan (1979)
Jaen	31-12-1978

Source: Own elaboration

and a lack of coordination. The third (1965–1969), however, involved some interesting changes: there were more financing formulas, economic–urbanistic location criteria were established, the average surface area increased considerably and the Plan's Commissariat appeared as a collaborator. The programme foresaw the construction of 12 estates in all, plus 42 developed by the *Institito Nacional de Urbanización* (National Institute of Housing, or INUR, dependent on the Ministry of Housing), representing 4,874 ha, the location of which was intended to achieve several objectives: decongest large cities (Madrid, Barcelona, Bilbao); support the extension of pole sites within the same region (Zaragoza, La Coruña and Vigo); build such estates in several cities of some importance, and collaborate with the zones of preferential industrial location and some towns and cities in order to ensure their support. In general, the construction of the approved estates suffered numerous delays due to financing difficulties, which certainly limited their capacity to foster development and industrialisation.

The fourth and last industrial estate programme (1970–1976) had more modest goals (14 estates; 1,252.7 ha) and did not have the Commissariat's collaboration. Indeed, practically nothing was done because of the delays in completing the previous programmes. By the end of 1974, the estates completed represented a mere 3,486.9 ha, 38 per 100 of the industrial land created from 1964 to 1974 by the Administration, town councils and private organisations.

Some of these estates were subsequently designated as for "preferential industrial location", affording them fiscal and credit advantages, import facilities and lower overhead costs.

2.5.2.3 Promotion of Tourism

The growth of tourism in Spain since the early sixties has been spectacular. In 1959, the country was visited by 2,863,000 tourists spending $158.9 million; in 1975, at the end of the Third Plan, its visitors accounted 30,122,000, with $3,404.4 million in revenue.

From the regional development perspective, tourism provided a series of apparent and immediate advantages for the areas visited: more direct (in the catering and similar sectors) and indirect employment; income and demand effects with a strong impact on other service sectors, agriculture, fishing and some local arts and crafts activities; significant changes in the mentality and behaviour patterns of the local inhabitants, etc. Construction was a driving force in all these cases, although most of its inputs came from other industrialised parts of the country.

The opposite side of the coin was found in the problems caused by growing tourism: economic dualism in tourist areas (e.g. between coastal and inland zones), lack of infrastructures, disordered growth and destruction of the landscape and environment, urban congestion, seasonal unemployment, surplus accommodation in some cases, etc. All these problems, which were only to be expected, should never have arisen, with suitable planning and the control of tourist expansion in each area, none of which would have affected the significant official support provided for the tourist industry. Most of the action taken during the sixties, however, was only aimed at increasing the tourist supply (loans, non-returnable grants, designated centres of tourist interest, tax benefits, etc.) and depended on the Ministry of Information and Tourism, which was never closely connected to the Plan's Commissariat or to regional policy proper.

2.5.2.4 Transport Infrastructures

Transport infrastructures policy was always largely independent from the Development Plan system. The First and Second Plans formally included investments programmed for roads, railways and ports, but these and other projects affecting the transport sector (price policy, regulation and control of transport companies, credit facilities, etc.) were basically in the hands of the Ministry of Public Works and other organisations. This had two serious consequences: on the one hand, there was a clear lack of coordination in the policies applied to different transport modalities and, on the other hand, investment in infrastructures was a centralised decision, and did not consider the impact on the country's regional and urban context. Only in the Third Plan, transport was suggested as a possible driving force for regional development, playing a major role in structuring the territory, although the situation continued much as before.

The basic investment criterion used in the sixties and early seventies to increase transport infrastructures by road was the dimension and evolution of *traffic demand*. The World Bank's report of 1962 said "we constantly urge that top priority be afforded to the improvement of the high-volume routes, and to the means of conveyance operating along them" and that was the basic principle followed in *Plan General de Carreteras* (General Road Plan) 1962–1977, the REDIA Plan, toll road concession priorities, the Spanish railway 10-year modernisation plan (1964) and other measures. Naturally, this meant that the more developed and dynamic areas in the country would receive more attention than others, although this was not always the case. The above plans also improved the communications between Madrid and other cities, reinforcing the *centralisation* approach (roads and railway) seen for nearly a century. For example, Table 2.13 shows the routes affected by the "REDIA" Plan and average traffic intensity figures for 1965. Nearly 75 per 100 of the affected network corresponds to roads to Madrid (even with low traffic intensity), ignoring other routes (*Valle del Ebro*, Leon-Extremadura-inland Andalusia, for instance) which could have played an important role in the development of some of the country's most depressed areas.

Finally, it must be pointed out that transport policy at the time tended to indiscriminately favour road transport. Although the modernisation plan was created for the railway system, and other programmes were subsequently devised, investment volume was not enough to create a system fit for a modern country. Ports and coastal maritime transport were also inadequately funded, partially due to pressure from large construction firms and the car industry.

Evidently, these three basic features do not cover all the characteristics of transport policy in this period. We should also consider the approach to motorway

Table 2.13 Network of road routes

Routes	Length (km)	Average traffic intensity (1965)
Madrid–Irun	497.5	4,023
Madrid–Barcelona	639.6	4,486
Madrid–Valencia	355.7	2,659
Madrid–Cadiz	690.5	3,540
Madrid–Badajoz	404.9	1,539
Madrid–Ponferrada	389.3	2,546
Ponferrada–La Coruña–El Ferrol	271.0	1,507
Madrid–Alicante	352.2	2,359
Alicante–La Junquera	710.2	6,222
Malaga–La Línea	134.4	3,898
La Linea–Cadiz	116.3	1,758
San Sebastián–Oviedo	367.1	2,917
Total	4.928.7	3,520

Source: Ministry of Public Works

and airport construction, which has a greater regional impact than other factors, the lack of coordination between different transport modalities, the state of the secondary road network, which is of decisive importance for regional integration, and many other aspects related to this sector. Although we are unable to analyse each of these factors in depth here, references can be found in other, more specialised, texts. However, following are a few notes on the relationships between each of the three Development Plans and specific transport programmes.

The *Plan General de Carreteras* 1962–1977 was based on the principle of concentrating investment (62,000 million pesetas over a 10-year period) on the routes with the greatest actual or potential demand, as suggested in the World Bank Report of 1962. Construction also started on toll motorways during the First Plan, managed by the Ministry of Public Works. The first concessions (Barcelona–La Junquera and Mongat-Mataró) involved State guarantees, important tax benefits and other advantages. The REDIA Plan, approved in 1967, involved an investment of 20,000 million pesetas over a 6-year period, aimed at improving a series of national routes. The National Motorway Programme also became effective in 1967, with over 500 km of motorways approved in 3 years, most of them around major industrial locations, except for the Seville-Cadiz road, which was due to political reasons. Practically, all the roads foreseen in the programme were adjudicated in the early 1970s.

2.6 Summary

To summarise, it is possible to highlight several aspects of regional policy in the 1960–1975 period and earlier (Primo de Rivera dictatorship, Second Republic and the first 20 years of the Franco regime).

The first is that there was no such thing as regional policy proper. Regions were not even recognised as such and regional measures were always controlled and enforced by the central government. Some of them certainly had a regional impact (e.g. river basin authorities, roads, irrigation or reservoirs). Neither were the subsequent Development Plans based on a regional approach, because regions continued to go unrecognised.

However, regional development in the Development Plans was based on ideas being put into practise in other countries (particularly France), where they had a clear "regional development" profile. In this respect, the poles policy was the most significant, but there were also others, such as industrial estates, zones of preferential location (for industry or tourism) or the Large Areas to which the Third Plan referred. Although the Development Plans were based on what was essentially a sectoral approach, they also had a "regional" profile which aimed to develop the country's most backward areas.

The results of all these policies are difficult to evaluate, at least with reference to their impact on reducing interregional differences. The effect of migration on reducing regional disparities in per capita income can be estimated at just over 50%. Migration to what were then the most dynamic and industrialised regions (Madrid, Basque Country and Catalonia) represented significant losses of population in regions, such as Galicia, Castilla-La Mancha, Andalusia, Murcia and Castilla y Leon. This automatically improved the per capita income of the regions producing these emigrants (who also moved to Europe), with the recipient regions seeing this indicator reduced. Table 2.14 shows some information of interest.

Table 2.14 Regional disparities 1940–1975 (Values in constant pesetas of 1995)

	% Weight of production value		Per capita GDP Spain=100	
	1940	1975	1940	1975
Andalusia	12.74	11.69	69.8	72.1
Aragón	3.76	3.27	100.5	96.32
Asturias	3.36	3.24	100.1	96.81
Balearic Islands	1.77	1.99	147.8	151.8
Canary Islands	2.32	2.87	92.8	95.0
Cantabria	1,72	1.54	99.2	97.4
Castilla-La Mancha	4.60	3.43	72.1	72.0
Castilla y Leon	7.42	5.93	77.1	79.9
Catalonia	22.22	21.51	148.1	121.0
Extremadura	2.28	1.59	54.0	56.2
Galicia	5.52	5.66	73.3	75.7
Madrid	11.47	14.74	189.8	139.5
Murcia	2.02	2.03	82.2	80.3
Navarre	1.52	1.19	106.4	110.6
Basque Country	7.91	8.82	150.4	123.4
La Rioja	0.87	0.75	100.1	98.7
Valencia	8.50	9.28	99.8	99.1
Spain	100	100	100	100

Source: Data from BBVA, Alcaide (2003)

As we can see, in the 1940–1975 period, production tended to be concentrated in some specific regions, such as Madrid, the Basque Country and Catalonia (in spite of some decline) and even Valencia. By the end of 1975, these four regions (now autonomous) represented 54.35 per 100 of the country's production, while some of the most underdeveloped regions in 1940 had lost weight (this was true of Andalusia, Aragon, Cantabria, Castilla-La Mancha, Castilla y Leon, Extremadura and La Rioja).

This does not mean, however, that the disparities in terms of per capita GDP were greater, as migration and some development in the most backward regions helped to improve their respective indicators relative to the national average, while the opposite occurred in the most dynamic and developed areas.

References

Alcaide, J. (2003). *Evolución económica de las regiones y provincias españolas en el siglo XX*. Madrid: Fundación BBVA.
Cuadrado-Roura, J. R. (1977). El INI y el desarrollo regional. *Libre Empresa, 1*, pp. 117–136
Cuadrado-Roura, J.R. (1980). Sociedades de Desarrollo Regional con participación pública: el caso español. In *VV.AA. Empresa Pública española*. Madrid: Instituto de Estudios Fiscales.
Cuadrado-Roura, J. R. (1981). La Política Regional en los Planes de Desarrollo (1964–1975). In *VV.AA.: La España de las Autonomías* (pp. 545–607). Madrid: Ec. Espasa-Calpe, tome 1.
Donges, J. (1976). *La industrialización de España*. Barcelona: Ed. Oikos-Tau.
Fernández, F. (dir.) (1975). *Evaluación de los Planes de Badajoz, Jaén y Tierra de Campos*. Madrid: Inst. de Estudios Económicos.
Fuentes Quintana, E. (1963). Compiler: El desarrollo económico de España. In *Juicio crítico del Informe del Banco Mundial*. Madrid: Revista de Occidente.
Fuentes Quintana, E. (1984). El Plan Nacional de Estabilización Económica de 1959, 25 años después. *Inf. Com. Española*, 612–613.
Fuentes Quintana, E. (1988). Tres decenios de la economía española en perspectiva. In J. L. García Delgado (dir). *España. Economía* (pp. 1–75). Madrid: Ed. Espasa-Calpe.
González, M. J. (1981). El desarrollo regional frustrado durante treinta años de dirigismo. In *VV. AA.: La España de las Autonomías*, vol. 1 (pp. 483–543). Madrid: Espasa-Calpe.
Macías Picavea. (1899). *El Problema Nacional (hechos, causas y remedios)*. Madrid: Librería General de V. Suárez.
Mortes, V. (1963). Las Obras Públicas. In *El Nuevo Estado Español*. Madrid: I.E.Politicos, Editora Nacional.
Ortega, P. (1973). *Dieciséis años del Plan Jaén*. Jaén: Cámara O. de Comercio e Industria.
Richardson, H. W. (1976). *Política y planificación del desarrollo regional en España*. Madrid: Alianza Universidad. (published also in English: Regional Development Policy and Planning in Spain (1975), D.C. Heath Ltd., UK and US).
Siguán, M. (1963). *Colonización y Desarrollo Social. Estudio en el marco del Plan Badajoz* (4 vols). Madrid: Presidencia del Gobierno, Secretaría Gestora del Plan Badajoz.
Tamames, R. (1973). *La República. La Era de Franco*. Madrid: Alianza Universidad.
Velarde, J. (1968). *Política Económica de la Dictadura*. Madrid: Ed. Guadiana.

Chapter 3
The Evolution of Spanish Regional Policy, 1977–2008

Tomás Mancha-Navarro and Rubén Garrido-Yserte

This chapter offers an overview of the evolution of Spain's regional policy since joining the European Union (EU). A simplified reference is also made to the virtual disappearance of regional operations carried out during the period of impact of the economic crisis (1975–1985). The chapter analyses the general orientation of the regional policies applied and their operational performance, both from a national and a European perspective.

The impact of Spain's entry into the current EU had a very important impact on Spanish regional policy and implied a radical change of direction in performance. The Spanish legal and operational framework had to be adapted and the country had to learn the new "rules of the game" in order to acquire important financial resources allocated to regional operations.

To be precise, it can be said that with the beginning of the programming stage between 1989 and 1993, Spanish regional policies – under European regional policy orientation and together with a timid but clear consolidation of the decentralisation process started in 1978 – started a brilliant period. This period ended in 2006, the closing year of a golden phase when European financial resources were obtained. These resources undoubtedly helped Spanish regions to improve their position in the European regional ranking in a wide variety of variables (economic, physical infrastructures, social, etc.).

The structure of this chapter is as follows: The first section briefly outlines Spain's general economic evolution from 1977 to date. This is then used as a general framework for more detailed analysis of regional policy. The second section begins with a brief reference to the period of decline between 1975 and 1985. It then offers a short summary of the most outstanding milestones reached and relates these to the performance of Spanish regional policy during periods which coincide with various programming stages of European regional policy:

T. Mancha-Navarro (✉)
Universidad de Alcalá, Departamento de Economía Aplicada, Pl. Victoria, 2, 28802 – Alcalá de Henares. Madrid, España,
e-mail: tomas.mancha@uah.es

1989–1993; 1994–1999 and 2000–2006. The third section analyses the current direction of regional policy (2007–2013) and the position of Spanish policy within a framework of significant changes in Europe. The fourth section explains the operational performance of Spanish regional policies, from the perspectives of its own instruments (*Fondo de Compensación Interterritorial* – Interterritorial Compensation Fund- and *Sistema de Incentivos Económicos Regionales* – Regional Economic Incentives System) and of Structural Funds. Finally, the fifth section assesses some relevant aspects of European influence on the development of Spanish regional policy from both quantitative and qualitative perspectives.

3.1 An Overview of the Spanish Economy Evolution Between 1977 and 2008

This analysis takes into account the different governments that were in office and their respective economic contexts. Special attention is paid to the evolution of three fundamental macroeconomic variables: economic growth, inflation and unemployment.

Within a framework of political change, where the basic focal point was to establish and consolidate a democratic system, Adolfo Suárez's political party, the Unión de Centro Democrático (UCD), had to assume, during its two terms of office (from June 1977 to October 1982), a serious economic situation characterised by three basic facts: decrease of economic growth, increase of unemployment and increase of inflation. The evolution of these variables demonstrated a clear objective: to fight against inflation. However, this had only limited success, with consequent negative evolution of unemployment[1] (see Fig. 3.1).

Due to negative economic records, the economic situation inherited by the new socialist government (Partido Socialista Obrero Español, PSOE) was quite discouraging. Therefore, it is no wonder that the first socialist term of office was notably pragmatic. Instead of applying the electoral programme presented in October 1982 when they won the elections, they tackled the core problems affecting the Spanish economy. Although the results of this adjustment policy were not particularly outstanding, towards their final stage they caused a change in the trend (from the second half of 1985),[2] which placed the Spanish economy into a

---

[1] During the first term of office of UCD, the so-called Pactos de la Moncloa (Moncloa Agreements), signed by the Government and all political parties with parliamentary representation, trade unions and employers associations, focussed on real problems of Spanish economy to reduce the inflation spiral. Although it could not stop the high increase in unemployment, it resulted in improving the serious external imbalance.

[2] This change of trend was unforeseen by the Decree Law of 30 of April, 1985. Its preamble expressed a clear message from the Ministry of Economy and Finance, still under the direction of Mr. Boyer that hard times were coming to an end. There were clear signs of a change of trend and a new positive turn in the economic situation. In other words, the crisis adjustment was over.

3 The Evolution of Spanish Regional Policy, 1977–2008

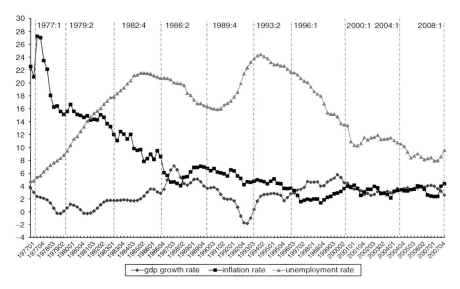

Fig. 3.1 Evolution of main macroeconomic variables (1977–2007)
Source: Mancha (2008)

context of economic recovery such as that of the second socialist term (June 1986–October 1989) (see Fig. 3.1).

The second socialist term of office, with Felipe González still president, was a *missed opportunity* to channel the Spanish economy not only toward the path of economic growth and stability, but also toward the path of fiscal consolidation. The commitments of the 1990s regarding big international events (the Expo '92 in Seville and the 1992 Olympic Games in Barcelona) and certain political components (the general strike in December 1989 and the breaking-off with trade unions) led the government to forsake the coherence characterised by the first term of office. This led to relaxed fiscal rules, which immediately held negative consequences for the evolution of the Spanish economy. In fact, from 1991, Spain entered into a crisis that, although less pronounced than that of the 1970s, led to a decline in economic growth and to a new rise in unemployment.

The following Socialist office terms (1989–1993 and 1993–1996) presented clear differences in the economic situation. The third electoral success occurred just some months after the incorporation of the Spanish currency – the peseta – into the European Monetary System (June 1989). This was the start of a failed strategy of *competitive disinflation*,[3] which had to be renounced after the signing of the

---

[3] The key element of this strategy of competitive disinflation is that the exchange rate of the peseta, clearly overvalued, required the moderation in growth of internal prices. However, this was not achieved, and the situation grew worse. This was due to high exchange rates that attracted important foreign capital flows, making monetary control more complex and becoming an additional factor encouraging price increase.

Maastricht Treaty in 1992. This treaty established well-known convergence criteria, to which the economic policy was subordinated.

The serious monetary and financial problems of September 1992 that led, among other difficulties, to four consecutive devaluations of the peseta, made the objectives set in the Convergence Programme drawn up for the period between 1992 and 1996 unfeasible. Once the PSOE won the elections in 1993, the new minister in charge of economic affairs, Pedro Solbes, changed the strategy in order to fulfil the requirements established in the Maastricht Treaty for the year 1997. In fact, the worst records of almost 14 years of socialist government are registered in this third term of office. Growth declined to negative rates during the quarters before the elections of 1993; unemployment reached a rate of nearly 22% and only inflation, within a clearly recessive context, reduced to 4.5%.

Despite the correct reorientation of the economic policy by the then Minister of Economy, Mr. Solbes, and the serious deterioration of the political image of the last socialist government, the comparatively modest economic results allowed Spaniards to foresee a possible change of government. This finally occurred in the elections held on 1 March 1996 with the victory of José María Aznar and the assumption of power by the Partido Popular (PP), which, although not achieving an absolute majority, was the most voted minority.

The clearest directive in the economic approach of the PP was the achievement of *budgetary consolidation*, as well as economic liberalisation, to meet the aforementioned convergence criteria of Maastricht. In order to do so, they took advantage of the final period of the socialist term, ending their first 6 months of government with excellent results regarding the three variables under analysis herein. The economic evolution in the following years corroborated these results, and confirmed their first term of office with good results. Spain then fulfilled integration into the European Monetary Union (EMU) at its beginning (1999), while the most favourable performances of the whole democratic period: high and steady economic growth, reduction of unemployment and price stability (see Fig. 3.1).

The achievement of *budgetary consolidation* was based on three foundations:

1. *Strict budgeting:* This principle of action took into consideration the following aspects: avoiding and preventing, in advance, the incremental nature of the budget; establishing quantity and time limits for all public expenditure commitments; and reforming the *Ley General Presupuestaria* or LGP (General Budget Law) to avoid lax budgeting practises and uses.
2. *Reinforced presence of executive power in different stages of the budgeting cycle:* One of the most obvious sign was the 2001 approval of the Partido Popular, a *Ley de Estabilidad Presupuestaria* (Budgeting Stability Law), during the second term of office.
3. *Implementation of structural reforms in strategic areas* (pensions, unemployment, public health, labour market, financing of autonomous regions and privatisations).

The economic approach of the current government by Mr. Zapatero, based on the electoral victory of the PSOE in March 2004, has not meant important changes to the general orientation of economic policy applied by the Partido Popular. This emerged from the updating of the 2005–2008 Annual Stability Programme, whose three basic priorities were: reinforcement of budgeting stability, in accordance with the new considerations of the reformed Stability and Growth Pact (Spring 2005); improvement of the competitive environment and promotion of productivity between 2005 and 2010, supported by the March 2005 *Plan de Dinamización de la Economía e Impulso a la Productividad*[4] (Plan to dynamise the economy and enhance productivity), and an October 2005 *Programa Nacional de Reformas* (National Reform Plan); and, finally, greater transparency and higher quality regulatory framework.

The clear signs of deceleration, already noticed in 2007, and the international financial crisis have put a brake on the Spanish economy, which had been running positively since 1996. Moreover, these resulted in an internal economic crisis considered as *unavoidable* by some economists. In fact, within the current economic climate, where no fundamental correcting measures have been applied during the second term of Mr. Zapatero, the crisis has hit the economy with two serious problems: an important inflation differential and an external unbalance (around 10% of GDP), which makes Spanish economy highly vulnerable, not even taking into consideration the explosion of the so-called "housing bubble". This has led the Spanish economy to the prelude of a recession and to a high increase in unemployment. It also halted the excellent results of public finance (which has in 2008 gone back into the red). In short, the Spanish economy is facing a worrying situation for which no immediate solutions are foreseen, and one which will be more difficult to overcome than initially expected.

3.2 Spanish Regional Policy Within the European Union (1975–2006)

3.2.1 Background of the Period 1975–1985: The Disappearance of Regional Policy

The negative impact of the mid-1970s economic crisis caused a change of trend that had an important impact on the evolution of regional policy. Despite the apparent concern of public (central and regional) authorities, this type of policy weakened considerably, and more or less disappeared until 1985.

---

[4]The Spanish Plan to Dynamise Economy and Enhance Productivity arose from the Spanish economy's need to find a durable and balanced growth pattern, based on the increase of productivity and employment. Moreover, this plan falls in line with the relaunching of the Lisbon Strategy (renewed since mid 2005) to increase competitiveness and welfare in the Spanish economy, which are the real final objectives of the Plan itself.

Three basic explanatory reasons underlie the aforementioned statement (Cuadrado and Mancha, 1995):

1. The seriousness of macroeconomic problems derived from the crisis of the 1970s.
2. The renunciation of planning system, and the obligatory need to resolve the short-term problems.
3. The redistribution of capabilities among the different public administrations, which resulted in a temporary uncertainty regarding the responsibility of regional actions.

This situation did not lead, however, to the disappearance of certain tools and mechanisms of regional promotion inherited from the previous period. Examples include regional incentives, SODIs (Societies of Industrial Development), areas of preferred industrial localisation, etc. These continued to run up until their legal expiration date.

A change of trend could be appreciated from the end of 1985, with clear signs of activity in areas related to regional policy. Two basic facts help to explain this situation: (1) a progressive consolidation and adjustment of the so-called *Estado de las Autonomías* (State of Autonomies) set in the Spanish Constitution of 1978; and (2) the entry of Spain into the then-called European Community, which started to be negotiated in 1977.

From the perspective of the State of Autonomies, the dynamisation of Spanish regional policy was also reinforced by the incipient but already noticeable decentralisation process, where regional governments started to consolidate a notable prominence.[5] As we shall see below, the implementation of the *Fondo de Compensación Interterritorial* (Interterritorial Compensation Fund, ICF) established in the Constitution of 1978, imposed on all Autonomous Regions the obligation of drawing-up a *Plan de Desarrollo Regional* (Regional Development Plan, RDP) with a common methodology also inspired by the legal requirements set for European Commission.

From the viewpoint of integration into Europe, the entry of Spain as a full member of the European Community forced its adaptation in all areas of the *European Union acquis*. Within the area of regional policy, this reflected the need to elaborate and present a RDP for the new programming period (1986–1989) in order to access EU resources allocated to regional development, especially to the European Regional Development Fund (ERDF).

---

[5]This new political-administrative framework was not exempt from problems, such as the existence of three interlocutors: Central government, regional authorities and local councils. Each of these needed to agree upon approve the framework within which the commitments of each party involved were established, as well as the economic and financial nature of such commitments. Nevertheless, this book will not analyse the regional policy designed and implemented by regional and local authorities, which does in no way mean that these are insignificant. On the contrary, they acquired an outstanding prominence from the 1990s onwards.

The years immediately following strengthened this line of action through the review, reorganisation and adaptation of regional incentives, the new regulations of the ICF and the drawing-up of a new RDP with forecasts for the 1990s, pursuant to the reform of the Community Structural Funds approved in the middle of 1988.[6]

At the end of the 1980s, the *emergence of regional policy* in Spain was clearly noticeable, as a RDP and a *Plan de Reconversión Regional y Social* (Regional and Social Restructuring Plan, RSRP) had to be prepared for the period between 1989 and 1993. Based on these, the two Community Support Frameworks (CSF1 and CSF2) had to be negotiated, not forgetting the *Plan de Desarrollo para las Zonas Rurales* (Rural Areas Development Plan, RADP).

3.2.2 The Ten-year Period from 1989 to 1999: A Strong Emphasis on Infrastructures

The strategy of Spanish regional policy designed for the two programming periods within the decade of the 1990s (1989–1993 and 1994–1999) was the result of the logical principle objective of *reducing interregional disparities*. For this reason, a durable and sustainable growth was essential to advance towards convergence with the EU average income per inhabitant.[7]

The accomplishment of this objective was based on various *strategic axes* related to a group of secondary objectives: consolidation of the growth trend in those areas registering more notable recovery and higher dynamism (Madrid, the Ebro Valley and the Mediterranean Axis); more concentrated efforts to stop the decline in the Cantabrian coast area and the recovery of its former growth potential; strong drive for the take-off of Andalusia and Murcia, incorporating these into the Mediterranean Axis; reinforced support to all other regions on the basis of promoting their most dynamic centres by means of important investments in infrastructures, diversification of their productive structure, and boosting their most competitive sectors; and finally, special attention given to rural areas.

From a global point of view, the strategy designed seemed to be clearly *maximalist* and *disperse*. However, the *instrumental priorities* – in view of the forecast financial resources that were later agreed in the two CSF – were more precise

---

[6] Three basic aspects, among others, could be highlighted for this new period of European regional policy. Firstly, the high financial increase in Structural Funds; secondly, their concentration on various objectives, which clearly benefited Spain due to the relatively worse situation of its interregional disparities, and finally, the strict European requirements related to the application of funds and reflected on the principles of additionality, coordination and co-participation.

[7] For a more detailed analysis of the strategy for each of the periods, see Mancha and Cuadrado (2000).

Table 3.1 Distribution of public investment according to strategic orientations (1989–1993) (in thousands of millions of current pesetas)

	RDP	RSRP	RADP	Total
Infrastructures	4,015.3 (50.1%)	1,034.7 (32.8%)	64.7 (70 %)	5,414.7 (46.3%)
Social equipments	1,936.4 (24.1%)	949.2 (30.1%)	–	2,885.6 (24.7%)
Incentives and promotion	718.1 (9%)	403.7 (12.8%)	–	1,121.8 (9.6%)
Other	1,350.2 (16.8%)	767.3 (24.3%)	156.7 (30%)	2,274.2 (19.4%)
Total	8,020.0	3,154.9	521.3	11,696.2

Source: Cuadrado and Mancha (1996)

and focused on three basic points. These were placed in order according to the importance of the financial resources allocated to each as follows (see Table 3.1):

- *Infrastructures*, with a marked emphasis on transport, but also including other infrastructures for the support of economic activity (hydraulic resources, farming infrastructures, etc.).
- *Allocation of social equipments*, particularly related to education, health and housing.
- *Incentives and promotion of productive activities*.

The *provision of infrastructures*, which absorbed almost half of the European resources, was justified by the Spanish authorities by the existence of high deficits in this area. Such deficits were partly the result of insufficient and scarce investments in the past, which were an important setback in the development of the most backward regions. From the opposite perspective, this exceptional investing bias strongly contrasts with the shortage of resources allocated to support productive activity, as the promotion and incentive axis do not even reach 10% of total funds budgeted in all regional plans.

The distribution by investment axes for the Spanish objective 1 regions from 1994 to 1999, within a new programming stage, shows that the strong concentration in infrastructures was partially modulated. The influence of the Commission was decisive. The CSF approved for the period 1994–1999 already included a clear strategic reorientation of Spanish regional policy. This reflects the increase of funds assigned to the *development of productive* tissue and to the *valorisation of human resources*. The priorities of Spanish regional policy were more specific than before, correcting the already criticised maximalist nature of the strategy[8] (see Table 3.2).

---

[8] In fact, the basic priorities focussed on connecting adequately the worst-funded regions with the transeuropean transport axis in order to reach minimum accessibility thresholds, and to improve the competitiveness of regional productive sectors by means of providing more support to small- and medium-sized enterprises.

Table 3.2 Distribution of investments per development axis for the Spanish objective 1 regions (1989–1999). In %

Development axes	CSF (1989–1993)	RDP (1994–1999)	CSF (1994–1999)
1. Integration and territorial articulation	37.09	34.23	27.23
2. Development of economic tissue	8.32	8.32	15.37
3. Tourism	1.38	2.71	2.29
4. Agriculture/rural development	14.84	9.93	7.89
5. Fishing	–	1.12	3.60
6. Infrastructures for the support of economic activities	18.30	27.38	20.37
7. Valuation of human resources	19.86	16.31	22.62
8. Technical assistance, support and Information	0.21	–	0.64
Total	100.00	100.00	100.00

Source: Mancha and Cuadrado (2000)

3.2.3 Spanish Regional Policy from 2000 to 2006: The Start of the Cutbacks

After long and arduous negotiations, the financial outlook was approved in the Berlin Summit (March 1999) for the programming period 2000–2006. This outlook set a different scenario to that of European regional policy in the 1990s. It can be defined by two basic parameters: (1) the *freezing* of financial resources assigned to Structural Funds; and (2) the enlargement of the EU to new countries, almost all of them with an income level quite lower than the EU average.

The starting period went through more uncertainties and difficulties than previously, particularly because the two aforementioned parameters hindered the conciliation of interests of all possible beneficiaries of these structural interventions.

In order to gain a better understanding of the performance of Spanish regional policy, it is worth explaining that the following general guidelines for regional and cohesion policies for the period 2000–2006 were set at a European level:

1. *Maintaining the effort put into the economic and social cohesion* as a political priority within a framework with an austere budget, limiting financial solidarity to 0.46% of the EU GDP. The final result was an allocation of €213.5 billion to regional policy, a higher amount than the 200 billion allocated for the period 1994–1999 (although part of the 21 billion reserved for the future new Member States should also be added to this). Furthermore, an additional limit was established so that no country would receive a total annual aid for structural interventions, including the Cohesion Fund, higher than 4% of its GDP.

2. *More concentrated objectives*, with a clear decrease in the population benefiting and a reduction of the five previous objectives to the following three:
   - *Objective 1*: Development and structural adjustment of less-developed regions. Strictly speaking, these have a GDP lower than 75% of the EU average.[9]
   - *Objective 2*: This was redefined to focus on the economic and social restructuring of those areas with structural problems, either industrial, urban, rural or fishing areas. Therefore, the aim of the new programmes for supporting such areas should be to diversify the productive structure, and the aids should focus on the support of SMEs and innovation, vocational training, environmental protection, promotion of human resources and development of rural areas.
   - *Objective 3*: This objective covered those regions not included in the two previous objectives. The aim was to aid Member States in their adaptation and modernisation of their policies and education systems, training and employment.
   - The Cohesion Fund was maintained, but with a lower allocation than the one initially established in the 2000 Agenda for the so-called *cohesion countries* (Spain, Greece, Ireland and Portugal). This decision was reached after long discussions on whether those previously benefiting from this fund, that met the Maastricht convergence criteria, should or should not keep on benefiting from these aids.
3. *A simplified and decentralised application of regional policy:* After approval of the regional development programmes by the Commission, this new stage implied distribution of responsibilities. In complementary programmes, the Member States defined the measures and projects to be implemented.
4. *Reinforcement of efficiency and improvement of control:* Pursuant to the previous guidelines, the fulfilment of the additionality principle was necessarily simplified, not only with regard to the content of each of the three assessments to be carried out, but also with regard to its implementation as set by previous guidelines. Additionally, in order to reward the most efficient regions regarding the achievement of the objectives, the so-called performance reserve scheme[10] *was launched.*

EU structural resources assigned to Spain, after the agreements reached in the Berlin Summit, resulted in 6,300 billion pesetas for objective 1; 3,300 billion for objectives 2 and 3; and 1,860 billion for the Cohesion Fund and EU initiatives. Despite the previous negotiating tension, Spain became again, in absolute terms, the

---

[9] However, a transitory support was established until the year 2005 for those regions eligible as objective 1 in 1999, but not meeting this condition for the year 2000, and until 2006 for those regions now eligible within the new objective 2. For the rest of regions, the aid would continue only by means of the EAGGF Guidance, ESF and FIFG during a period of time not exceeding the year 2006. Within this objective, outlying regions were also included, as well as the regions formerly assigned to objective 6.

[10] An analysis of the motivation and its basic content can be found in Mancha et al. (1999), and an assessment of its implementation in Mancha Navarro et al. (2005).

most favoured country as far as the allocation of EU funds is concerned, particularly regarding objective 1, where about 30% of the total was given. This amount was outstandingly higher than that corresponding to Italy, which took second place and was allocated just slightly over 17%.

The European Union's increasing role in the formulation of the regional policy of each member state is clear. In the Spanish case, this is demonstrated by the design of priorities for the objective 1 regions in the period 2000–2006, and is summarised in the pursuance of two broad objectives (see Mancha Navarro and Garrido Yserte, 2004; Garrido et al., 2007; and Cuadrado and Mancha, 2008):

1. Favouring the process of real convergence of the regions with lower income levels by achieving a series of intermediate objectives, such as:

   - Promoting business and territorial competitiveness
   - Facilitating structural adjustment and development of the productive tissue
   - Making better use of endogenous growth and the sectoral comparative advantages.

2. Favouring employment creation by improving the conditions of employability and equal opportunities.

Another two horizontal objectives were added to the previous two: the promotion of equal opportunities and sustainable development.

The CSF negotiated by Spanish and European Commission for the objective 1 regions established an amount of over €39.5 billion for the period between 2000 and 2006, distributed into nine large *intervention axes* (see Fig. 3.2). Despite certain formal changes, it was clear that the Spanish regional policy continued emphasising *the provision of physical infrastructures*, although with less accent mainly due to the Commission's reluctance to approve Spain's initial demands. Proof of this reluctance is a request in the RDP for infrastructures of virtually 30% of the funds; the final agreement was reduced to 23% of the approved CSF.

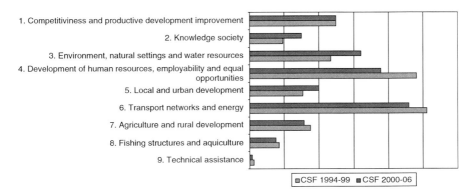

Fig. 3.2 Priorities of Spanish Regional Policy for 2000–2006. Objective 1 regions. (% of total foreseen expenditure)
Source: Ministry of Economic and Finance (several years). Own elaboration

The priorities of the Commission and the political orientations of the different European Councils are reflected in the structural policy through the fostering of the environment and measures for the development of the Knowledge Society, which became of more importance than in the previous programming period. However, the commitment to the development of human resources remains constant taking into account that it is focused not only on axis 4 but also on axes 1, 2 and 5.

3.3 Regional Policy in the Current Programming Period (2007–2013): The Difficult Balance of Sharing Fewer Resources Among More Countries

The aforementioned problems of implementing the European regional policy in the year 2000 became more severe in the current programming period. There are two basic explanations: the enlargement of the EU to 27 countries and the freezing of resources.

In this context, it is not hard to imagine the difficulties in coming to satisfactory agreements. However, the difficult trade-off among the three objectives which were initially almost irreconcilable was finally achieved. Firstly, the members of the old EU-15 would maintain some kind of benefit from the European Community Regional Policy (ERP); secondly, the new Member States would receive a significant share of the resources available; and finally, the net contributing countries would not change their condition, but would reduce their contribution.

The main innovations of the ERP for the current period can be summarised as follows (Cuadrado and Mancha, 2008):

- A more strategic approach to the programming focussed on the priorities of EU-27.
- Greater thematic and budgetary concentration.
- Greater decentralisation and simplification.

Regarding the first point, the time sequence of the programming is shown in Fig. 3.3. The new elements of significance are, on the one hand, the prominence of the strategic elements of the Commission, leaving the OP management and the selection of operations to national and regional authorities; and on the other hand, the key mechanism of National Strategic Reference Frameworks (NSRF), which substituted the previous CSFs and guaranteed that the national regional policies agreed with those established in Brussels.

The level of concentration has been improved by seeking a point of balance between the geographical, thematic and financial questions. This implies the substitution of the former objectives by three new ones, i.e.: *convergence*,[11] the most

---

[11] Formerly objective 1, it covers regions that have a GDP per capita of less than 75% of the EU average, as well as phasing-out regions (those regions which would have been eligible for funding in terms of the EU-15, but with a GDP per capita higher than the threshold of 75% in terms of the UE-27).

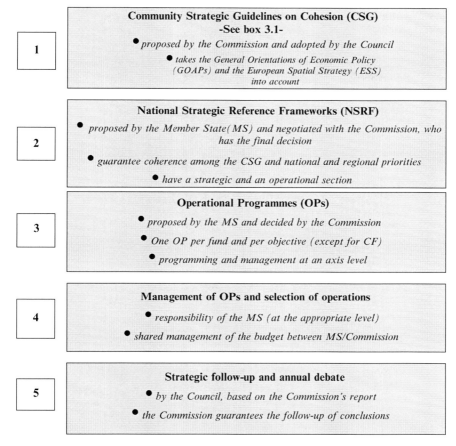

Fig. 3.3 Time sequence of the programming period 2007–2013 of the CRP and basic contents
Source: European Commission (2007)

important one from the viewpoint of financial resources (almost 80% of the total); *regional competitiveness and employment;*[12] and *European territorial cooperation.*

However, the interventions should prioritise the objectives of the so-called Renewed Lisbon Strategy (RLS); research and technological development, innovation and business spirit and information society are among the most important. All this is reinforced with the requirement of reserving specific percentages of the Structural Funds received for such objectives (*earmarking*): 60% for the regions eligible for the "convergence" objective and 75% for those eligible for the "regional competitiveness and employment" objective. Moreover, it is worth highlighting the preferential and significant treatment of the outermost regions and the most distinguished simplification of the instrument panel of regional policy.

---

[12] It includes those EU regions not included in the convergence objective.

Since early summer 2006, Spanish authorities have been negotiating with the Commission with regard to the content of the NSRF. The content was finally approved in the following year, while the Operational Programmes were being discussed in Brussels. This has meant that the effective date of the new programming period occurred before the negotiations had been fully terminated. This pattern has been repeated in the majority of countries.

In this negotiation process, a fundamental strategic reference has been present on which the future application of Structural Funds will be based: the RLS. This has been translated so that the *Community Strategic Guidelines* on cohesion concentrate on three broad priorities (see Box 3.1):

1. Improvement of territorial appeal.
2. Support for innovation, promotion of business spirit and growth of knowledge economy.
3. Creation of more and better jobs.

Therefore, the regional development strategy in Spain will be based on the key factors of competitiveness. To this end, the Spanish National Reference Strategy Framework (NRSF) 2007–2013 has three basic objectives:

1. To turn Spain into a more attractive place to invest and work.
2. To improve knowledge and innovation in favour of growth.
3. To create more and better jobs.

According to the above, the Spanish NRSF has established that Spanish regional policy can contribute to achieve a higher convergence and to increase the competitiveness of the European economy by the following means:

– Enlarging and improving its internal market
– Increasing the endowment of technological capital

Box 3.1 Community Strategic Guidelines for ERP

---

1. Making Europe and its regions a more attractive place to invest and work.
  1.1 To expand and improve transport infrastructures
  1.2 To improve the environmental contribution to growth and jobs
  1.3 To address the intensive use of traditional sources of energy

2. Knowledge and innovation for growth.
  2.1 To increase and improve investment in Technological R&D
  2.2 To facilitate innovation and to promote entrepreneurship
  2.3 To promote the Information Society for all
  2.4 To improve access to financing

3. More better jobs.
  3.1 To attract and retain more people in employment and to modernise the social protection systems
  3.2 To improve the adaptability of workers and companies and the flexibility of labour market
  3.3 To increase investment in human capital through better education and skills
  3.4 Administrative capacity
  3.5 Health and the labour force

- Improving the endowment of physical structures
- Improving the efficiency in the use of energy and the composition of energy supply
- Increasing the number of firms and entrepreneurship spirit
- Creating more and better jobs
- Improving education and the quality of its human capital
- Improving social cohesion
- Promoting equal opportunities between men and women and social integration
- Recovering and preserving the environment

The specific objectives of the NRSF for the period 2007–2013 are the following (Ministry of Econimic and Finance (2007)):

1. Increasing production in order to reach an income per capita similar to or higher than the European Union average. This requires a global employment rate higher than 70%, a female employment rate higher than 57%, and an increase in productivity per employee.
2. The productivity improvement must be based on a higher research effort. This implies exceeding 2% of the GDP and, more specifically, a higher private effort in order to reach 55% of the R&D expenditure.
3. The information society should reach levels of penetration much higher than current levels not only in companies (99% of companies with more than ten employees have an Internet connexion), but also in the whole population (65% of the population connects to the Internet on a regular basis), thus intensifying efforts to reduce the digital gender gap.
4. The investment in human capital must become another key pillar for the increase in productivity. In order to do so, the early school leaving rate must be reduced to 15%, and participation in lifelong learning must be increased to reach levels similar to those of the EU.
5. Sustainable use of natural resources, especially water, in order to fulfil the commitments of reducing CO^2 emissions to 24%.
6. Significant improvements in mobility, in both the transport of people and of goods, improving considerably railway transport (increase and extension of the network up to 35 km per 1,000 km).
7. Avoiding depopulation of certain areas, especially rural, where it is necessary to guarantee the sufficiency of urban and social infrastructures. At the same time, to ensure that cities and municipalities could become integrated sites for opportunities and employment generation, where it is necessary to guarantee an adequate quality of life by protecting and preserving the environment.

The details of the intervention axes of the European regional policy in Spain allow us to show how lines of action eligible for Structural Funds in the current programming period 2007–2013 include, in the case of "convergence" regions, investments which will not be applicable in the regions of the "competitiveness" objective. In particular, the Community financing of large transport infrastructures (motorways and highways), as well as social equipments (sanitary, educational and for attention of certain groups of population) will only be possible in the less-developed regions of the country (see Table 3.3).

Spanish regions have been classified for this programming period according to their different economic evolution in recent years as follows:

- Regions within the convergence objective:
  - Below 75% of GDP per EU inhabitant: Andalusia, Castile-La Mancha, Extremadura and Galicia.
  - Phasing-out regions:[13] Asturias, Murcia, Ceuta and Melilla.
- Regions within the regional and employment competitiveness objective:
  - Cantabria, Aragon, the Balearic Islands, Catalonia, Madrid, the Basque Country, Navarre and La Rioja.
  - Phasing-in regions:[14] Valencia, Castile-Leon and the Canary Islands.

The resources finally allocated to Spain in Structural and Cohesion funds have amounted to almost €35 billion, which is clearly below the €61.89 billion received for the period between 2000 and 2006. Despite this substantial decrease, Spain

Table 3.3 Priority axes of intervention of the European regional policy in Spain (2007–2013)

Priority axes of intervention of the European regional policy in Spain (2007–2013) through the ERDF

Convergence objective	Competitiveness and employment objective
1. Development of knowledge economy (R&D, information society and ICT)	1. Business innovation and development and knowledge economy
2. Business development and innovation	2. Environment and risk prevention
3. Environment, natural settings, water resources and risk prevention	3. Accessibility to transport networks and services
4. Transport and energy	4. Local and urban sustainable development
5. Local and urban sustainable development	5. Technical assistance
6. Investment in social infrastructures	
7. Technical assistance and reinforcement of institutional capabilities	

Priority axes of intervention of the European regional policy in Spain (2007–2013) through the ESF in the "convergence" and "competitiveness" regions

1. Promotion of entrepreneurial spirit and improvement of worker's adaptability
2. Promotion of employability, social inclusion and equal opportunities between men and women
3. Increase and improvement of human capital
4. Promotion of transnational and interregional cooperation
5. Technical assistance

Source: Mancha Navarro et al. (2008)

---

[13] So-called the regions eligible for funding in terms of the EU-15, but whose per capita GDP is higher than 75% of the EU-27 average. Include those regions affected by the "statistical effect".

[14] So-called the regions that would exceed the threshold of 75% of the former EU-15 average, but were objective 1 regions during the programming period 2000–2006. The financial support is limited to the current programming period.

remains as one of the main recipients of Structural Funds, exceeded only in absolute terms by Poland in the current programming period.

A more detailed analysis of the internal structure of the NSRF allows us to demonstrate that only Axes 1 (Development of knowledge economy) and 2 (Development of business innovation) of the ERDF designate 100% of their actions to the objectives of the RLS. In other words, the objective of fostering the competitiveness of Spanish regions fully coincides with the Community policy which supports the progressive establishment of a European research area, where a regional dimension plays an important role within the research policy (Table 3.4).

The next most significant contribution to the RLS is shown in Axis 4, transport and energy, in the "convergence" regions, where a substantial amount of budgeted investments are included in the *earmarking*. This is due to the fact that such investments boost, to a large extent, the development of economic activities and long-term employment.

The actions taken by the ESF contribute to the RLS more clearly than those of the ERDF. In fact, most of the actions integrated in the five Axes of this Fund, except for that of technical assistance, favour compliance with the RLS. The base of this approach is justified because the effort made in favour of the European employment strategy will be a stimulus to the development of human resources, allowing a more efficient response to the needs of the labour market at a local level,

Table 3.4 Percentage of forecast actions linked to the RLS over all types of actions

ERDF	Convergence regions (%)	Competitiveness regions (%)
1. Development of knowledge economy (R&D and information society)	100	100
2. Development and business innovation	100	100
3. Environment, natural settings, water resources and risk prevention	18	22
4. Transport and energy	70	38
5. Local and urban sustainable development	0	0
6. Social infrastructures	25	–
7. Technical Assistance	0	0
Total	57	47

ESF	Convergence regions (%)	Competitiveness regions (%)
1. Promoting entrepreneurial spirit and improvement of the adaptability of workers, companies and employers	100	100
2. Promoting employability, social inclusion and equal opportunities between men and women	100	100
3. Increasing and improving human capital	71	71
4. Promoting transnational and interregional cooperation[a]	–	–
5. Technical Assistance	0	0
Total	75	75

[a]During the programming period 2007–2013, the ESF will support interregional and transnational actions among Member States, continuing those undertaken under the Equal Community Initiative
Source: Mancha Navarro et al. (2008)

as well as to the employment possibilities. Consequently, it will be easier to improve the regions' productive capacity and to apply an active employment policy, pursuant to the objectives set out in Lisbon to this respect.

The reformulation of the Regional Policy and its orientation towards the competitiveness parameters fixed in the RLS mean the recognition of a development economic model combining market dynamism, social cohesion and environmental responsibility. Furthermore, Structural Funds are bound to play a fundamental role in order to exploit their full potential, as these are one of the most solid channels toward growth and employment in Spain and Europe.

However, it is worth highlighting that although the percentage of measures associated to the RLS regarding all the actions eligible in each objective of the new ERP is higher in the "convergence" regions, the real programmed effort, with respect to the total of the financial resources available, is almost 20 points lower (68.5%) than that of the "competitiveness" regions (85.3%) (see Table 3.5).

This reconversion of regional policy, putting it at the service of the RLS, introduces some uncertainties as to the type of results to be generated, particularly from the perspective of economic and social cohesion. A good example for the Spanish case is investment related to the water cycle. Undoubtedly, the availability of water resources is a key element for economic growth which, in some areas of the country, is starting to act as a limiting factor to their development. In fact, access to water affects the location for productive activities. In cases where the supply is inadequate, territorial disparities could be intensified considerably.

Therefore, it is reasonable to consider hydrological policy as one of the basic pillars of the cohesion strategy and, consequently, that Structural Funds are used to guarantee the quality and quantity of the available water resources. However, its contribution in making the economy more dynamic and competitive, which is at the same time the principal aim of the RLS, is more than dubious. It would be contradictory not to consider other actions in the same way, whose investments are not taken into account for fulfilling the *earmarking* (such as those for improving the allocations of land transport infrastructures), but which are very important in the medium- and long-term development of any region.

From a complementary viewpoint, another noteworthy problem in the Spanish case lies in the great attention paid to R&D&I, which could present problems in its implementation. The reason is that a paradox could arise: the existence of sufficient

Table 3.5 Comparison of Community aids related to the RLS during the programming periods 2000–2006 and 2007–2013

	2000–2006		2007–2013	
	Aid linked to RLS*	% over total	Aid linked to RLS*	% over total
Pure convergence regions	10,726,492,528.00	53.11	14,267,107,522.00	68.54
Phasing-out regions	2,209,404,248.00	54.10	1,350,656,845.00	74.11
Phasing-in regions	6,587,622,662.00	58.16	3,174,352,779.00	67.18
Competitiveness regions	2,028,498,084.00	62.86	3,201,976,779.00	85.32

*In current euros
Source: Own elaboration

financial resources and the inability of Spanish regions to use them if they lack appropriate projects or initiatives. In fact, during the programming period 2000–2006, great difficulties were observed by many objective 1 regions in the use of public funds allocated to innovation.

In conclusion, it is worrying that a certain imbalance could be created due to the difficulty of reaching a trade-off between a list of new objectives at the service of the RLS, focussed on increasing competitiveness and implementing certain financial instruments (i.e. Structural Funds) conceived for increased cohesion.

3.4 The Instruments Used in the Spanish Regional Policy

Two basic facts marked the design and implementation of Regional Policy in Spain: the configuration of the new State of Autonomies, set out in the Constitution of 1978, and the entry of Spain into the then-called European Community in 1986. In this context, two wide groups of instruments can be differentiated: those specific to the Spanish Regional Policy and those that come from the European regional policy.

3.4.1 Specific Instruments of Spanish Regional Policy

There are two instruments specific to the Spanish Regional Policy: the ICF and the *Regional Economic Incentives System (REIS)*.

3.4.1.1 Interterritorial Compensation Fund

As mentioned previously, the ICF was established under the 1978 Constitution as an instrument conceived to reduce disparities among the regions, and whose ultimate aim was to make the interregional solidarity principle effective. Its legal regulation, pursuant to article 157 of the Constitution, was expressed in the *Ley Orgánica de Financiación de las CC.AA.* or LOFCA (Organic Law on the Financing of the Autonomous Communities), where the basic aspects were set out; the distribution criteria were established by ordinary law.

At the beginning, after the enactment of the Law of 1984, the ICF did not only met its purpose established in the Constitution of being an instrument to reduce regional disparities, but it was also used as an instrument to finance the investment for the services transferred from Central Government to Regional Governments. Under this approach, all Autonomous Regions were recipients of this Fund, which was a percentage of the new civil investment carried out by the State and was distributed according to several criteria. Among these criteria, a lower income per capita was top priority.[15]

In practise, the concept of the ICF with its aforementioned double purpose caused some important dysfunctions derived from the decentralisation process itself. This was clearly favourable for certain regions depending on the legal framework of their Autonomy Statutes, which were not precisely the least developed and that, after assuming new competencies, received more resources. Additionally, the unequal level of economic development reached by Spanish regions profoundly affected the distribution process, with a remarkable change regarding migratory flows.

The essential reform needed by the ICF was undertaken in 1990 and can be summarised in two basic points: the beneficiary regions would be designated every year in the Spanish State Budget, being those considered as objective 1 regions of the European regional policy; and the distribution criteria would be modified.[16]

The last reform of this Fund, approved in 2001, introduced two significant changes: the destination of the resources allocated to it and the establishment of its beneficiaries. The first change was to split the ICF into the existing Compensation Fund and a new one called the Complementary Fund,[17] whose objective was to finance through the ICF not only the investment expenditure, but also current expenditure related to it.

The ICF has been used to finance the expenditure priorities in investments of the autonomous regions, and its high amount has favoured the consolidation and promotion of a capitalisation process particularly significant for Spanish objective 1 regions. Nevertheless, the ICF is an instrument not conditioned to undertake certain actions, so it responds to the preferences of the different autonomous governments. Nevertheless, transport infrastructures have been the main destination of ICF in recent years (around 25%).

---

[15] 70% inversely proportional to GDP per capita; 20% directly proportional to migratory balance; 5% directly proportional to the area; and 5% directly proportional to regional unemployment rate. A correcting factor of 'insularity' was also added, which meant another 5% for the Balearics and Canary Islands, plus 1% for each 50 km of distance between their territory and the Iberian Peninsula, proportionally subtracting the resulting amount from the rest of regions.

[16] 87.5% directly proportional to relative population. 1.6% directly proportional to migratory balance. 1% directly proportional to unemployment rate, 3% directly proportional to the area of each region. 6.9% directly proportional to dispersion of population within the territory. Once the ICF is distributed according to the previous criteria and weightings, the result obtained is corrected according to the following criterion: The inverse of the GDP per capita of each region and the 'insularity', which will increase by 63.1% the amount corresponding to the Autonomous Region of Canary Islands based on the aforementioned criteria. The increase obtained will be subtracted from the rest of the autonomous regions proportionally to the quantities that would have corresponded to them for the same aforementioned paragraphs.

[17] The Complementary Fund has an annual allocation equivalent to 33.33% of its respective ICF. This will be allocated to finance the investment expenditures, and also the expenditures required to launch and implement those investments debited against the ICF or the Complementary Fund during a maximum period of 2 years.

3.4.1.2 Regional Economic Incentives System

Incentives for business investment are, undoubtedly, one of the oldest instruments of regional policy, and it was profusely used during the 1960s. The accumulation of different figures, their limited transparency and the relative lack of selectivity led to its abandonment due to its low effectiveness.

It was not until 1985 that this system was reorganised and made compatible with the Community regulations under Law 50/1985,[18] thus suppressing the multiplicity of existing figures through the differentiation of just three types of zones: *Economic Promotion Zones* (EZP); *Industrial Decline Zones* (IDZ); and the so-called *Special Zones* (SZ).[19] Once the affected zones were defined according to the previous criteria, the economic territory was classified according to its level of development in type I, II, III and IV zones, which resulted in the establishment of the subsidy ceiling (75%).[20]

From 1988 to 2007, the REIS materialised in the approval of 13,607 files, with aid granted of €7.447 billion, with an investment of over €52.517 billion, which allowed the creation of 238,000 jobs and the preservation of over 711,000 (see Table 3.6).

The regional distribution shows that the regions that benefited the most from this system are Andalusia, Castile-Leon and Galicia. Data demonstrate that, due to the subsidies, this mechanism plays a relatively re-balancing role, as it favours the less-developed regions, which are those with the highest subsidy ceilings.

3.4.1.3 The Participation of European Regional Policy in Spain

Until 1988, European regional policy was a kind of subsidiary policy of the State member. For this reason, it was seen as a way to increase the returns of the Community budget by the less-developed countries, rather than as a real instrument for regional development.

The aforementioned 1988 reform changed its approach with an important budgetary increase regarding Structural Funds and the reorientation of their basic objectives. It now focussed on reinforcing economic potential, supporting structural

---

[18] This legal regulation was modified in 1995 only with regard to the establishment of zones and subsidy ceilings. This implied an increase in the percentage of the population that benefit, which rose from 63 to 75%.

[19] EZP comprise the less-developed geographical areas, defined according to the following criteria: GDP per capita, unemployment rate and other indicators representative of the intensity of national problems. IDZ comprise those areas affected by industrial restructuring processes that would have had a negative impact on the activity and employment level. Finally, SZ were considered to include special situations in areas that, due to the characteristics of their population, geographical situation, GDP, etc., would need a specific treatment and were not considered to be EZP or IDZ.

[20] The possibility of providing public aids through the REIS is an exception to article 92 of the Rome Treaty, which expressly declares incompatible with the state aids which distort or threaten to distort competition.

Table 3.6 Regional incentives evolution (1988–2007)

Zone	Number of records	Approved investment*	Subsidy*	Jobs to be created	Jobs to be preserved
Andalusia	3,237	12,262.4	1,748.0	60,089	137,679
Aragon	520	1,886.4	201.2	10,743	17,670
Asturias	596	2,651.3	465.7	9,136	27,707
Asturias (DIZ)	47	129.7	34.9	1,333	763
Canary Islands	565	3,046.9	391.3	1,5276	25,049
Cantabria	219	997.6	125.1	4,290	24,637
Cantabria (DIZ)	30	58.9	9.8	421	5,301
Cast.-la Mancha	1,003	3,036.6	425.5	2,0112	39,622
Cast.- Leon	2,162	8,956.0	1044.6	3,6708	152,210
Ceuta	16	29.6	4.9	262	237
Extremadura	892	2,139.4	368.6	1,3148	20,636
Extremadura (ZID)	79	98.9	44.8	1,357	467
Ferrol	79	216.8	99.5	1,904	1,064
Galicia	1,687	5,018.1	757.2	24,709	87,932
Melilla	10	21.5	3.3	197	22
Murcia	677	5,036.0	1162.4	1,4211	49,495
Basque C.	216	293.3	44.0	2,032	13,425
Valencian community	1,552	6,366.9	517.2	22,603	107,417
Total	13,607	52,157.6	7,447.9	238,531	711,333

*In millions of current euros
Source: Ministry of Economic and Finance (several years). Own elaboration

adjustment and boosting economic growth and long-term employment in the aided areas. Structural Funds always operate on a co-financing principle between Member States and the European Commission.

According to the concentration principle, the European regional policy until 2006 devoted the majority of its resources (almost 70% of the budget) to objective 1 regions, i.e. those with a GDP per capita below the Community average of 75%. Another 24% was allocated to the rest of the objectives, and the remaining percentage was basically assigned to Community Initiatives.[21]

From a financial point of view, since 1989, Spain has been the main beneficiary country in absolute terms, with an allocation of almost 26% of the total Structural and Cohesion Funds. However, in per capita terms, it has been surpassed by Greece and Ireland. Even so, more than 31 million people in Spain live in an objective 1 (23.2 million) or objective 2 region (8.8 million). From the perspective of investment flows received, the ERDF is, without a doubt, the most important fund quantitatively speaking. In fact, if we compare this with the ICF and the REIS, its prominence is clear (see Table 3.7).

---

[21] The rest of the objectives are summarised in objective 2 (regions with socio-economic restructuring problems) and objective 3 (dedicated to human resources). However, there were four Community Initiatives: Interreg (crossborder cooperation); Urban (actions in cities); Leader (rural development) and Equal (equal opportunities).

3 The Evolution of Spanish Regional Policy, 1977–2008   75

Table 3.7 Resources allocated to Regional Policy in Spain (1986–2006) (in millions of current euros)

Years	ICF	REIS	ERDF	EAGGF Guidance	ESF	Cohesion fund	EAGGF guarantee
1986	1178		242.8	0.4	144.2		224.8
1987	848.6		290.1	14.4	229		737.4
1988	908.4		418.3	62.5	229		1,687.8
1989	1291	1,247.1	694.8	222.1	394.3		1,486.1
1990	721.2	557.1	830.6	164.7	338.6		1,812.5
1991	774.1	211.6	1,702.1	496.1	816.6		2,721.5
1992	774.1	72.1	1,883	508.7	658.5		2,920.3
1993	774.1	175.5	1,682.8	670.7	645.2	194.3	4,149.1
1994	774.1	451.4	1,560.2	311.6	464.2	364	4,674.3
1995	774.1	206.7	2,704	861.7	1,472.1	1,023	4,940
1996	774.1	170.7	2,530.3	942.6	1,277	1,265.1	4,845.6
1997	800.5	385.2	2,547.1	733.5	1,818.2	722.6	5,111.3
1998	818.6	397.3	2,823.6	1,098.8	1,744.8	1,184.1	5,410.6
1999	833.5	420.5	3,726.5	1,412.7	1,968.8	1,110.7	5,237.2
2000	850.3	306.3	2,818.9	521.3	796.6	1,197.1	5,803.2
2001	880.9	569.2	3,380.6	630.3	1,084.8	868.3	6,302.6
2002	894.7	322.2	4,047.8	981.3	1,795.6	2,121.6	6,562.1
2003	955.8	612.8	5,343.7	1,276.7	1,652.7	1,800.10	6,422
2004	1,011.2	198.7	4,712.2	1,129.8	1,773.7	1,906.40	6,732
2005	1,061.8	473.9	3,851.4	1,272.4	1,784.2	1,391.40	6,267.9
2006	1,159.9	363.4	2,214.1	1,094.5	1,246.5	1,283.40	6,202.5
TOTAL	18,859.0	6,667.8	50,004.9	14,406.8	22,334.6	16,432.1	90,250.8

Source: Ministry of Economic and Finance (several years). Own elaboration

Aside from the aforementioned resources, those from the Cohesion Fund can be added from 1993. This fund contributed to financing investments in transport and environmental infrastructures in the four countries that, due to their poorer situation, were to be affected by the Economic and Monetary Union (Spain, Portugal, Greece and Ireland). Table 3.6 also shows the flow received from the EAGGF (European Agricultural Guidance and Guarantee Fund) Guarantee Section due to the implementation of the Common Agricultural Policy (CAP) which, although not designed with a regional end does have an important territorial impact, aside from the substantial amount of its resources. In fact, the CAP is frequently and with good reason assessed as a territorially unbalancing policy at a European level, because it provides more generous protection schemes for continental products than for Mediterranean products. However, in Spain, the CAP continues to have certain redistributing impacts as it benefits some less-developed areas with agricultural model similar than continental European one. The clearest example is Castile-Leon.

The Spanish evolution from the viewpoint of the resources received from the current European Union has clearly been ascending up until 2006, when it reached its peak. The already mentioned reform of the European regional policy for the period 2007–2013 has resulted in a more than notable reduction of structural aids, which have decreased dramatically (see Table 3.8).

Table 3.8 Resources received by Spain in structural aids since 1986 (in millions of euros 2004)

	1986–1988	1989–1993	1994–1999	2000–2006	2007–2013
Structural Funds	–	–	41.080	49.569	31.114
Cohesion Fund	–	–	9.574	12.322	3.543
Total	4.822	18.707	50.654	61.890	34.657

Source: Ministry of Economic and Finance (several years)

3.5 Some Relevant Results of Regional Policy in Spain

An evaluation of Spain's regional policy must take into account the influence of the current European Union on its design, implementation and effectiveness, not only from a qualitative, but also from a quantitative perspective.

From a qualitative viewpoint, Community regulations, particularly after the last legal reforms, have *strengthened the role of regional public authorities* in the process of elaborating Spanish regional policy. However, the *introduction of much more realistic selectivity criteria* has been remarkable, depending on the contribution to development of less-developed regions in terms of the actions designed, especially those devoted to the promotion of productive activity.

Spanish regional policy has also benefited from the integration process in Europe in two additional ways. On the one hand, some *order* has been put into a field where, after the period 1975–1985, regional actions had virtually disappeared. The most plausible explanation is connected with the duty to present a RDP according to a specific and strict methodology. This has avoided a problem by which regional actions would have been set out and executed in uncoordinated manner and without a clear definition of medium-term objectives.

On the other hand, European regional policy has introduced a higher level of *discipline and financial control*. In fact, Community regulations have forced the Spanish authorities to present their programmes and actions with a financial table scheduled by year and with commitments assumed by each and any of the possible authorities involved. It is remarkable that it has been necessary to implement specific mechanisms to be feasible the evaluation of the regional projects efficiency.

The assessment of the effectiveness of regional policy from a quantitative perspective is not an easy task. However, thanks to the existence of simulation exercises such as those made by Sosvilla (2007), we can state that the impact of Structural Funds on the Spanish economy is more than positive in terms of growth, gross capital formation (where funds contribute more than 5%), improvement of capital stock and employment, with policies for the valorisation of human resources. Moreover, these are long-term impacts, which imply that the positive differential effects go beyond the year 2006 (see Fig. 3.4).

The data confirm the regional policy's aforementioned emphasis on infrastructures over these years (more than 60% of the total resources allocated), followed at a considerable distance by those resources allocated to human capital and aids for companies (see Table 3.9).

3 The Evolution of Spanish Regional Policy, 1977–2008

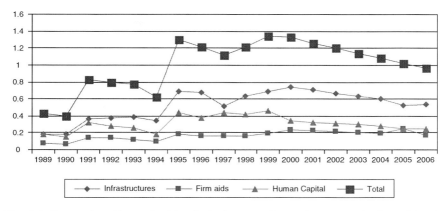

Fig. 3.4 Community aids received by Spain in proportion to its real production (GDP) by programming period and type of action
Source: Sosvilla (2007)

Table 3.9 Community aids received by Spain by programming period and types of action between 1989 and 2006 (in millions of euros in the year 2000)

Programming period	Infrastructures	Firm aids	Human capital	Total
Average (1989–1993)	1,008	362	798	3,096
Average (1994–1999)	3,859	1,026	2,534	6,229
Average (2000–2006)	5,021	1,703	2,334	7,891
Average (1989–2006)	3,519	1,105	1,974	6,005
Total (1989–2006)	63,341	19,892	35,535	108,098

Source: Sosvilla (2007)

One result that frequently goes unnoticed is the benefit that European regional policy generates for advanced regions. This fact is perfectly reflected in the external sector's accounts. Capitalisation processes carried out for objective 1 regions and cofinanced with Structural Funds are also of benefit to the rest of European regions, thanks to their imports Mancha Navarro and Garrido Yserte (2008).

Regional policy plays an obvious redistributive role as well. In fact, a great part of the co-financing received for the capitalisation of objective 1 regions is for redistributive purposes rather than for efficiency. By using simple indicators, such as Lorenz concentration curves and the Gini Index, several research studies have analysed the regional distribution of Regional Funds and their redistributive incidence.[22] Results show that concentration is particularly outstanding in the case of the ERDF, at a European level, and in Regional Incentives in the case of Spanish

---

[22] One of the first works was carried out by the European Parliament (1991), which designed a methodology later used for the Spanish case in other researches, such as those by Cordero et al. (1995), Lázaro and Cordero (1995), Correa et al. (1995) and Correa and Manzanedo (2002) and Mancha and Cuadrado (1996). These research studies concluded that such funds positively influence Spanish regions.

Table 3.10 Participation of Spanish regions in the resources allocated to Regional Policy (1983–2006). In %

	Spanish regional policy (1983–1999)	Spanish regional policy (2000–2006)	European regional policy (1986–1999)	European regional policy (2000–2006)
Andalusia	21.39	35.87	29.06	27.46
Aragon	3.43	0.64	2.02	5.54
Asturias	4.35	3.93	2.91	2.87
Balearics	0.79	0	0.61	0.44
Canary Islands	5.49	5.04	5.05	3.70
Cantabria	1.77	1.37	0.89	1.09
Cast.-Leon	10.03	9.85	8.87	13.79
Cast.-La Mancha	7.41	7.02	7.19	11.00
Catalonia	7.83	0	6.87	5.58
Valencian C.	8.45	7.63	5.65	4.87
Extremadura	5.15	6.95	7.24	8.99
Galicia	11.00	15.10	12.29	6.35
Madrid	4.4	0	4.02	1.54
Murcia	3.01	5.77	2.78	2.54
Navarre	0.89	0	0.36	1.51
Basque C.	3.66	0	3.53	2.04
Rioja (La)	0.42	0	0.36	0.53
Ceuta and Melilla	0.53	0.84	0.28	0.18
Total	100	100	100	100.00

Source: Correa and Manzanedo (2002) and own elaboration

instruments. The lowest impacts correspond to the ESF, as because of its aim it affects a horizontal objective, not regional, and the Cohesion Fund, with no regional criteria in order to be distributed.[23]

As a result of the aforementioned trend, the regions that obtain the greatest benefit from regional policy, both from the use of national and Community instruments are Andalusia, Galicia, Castile-Leon and Extremadura. The relationship between the support received and income level per capita is clear, showing that the financial efforts made have been particularly allocated to the less-developed regions. However, it is also worth mentioning the aforementioned positive effect generated by the intense capitalisation process of less-developed regions on high-developed areas. The absorption of Spanish and European resources by Andalusia is particularly significant, followed at a considerable distance by both Castile regions, Galicia and Extremadura. These five regions took up three-quarters of the resources allocated by Spanish regional policy and two-thirds of European resources between 2000 and 2006 (Table 3.10).

---

[23] Absolute values obtained from the concentration index calculated for the period 1986–2006 are: ERDF, 0.35; ESF, 0.15; EAGGF Guidance section, 0.24; FCI, 0.18 and SIER, 0.41.

References

Cordero, G., Gayoso, A., Pavón, A., & Rodriguez, E. (1995). *La política de cohesión económica y social de la UE y el presupuesto comunitario.* Working Paper. Madrid: General Direction of Planning. Ministry of economy and Finance.

Correa, M. D., & Manzanedo, J. (2002). Política regional española y europea. Working Paper. *Dirección General de Análisis y Programación Presupuestaria.* Madrid: Ministry of Economy and Finance.

Correa, M. D., Fanlo, A., Manzanedo J., & Santillán, S. (1995). *Fondos comunitarios en España: regionalización y análisis de su incidencia.* Working Paper. General Direction of Planning. Madrid: Ministry of Economy and Finance.

Cuadrado, J. R. and Mancha, T. (1995). Política regional comunitaria: ventajas e implicaciones para España. *Economistas,* 13, pp. 66–67.

Cuadrado, J. R., & Mancha, T. (2008). Política regional y de cohesión. In J. M. Jordán Galduf (Ed.), *Economía de la Unión Europea.* Madrid: Thompsom.

European Parliament (1991). Regional Effects of Community Policies. Luxembourg.

European Commission (2007). *Cohesion Policy 2007–2013. Comments and oficial texts.* Brussels. European Commission.

Garrido, R., Mancha, T., & Cuadrado, J. R. (2007). La política regional europea. 20 años de avance y un futuro nuevo. *Investigaciones Regionales* 10.

Lázaro, L., & Cordero, G. (1995). La política de cohesión económica y social de la UE: evaluación desde la perspectiva española. *Papeles de Economía Española* 63.

Mancha Navarro, T. (1999). Desequilibrios regionales e integración económica: algunas consideraciones para el caso español, *Economía Aragonesa,* February

Mancha Navaarro, T. (2008). "El ciclo político-económico en la democracia". In L. Gámir (Ed.), *Política Económica de España.* Madrid: Alianza Editorial.

Mancha, T., & Cuadrado, J. R. (1996). La convergencia de las regiones españolas: una difícil tarea. In J.R. Cuadrado and T. Mancha (Ed.), *España frente a la Unión Económica y Monetaria.* Madrid: Civitas.

Mancha, T., & Cuadrado, J. R. (2000). Política regional. In Gámir (Ed.), *Política Económica de España.* Madrid: Alianza.

Mancha, T., Cuadrado, J. R., & Garrido, R. (1999). *Evaluación de resultados y reserva de eficacia: un desafío para la política regional en la Unión Europea.* Communication presented to the III Jornadas de Política Económica. Alicante, April.

Mancha Navarro, T., & Garrido Yserte, R. (2004). La Política regional de la Unión Europea: quo vadis? *Cuadernos de Economía, 27*(73), 13–35.

Mancha Navarro, T., & Garrido Yserte, R. (2008). Regional policy in the European Union: The cohesion-competitiveness dilemma. *Regional Policy and Practice, 1*(1).

Mancha Navarro, T., Garrido Yserte, R., & Pablo Pindado, F. (2005). *Evaluación de la calidad de la gestión y ejecución de la política regional: la Reserva de Eficacia y los progresos en la consecución de los objetivos planteados.* Communication presented to the IV Conferencia Sociedad Española de Evaluación. Madrid, June.

Mancha Navarro, T., Garrido Yserte, R., Pablo Pindado, F., & Fernández, N. (2008). La política regional europea y el dilema entre competitividad y cohesión. In J. M. Jordán, and A. Sánhez (Eds.), *Desafíos actuales de la política económica.* Madrid: Civitas-Thompson.

Ministry of Economic and Finance (several years). La planificación regional y sus instrumentos. Informe Anual. Madrid: Ministerio de Economía y Hacienda.

Ministry of Economic and Finance. (2007). *Marco de Referencia Estratégico Nacional 2007–2013.* Madrid: Ministerio de Economía y Hacienda.

Parlamento Europeo. (1991). *Efectos regionales de las políticas comunitarias.* Serie Política regional y transportes. Luxemburg: Parlamento Europeo.

Sosvilla, S. (2007). *La economía española y la política de cohesión europea.* Communication presented to the VIII Jornadas de Política Económica, Valencia, October.

Part II
Regional Growth, Structural Changes and Convergence

Communication service providers have been active in adopting software technology for OSS/BSS processes as a means to improve productivity. The first section of this chapter starts with a general analysis on when and how software can be used as a means to improve enterprise productivity, and the second section continues with a small-scale quantitative analysis on the impact of software usage to CSP performance. The third section uses interviews of CSP representatives to gain internal view to the use of software in telecom operators. The interviews from Europe and the Far East disclose CSPs' criteria about when to buy software instead of making it in-house and give some background on the CSP business environment in China and Taiwan. Section four targets the OSS/BSS software market evolution and analyses it using multiple market development models.

Chapter 4
Macroeconomic Effects of the European Cohesion Policy in the Spanish Economy

Simón Sosvilla-Rivero

4.1 Introduction

Since its joining of the today's European Union (EU), on 1 January 1986, the Spanish economy has experienced a strong impulse based on several factors (Polo and Sancho, 1993). Among these factors, we can cite the liberalisation, both internal and external, that entry to the club implied the massive reception of structural aid, participation in the co-ordination of macroeconomic policy, at the beginning, and the adoption of the euro and the stability and growth pact, later on.

Among the factors cited above are the structural and cohesion aid that Spain has received, in a preferential manner, at least in absolute terms, since its incorporation and even more-so, since the structural funds were reformed in 1987. The aim of this chapter is to assess the impact of such funds on the Spanish economy. We analyse both the 1989–2006 period and the current 2007–2013 budgetary period. Our evaluation is based on the observed evolution (and a projection up to a given year) of per-capita real income and relative income per-capita between Spain and the average of the EU15, from which we extract the effects that we can supposedly attribute to the EU aids. These effects are obtained using the HERMIN macro-econometric model of the Spanish economy. Proceeding in this way, we can produce a counter-factual scenario that we can then compare with the observed (and projected) evolution. This counter-factual method will always be limited since, had the EU structural and cohesion aid not been received, other developments and alternative policies that are impossible to imagine now would have taken place. Therefore, the effects attributed to the EU programmes cannot be understood as benefits, whenever they are positive, as the Spanish economy would not have been

---

S. Sosvilla-Rivero
Universidad Complutense, Facultad de Ciencias Económicas y Empresariales, Departamento de Fundamentos de Análisis Económico, Campus de Somosaguas, 28223-Madrid, España
e-mail: sosvilla@ccee.ucm.es

able to compensate, to a greater or lesser degree, with other alternative policies in the absence of the former.

In Sect. 2, we discuss the methodology used. Section 3 briefly describes European regional policy, offering a quantification of the structural and cohesion aid that Spain has received or will receive during the period 1989–2006 and the programmed aid for the period 2007–2013. In Sect. 4, we offer an ex-post evaluation for the period 1989–2006, while Sect. 5 presents an ex-ante evaluation for the period 2007–2013. Finally, Sect. 6 provides some concluding remarks.

4.2 Methodology

4.2.1 Clarifying the Effects of European and Cohesion Aids

European structural and cohesion aids influence the economy through a mixture of supply and demand effects. Short-term demand (or Keynesian) effects arise in the model as a consequence of increases in the expenditure and income policy instruments associated with structural and cohesion policy initiatives. Through the multiplier effects contained in the model, there will be a knock-on increase in all the concepts of domestic expenditure (e.g. total investment, private consumption, the net trade surplus, etc.) and the components of domestic output and income. These demand effects are of transitory importance, and are merely a side-effect of structural and cohesion aids. Rather, these interventions are intended to influence the long-run supply potential of the economy. The supply-side effects steaming from increased capacity (infrastructure, private capital and human capital) operate through lower costs, higher productivity and increased competitiveness, stimulating production, reducing imports and increasing exports. As income increases, we also note the inflationary pressure that originates in the demand-side of the model. These supply-side effects arise through policies designed to

1. Increase investment in order to improve physical infrastructure as an input to private sector productive activity (see, for example, Gramlich, 1994)
2. Increase in human capital, due to investment in training, an input to private sector productive activity
3. Channel public funding assistance to the private sector to stimulate investment, thereby increasing factor productivity and reducing sectoral costs of production and of capital

Providing more and better infrastructure, increasing the quality of the labour force or providing investment aid to firms, are the mechanisms through which structural and cohesion interventions improves output, productivity and cost competitiveness of the economy. In a certain sense, these policies create conditions where private firms enjoy the use of additional productive factors at free of cost to themselves. Alternatively, they may help to make the current private sector inputs, which firms are already using, available to them at a lower cost, or the general conditions under which firms operate are improved as a consequence. In all these ways, positive externalities may arise out of these structural and cohesion interventions.

Recent advances in growth theory have addressed the role of spill-overs externalities, which arise from public investments, for example, in infrastructures or in human capital.[1] Furthermore, this literature suggests that technical progress can be affected directly through investment in research and development, arising externalities when innovations in one firm are adopted elsewhere.[2]

In this sense, two types of beneficial externalities are likely to enhance mainly the demand-side (or Keynesian) impacts of well designed investment, training and aid policy initiatives. The first type of externality is likely to be associated with the role of improved infrastructure and training in boosting output directly. This works through mechanisms, such as attracting productive activities through foreign direct investment and enhancing the ability of indigenous industries to compete in the international market place. We refer to this as an output externality, since it is well-known that the range of products manufactured in developing countries changes during the process of development, and becomes more complex and technologically advanced.

The second type of externality arises through the increased total or embodied factor productivity likely to be associated with improved infrastructure or a higher level of human capital associated with training and education. We refer to this as a factor productivity externality. Of course, a side-effect of increased factor productivity is that, in the restricted context of fixed output, the labour is shed. The prospect of such "jobless growth" is particularly serious in economies where the recorded rate of unemployment is already high. Thus, the factor productive externality is a two-edge process: industry and market services become more productive and competitive, but labour demand is weaken if output is fixed. However, on the positive side, factor productivity is driven up, real incomes rise, and these effects cause knock-on multiplier and other benefits throughout the economy.

4.2.2 HERMIN: A Macro-Sectoral Modelling Framework

As we have mentioned already, in order to evaluate the macroeconomic effects of the European structural and cohesion aids, we use the HERMIN modelling

---

[1] For the Spanish case, see: Bajo-Rubio and Sosvilla-Rivero (1993) and Sosvilla-Rivero and Alonso-Meseguer (2005), respectively.

[2] The concept of externalities in production is central to the recent developments in the theory of endogenous growth, offering a more adequate representation of the process of economic growth by extending neoclassical growth theory to include the role of human capital, public capital and technology (see, for example, Sala-i-Martin, 1990).

framework,[3] which has been used on several occasions to compare the structural characteristics of the European periphery economies (Bradley et al., 1995b, 1995c), to evaluate the macroeconomic effects of the community support frameworks (CSF) (Bradley et al., 1995a; Herce and Sosvilla–Rivero, 1994; Christodoulakis and Kalyvitis, 2000) or the Single European Market (Barry et al., 1997), as well as the environmental consequences of CSF (Antón et al., 1999), the ageing of population (Herce and Sosvilla Rivero, 1998) or the effects for the Spanish economy of the eastern enlargement of the EU (Martín et al., 2002).

The theoretical underpinning of the HERMIN model is that of a two-sector small open economy model with a Keynesian role for domestic demand. The two-good model assumes two domestic sectors, one producing mainly internationally traded and the other mainly non-traded goods and services. The mainly traded sector is identified with manufacturing, while the mainly non-traded sector is identified with market services. Both the sectors produce with constant returns to scale technologies and with sector-specific physical capital.

The non-traded sector operates rather like a closed economy, where firms are price setters in the output market and price takers in factor markets. Therefore, they maximise their profits subject to the production function constraint. In the traded sector, business are assumed to be a mixture of domestically owned local firms and externally owned multinationals. With limited market power, the pricing behaviour of the traded sector goods is a mixture of both price taking and price setting behaviour. The extension of the supply-side of the traded goods sector towards a more realistic model allows output of the sector to be determined both by domestic factor costs as well as by external and internal demand.

The HERMIN model framework focuses on key structural features of the economy that are essential for the analysis of the European structural and cohesion policy (see Bradley et al., 1995a):

1. Economic openness, exposure to world trade, and response to external and internal shocks.
2. Relative sizes and characteristics of the traded and non-traded sectors and their development, production technology and structural change.
3. Wage and price determination mechanisms.
4. The functioning and flexibility of labour markets.
5. The role of the public sector and public debt, and the interactions between the public and private sector trade-offs in public policies.

To satisfy these requirements, the HERMIN framework is designed as a macro-econometric model composed of four sectors:[4]

---

[3] See Herce and Sosvilla-Rivero (1995) for a more detailed description of the Spanish version of the model, and Herce and Sosvilla-Rivero (1994) for an exposition of the macroeconomic treatment of the European structural and cohesion funds.

[4] The choice of the sectoral disaggregation is justified by the desire of keeping the model as small and simple as possible while separating sectors with different behaviour and driven by different forces.

1. Manufacturing (*T*), the exposed tradable sector driven by both domestic and foreign demand, and by international cost competitiveness.
2. Market services (*N*), the protected non-tradable sector driven by domestic demand.
3. Agriculture (*A*), treated as mainly exogenous, and
4. Public sector or non-market services (*G*), depending on Government policy decisions, with expenditure and tax revenues as instruments.

The Spanish model consists of 178 equations distributed in three main blocks (see Herce and Sosvilla-Rivero, 1995):

- A supply-side, determining output, factor inputs, wages, prices, productivity, etc.
- An absorption side, determining the expenditure side of the national accounts, such as consumption, stock changes, etc.
- An income distribution side, determining private and public sector income.

Conventional Keynesian mechanisms are at the core of the HERMIN model. Therefore, the interaction of the expenditure and income distribution blocks generates the standard multiplier properties of the HERMIN model. However, the model also incorporates several neoclassical characteristics, above all associated with the supply-side of the model. Thus, private sector production is not determined exclusively by demand, but rather it is also influenced by competitiveness in costs and prices, within a context of firms acting with an objective of minimising productive costs Bradley and Fitz Gerald, (1988). The model incorporates a constant elasticity of substitution (CES) production function, in which the capital/labour ratio responds to the relative prices of these factors. Finally, the inclusion of a Phillips curve mechanism in the wage negotiation procedure introduces further relative price effects into the model.

The national accounts define three ways of measuring gross domestic product (GDP): the output basis, the expenditure basis and the income basis. On the output basis, HERMIN disaggregates output for the four sectors. On the expenditure side, HERMIN disaggregates into five components: private consumption, public consumption, investment, stock changes and net trade balance. National income is determined on the output side, and disaggregated into private and public elements.

Since all the elements of output are modelled, the output-expenditure identity is used to determine net trade surplus/deficit residually. The output-income identity is used to determine corporate profits residually. Finally, the 178 equations in the model can be classified as behavioural or identity. In the case of the former, economic theory and calibration to the data are used to define the relationships. In the case of the identities, these follow from the logic of the national accounts, but have important consequences for the behaviour of the model as well. There are 138 identities and 40 behavioural equations in the Spanish HERMIN model.

The model functions as an integrated system of equations, with interrelationships between all their sub-components and blocks. The essential core of the model consists of a small number of equations, of which only 20 are behavioural in the economic sense. The main behavioural equations are the following:

- Manufacturing
  - GDP in manufacturing
  - Joint factor demand system in manufacturing (employment and investment)
  - Manufacturing GDP deflator
- Average annual earnings in manufacturing
  - Market services
  - GDP in marketed services
  - Joint factor demand system in marketed services (employment and investment)
  - Marketed services GDP deflator
- Agriculture
  - GDP in agriculture, forestry and fishing
  - Labour in agriculture, forestry and fishing
  - Investment in agriculture, forestry and fishing
- Demographics
  - Male labour force participation rate
  - Female labour force participation rate
- Absorption
  - Household consumption

The model is calibrated using homogeneous time series of national accounts data from the period 1964–2006 offered by the data base BDMACRO (Díaz Ballesteros et al., 2008). The HERMIN model databank is developed in Excel and TSP format, and model calibration is carried out using TSP. The model is constructed and simulated using the WINSOLVE software package.

4.2.3 Incorporating the Externality Mechanisms into the Model Structure

As we have already seen, it is assumed that the economic effects derived from European structural and cohesion aids hit first the economy as stimuli to aggregate demand and then as supply externalities, as the extra productive capacity they contribute to create comes into operation. In the case of externalities, we attempt to capture the effects by modifying the key equations in this model (mainly the production functions and the demands for factors).

Regarding the output externalities, we posit a hybrid supply–demand equation to determine manufacturing sector output (OT):

$$\log(\text{OT}) = a_0 + a_1 \log(\text{FDDWOT}) + a_2 \log(\text{OW}) \\ + a_3 \log(\text{CCOMPT}) + a_4 \text{ TIME},$$

where FDDWOT represents the influence of domestic absorption, OW represents the crucial external (or world) demand, CCOMPT represents costs competitiveness and TIME is a time trend. To take account of output externalities associated with infrastructure, human capital and private investment, the following three terms are added to the above equation:

$$\eta_1(\text{KGINF}_t/\text{KGINF}_0) + \eta_2(\text{KH}_t/\text{KH}_0) + \eta_3(\text{K}_t/\text{K}_0),$$

where the output of the manufacturing sector is now directly influenced by any increase in the stock of infrastructure, human capital and private capital (KGINF, KH and K, respectively) over and above a baseline values for these stocks (KGINF$_0$, KH$_0$ and K$_0$, respectively). η_1, η_2 and η_3 represent the corresponding elasticities.

With respect to the factor productivity externalities, consider the following CES production function:

$$O = A\{\delta(\exp(\lambda_L t)L)^{-\rho} + (1-\delta)(\exp(\lambda_K t)K)^{-\rho}\}^{-(1/\rho)},$$

where O, L and K represent, respectively, GDP, employment and the *stock* of capital, A is a scale parameter, $\frac{1}{1+\rho}$ is the elasticity of substitution, δ is a parameter of factor intensity and λ_L and λ_K are the rates of technical change incorporated in labour and capital, respectively. Externality effects can be incorporated by making the scale parameter endogenous, for example, by making it depend upon public investment in infrastructure (KGINF), human capital (KH) and the private capital (K), in the following way:

$$A_t = A_0(\text{KGINF}_t/\text{KGINF}_0)^{\eta_1}(\text{KH}_t/\text{KH}_0)^{\eta_2}(\text{K}_t/\text{K}_0)^{\eta_3},$$

where, as before, the sub-indexes t and 0 denote the accumulated stock with and without European structural and cohesion aids, and η_1, η_2 and η_3 represent the corresponding elasticities.

In our empirical application, we adopt the following values for the different elasticities: $\eta_1 = 0.20$, $\eta_2 = 0.07$ and $\eta_3 = 0.10$. These values are approached gradually as the different investments within the CSF package mature. As far as the value used for the elasticity $\eta_1 = 0.2$ is concerned, we have used the estimations of Bajo-Rubio and Sosvilla-Rivero (1993) and Argimón et al. (1994) as a base. The value for the elasticity $\eta_2 = 0.07$ has been taken from the estimations on the social return of education and professional training in Spain obtained by Corugedo et al. (1992). This elasticity is actually the estimated coefficient for the education variable in a model, which attempts to explain the net wage earned by a worker in his or her current job, and it corresponds to the internal rate of return for education proposed by Mincer (1974). Finally, the value of the elasticity $\eta_3 = 0.1$ was chosen based on detailed field evidence on the effects of the CSF 1989–1993 (Herce, 1994).

This manner of introducing supply effects into a conventional econometric model is, without doubt, an *ad hoc* attempt within a treatment that has yet to be fully explored. With the objective of limiting risks, we have taken the most moderate values for the elasticities that are suggested from the previous literature, and in the simulations, we have made their effects to mature progressively. It is clear that the results concerning the supply effects of the European structural aids will depend on both the size of the externalities and their rate of maturity.

4.3 European Cohesion Policy Towards Spain

4.3.1 EU Cohesion Policy

The European Regional Development Fund, the centrepiece of the European Union's regional policy, was established in 1975, but it was not until 1985 when Spain and Portugal were admitted into the then European Community that regional income differences became a priority issue on the community's agenda. The European Social Fund had existed since 1969, and agricultural policy was financed by the European agricultural guidance and guarantee fund, whose guidance section was assimilated to the structural funds during the early 1990s. In March 1988, the European Council in Brussels decided to allocate ECU 64 billion to the structural funds, which represented a doubling of annual resources over the period 1989–1993. On 24 June 1988, the Council adopted the first regulation integrating the structural funds under the umbrella of cohesion policy. This landmark reform introduced key principles, such as focussing on the poorest and most backward regions, multi-annual programming, strategic orientation of investments and the involvement of regional and local. Five priority objectives were agreed in 1988:

- Objective 1: Promoting the development and structural adjustment of regions whose development is lagging behind.
- Objective 2: Converting regions seriously affected by industrial decline.
- Objective 3: Combating long-term unemployment.
- Objective 4: Facilitating the occupational integration of young people.
- Objective 5: (a) Speeding up the adjustment of agricultural structures and (b) promoting the development of rural areas.

Agreed in Maastricht on 7 February 1992, the Treaty on European Union and the revised Treaty on the European Communities (TEC) entered into force on 1 November 1993. In respect to Cohesion and Regional Policy, the TEC established a new instrument, the cohesion fund, and a new institution, the Committee of the Regions, as well as the introduction of the subsidiarity principle. In December 1992, the European Council decided on the new financial perspective for the period 1994–1999 and ECU 168 billion were set aside for the structural and cohesion funds. This represented a doubling of annual resources and equalled a third of the EU budget. New Cohesion Policy regulations were adopted by the Council on 20 July 1993, which now included the financial instrument of fisheries guidance and the cohesion fund. The new regulations confirmed the policy's key principles (concentration, programming, additionality and partnership) and kept the five existing objectives more or less unchanged. Some provisions were strengthened, such as the involvement of other EU institutions, in particular the European Parliament, and the rules on partnership, evaluation and publicity. Upon the accession of Austria, Finland and Sweden on 1 January 1995, an amending regulation defined a sixth objective favouring the extremely low populated regions of Finland and Sweden and a financial allocation for the three new Member States.

A move towards simplification of Cohesion Policy's design and procedures in parallel with preparation for enlargement were the two major themes of the period 2000–2006. "Agenda 2000" had been in preparation since the second half of 1990s and it paved the way for the biggest ever enlargement of the EU, with ten new Member States joining in May 2004. This historic enlargement brought a 20% increase in the EU's population, but only a 5% increase in the Union's GDP. With enlargement came increased disparities in income and employment, as the average GDP per head in these new member countries was under half the EU average and only 56% of their population were in active employment, compared to 64% in EU-15. The new Member States' territory almost completely fell under Objective 1, eligible for the highest possible level of support from the structural and cohesion funds. However, work began before enlargement including making pre-accession instruments available to help the then candidate countries to prepare for Cohesion Policy. Following a decision taken by the European Council of Berlin in March 1999, the 2000–2006 budget for Cohesion Policy totalled €213 billion for the 15 Member States. An additional allocation of €22 billion was provided for the new Member States for the period 2004–2006. The "Lisbon Strategy" was agreed by the European Council in Lisbon in March 2000; with its focus on growth, employment and innovation, it became more and more the leitmotiv of many EU policies and was the momentum for a paradigm shift in Cohesion Policy.

The highest concentration ever of resources on the poorest Member States and regions, the inclusion of all regions, and a shift in priorities set to boost growth, jobs and innovation, are essentially the major changes to EU Cohesion Policy during the 2007–2013 period. The new priority objectives are defined as follows:

- Convergence: aims at speeding up the convergence of the least-developed Member States and regions defined by GDP per capital of less than 75% of the EU average
- Regional Competitiveness and Employment: covers all other EU regions with the aim of strengthening regions' competitiveness and attractiveness as well as employment, and
- European Territorial Cooperation: based on the Interreg initiative, support is available for cross-border, trans-national and interregional cooperation as well as for networks

In the EU of 27 Member States, one in three EU citizens now live in the poorest regions, which receive assistance under the "Convergence" objective. Economic and social disparities have significantly deepened with recent enlargements. The European Council agreed in December 2005 on the budget for the period

2007–2013 period and allocated €347 billion to Structural and cohesion funds, of which 81.5% are planned to be spent in the "Convergence" regions. Based on simplified procedures, nearly all of the 436 programmes covering all EU regions and Member States were agreed before the end of 2007. The radical shift in their priorities means that a quarter of resources is now earmarked for research and innovation and about 30% for environmental infrastructure and measures combating climate change.

4.3.2 EU Aids Received by the Spanish Economy

The balance of resources provided by and obtained from the overall community budget could not have been better for Spain within the primary terms of the implied flows, going back to the early 1990s with a net balance close to €6 billion per year in its favour. The structural and cohesion aid received by Spain has been of a similar, or even greater, magnitude, and Spain has been the country that has most benefited, in absolute terms, from the community's cohesion policy. As shown in the analysis that follows, the macroeconomic impact of this aid has been both substantive and long-term. In Table 4.1, we detail the community aid that has been provided to Spain by both the structural funds and the cohesion fund, according to programming periods and functional category. Independently of the funds or instruments from which the funds originate, in order to carry out our evaluation, we have divided the aid into the following sections: public investment in infrastructure, aid for private productive investment, and investment in human resources. We have used information on actual expenses for the years 1989–1999 (Correa and Manzanedo, 2002), whereas for the programming period 2000–2006, we have simply used the amounts envisaged in the Agenda 2000 plan (Ministerio de Hacienda, 2001). Finally, total data for the 2007–2013 period come from Ministerio de Hacienda (2008) and the detailed disaggregation was kindly provided by Angeles Gayoso.

Table 4.1 European structural and cohesion aid received by Spain, by programming period and aid category for the period 1989 to 2006 (in million euros, at 2000 prices)

Programming period	Production aid	Human capital	Infrastructure	Total
1989–1993	2,000	4,259	5,947	12,206
1994–1999	4,196	10,504	15,759	30,459
2000–2006	11,733	15,830	34,062	61,624
2007–2013	5,618	10,274	18,273	34,165
(Annual average 1989–2006)	1,007	1,727	3,126	5,861
(Annual average 1989–2013)	950	1,655	2,982	5,586
Total aid 1989–2006	18,130	31,093	56,272	105,495
Total aid 1989–2013	23,748	41,367	74,545	139,660

Sources: Correa and Manzanedo (2002), Ministerio de Hacienda (2001, 2008) and own computations

In this way, the total amount of EU aid destined for Spain over the period 1989–2006 is €105,495 million as of 2000 prices, of which 91,693 million correspond to the structural funds and 13,802 million to the cohesion fund. As can be seen in Table 4.1, over this period, an average of 53.34% of the aid is dedicated to infrastructures, a total of €56,272 million as of 2000, which represents an annual average over the period of €3,126 million as of 2000. The next most important category is the aid destined to enhance human capital, with a sum total of €31,093 million as of 2000, or 29.45% of the total European structural and cohesion aid, representing an annual average over the period 1989–2006 of €1,727 million as of 2000. Finally, we have €18,130 million as of 2000 dedicated to productive aid to firms that is a total of 17.19% of the total aid package, which represents an annual average over the period 1989–2006 of €817 million as of 2000. Regarding the current period (2007–2013), the total amount is €34,165 million as of 2000, the 53.48% of which is expected to be allocated to infrastructures (€18,273 million as of 2000), being the 30.07% dedicated to enhance human capital (€10,274 million as of 2000) and the remainder 16.44% is programmed to be invested in private firms (€5,618 million as of 2000). During the 2007–2013, 90.86% of the ERP will be arriving via the structural funds, while the remainder 9.14% will be received via the cohesion fund.

Figure 4.1 shows the EU structural and cohesion aid as a percentage of Spanish GDP for each programming period, as of 2000 prices. As can be seen in this graph, the Community aid would have implied a positive shock on the economy equivalent to 0.45% of annual real production over the period 1989–1993, which increases to 1.03% for 1994–1999, and after representing 1.30% of GDP for the 2000–2006 period, reduces sharply to 0.60% of GDP for the current 2007–2013 period. Over the entire period (1989–2013), the annual average of European structural and cohesion aid as a percentage of real GDP is expected to be 0.87%. We can also note in the graph, the relative importance of each functional shock received by the Spanish economy in each period.

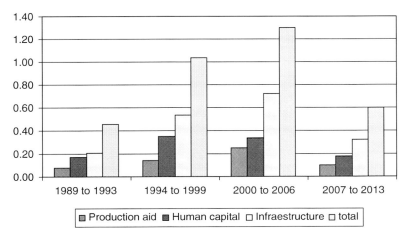

Fig. 4.1 European structural and cohesion aid received by Spain as a percentage of GDP by programming period and category of aid – 1989 to 2013 (annual average)

4.4 Ex-post 1989–2006 Evaluation

Given that the main objective of the European structural and cohesion funds is to promote economic and social convergence, we shall focus our attention on the impact on of real per-capita income, proxied by per-capita GDP as of 2000 prices over the period 1989–2006. The effects are compared with the situation that would have existed when the aids have not been given (the benchmark scenario). The approach adopted is especially important in that the fact that a particular economy has not "improved" its performance in spite of having received the EU grants does not necessarily imply that the aids received had been ineffective, since the economy could feasibly have been in an even worse position had these not been received (see Sosvilla-Rivero et al., 2002).

It should be noted that, ideally, we should use the actual ex-post realised EU Cohesion expenditures, but they were not available for the 2000–2006 period. Therefore, and previously stated, we use realised expenditures for the 1989–1999 period and programmed expenditures for the 2000–2006 period.

In Table 4.2, we present the results for each programming period in terms of this variable for three simulations: the first shows only the demand effects; the second only takes into account the supply effects; and the third considers both total supply and demand effects. As can be seen in that table, for the programming period 1989–1993, the results of our simulations suggest that the per-capita income was, on average, €215 as of 2000 greater than what it would have been without EU aids. Over the second programming period (1994–1999), the difference increases to €692 (as of 2000 prices), and this increases to €1,083 for the 2000–2006 period. Finally, over the entire period analysed (1989–2006), we obtain an average difference of €674 as of 2000 between the scenarios with and without structural and cohesion aids. Given that the average of per-capita EU aid during the period was €142 of 2000, our results imply that Spaniards could have profited more than four times as much as the amounts from Brussels, indicating the capacity of the EU aids induced investments to generate income and wealth. Finally, although the average growth rate of real income per-capita was 2.28% during the 1988–2006 period, the simulation results suggests that such average rate would have been 2.10% without demand effects and 1.90% without total (demand and supply) effects. That is, the structural and cohesion community aids would have implied that per-capita real income in Spain has grown at almost 0.4% points above the rate it would be observed in the absence of such aids.

Table 4.2 Effects of European structural and cohesion aid on the real per-capita income in Spain (annual average, in euros of 2000)

	With EU aid (supply and demand effects)	Without demand effects of EU aid	Without EU aid	Difference between first and third column
1989–1993	12,516	12,325	12,301	215
1994–1999	13,694	13,225	13,001	692
2000–2006	16,312	15,731	15,229	1,083
1989–2006	14,231	13,818	13,557	674

Table 4.3 Relative per-capita income in Spain (PPP adjusted, EU-15=100)

	With EU aid	Without EU aid	Difference
Index in 1988	74.34	74.34	0.00
Index in 1993	78.83	76.95	1.88
Index in 1999	83.54	77.41	6.13
Index in 2006	89.39	83.61	5.78

Source: Own calculations using the HERMIN-Spain model, and AMECO database (DG ECFIN, EU Commission)

Table 4.3 shows the relative situation of income per-capita between Spain and the average of the European Union of 15 before May 2004 in terms of purchasing power standards (PPS) and expressed as index numbers with a value of 100 for the average of EU-15 for each year. As can be seen, in 1988, Spain's per-capita income was only 74.34% of the average of the EU-15. The results of our simulations suggest that by the end of the first programming period, the Spanish economy had achieved an index that was greater by 1.88% points than what would have been the case without EU aid, a real convergence result. This difference increases to 6.13% points for the second programming period. Finally, for the 2000–2006 period, our results indicate that the difference in the index between the scenarios with and without EU aid could be 5.78% points, with the relative Spanish per-capita income being close to 90% of the EU-15 average, quite a real progress by any standard.

From a dynamic point of view, Table 4.3 shows that without the investments corresponding to EU structural and cohesion aids, the process of real convergence would have advanced more slowly, both between 1993 and 1999 (4.71% points compared to 0.46) as well as between 1993 and 2006 (10.56% points compared to 6.66). In terms of average values per budgeting period, the simulations indicate that the difference in relative income between the scenarios with and without EU aids is 1.33, 4.01 and 5.76% points for the periods 1989–1993, 1994–1999 and 2000–2006, respectively. This implies that real convergence has advanced by 2.44% points between the first and the second periods, and by 8.98% points between the first and the third. This compares with the figures of −0.24% points that would have been achieved between 1989–1993 and 1994–1999, and 4.55% points between 1989–1993 and 2000–2006, when no aids had been given.

4.5 Ex-ante 2007–2013 Evaluation

As we have seen before, after the EU enlargement, Spain has seen the amounts received from the structural and cohesion funds considerably reduced for the 2007–2013 period, as it could not have been otherwise given the rapid convergence experienced by the whole country and many of its regions since the European structural and cohesion aids were reformed in 1987. What could possibly be the consequences of this scenario for real convergence in Spain?

Table 4.4 Effects of European structural and cohesion aid on the real per-capita income in Spain (euros of 2000)

	With EU aid (supply and demand effects)	Without EU aid	Difference
2006	18,483	18,483	0
2007	19,097	18,898	199
2008	19,273	18,882	391
2009	19,148	18,743	405
2010	18,870	18,453	417
2011	19,244	18,817	426
2012	19,702	19,271	431
2013	20,114	19,686	428
Average 2007–2013	19,350	18,964	385

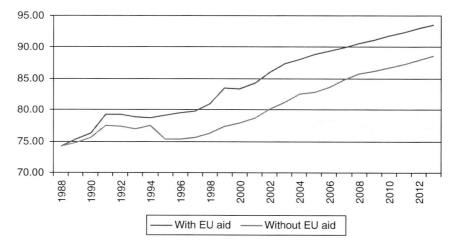

Fig. 4.2 Spanish per-capita income (adjusted by PPS) as a percentage of the corresponding EU-15 figure for 1988–2013 (EU-15=100 across the period). Source: Sosvilla-Rivero and Herce (2004). See main text for a description of scenarios

Table 4.4 reports the results of real per-capita income for the 2007–2013 period, assuming a counter-factual scenario of absence of EU Cohesion aid from 2006. As can be seen in that table, our simulations suggest that the per-capita real income is expected to be, on average, €385 as of 2000 greater than what it would be expected EU aids. The average growth rate of real income per-capita is expected to be 1.21% during the 2007–2013 period with EU aids and 0.90% without such structural and cohesion investments.

Regarding convergence, Fig. 4.2 offers the projections results for the 2007–2013 period To facilitate comparisons, the figure also contains the observed evolution of per-capita income of Spain relative to the EU-15 average since 1989 (EU-15 = 100 over the whole period) and the "without aids" scenario of the previous sections.

Firstly, and we have just seen, over the period 1989–2006, relative per-capita income in Spain would have gone from 74.34% of the EU-15 average in 1989 to 89.39% in 2006, with a gain of 15% points. However, if the structural and cohesion aids had not been received, then this improvement would have been almost 6% points less (i.e. only 9.27% points). Although due to the nature of our calculations, we cannot make a concrete statement as to the final effect, we can note that it is quite likely that by 2006, EU structural and cohesion aids would have contributed just over a third of the improvement in real convergence between Spain and the European Union.

As far as the period that we are really interested in throughout this section (2007–2013) goes, in Fig. 4.2, we show that the indicator of relative income is expected to rise from 89.39 in 2006 to 93.56 in 2013, therefore adding another 4.16% points in the convergence process (being 19.21% points the cumulative gain from 1989). Our simulation results suggest that, without EU aids, relative per-capita income would be expected to be 88.86% of the EU-15 average in 2013.

4.6 Concluding Remarks

The Spanish economy has benefited from important effects on its principal macroeconomic indicators and its real convergence to the European Union, thanks to substantive structural and cohesion aids that it has been receiving since 1989. In this chapter, we have presented an evaluation of their effect on per-capita income and on convergence to EU-15 per-capita income both for the 1989–2006 period and the 2007–2017 period.

In short, our results suggest that EU Cohesion Policy would have allowed about a third of the 15% points that the Spanish per-capita income has caught up on the EU-15 average over the 1988–2006 period. These results are similar to those obtained in earlier studies, although for shorter periods of analysis, both by the current authors and by others (de la Fuente, 2003).

As regards projections for 2007–2013, our projections indicate that, even though Spain is going to receive considerably less funds as in the recent past, the EU structural and cohesion aid will contribute with 4.2 extra convergence points on top of the endogenous capacity of the Spanish economy to continue its real convergence process towards the EU.

As in every empirical analysis, the results must be taken with caution, since it is based on a set of assumptions and on a given evaluation framework. First, the beneficial impacts of EU aid are likely to operate in conjunction with other policy shocks (e.g. fiscal, monetary, industrial, social, labour market, etc.) and other external shocks (developments in the world growth, oil shocks, etc.), and it may be difficult or impossible to disentangle the isolated impacts of such aid programmes in a completely satisfactory way. Second, the manner of incorporating the EU structural and cohesion policy into the HERMIN model draws on very recent economic research that itself has only begun to address the questions of the relationship between increased public investment and the consequences for economic growth and development. Third, our results are expressed in terms of counter-factual scenarios that are, by nature, not observable, since we simply do not know what would have happened had the EU aid not existed. Finally, we should also take care when considering the possible crowding-out effects that the structural aids may have had on private initiatives (de la Fuente, 1997, 2003), and the debatable overall efficiency of the regional community policy (Canova, 2001). All in all, we believe that the structural aid packages for Spain have had a positive effect of the order of magnitude mentioned above.

References

Antón, V., de Bustos, A., Herce, J. A., & Sosvilla-Rivero, S. (1999). Environmental consequences of the community support framework 1994–99 in Spain. *Journal of Policy Modelling, 21,* 831–850.
Argimón, I., González-Páramo, J. M., Martín, M. J., & Roldán, J. M. (1994). Productividad e infraestructuras en la economía española. *Moneda y Crédito, 198,* 207–241.
Bajo-Rubio, O., & Sosvilla-Rivero, S. (1993). Does public capital affect private sector performance? An Analysis of the Spanish case, 1964–1988. *Economic Modelling, 10,* 179–185.
Barry, F., Bradley, J., Hannan, A., McCartan, J., & Sosvilla-Rivero, S. (1997). *Single market review: aggregate and regional aspects: The cases of Greece, Ireland, Portugal and Spain.* Luxemburg: Office of Official Publications of the European Communities.
Bradley, J., & Fitz Gerald, J. (1988). Industrial output and factor input determination in an econometric model of a small open economy. *European Economic Review, 32,* 1227–1241.
Bradley, J., Herce, J. A., & Modesto, L. (1995). The macroeconomic effects of the CSF 1994–99 in the EU periphery: An analysis based on the HERMIN model. *Economic Modelling, 12,* 323–333.
Bradley, J., Modesto, L. & Sosvilla-Rivero, S. (1995a): HERMIN: A macroeconomic modelling framework for the EU periphery, *Economic Modelling, 12,* 221–247.
Bradley, J., Modesto, L., & Sosvilla-Rivero, S. (1995b). HERMIN: A macroeconomic modelling framework for the EU periphery. *Economic Modelling, 12,* 221–247.
Bradley, J., Modesto, L., & Sosvilla-Rivero, S. (1995c). Similarity and diversity in the EU periphery: A HERMIN-based investigation. *Economic Modelling, 12,* 313–322.
Canova, F. (2001). Are EU policies fostering growth and reducing regional inequalities? Opuscle No. 8, CREI-Universitat Pompeu Fabra. Available at http://www.econ.upf.es/crei/research/opuscles/op8ang.pdf.
Christodoulakis, N. M., & Kalyvitis, S. (2000). The effects of the second community support framework 1994–99 on the Greek economy. *Journal of Policy Modelling, 22,* 611–624.
Correa, M. D., & Manzanedo, J. (2002). *Política regional española y europea, Documento de Trabajo SGFCC-2002–05.* Spain: General Budgetary Office, Ministerio de Hacienda.
Corugedo, I., García, E., & Martínez, J. (1992). Educación y rentas. Una aplicación a la enseñanza media en España: Una nota. *Investigaciones Económicas, 16,* 299–304.
de la Fuente, A. (1997). *Fiscal policy and growth in the OECD,* Discussion Paper No. 1755. London: Centre for Economic Policy Research.
de la Fuente, A. (2003). *The effect of Structural Fund spending on the Spanish regions: an assessment of the 1994–99 Objective 1 CSF, Working Paper 2003–11.* Madrid: FEDEA.
Díaz Ballesteros, A., García, E., & Sosvilla-Rivero, S. (2008). *Base de Datos Macroeconómicos de España (BDMACRO).* Madrid: Cátedra FEDEA-Caja Madrid de Economía Regional.

Gramlich, E. (1994). Infrastructure investment: A review essay. *Journal of Economic Literature, 32*, 1176–1196.
Herce, J. A. (1994). (Coord.). *Evaluación del Marco de Apoyo Comunitario 1989–93* (Mimeo). Madrid: FEDEA.
Herce, J. A., & Sosvilla-Rivero, S. (1994). *The effects of the Community Support Framework 1994–99 on the Spanish economy: An analysis based on the HERMIN model, Working paper 94–10R*. Madrid: FEDEA.
Herce, J. A., & Sosvilla-Rivero, S. (1995). HERMIN-Spain. *Economic Modelling, 12*, 295–311.
Herce, J. A., & Sosvilla-Rivero, S. (1998). *Macroeconomic consequences of population ageing in Spain: A preliminary evaluation*. Paper presented to the XIIth Annual Conference of the European Society of Population Economics, Amsterdam.
Martín, C., Herce, J. A., Sosvilla-Rivero, S., & Velázquez, F. J. (2002). *European Union Enlargement. Effects on the Spanish Economy*. "la Caixa" Economic Studies Series No. 27. Barcelona: la Caixa Economic Studies. Available at http://papers.ssrn.com/sol3/papers.cfm?abstract_id=329123.
Mincer, J. (1974). *Schooling experience and earnings*. New York: National Bureau of Economic Research.
Ministerio de Hacienda. (2001). *Marco Comunitario de Apoyo 2000–2006 para las Regiones Españolas del Objetivo 1*, Madrid: Ministerio de Hacienda. An English summary of this document can be downloaded at http://europa.eu.int/comm/regional_policy/funds/prord/document/resu_en.pdf.
Ministerio de Hacienda. (2008). *Spain's National Strategic Reference Framework for 2007 – 2013*. Madrid: Ministerio de Hacienda. Downloaded at http://www.dgfc.sgpg.meh.es/aplweb/pdf/DescargasFondosComunitarios/(490)Resumen_ejecutivo_ingl_s.pdf.
Polo, C., & Sancho, F. (1993). An analysis of Spain's integration in the EEC. *Journal of Policy Modelling, 15*, 157–178.
Sala-i-Martin, X. (1990). *Lecture notes on Economic Growth (I): Introduction to the literature and the neoclassical model*, Working Paper 3563. New York: NBER.
Sosvilla-Rivero, S., Gadea, M. D., Herce, J. A. & Montañés, A. (2002): Los Efectos de las Ayudas Comunitarias en Aragón. Zaragoza: Consejo Económico y Social de Aragón.
Sosvilla-Rivero, S., & Herce, J. A. (2004): La Política de Cohesión Europea y la Economía Española: Evaluación y Prospectiva, Documento de Trabajo 52/2004, Real Instituto Elcano de Estudios Internacionales y Estratégicos. Available at http://www.realinstitutoelcano.org/documentos/141/141.pdf.
Sosvilla-Rivero, S., & Alonso-Meseguer, J. (2005). Estimación de una Función de Producción MRW para la Economía Española, 1910–1995. *Investigaciones Económicas, 29*, 609–624.

Chapter 5
The Spanish Regional Puzzle: Convergence, Divergence and Structural Change

Rubén Garrido-Yserte and Tomás Mancha-Navarro

Regional growth and analysis of the factors which contribute to the process of economic convergence is a research area of great interest among regional economists. Resurgence has been witnessed since the 1990s, due to research carried out by Sala-i-Martin and Barro and the renewed debate about regional convergence and its assessment.

Nowadays, the analysis of regional disparities continues to be of great interest to professional economists and geographers, as well as to those dedicated to the design and implementation of regional development policy. This need for analysis is due to the lack of a unified sole theoretical response regarding the evolution of regional economic disparities and the need to demonstrate under which circumstances these disparities tend to diminish. It is also due to an empirical approach: the discovery that regional disparities tend to decrease gradually and, sometimes, even to show divergent behaviour.

However, a clear consensus seems to exist that one of the factors determining GDP per capita and its evolution in the different regions lies on the behaviour of productivity. Examples include the introduction of new technologies (generally linked to capitalisation processes); the abandonment of certain low-production activities in favour of more productive ones; the strong restructuring processes registered in the employment figures in some regions; and improvement of human capital. These examples highlight the heterogeneous nature of this phenomenon, particularly from a regional perspective.

The principal aim of this chapter is to provide new empirical evidence on the evolution of regional disparities in Spain, and to relate such evolution to the structural changes that occurred in the Spanish economy and its regions throughout a broad, 20-year time span (from 1986 to 2007). A new database by the *Instituto Nacional de Estadística* or INE (Spanish National Statistics Institute) is used, which homogenises

R. Garrido-Yserte (✉)
Universidad de Alcalá, Departamento de Economía Aplicada, Pl. Victoria, 2, 28802 - Alcalá de Henares, Madrid, España
e-mail: ruben.garrido@uah.es

data on Spanish Regional Accountancy from 1986 to 2007 with accounting criteria and the sectorisation of the ESA-95. Chain-linked volume series data have been used in order to elaborate a data series in constant euros of the year 2000.

It is always difficult to choose a period of time for the analysis of processes in order to demonstrate the changes in tendencies. Nevertheless, 1986 was chosen as the starting year for this analysis. This choice was not only restricted by the data used (data prior to this date are unavailable), but 1986 was also the year that Spain entered the European Economic Community. As discussed in other chapters of this book, from a territorial perspective, Spain's entrance was a clear turning point for Spanish Regional Policy.

The signing of the Treaty of Accession in June 1985, after previously applying in 1962 and 1977, introduced Spain to a new international context of "no-return". This promoted important changes required for the Spanish economy to function in a new global scene characterised by broader European integration and business internationalisation.

The response by the Spanish economy indicated the start of a clear stage of economic recovery that has extended virtually until 2006, with a slight inflection between 1993 and 1995. At a territorial level, this resulted in important advances for all the Spanish regions, as we will discuss later.

At the same time, the Statutes of Autonomies foreseen in the 1978 Constitution were developed during this period. All Autonomous Regions were allocated with increasing competences, under a more de-centralised administration design. Moreover, they were provided with more financing mechanisms in order to fulfill the new competences transferred (essentially health and education) and to develop capitalisation processes through the Inter-territorial Compensation Fund set out in 1978 Constitution. This fund was created as a basic instrument for regional development, "regionalising" investment made by the State with criteria of territorial reequilibrium.

The above imply that, from a Spanish viewpoint, the regional analysis has clearly improved. Studies on regional disparities have been developed with a double objective: firstly, to understand the evolution of such disparities and the basic mechanisms of regional convergence; and secondly, to assess the success of regional policies implemented (fostering with EU Regional Policy in Spain).

With this perspective, the aim of this chapter is to trace the evolution of regional disparities from 1986 to the present. This chapter attempts to answer the *Spanish Regional Puzzle*: How is it possible to combine convergence in relative terms, particularly significant in the case of productivity, with an increase of divergence in the most important absolute variables: gross value added (GVA), employment and population?

The answer lies in regional structural change. The important *tertiarisation* process of the Spanish economy in these years has caused regional productivity levels to reduce their differences, although at the expense of a greater difference in the distance between the most- and the least-developed regions, with regard to their participation in GVA and employment.

This chapter is divided into five sections. Firstly, the evolution of regional disparities in relative terms is analysed, taking into consideration the growth of

GDP per capita and apparent labour productivity. The second section examines regional distribution of employment, production and population. The third section is devoted to aspects related to structural change and its spatial reflection. The fourth section shows the records in terms of beta-convergence in productivity and explains the role of productive structure in this process. The chapter ends with conclusions set forth in the fifth section.

5.1 The Evolution of Regional Disparities in Relative Terms: GDP Per Capita and Productivity

Between 1986 and 2006, the cumulative average rate of GDP growth for Spanish economy was 3.2%. However, the Spanish economy has experienced several cyclical phases: An expansive phase from 1986 to 1991; a cyclical deceleration stage between 1992 and 1995, with some years of negative growth; and finally, from 1996 to 2006, an average growth exceeding 3.5%.

These results are positive compared with those of the European Union. Together with a relatively modest population growth (less than 1% of annual average between 1986 and 2006) and birth rates among the lowest in Europe, these results explain the important process that Spain and its regions are undergoing to approach the European average in terms of income per capita.

In 1988, the Spanish GDP per capita, in terms of purchasing power, was 74 of EU average. Ten years later, the value was 81. In 2005, Spain exceeded the Community average with a value of 103, which was caused not only by an important differential growth in the Spanish economy, but also by the Eastern countries adhesion, which reduced the EU average by almost ten points. This means that Spain could currently have an index around 95 at EU-15 level. Nonetheless, the catch-up has been quite remarkable.

Regional performance has been highly significant during this period. According to Eurostat, eight regions currently exceed the European average per capita (Madrid, Navarre, the Basque Country, the Balearics, Catalonia, La Rioja, Aragon and Cantabria), with values ranging from 133 (Madrid) to 100 (Cantabria). On the contrary, Extremadura, Andalusia and Galicia register the lowest values, with indices of 70, 80 and 82 respectively (Table 5.1).

Although convergence with the European Union figures is an important characteristic during this period, regional convergence with Spanish figures shows a very low reduction of disparities, with a relative stagnant convergence.

Less-developed regions have experienced some improvement (Extremadura, Andalusia and Galicia), although advances are fairly slight in certain cases, and their levels remain below the Spanish average. It is worth highlighting the notable decline experienced by Asturias and the Balearics.

However, the most-developed regions (La Rioja, the Basque Country, Navarre, Catalonia and Madrid) have registered a relative improvement. This implies that the distance between more- and less-developed regions was initially maintained and then became more pronounced, especially after 1996. Thus, around 2007, the

Table 5.1 Evolution of regional income per capita (Spain=100)

	1985	1995	2006
Andalusia	72.10	73.12	76.27
Aragon	107.00	105.78	107.97
Asturias	94.60	87.41	88.93
Balearics	135.90	132.00	106.01
Canary Islands	86.50	100.35	89.76
Cantabria	106.60	94.26	97.63
Castile-Leon	87.70	94.34	96.93
Castile-La Mancha	73.80	80.57	78.65
Catalonia	123.80	122.96	118.22
Valencian C.	105.00	95.02	90.93
Extremadura	65.10	62.93	69.35
Galicia	78.30	81.39	82.71
Madrid	138.90	130.06	131.44
Murcia	81.30	82.67	81.58
Navarre	108.00	124.21	128.01
Basque Country	108.60	119.32	129.30
Rioja (La)	109.20	114.63	108.29
Spain-EU (27)			103 (2005)
Spain-EU (13)			93 (2005)
Spain-EU (15)	74 (1988)	81 (1998)	

Source: Banco de Bilbao-Vizcaya: Spanish National Income–provincial distribution, INE (Spanish National Statistics Institute), Eurostat and own elaboration

income per capita of the richest regions was 60% higher than that of regions with lower income per capita. This has remained true for 20 years (Fig. 5.1).

Undoubtedly, sigma-convergence is one of the most widespread measures in literature regarding economic growth, especially in the area of regional disparities. Sigma-convergence assesses how inequalities among different economies evolve over time, taking a specific economic variable as a reference (GDP per capita, GDP per employee, etc.).

Figure 5.2 shows the results obtained for the period between 1986 and 2007, and reinforces the idea of a stagnant reduction in disparities. The variation of sigma-convergence is hardly significant over the whole period. Only a slight reduction of disparities is observed in the last 5 years.[1]

The classification of Spanish regions into income quartiles groups offers a complementary analysis of these results (Fig. 5.3). For almost all groups, dispersion has been reduced very considerably, and particularly in central distribution groups (2 and 3).

In 1986, the intra-group differences were highly significant, as demonstrated by the values of groups 4 and 2. In 2007, intra-group dispersion was quite low, which

---

[1] For those not familiar with this terminology, we say that there is sigma-convergence if a reduction in dispersion is observed (measured by standard deviation) in the analysed variable, in this case GDP per head.

5 The Spanish Regional Puzzle: Convergence, Divergence and Structural Change

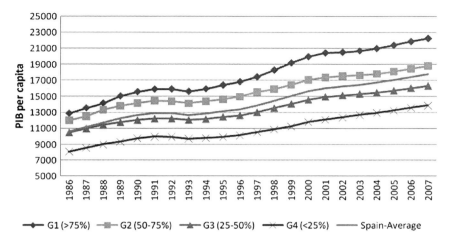

Fig. 5.1 Evolution of the GDP per capita by regions (classified by income quartiles)

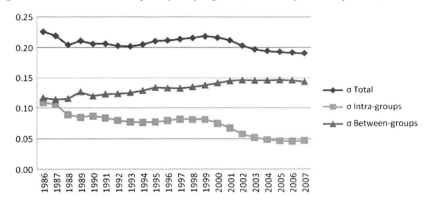

Fig. 5.2 Overall and intra- and inter-groupal sigma-convergence (regions classified by income quartiles).
Source: Own elaboration

demonstrates that dispersion among the groups was the principal reason for the existing deviation (between-groups dispersion). In fact, while in 1986, total dispersion was caused in inter- and intra-group virtually at 50%, the distance between the groups of regions explained 75% of disparities in 2007.

These changes are the result of differentiated regional behaviours in their growth-paths. Therefore, in terms of GDP per capita, we can set out three groups (see Figs. 5.4 and 5.5):

1. Regions with a *divergent* path, such as Aragon, Madrid, Catalonia, Navarre and the Basque Country, are within the group of regions with above average income levels. Murcia and the Valencian Community are among the regions with levels below the national average.

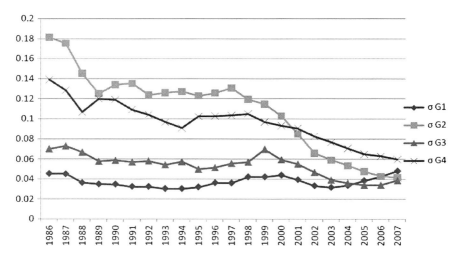

Fig. 5.3 Sigma-convergence by groups of regions (classified by income quartiles).
Source: Own elaboration

2. Regions with a *stagnant* path are Castile-La Mancha and Andalusia.
3. Regions with a *convergent* path are those that have progressively evolved towards the average. These include areas of high values, such as the Balearics and La Rioja, to regions of below-average values, such as Extremadura, Galicia and Cantabria.

Behind these results, changes can be observed in regional variables, specifically in employment figures. As we will see in the next section, these explain the convergence in regional productivity. In other words, the lessening of regional disparities is explained through the behaviour of employment, which affects productivity dynamics.

Taking into consideration that GDP per capita can be decomposed in two factors (apparent labour productivity and labour per inhabitant), the Theil's inequality index[2] allows us to assess which part of income inequality is due to productivity differences, and which part is caused by differences regarding the employment–population ratio.

The results show that most of the inequality regarding the existing GDP per capita can be explained through regional employment disparities rather than

---

[2] The Theil index used decomposed the inequality in two factors:

$$IT = \sum_i \frac{Y_i}{Y} \ln\left(\frac{Y_i/E_i}{Y/E}\right) + \sum_i \frac{Y_i}{Y} \ln\left(\frac{E_i/P_i}{E/P}\right).$$

5 The Spanish Regional Puzzle: Convergence, Divergence and Structural Change   109

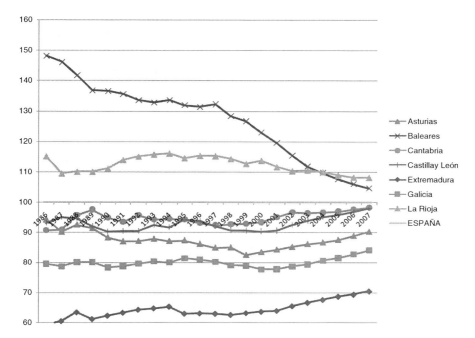

Fig. 5.4 Regions with convergent behaviour in GDP per capita (Spain = 100).
Source: Own elaboration

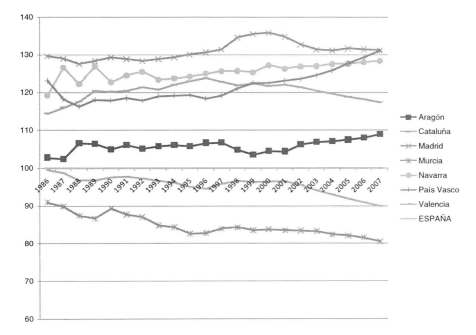

Fig. 5.5 Regions with divergent behaviour in GDP per capita (Spain = 100)

through differences in regional productivity. This is especially significant from the mid-1990s (Fig. 5.6).

In fact, the Theil index allows us to illustrate two important aspects. Firstly, and according to what is obtained in the sigma-convergence, disparity levels tend to stabilise throughout the entire period.

Secondly, it is important to note that behind this result, a process occurs that highlights two contrary economic strengths: a significant convergence in productivity, and an important increase in differences in the employment–population ratio. A highly pronounced trend towards divergence is observed from 1986 to 1999, and which becomes more moderate from this date until 2007. In 1986, the existing divergences in relative employment explained 38% of existing inequality. Twenty years later, inequality has hardly reduced, but regional disparities in the employment–population ratio explain almost 85% of the inequality.

These results lead to the Spanish Regional Puzzle: convergence in relative variables, such as income per capita and specially productivity, and, at the same time, divergence and higher regional concentration in those variables integrating ratios such as production, employment or population.

As indicated in other parts of this book, the important convergence process observed in the 1960s has the same features, partly due to the crisis of the 1970s. During the development process of the 1960s, the notable migratory flows – both international and interregional – allow us to talk about a *downward* convergence process to the extent that the most advanced regions show a relative dynamic that brings their levels closer to national averages.

In turn, the crisis of the 1970s mainly affected those regions that led Spanish economic growth, which also caused a reduction in distances. Since 1986, growth in Spain has been revitalised. Again, the most advanced regions seem to have led the growth process, which could explain why the reduction of disparities came to a halt.

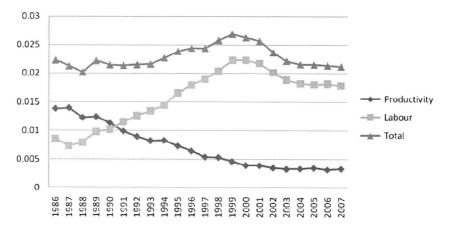

Fig. 5.6 Theil index for Spanish regions.
Source: Own elaboration

5 The Spanish Regional Puzzle: Convergence, Divergence and Structural Change

At the same time, however, these regions have been the principal focus of attraction for employment and, thus, for population. As we will see below, this makes it possible to state that there has been an increase in regional concentration with regard to these variables.

5.2 Regional Divergence in Absolute Terms: GDP, Employment and Population

Throughout the last 20 years, there have been highly significant structural changes in the Spanish economy. Later in this book, we will refer to these changes in productive structure; other authors will also mention important changes experienced by the Spanish economy with regard to key aspects such as productive capitalisation, human capital and competitiveness.

Moreover, this period has also been of use in consolidating the process of concentration of activity, employment and population in the most prosperous regions. Therefore, if we calculate the Herfindahl concentration index (Fig. 5.7), which is the sum of the squares of the production share of each region within the total national share (regarding GDP and employment and population), the results obtained allow us to emphasise three important aspects:

1. Concentration was accentuated between 1986 and 2007 and for all three variables under analysis.

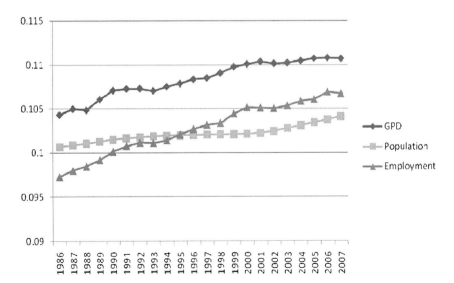

Fig. 5.7 Evolution of production, employment and population concentration. Herfindhal index.
Source: Own elaboration

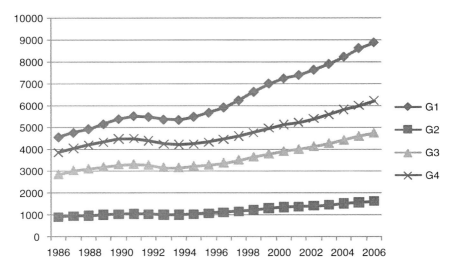

Fig. 5.8 Evolution of employment by regions (classified by income per capita).
Source: Own elaboration

2. This concentration is clearly higher in terms of GDP than employment and population (Fig. 5.8).
3. The evolution of employment concentration is highly significant and corroborates the idea that the reduction in territorial disparity regarding productivity was congruent with the concentration process applied, as shown by the Theil index in the previous section[3].

The economies of Catalonia, Madrid, Andalusia and the Valencian Community remain those with the highest weights in the whole GDP generation (altogether, these regions accounted for 60% of the GDP in 2006). These economies also increased their individual relative share over the last 20 years (Fig. 5.9).

With regard to employment and population, trends towards concentration are evident. The four largest Spanish regions generated 53% of employment in 1986 (55% of population); in 2006, that figure rose to 60% (58% of population). Figure 5.8 shows that the richest regions are those registering the highest growth in terms of labour variables, which have a clearly divergent pattern during this period.

These results cannot be understood without considering a recent but intense phenomenon: immigration. The Spanish economy has evolved from an emigrant economy to becoming a receptor of a foreign population, amounting to approximately 10%. Although this figure is comparable to or even lower than that for other

---

[3] Garrido-Yserte (2001) and Goerlich and Mas (2001) shows similar results using another territorial disaggregation (provinces levels). Goerlich et al. (2002) shows the relationship between concentration and convergence using another methodology.

Fig. 5.9 Communities gaining relative participation between 1986 and 2006.
Source: Own elaboration

neighbouring economies, it has doubled in comparison to the Spanish economy in 2002.

Catalonia, Madrid, the Valencian Community, Andalusia and the Canary Islands concentrate around 70% of the immigrant population. Without the contribution of immigrants, the notable growth experienced would not have been possible[4]. The development of construction and services sector, which have been essential in the last Spanish cycle of growth would also not have been possible.

5.3 Structural Change of the Spanish Economy and Its Regional Impact

Undoubtly, the *tertiarisation* process led by employment is a remarkable characteristic of these last 20 years of Spanish growth. Using data from the *Contabilidad Regional de España* (Spanish Regional Accounting), Service and Construction activities increased their share in employment significantly over these 20 years (1986–2006). On the contrary, a serious decline in agricultural activities, which reduced their share from 14% to 5%, can be observed (Fig. 5.10).

In general, regional industrial mix is more similar now than in 1986, although it is worth highlighting that the sectoral contribution to existing disparities in industrial mix has drastically changed. Thus, Fig. 5.11 shows that while differences in employment regarding regional agricultural structures accounted for almost 40% of the existing differences and 30% of services, the most remarkable regional differences are registered in 2006 by service activities (almost 50% of disparities in employment regional structure), followed by the manufacture sector and construction, which is growing at a significant rate.

The regional concentration in service and construction employment during this period lags behind these results. This leads us to believe that, by territory, the structural change was relatively unequal in a disaggregated view, despite their common patterns at more aggregate levels.

---

[4] Raymond and García Greciano (1996) show the impact of inter-regional migrations on spanish convergence using a long-term series.

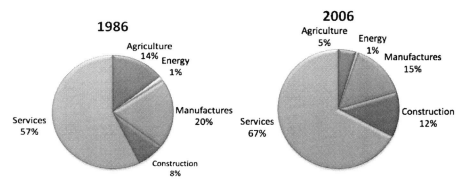

Fig. 5.10 Structural change of the Spanish economy.
Source: Own elaboration

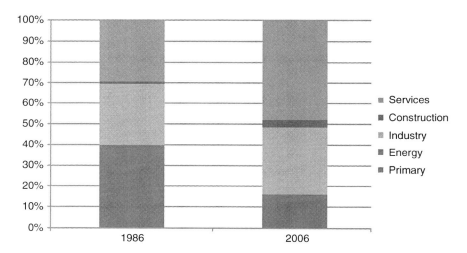

Fig. 5.11 Inequality in regional productive structure. Sectoral contribution.
Source: Own elaboration

Regarding sectoral share in employment, half the employed people in Spain (49.5%) work in the *market service* sector, while *secondary* and *non-market service* sectors (with 18% and 15% of total employees respectively) follow in terms of employment generation. The majority of employees within the *market service* sector are concentrated in Madrid, Andalusia and Catalonia; employees within the *secondary* sector are mainly based in Catalonia, the Valencian Community and Madrid; and employees within *non-market services* are located principally in Andalusia, Madrid and Catalonia.[5]

---

[5] The *Contabilidad Regional de España* (Spanish Regional Accounting) does not allow us to differentiate between market services and public services. These comments have been made using the IVIE (Valencian Economic Research Institute) databases.

This characterisation is more clearly shown in the results of the specialisation index. On average, 11 out of the 17 Spanish autonomous regions show a certain level of specialisation. On the contrary, the most diversified regions are Madrid, the Balearics, the Basque Country, Catalonia, the Canary Islands and the Valencian Community.

Figure 5.12 includes the specialisation indices by sectors and regions. It is worth mentioning the specialisation in the primary sector (agriculture, stockbreeding and fishing) shown by regions, such as Galicia, Murcia and Extremadura and, to a lesser extent, Castile-La Mancha and Andalusia.

However, the highest level of relative specialisation in the secondary sector (energy and manufactures) is registered in Navarre, the Basque County, La Rioja, Catalonia and Aragon. With regard to the construction sector, Castile-La Mancha and Extremadura, together with Andalusia, register the highest levels of employment specialisation. Finally, within the sale services sector, the highest specialisation is shown by Madrid, both archipelagos, Catalonia, the Valencian Community and Cantabria.

These territorial specialisation patterns can explain three points: (1) the stagnation of disparities in terms of sigma-convergence; (2) the increase in the territorial concentration processes; and (3) as we will see below, these patterns will be used as a basis to understand the productivity convergence regarding growth rates or beta-convergence.

5.4 Regional Convergence and Structural Change

As previously specified, inequality levels, measured in terms of sigma-convergence, are relatively stable. However, a necessary but insufficient condition for the occurrence of sigma-convergence is the existence of an inverse relationship between the starting levels of productivity or income per head and the growth observed, in order to achieve a "catching-up" effect.

Initially, this concept of convergence was developed on the basis of the neoclassical growth model, which predicts that income per capita tends toward steady-state level. In this case, we are before a so-called beta-convergence. Sala-i-Martín (1990 and 1994) contrasted the beta-convergence hypothesis in discrete time using the following formula:

$$(1/T)\ln(y_{it+T}/y_{it}) = \alpha + \beta_1 \ln y_{it} + e_i \tag{5.1}$$

The existence of a $\beta < 0$ parameter would indicate the occurrence of the aforementioned "catching-up" process. This concept of beta-convergence has been subject to criticism, mainly in its original formulation: the use of cross-section data to contrast a negative relationship between growth rates and initial income or productivity levels (See Quah, 1996; Ben-David, 1994 or Adams and Pigliaru 1999). More specifically, those considering that the estimation of a relationship using this formula could downwardly bias the calculation of convergence to the extent that long-term trends would be assumed to be the only ones existing for all the economies under analysis.

For this reason, *extended* formulations of the (1) have been considered, allowing the economies to differ from the fundamentals determining the steady-state. This approach is also coherent with the empirical evidence showing that convergence occurs between similar economies, or when included within the same economic areas (Baumol, 1986 and 1994; Cánova and Marcet, 1995).

These interpretations introduced the concept of conditional beta-convergence in specialised literature: the trends of the economies analysed are towards convergence, once the variables determining the steady-state (investment, technology, etc.) are *controlled*.

However, the existence of absolute or conditional beta-convergence is not only the object of methodological and econometric discussions. The implications of economic policy derived from both areas are completely different. Admitting the possible existence of diverse regional realities determining different long-term trends means providing a much broader scope for public policies than demonstrating the existence of non-conditional economic convergence. In the first case, economic policies could or should aim to remove obstacles preventing or hindering the evolution of a region and reducing the level of relative underdevelopment.

Such obstacles could be related to their productive structure, but also to the lack of infrastructures, human capital and availability of other soft-factors like innovation, etc. In the case of non-conditional convergence, virtually, the only role of economic policy would be to guarantee the free functioning of the market.

From a conceptual perspective, the differences between conditional or absolute beta-convergence should not be seen as irrelevant. Accepting that regional economies are becoming progressively closer but forming groups or "clubs", could be considered a *second-best*. Admitting that economies approach their income or productivity levels at different long-run levels is tantamount to a contradiction. The spotlight might shift the focus from the speeds of convergence to the factors determining long-term inequality. The contrast of conditional convergence implies moving the interest in calculation from how (speed of convergence) to where (amplitude of the observed regional disparities). Overall, this demonstrates that differences among the economies under analysis tend to become more stable over time.

From the viewpoint of estimation, the convergence equation (1) would be as follows:

$$(1/T)\ln(y_{it+T}/y_{it}) = \alpha + \beta_1 \ln y_{it} + \eta_i + e_i \tag{5.2}$$

where regional effects (η_i) would include all those specific factors of regional economies determining their steady-state, which in many cases are very difficult to quantify.

The availability of panel data allows us to contrast both concepts jointly. Raymond and García Greciano (1994) suggest the following estimated relationship:

$$\Delta y_{it} - \Delta \overline{y_t} = \alpha_i + \beta(\overline{y_{t-1}} - y_{it-1}) + v_{it} \tag{5.3}$$

5 The Spanish Regional Puzzle: Convergence, Divergence and Structural Change

In the first member of the equation, the differences in the growth of a region i are analysed compared to the average national growth. These differences will depend positively on that existing during the period $t-1$ between the value of the national productivity level and the value of the region i, i.e. of the existing gap.

The use of panel data makes contrasting the hypotheses underlying the analysis of absolute beta-convergence possible: the same speed of convergence for all regions ($\beta_i = \beta$) and/or the existence of regional parameters defining the same steady-state ($\alpha_i = \alpha$).

The results of the estimations from the beta-convergence are summarised in Table 5.2 and are consistent with the evolution of sigma-convergence highlighted in the first section.

In the first place, and for the whole period, the convergence process is much more important for apparent labour productivity than for GDP per capita. Regional disparities regarding income per head would reduce by half at a speed of 1.2%, while the productivity breach would register a fall of 1.9%. These estimated speeds are relatively low, and demonstrate that the existing breach would reduce by half over approximately 55 years in the case of income and 37 years in the case of productivity.

Nevertheless, the most interesting result is that derived from the use of panel data to contrast the presence of regional fixed effects, that is to say, a series of

Table 5.2 Beta-convergence among the Spanish regions in GDP

	1986–1995		1996–2007		1986–2007	
per capita						
β	−0.02130	−0.13071	−0.01224	−0.01868	−0.01191	−0.01777
	(−4.78)[c]	(−13.54)[c]	(−5.66)[c]	(−5.58)[c]	(−5.92)[c]	(−5.76)[c]
Fixed effects	No	Yes	No	Yes	No	Yes
F-test ($u_i=0$)		9.68		3.31		1.75
(probability)		(0.0000)[c]		(0.0000)[c]		(0.0334)[b]
R^2	0.5616	0.5616	0.1364	0.1364	0.0846	0.0846
F-test		183.21		31.12		33.17
(probability)		(0.0000)[c]		(0.0000)[c]		(0.0000)[c]
Observations	162	162	216	216	378	378
per employee						
β	−0.01516	−0.05554	−0.02453	−0.05459	−0.01892	−0.02951
	(−4.43)[c]	(−4.41)[c]	(−5.94)[c]	(−7.49)[c]	(−7.59)[c]	(−6.85)[c]
Fixed effects	No	Yes	No	Yes	No	Yes
F-test ($u_i=0$)		1.55		5.83		2.12
(probability)		(0.0869)[a]		(0.0000)[c]		(0.0061)[c]
R^2	0.1196	0.1196	0.2219	0.2219	0.1155	0.1155
F-test		19.43		56.17		33.17
(probability)		(0.0000)[c]		(0.0000)[c]		(0.0000)[c]
Observations	162	162	216	216	378	378

[a]Significant at 10%; [b]Significant at 5%; [c]Significant at 1%.
Source: Own elaboration

factors conditioning, positively or negatively, the convergence process and signalling the existence of an important equilibrium inequality.

For all the adjustments carried out, convergence is a phenomenon clearly conditioned by these starting conditions (technology, training, productive structure, etc.). These conditions are not explicitly included in the model and, although they would speed up the process of reduction of disparities, they would tend to have clearly differing regional equilibrium levels.

In fact, the estimated equilibrium levels are clearly related with an uneven production structure, as shown in Fig. 5.12, including a negative relationship between the levels of equilibrium income and productivity and the importance of agricultural employment.

As we will see below, these results demonstrate the importance of production structure and structural change when explaining not only the estimated levels of equilibrium inequality, but also the convergence process in productivity (Adams and Pigliaru, 1999).

From the perspective of structural change, regional gains in productivity come from two sources: the increase in *intra-sectoral* productivity and the improvement resulting from a change in the regional production structure, where low-productive activities lose weight in favour of more productive activities (composition effect), or a combination of both.

The aforementioned implies that convergence processes can be explained by a wide variety of factors, which can be grouped together into two categories: neoclassical convergence mechanisms, where simultaneous global and sectoral convergence processes can be appreciated; and processes of structural change that explain global convergence and sectoral divergence (Bernard and Jones, 1996 and Ciccone and Hall, 1996).

From this viewpoint, and like Paci and Pigliaru (1997) do for Italian regions, the fact that the most underdeveloped regions show higher growth rates in income and productivity could be compatible with other, non-neoclassical growth models.

In other words, coexistence is possible between economic phenomena that could lead to convergence. It may not be related to the assumptions in the Solow-type growth models, but to changes in the sectoral composition of the output compatible with endogeneous growth models. This was demonstrated by Barro and Sala-I-Martín (1995), with a neoclassical basis or with models where the growth propellant was not only due to inter-sectoral supply, but also to demand, in a *Kaldorian* perspective.

In Spain, as examined previously, regional economic development since the end of the 1970s, but particularly between 1986 and 2007, has mainly been due to the improvement in services. This phenomenon has been more significant in those regions with medium and high productivity levels. Therefore, an almost automatic convergence process was seen supported by the gradual divergence observed in variables regarding the labour market.

This pattern also adapts to the growth models suggested by Kaldor, who stated that *the advanced, high-income areas are inevitably those which possess a highly*

5 The Spanish Regional Puzzle: Convergence, Divergence and Structural Change

developed modern industry.[6] These postulates have been frequently contrasted in specialised literature on national and regional growth.[7]

According to these approaches, the value of explaining regional differences depending on factor endowments can be controversial. If demand plays an important role, the cause could be mistaken for the effect of these differences.

The core of the approach is the existence of some form of scale returns that lead to the principle of cumulative causation. On one hand, these returns are not necessarily internal to the company – scale returns. In current literature, these factors are known as external economies, mainly reached through specialisation.

On the other hand, the processes of services outsourcing or changes in their industrialisation could also be seen as the foundations of a cumulative pattern where intermediate demand causes an improvement in economic productivity (Fixler and Siegel, 1999).

From the aforementioned point, the estimation of the so-called Kaldor's third law is set out. The original formulation of this "third law" was based on the fact that industrial growth also causes an increase in productivity in other sectors to the extent that it favours the transfer of the labour force from such sectors to industry. Nowadays, the same effect could occur, not only in these activities, but also in services[8].

In order to verify this fact, we have contrasted two alternative relationships: one for industry:

$$\dot{y}_{tot} = a + b_1 \dot{q}_m + b_2 \dot{e}_{nm} + \varepsilon_4 \quad \text{with} \quad b1 > 0 \text{ and } b2 < 0 \qquad (5.4)$$

and another for market services:

$$\dot{y}_{tot} = a + b_1 \dot{q}_{sdv} + b_2 \dot{e}_{nsv} + \varepsilon_4 \quad \text{with} \quad b1 > 0 \text{ and } b2 < 0, \qquad (5.5)$$

where a direct relationship is expected to exist between overall productivity growth and productive growth in industry or services, and an inverse relationship between employment growth in non-industrial sectors (in the case of the original relationship) or outside the services sector in the case of the (5).

Table 5.3 shows the results obtained with cross-section data, which seems to indicate that productivity growth could also be explained by a process of inter-sectoral reassignment. This process, together with other restructuring processes in the rest of the activities, contributes to an increase in the aggregate productivity levels.

The results obtained show some remarkable characteristics for the Spanish case. These are similar to countries, such as Italy (see works by Paci and Pigliaru cited in

---

[6]Kaldor (1970) p. 339
[7]See McCombie and Thirwall (1984), Drakopoulos and Theodossiou (1991), Sonmez (1993), Bernard (1996), and Pons and Viladecans (1999).
[8]Cuadrado et al. 2000 show the contribution of public services to convergence process in Spain.

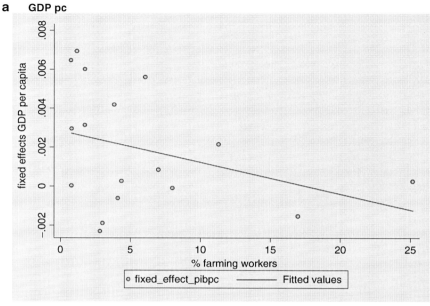

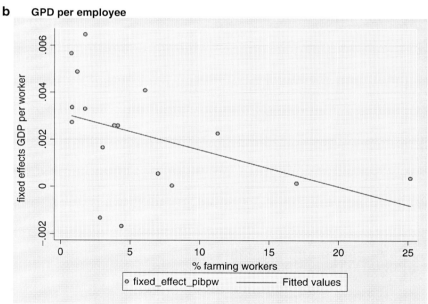

Fig. 5.12 Relationship between fixed effects and agriculture shares of employment. (**a**) GDP pc. (**b**) GPD per employee.
Source: Own elaboration

Table 5.3 Estimation of Kaldor's third law. 1986–2006 Cross-section data

Variable	Equation (4)	Equation (5)
B_1	0.289	0.10
Prob.	(2.37)	(0.256)
B_2	−0.56	−0.386
Prob.	(−7.91)	(−2.71)
F-Snedecor	31.6	6.07
	(0.829)	(0.014)
R^2	0.555	0.483

Source: Own elaboration

the references below), but differ significantly from other countries, while showing certain idiosyncrasies with regard to the assessment of gains in productivity:[9]

1. Firstly, the importance of structural change is revealed through the estimated labour parameters for both equations. In the case of the employment growth in the sectors, the absolute value of the parameter is higher than the contribution of industrial production to overall productivity which is, in turn, positive and significant.
2. The previous result is corroborated when the estimation is carried out in the case of services. The impact of services growth in the apparent labour productivity of the whole economy is not significant, while the effects of sectoral reassignment of employment are significant and show the expected result.
3. These results demonstrate the importance of inter-sectoral structural change when explaining the advances in productivity. This also partly highlights the growth pattern of the Spanish economy in recent years, which is led by employment and registers a relatively modest growth in overall productivities.

5.5 Final Remarks

The Spanish economy experienced significant changes in the period from 1986 to 2007. There has been a convergence process to EU average. From a territorial perspective, virtually all regions improved their position. Nevertheless, differentiated patterns of change and downward convergence processes can be appreciated, which result in an overall stagnant disparity regarding income per capita.

The important *tertiarisation* of the economy throughout this period demonstrates how to combine a process that favours convergence in relative variables and, at the same time, increases concentration, particularly regarding employment in the most advanced regions.

Far from being homogeneous by territory, this change has contributed to the consolidation of the existing relative differences. Those economies more specialised in primary activities, despite the marked "de-agrarisation" process

---

[9] See the work carried out by Cuadrado et al. (1998) and Cuadrado and Parellada (2002) from European perspective in this respect.

experienced, did not reach an equivalent dynamism in other activities (mainly service activities). This implies a certain loss of weight within overall employment and a clear consolidation of their specialisation patterns, which are only tinged with a higher presence of construction and public services activities.

On the contrary, the communities founded on a productive structure more linked to industry or services have experienced a sectoral change that has consolidated such a specialisation. These have also played a leading role in the intense tertiarisation process of the Spanish economy, but led by employment rather than by the production variables, which has translated into a relatively low performance in productivity.

At the same time, these changes in the employment variables suggest that those territories more related to agriculture show higher productivity gains than those specialised in the services sector, for example, with gains clearly lower than the average, thus resulting in a kind of convergence process.

However, these are not neutral effects for two reasons: firstly, this convergence mechanism is clearly limited by the fact that the decrease in employment in low-productive sectors constitutes an end in itself; and secondly, specialisation determines long-term productivity and income levels.

Therefore, as the results seem to indicate, if tertiarisation implies an increase in productivity and income levels of the whole economy, the most advanced territories will remain ahead of the others. But if tertiarisation is synonymous with a higher territorial competitiveness (availability of services improving industrial margins) and becomes the economic base of many regions (i.e. tourism), the structural change is not neutral, especially in the long-run.

As far as regional policy is concerned, formulating the objectives only according to income per head or to apparent labour productivity could bias our analysis. Political recommendations could arise towards situations with a desirable result (higher levels of income per capita), without taking into consideration how the gains are obtained (Cuadrado et al., 1997, 2002).

As demonstrated in this chapter, many of the regions registered the highest levels in productivity at the expense of employment increases, much below the average.

Currently, convergence in productivity does not seem to be compatible with convergence in employment. Again, this is not neutral in the long-term and, obviously, does not favour the attainment of the objectives included in the renewed Lisbon agenda.

However, and although not included in the objectives of this research, the influence of economic variables on demographic variables deserves special attention. Employment determines income generation and consumption, and can be used to establish the population in the territory. Many of the least dynamic regions register low population densities and regressive growth dynamics (Raymond and García Greciano, 1994). This is especially significant in the case of large regions with a highly significant rural component.

These statements are not only of interest for economic reasons, but also for political reasons and for formulating regional development policies (Armstrong, 2002). Until relatively recently, Spanish regional policy focussed mainly on improving public capital endowment of the economy, particularly their infrastructure. Undoubtedly, this investing effort is related to the existing needs and the positive impact of the Spanish economy on productivity. This impact, however, could lead to a decrease in returns. It is therefore advisable to focus on other priorities, as in the previous period (2000–2006) and more frequently in the current period (2007–2013) of regional programming.

The formulation of programmes should now take into consideration the weaknesses of regional productive structure and the improvement of its change or competitiveness capacities. These policies normally use fewer resources, which is a benefit within the current situation of less structural funds. Although their results are more uncertain, their maturing periods are longer and they need the collaboration and promotion of the private sector (small and medium enterpresite) of regional economy.

Such policies require a critical mass in order to have a positive and catalysing effect on regions, so that productivity gains are not led by employment restructuring processes, but start to be built on gains on a production level and towards achieving a future *virtuous circle of regional development.*

References

Adams, J., & Pigliaru, F. (1999). *Economic Growth Change. National and Regional Patterns of Convergence and Divergence*. Cheltenham: Edward Elgar.
Armstrong, H. W. (2002). European Union regional policy: Reconciling the convergence and evaluation evidence. In Cuadrado and Parellada (Eds.), *Regional convergence in the European Union. Facts, prospects and policies*. Berlin: Springer.
Barro, R. J., & Sala-I-Martín, X. (1995). *Economic Growth*. London: McGraw-Hill.
Baumol, W. J. (1967). Macroeconomics of unbalance growth: the anatomy of urban crisis. *American Economic Review, 57*, 415–426.
Baumol, W. J. (1986). Productivity growth, convergence and welfare: What the long run data show. *American Economic Review, 78*(5), 1155–1159.
Baumol, W. J. (1994). Multivariate growth patterns: Contagion and common forces as possible sources of convergence. In Baumol, Nelson, and Wolff (Eds.), *Convergence of Productivity*. New York: Oxford University Press.
Ben-David, D. (1994). *Convergence clubs and diverging economies (working Paper)*. Londres: CEPR.
Bernard, A. (1996). Does manufacturing matter? A spatial econometric view of Kaldor's laws. *Journal of Regional Science, 36*, 463–477.
Bernard, A., & Jones, C. (1996). Productivity and convergence across U.S. States and industries. *Empirical Economics, 21*, 113–135.
Cánova, F., & Marcet, A. (1995). The poor stay poor: Non-convergenge across Countries and regions. CEPR Discussion Paper no. 1265. Londres: CEPR.
Ciccone, A., & Hall, R. (1996). Productivity and density of economic activity. *American Economic Review, 86*(1), 55–70.
Cuadrado, J. R., Mancha, T., & Garrido, R. (1997). Tendencias de la productividad regional española, 1964–1993 Información Comercial Española. *Revista De Economía, 762*, 87–110.
Cuadrado, J. R., Mancha, T., & Garrido, R. (1998). *Convergencia regional en España. Hechos, tendencias y perspectivas*. Madrid: Fundación Argentaria–Visor dis.
Cuadrado, J. R., Mancha, T., & Garrido, R. (2000). *Servicios públicos y convergencia regional en España*. Madrid: SERVILAB Documento de trabajo.

Cuadrado, J. R., Mancha, T., & Garrido, R. (2002). Regional Dynamics in the European Union: Winners and Losers in Cuadrado y Parellada (2002) eds.
Cuadrado, J. R., & Parellada, M. (2002). *Regional Convergence in the European Union*. Springer-Verlag.
Drakopoulos, S. A., & Theodossiou, I. (1991). Kaldorian approach to Greek economic growth. *Applied Economics, 23*, 1683–1689.
Fixler, D., & Siegel, D. (1999). Outsourcing and productivity growth in services. *Structural Change and Economic Dynamics, 10*(2), 177–194.
Garrido-Yserte, R. (2001). *Cambio estructural y desarrollo regional en España*. Madrid: Pirámide.
Goerlich, F. J., & Mas, M. (2001). *La evolución económica de las provincias españolas (1955–1998)*. Madrid: Fundación BBVA.
Goerlich, F. J., Mas, M., & Pérez, F. (2002). Concentración, convergencia y desigualdad regional en España in *Papeles de Economía Española*, 93, Fundación de las Cajas de Ahorro, Madrid.
Kaldor, N. (1970). The case of regional policy, *Scottish Journal of Political Economy, 17*, 337–348.
McCombie, J., & Thirwall, A. P. (1984). The Verdoorn law controversy: some new empirical evidence using US state data. *Oxford Economic Papers, 36*, 268–84.
Paci, R., & Pigliaru, F. (1997). Structural change and convergence: an Italian regional perspective. *Structural Change and Economic Dynamics, 8*, 297–318.
Pons, J., & Viladecans, E. (1999). Kaldor's laws and spatial dependence: Evidence for the European regions. *Regional Studies, 33*(5), 443–451.
Quah, D. (1996). *Regional convergence clusters across Europe*, Working Paper no. 1286. Centre for Economic Performance, London
Raymond, J. L., & García Greciano, B. (1994). Las disparidades en el PIBpc entre las CC.AA. y la hipótesis de convergencia. *Papeles de Economía Española, 59*, 37–58.
Raymond, J. L., & García Greciano, B. (1996). Distribución regional de la renta y movimientos migratorios. *Papeles de Economía Española, 67*, 185–201.
Sala-i-Martín, X. (1990). On growth and states. Ph. D. dissertation, Havard University, MA, USA.
Sala-i-Martín, X. (1994). La riqueza de las regiones. Evidencia y teorías sobre crecimiento regional y convergencia. *Moneda y Crédito, 198*, 13–80.
Sonmez Atesoglu, H. (1993). Manufacturing and economic growth in the United States. *Applied Economics, 25*, 67–69.

Chapter 6
The Sources of Spanish Regional Growth

Matilde Mas, Francisco Pérez, and Javier Quesada*

Over the last 20 years, the Spanish economy has followed a sustained growth trend – with the exception of a very short recession in 1993 – interrupted by the current global crisis initiated in the middle of 2007. Spain's growth has been driven both by a very intensive process of labour employment creation – accompanied by large improvements in qualification – and a great effort made in capital accumulation. Across the board the results have been positive, especially from the labour market perspective. The slashing of the unemployment rate (a chronic problem in Spain for more than 20 years) has been remarkably positive, concurrent with a fast increase in the participation of women in the labour force. The fact that Spain has turned from a country of emigrants into a country with immigrants clearly shows this process, indicating that in recent years foreigners have found good job and welfare opportunities in the country.

In spite of these undeniably positive results, Spain has also shown some weaknesses that threaten to condition its future recovery. Probably the most serious problem today is the poor performance of labour productivity. The origin of this problem is twofold: firstly, a product specialisation in activities that are very intensive in labour and have low value added; and secondly, the inefficient use of the production factors capital and labour. Although both determinants are common to most of the other EU countries, they have been aggravated in the Spanish case by the high and increasing weight of the construction sector (including real estate activities) characterised by the intensive use of labour – particularly unqualified – slow penetration of technical progress; and with high risk of suffering cyclical speculative bubbles that sooner or later burst and cause the collapse of other key industries.

M. Mas (✉)
IVIE, Guardia Civil, 22, esc.2-1, 46.020-Valencia, España
e-mail: matilde.mas@uv.es

*The authors are grateful to Juan Carlos Robledo for research assistance. Financial assistance from Ministerio de Ciencia y Tecnología/FEDER SEC2008-03813/ECO and Fundación BBVA-Ivie research programme is also gratefully acknowledged.

The two historical episodes that have probably been the most decisive in shaping the current territorial configuration of Spain are the *Stabilisation Plan* of 1959 and the Constitution of 1978, which led to the creation of the State of the Autonomies[1] (Pérez, 2007). The 1959 Plan put an end to the autarchy period that had started at the end of the Spanish Civil War in 1939. It was the beginning of new economic policies implying the external opening and modernisation of the country. Until then, Spain had basically been an agricultural country with a few industrial sites in Catalonia (textile and light industry), the Basque Country (steel and metallurgic), or Asturias (mining). These regions attracted the labour force expelled from the farming fields, while the capital of the nation, Madrid, attracted the most qualified workers to the Administrative Institutions of the Central State. In the mid-sixties, two additional regions became an important focus for attracting population: the Balearic Islands and the Valencian Community. Both regions are located on the Mediterranean coast and given that they enjoy good climate conditions and landscapes at good prices, many Europeans chose them as a favourite destination either for holidays or for retirement.

As a result of these changes, Spain suffered a territorial fracture over the sixties and seventies (Goerlich and Mas (2006)). The Southern and the Western parts of the country lost population, whereas in the East, the Basque Country and Madrid concentrated the gains. There was an exodus from the central part of the country to the coastal provinces and also from the mountains to the valleys (Goerlich and Mas, 2008).

After Franco's death in 1975, the new State of the Autonomies ended the former centralism of the dictatorship. With the creation of the new Autonomies, the regional governments were able to develop public expenditure policies favouring regional development. At the same time, the new welfare state created over the eighties made substantial improvements in unemployment benefit and the pension system, as well as greatly extending public education and health services all over the country. As a result, new public social guarantees improved all over the country, slowing down the process of the concentration of the population. In this way, public policies weakened the negative effects of the high unemployment rates, particularly in the poorest regions (Pérez, 2007; De la Fuente, 2008a).

In 1986, with Spain's entry into the EU, the European and regional policies reinforced each other. At the beginning, the relatively backward position of Spain and most of its regions made them eligible for Cohesion and Structural Funds from the EU. Both funds have the objective of promoting economic growth as well as social and territorial cohesion. In fact, both goals can be subsumed into one: favouring territorial convergence, that is, reducing the distance between the rich and the poor regions (Garrido et al., 2007). Two of the main instruments were very important for Spain: the European Regional Development Fund (ERDF) and the Cohesion Fund. Both funds have provided financial resources to improve public infrastructures, one of the main tools for promoting regional growth and

---

[1] We will refer to them as regions.

convergence. Unquestionably, the great investment effort made by all regions as a result of the double boost of the decentralisation process and the entry in the EU has changed the look of most of the cities and regions in Spain. The impact of public investment on regional growth and convergence has been analysed by different authors and from different perspectives.[2] The starting point of most of the studies was the seminal contribution of Aschauer (1989), who blamed the public infrastructures for the deceleration of productivity growth experienced by the US economy after the mid-seventies.[3]

In addition to public investment, the improvement of young generations' access to education has played a key role in Spain, showing much higher ratios of enrolment in secondary school and university studies. After the discovery of Solow's residual in 1957, Schultz (1961) argued that what was important from the growth perspective was not the number of workers but their level of education and skills. These quality variables had a direct effect on labour productivity. This consideration was included in the concept of human capital developed at the end of the fifties and early sixties by Jacob Mincer (1958) and Gary Becker (1964). The role of this intangible asset on Spanish growth has been analysed by different authors over the last two decades.[4]

The combination of public investment – both in infrastructures and human capital – with private investments – in machinery and equipment – comprises the process of accumulation of capital. This process allows the creation of employment and the improvement in productivity. From the mid-seventies, labour productivity in European economies increased faster than in the United States. However, this trend was inverted in the mid-nineties. The reason for this break was attributed initially to the development of new Information and Telecommunication Technologies (ICT). First, it was attributed to the ICT producing sector (Gordon, 2000, 2002, 2003). However, this effect was later extended to the ICT using sectors as well.[5] As a result, both the Lisbon 2000 and Barcelona 2002 EU summits placed the role of ICT in the core of the new growth strategy for the EU. The ambitious goals of the Lisbon Agenda depart from the results seen in the EU in recent years. In terms of productivity, they differ even more from the performance of Spain and its regions, where labour productivity advances have been very small and total factor productivity gains have been negative for many years.

In the following pages we develop some empirical evidence on these preliminary ideas. Section 1 revises the behaviour of Spain over the last few years. It provides a general framework for checking the particular performance of individual regions

---

[2] Mas (2006), Mas et al. (1995, 1996, 1998), Draper and Herce (1994), De la Fuente (2008a, 2008b).

[3] Today the same idea has been used by President Obama in his plan to promote growth after the great turbulence in which most of the western economies find themselves.

[4] Mas et al. (2002); Pérez and Serrano (2000, 2008); de la Fuente and Doménech (2006); De La Fuente (2008b).

[5] Jorgenson (1999, 2000, 2001), Jorgenson and Stiroh (2000); Jorgenson et al. (2002). See National Research Council (2007) for a review.

which are analysed in the following sections. Section 2 presents the basic facts of regional economic growth, highlighting the industry composition of output as well as the various sources of growth, namely, labour growth and capital accumulation and their corresponding composition. Section 3 analyses the regional convergence process and Section 4 concludes.

6.1 Spain's Growth

Once the long crisis of the seventies was over, Spain started to grow at an annual average of 3.3% in real terms between 1985 and 2007 (Table 6.1). The average growth rate of employment was 2.4% and labour productivity thus increased at a rate of 0.9%.[6] Around this long-term growth trend there were cyclical oscillations with different characteristics. For this reason, it is interesting to split the entire period into four different sub-periods with their specific features as shown in Table 6.1 and Fig. 6.1. The second half of the eighties was characterised by a very high growth of GVA and employment, 4.5% and 3.2% respectively, and a similarly high advance of labour productivity (1.4%). These were *virtuous* years for Spain with high growth rates of GVA, accompanied by a large creation of employment and positive advances of productivity.

The first half of the nineties offers quite a different picture. Growth substantially decelerated, being slightly negative in 1993, and there was employment destruction (−0.4% annual rate) instead of creation. Over this period, labour productivity grew at the highest pace of the whole period, almost 2% (1.97%). This experience should warn us about interpreting in an excessively simplistic way the evolution of labour productivity since –in the short run – great advances of productivity can be the result of a great reduction of employment.

After 1995, Spain's growth was quite significant, although it slowed down from 3.8% in 1995–2000 to 3.2% in 2001–2007. The slow down of the rate of employment creation was even more intensive, falling from 4.0% to 2.7%. However, the intensity of productivity deceleration concentrated in the first half (−0.15%),

Table 6.1 Rates of growth of real GVA, employment (hours worked) and labour productivity. Total economy Percentage

	1985–2007	1985–1990	1990–1995	1995–2007	1995–2000	2000–2007
Real GVA	3.28	4.53	1.53	3.49	3.83	3.24
Employment (hours worked)	2.38	3.17	−0.44	3.23	3.99	2.69
Labour productivity	0.90	1.36	1.97	0.26	−0.15	0.55

Source: INE and own elaboration

---

[6]More details in Maroto-Sánchez and Cuadrado-Roura (2006).

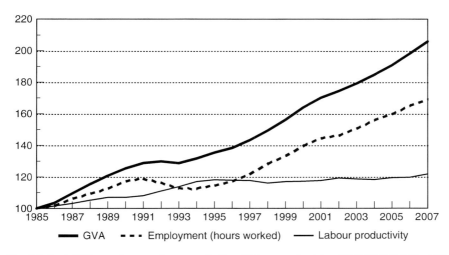

Fig. 6.1 Real GVA, employment (hours worked) and labour productivity. 1985–2007 (1985 = 100)
Source: INE and own elaboration

whereas between 2001 and 2007, there was a slight annual improvement of 0.6%. The uncertainties currently present in the western economies do not allow us to forecast their future evolution. Nevertheless, in the near future we should expect a deceleration in GVA and employment growth, as well as an improvement of labour productivity in line with what happened at the beginning of the nineties.

Spanish growth has been driven by an intensive process of capital accumulation. The effort in investment – measured as the ratio between investment (gross capital formation) and the gross domestic product (GDP) – has been one of the highest of the EU countries. A great part of this effort has been absorbed by the housing sector due to the high price increases of this asset. However, in real terms, the most intensive capital accumulation has taken place in non-residential assets, that is to say, assets that are part of the productive capital, including machinery and equipment (comprising ICT), and transport equipment.[7] The profiles of the accumulation of productive capital (excluding residential capital) over the last 20 years are shown in Fig. 6.2. Total capital shows a cyclical pattern around a very high average growth rate of 4%. ICT investment also shows a high average rate of accumulation, although it presented an intensive decrease during the short crisis of the early nineties. It was followed by a recovery period until 2000 and by a second downturn associated with the so called *dot com* crisis. Since then, we have seen a period of stable investment effort.

The composition of capital is shown in Table 6.2. We have considered three types of non-residential capital: infrastructures, ICT capital and the rest (non-infrastructures, non-ICT). The bulk of capital is made up of this last category

---

[7] Pérez (2008 y 2006).

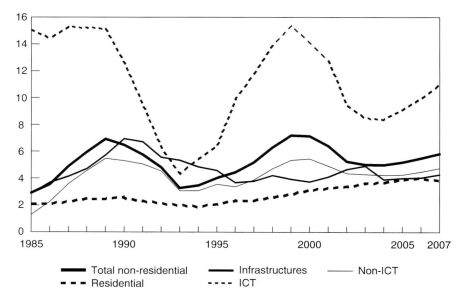

Fig. 6.2 Rates of growth of productive capital in Spain. 1985–2007 (Percentages)
Source: Foundation BBVA-Ivie and own elaboration

Table 6.2 Composition of net Non-Residential capital stock. Spain Percentage

	1985	1995	2000	2007
Total non-residential capital	100.00	100.00	100.00	100.00
Infrastructures	18.22	19.93	19.74	20.34
ICT	4.67	4.74	4.60	4.31
Non-infrastructures, Non-ICT	77.11	75.33	75.66	75.35

Source: Foundation BBVA-Ivie and own elaboration

with a relative weight of around 75%. Infrastructures are approximately 20% of total capital and ICT represents the remaining 5%.

With available data for different types of physical capital as well as for human capital, one can make a more precise analysis of the sources of labour productivity growth presented in Table 6.3. The most recent approaches consider that from the perspective of growth, quality improvements are as important as quantity increases. The higher the input quality is, the larger the impact of this factor will be on productivity. The way to approximate factor quality indices is to consider the price that one is willing to pay for them. Highly qualified workers are better paid than unqualified ones because they are more valuable to the firm. In the same way, different types of capital have different user costs – to cover for depreciation, the interest rate as a proxy for the opportunity cost, and the devaluation or revaluation of the capital asset. These user costs are the prices that a firm would be willing to pay if the assets were rented and they are proportional to the expected productivities.

6 The Sources of Spanish Regional Growth

Table 6.3 Growth accounting. Labour productivity. Spain. Private Sector. Percentage

	1985–2006	1985–1995	1995–2000	2000–2006
Labour productivity growth	0.81	1.87	−0.51	0.14
Contribution of:				
Infrastructures	0.07	0.15	−0.02	0.05
ICT capital	0.36	0.38	0.40	0.35
Non-Infrastructures, Non-ICT capital	0.48	0.70	0.05	0.39
Labour force qualification	0.51	0.71	0.34	0.82
Total factor productivity (TFP)	−0.61	−0.06	−1.28	−1.47

Source: Own elaboration

With the adequate information, growth accounting allows the origin of the advances in labour productivity to be broken down into the contribution of the inputs used in the production process. It identifies the contributions of infrastructures; ICT capital; non-infrastructures, non-ICT capital; labour qualification; and a residual factor or total factor productivity (TFP). The exercise has been carried out only for the private sector, excluding the production of public services. In this way, we do not run into the problems of measuring the real output values and quality levels of publicly provided services.

Over the 1985–2006 period, the average growth rate of labour productivity in the private sector was 0.8% (Table 6.3). The decomposition of this growth rate into its determining factors attributes 0.07% to investment in infrastructures; 0.36 to ICT capital investment; 0.48 to investment in non-Infrastructures, non-ICT capital; and, finally, 0.55 to the improvements in labour quality. Note the high contribution to labour productivity growth of factors that are intensive in knowledge; ICT explains 44.4% of this improvement but is only 5% of total net capital; human capital explains on its own 70% of the labour productivity growth. Additionally, non-infrastructures, non-ICT representing 75% of total capital contribute 59.2% to potential growth. Finally, infrastructures representing 20% of total net capital contribute only 8.6% to productivity growth.

Clearly these percentage contributions to labour productivity add up to more than one hundred. This means that productive factors have not been actually used up because we find a residual with a large negative contribution (−0.61): the TFP term. This negative contribution can be interpreted as the result of an inefficient assignment of resources in the production process. Taking into consideration not only the quantities but also the improvements in quality and composition, production has increased less than the resources used to generate it.

In the sub-periods, we find a decreasing role for infrastructures, a constant one for ICT and a very unstable one for non-infrastructure, non-ICT capital. We find a negative contribution of TFP in all sub periods that is particularly large in the last expansionary period, when labour productivity stagnates (even decreases) due to the intensive process of employment creation. This remarkable and persistent result cannot rule out the possibility that the growth accounting methodology overestimates the contribution of some of the productive factors. With this caveat in mind, we proceed with the regional analysis in the remaining sections.

6.2 Labour Productivity in Spanish Regions

In 2007, the levels of labour productivity in Spanish regions show differences that amount to 20% above and under the national average. The Community of Madrid and the Basque Country are the regions with the highest levels, whereas Extremadura, Castile-La Mancha and Murcia present the lowest values. The map of Spain is divided into three different geographical zones (Map 6.1). A central-axis with low productivity levels running East to West through Extremadura, Castile-La Mancha and Murcia. On both sides of this axis there are regions with productivity levels around the national average: on the southern part it comprises Andalusia, the Canary Islands, and the two autonomous cities; and on the other part the rest of the northern regions, the Valencian Community and the Balearic Islands. Finally,

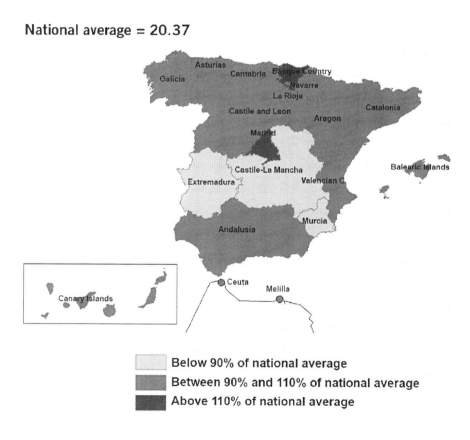

Map 6.1 Labour productivity. 2007 Euros per hour worked
Source: INE and own elaboration

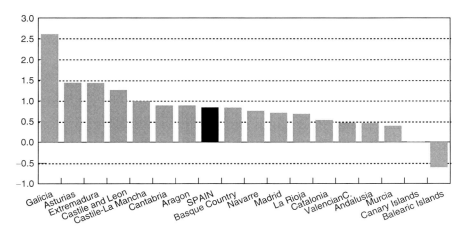

Fig. 6.3 Labour productivity. Rates of variation. 1985–2007 (Percentages)
Source: INE and own elaboration

we find the Community of Madrid and the Basque Country as the regions with productivity levels significantly above the national average.

It is important to identify not only the regional levels of productivity but also their dynamic behaviour. We find very significant differences over the period (Fig. 6.3). With the exception of the Balearic Islands, all regions improved their productivity over the period 1985–2007 although at different rates, from 0.4% to 2.6%. The highest growing region in terms of productivity was Galicia followed by Extremadura, Castile and Leon and Castile-La Mancha. These are regions that experience productivity gains more as a result of a slow growing population than because of a fast growth of output. On the opposite side, we find the Canary Islands, Murcia and Andalusia, which are very dynamic communities in terms of population and employment growth. This high trend has more than reversed the growth of GVA, making the indices of productivity gains in these regions the lowest ones in the country.

In the remaining part of this section, we consider two relevant determinants of the regional evolution of productivity: the differences in industry specialisation and in sources of growth.

6.2.1 *The Relevance of Specialisation*

The aggregate growth of one region is a combination of the behaviour of firms and sectors in the economy. Industries can follow different patterns of growth depending upon the opportunities brought about by their product specialisation, and the efficiency of their firms in exploiting the externalities associated to a specific location in a region. Following the proposal by Basu and Fernald (1995, 1997), and Stiroh and Kevin (2002), Table 6.4 decomposes labour productivity growth into the contribution of the growth experienced in each of the industries plus a reassignment factor of labour hours. While this latter element is positive whenever there is a movement of the labour force towards activities with higher value added, it is negative in the opposite case. At any rate, its importance at the aggregate level is very limited. The differences in productivity trends of each of the industries are much more relevant which, as shown, can be very substantial among economies.

The last two rows in Table 6.4 contain information on the EU-15 and the United States for the most recent period 2000–2005. They are a useful reference to compare the performance of Spain and its regions. Over this period, labour productivity increased in the US twice as fast as in the EU-15 and five times more than in Spain. This higher dynamism originated in the ICT producing sector (*Electric machinery, post and telecommunication*) rather than in the rest of *Manufacturing*. But indeed the main differences occurred in the service sectors. Note that in *Trade and Transport* industries, US productivity growth was 3.5 times higher than in Europe; in *Financial Intermediation and Business Services*, 6.6 times; and in *Personal and Social Services* US growth was positive (0.3 pp), while it was negative in the EU (−0.1 pp). Consequently, the great difference in productivity growth between the US and the EU-15 lies in the higher dynamism of the US service sectors and not so much in the manufacturing sectors, if one excludes the ICT producing sectors.

Data for Spain and its regions clearly show, once more, that advance in productivity has indeed been slow over the last period. In none of the regions did productivity grow at a rate close to the EU-15 average and much less to that of the US. Industry contributions to this modest advance in productivity are very striking. In nearly all regions, ICT producing industries (*Electric Machinery, Post and Telecommunications*) contributed positively to productivity enhancement. Note the positive contribution in the Community of Madrid, with 0.28 pp, as opposed to the rest of the regions where in most cases it is small or even negative. In all regions without exception, on one hand, *Manufacturing* contributed positively to productivity growth with Catalonia, the Basque Country and Navarre as the regions with the highest contributions. On the other hand, the *Construction* sector contributed negatively in most of the regions. The highest positive contribution was in Aragon and the most negative one in Murcia.

The three sub-sectors of services show completely different patterns of behaviour. *Financial Intermediation and Business Services* contributed positively in all regions without exception, being highest in the Community of Madrid but also relevant in other regions. On the contrary, *Personal and Social Services* contributed negatively in nearly all regions, with Extremadura being the only exception, although very marginally. Note that this sub-sector is the sector that has contributed most negatively to productivity growth not only in Spain but also in the EU-15. By contrast, the US shows a positive contribution over the last few years. Finally, *Trade and Transport* presents weak advances in productivity in comparison with what happened in the EU and the US; at the regional level, it has shown a pattern

6 The Sources of Spanish Regional Growth

Table 6.4 Industries contribution to labour productivity growth. 2000–2005. Percentage

	Labour productivity	ICT producing industries[a]	Manufacturing, excluding electrical	Construction	Other production	Distribution	Finance and Business Services	Personal services	Reallocation of labour effect
Aragon	1.33	0.17	0.46	0.30	−0.06	0.27	0.26	−0.14	0.07
Castile and Leon	1.23	0.10	0.24	0.19	0.12	0.20	0.23	−0.04	0.19
Basque Country	1.22	0.13	0.50	−0.09	0.15	0.19	0.34	−0.07	0.07
Extremadura	1.05	0.07	0.11	0.07	−0.09	0.32	0.19	0.10	0.28
Catalonia	1.01	0.12	0.48	0.21	0.05	0.03	0.45	−0.29	−0.04
Asturias	0.96	0.03	0.10	0.12	0.48	0.23	0.16	−0.21	0.04
Navarre	0.73	−0.01	0.54	−0.05	0.20	−0.14	0.37	−0.18	0.00
Madrid	0.73	0.28	0.39	−0.15	0.05	0.00	0.50	−0.26	−0.08
Galicia	0.66	0.03	0.21	0.05	0.21	−0.08	0.18	−0.10	0.16
Castile-La Mancha	0.66	0.03	0.14	0.05	0.25	−0.15	0.19	−0.10	0.25
Spain	0.61	0.07	0.27	−0.03	0.12	0.10	0.27	−0.18	−0.01
Andalusia	0.39	0.07	0.14	−0.20	0.08	0.11	0.24	−0.22	0.18
Valencian C.	0.27	0.05	0.32	−0.17	0.09	−0.07	0.17	−0.23	0.10
La Rioja	0.24	0.02	0.37	−0.08	−0.17	−0.03	0.21	−0.19	0.11
Cantabria	0.07	−0.01	0.22	−0.07	−0.08	−0.18	0.17	−0.02	0.05
Canary Islands	−0.10	−0.01	0.06	−0.14	0.14	−0.10	0.13	−0.18	0.00
Murcia	−0.62	0.01	0.23	−0.62	−0.07	−0.17	0.17	−0.21	0.04
Balearic Islands	−0.92	−0.04	0.15	−0.41	0.09	−0.11	0.17	−0.82	0.05
EU-15	1.36	0.25	0.45	0.04	0.24	0.34	0.09	−0.10	0.05
United States	3.18	0.53	0.75	−0.08	0.00	1.16	0.60	0.33	−0.11

[a] Electrical machinery, post and communication services

Source: EU KLEMS Database, March 2008, http://www.euklems.net, INE and own elaboration

somewhat more favourable in regions, such as Extremadura and Aragon, and negative in others (Cantabria and Murcia).

In conclusion, Spain and its regions show generalised weaknesses in productivity behaviour in practically all productive activities: with the exception of *Financial Intermediation*, productivity improvements in each of the industries are much smaller than those of the EU-15 and the US. These results can be both due to an inefficient use of productive factors or to the industry composition of each of the sectors. Both explanations may be related to one another, since intra-industry specialisation can be responsible for the inefficient use of productive factors, in particular those that are knowledge intensive.

6.2.2 Growth Accounting

Growth accounting allows the decomposition of productivity growth into the contributions of the capital per worker endowments, and a residual term which captures all factors different from capital deepening. We have mentioned how important it is to distinguish between the different types of capital because of their different impact on productivity. In this sense, available data for Spanish regions[8] allow us to evaluate the contribution to productivity of improvements in capital endowments (human; infrastructures; ICT; and non-infrastructures, non-ICT). Before showing the results of the growth accounting exercise, we briefly describe the regional endowments of the relevant variables.

Infrastructure capital is distributed in an irregular form between different regions (Mas et al., 2007a), although it is necessary to look at the indices of demand.[9] It is very common to use the level of employment, or the size of the territory, to normalise these indicators. In the first case, we get the capital labour ratio, which directly influences productivity growth. The size of the region is meaningful because a great part of infrastructures are related with the location of activities and the level of communications. However, Spain shows a radial structure for many of the transport infrastructures. This makes the region of Madrid –located in the centre of the country – the core connecting region for most of the territory. In 2006, using the capital labour ratio indicator, the regions with the highest endowments were Asturias, Aragon, Castile-La Mancha, Castile and Leon and Extremadura. On the opposite side, we find the Balearic Islands, Madrid, Catalonia, Murcia and the Valencian Community (Fig. 6.4a).

When we use the indicator of capital per square kilometre – excluding the two autonomous cities of Ceuta and Melilla – the rank changes very significantly.

---

[8] See Mas et al. (2007b) for capital stock and Mas et al. (2008) for human capital.

[9] The permanent inventory procedure used in the estimates of FBBVA-Ivie considers the investment made in the corresponding region, although its use – as in the case of the infrastructures of transport – is not limited to its residents or to the firms operating in the area. This fact makes the comparison of infrastructures among regions difficult.

6 The Sources of Spanish Regional Growth

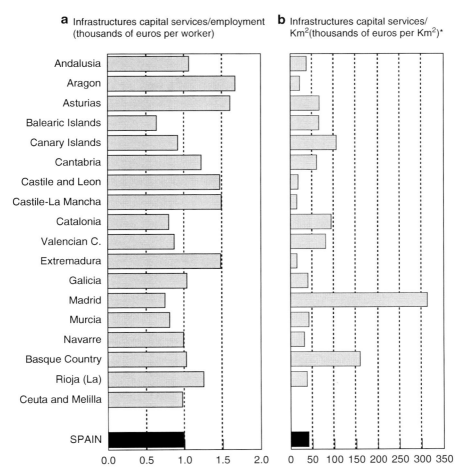

Fig. 6.4 Infrastructure capital services in the Spanish regions. 2006.
*Cevta and Melilla have not been included in the figure, with a value of 2 million euros per km²
Source: Foundation BBVA-Ivie, INE and own elaboration

The Community of Madrid, a small region in geographical terms, ranks first, well ahead of the second community, the Basque Country, followed by the Canary Islands and Catalonia. On the opposite side, we find Extremadura, Castile-La Mancha, Castile and Leon and Aragon, all of which are very large regions with a very low population density.

ICT capital includes three different assets: computer equipment referred to as *hardware*; *software*; and equipment and network lines of transport for voice and data associated with *telecommunications*. ICT capital per worker is an indicator similar to the capital labour ratio defined earlier for infrastructures. Figure 6.5a shows the relative position of the Spanish regions in 2006. We find the highest level

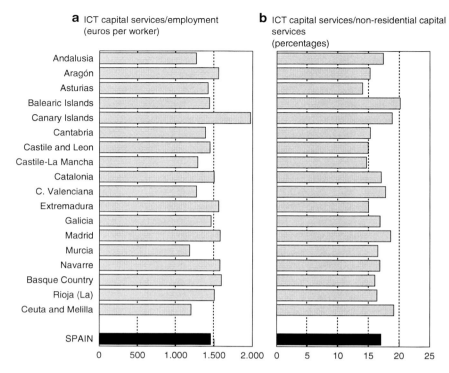

Fig. 6.5 ICT capital services in the Spanish regions. 2006
Source: Foundation BBVA-Ivie, INE and own elaboration

in the Canary Islands, followed by the most developed regions like Madrid, the Basque Country and Navarre, and also by Aragon and Extremadura.

The relative weight of the ICT capital services with respect to the total productive capital services is a complementary indicator of the degree of penetration of the new technologies by region (Fig. 6.5b). Above the national average, we find communities, such as the Balearic Islands, Madrid, the Canary Islands and the Valencian Community (besides Ceuta and Melilla). With a lower than the national average ICT capital labour ratio, we find the communities of Asturias, Castile-La Mancha, Extremadura, Castile and Leon, Cantabria and Aragon.

To evaluate the endowments in human capital, we have built a synthetic index which considers the average years of workers' education in the different regions. As shown in Fig. 6.6, the human capital endowments are highest in Madrid and the northern regions, and lowest along the belt of lowest productivity regions crossing the centre of the country, as shown in Map 6.1.

The growth accounting results provide a very different pattern among Spanish regions. These differences are more quantitative than qualitative. Table 6.5, referring to the period 1995–2006, shows the retrogressive movement of labour productivity in most of the regions, and substantial improvements only in Galicia,

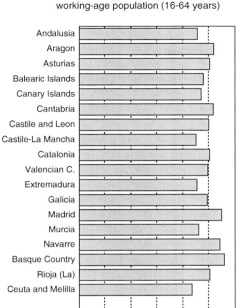
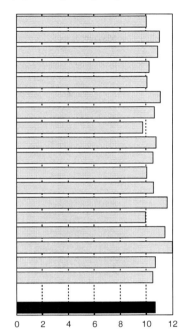

Fig. 6.6 Human capital in Spanish regions. 2006
Source: INE and own elaboration

Extremadura, Castile-La Mancha and Asturias. In all regions, without exception, TFP contribution to labour productivity was negative. The regions with the lowest negative values were the Balearic Islands, the Canary Islands, Castile-La Mancha, La Rioja, and Murcia.

With regard to the factor contributions, the results are as follows:

1. Changes in the composition of the labour force have shown positive –although uneven – effects in all regions, with the exception of the Basque Country and marginally Navarre. The regions affected most significantly are Galicia, Castile-La Mancha, the Valencian Community and La Rioja. The regions with lower intensity are Catalonia, Cantabria, the Balearic Islands and Aragon, together with the two already mentioned Basque Country and Navarre.
2. The contribution of infrastructures to productivity growth has been positive in general but small. It has been much lower than the attention received by public policies or their relative weight in total capital. While in seven regions the contribution was negative, it was only positive and significant in Asturias and Galicia.

Table 6.5 Growth accounting. Labour productivity. Private Sector (1995–2006)

	Labour productivity	Capital per hour worked ICT	Infrastructures	Non-infrastructures, Non-ICT	Labour force qualification	TFP
Andalusia	−0.37	0.43	−0.04	0.31	0.75	−1.83
Aragon	0.06	0.41	0.07	0.45	0.17	−1.04
Asturias	0.78	0.36	0.14	0.21	0.45	−0.38
Balearic Islands	−2.86	0.45	−0.03	0.19	0.17	−3.64
Canary Islands	−0.95	0.41	−0.01	0.10	0.77	−2.22
Cantabria	−0.70	0.34	0.03	−0.13	0.11	−1.05
Castile and Leon	0.60	0.41	0.09	0.39	0.55	−0.85
Castile-La Mancha	−0.40	0.40	0.02	0.23	1.01	−2.05
Catalonia	−0.56	0.31	0.01	0.11	0.14	−1.12
Valencian C.	0.16	0.43	0.02	0.49	1.01	−1.78
Extremadura	0.72	0.38	0.01	−0.18	0.89	−0.38
Galicia	1.95	0.50	0.14	0.68	1.23	−0.59
Madrid	−0.57	0.29	0.04	0.22	0.50	−1.63
Murcia	−0.35	0.41	−0.02	0.58	0.84	−2.16
Navarre	−0.42	0.41	−0.05	0.42	−0.01	−1.18
Basque Country	−0.02	0.36	−0.02	0.05	−0.23	−0.17
La Rioja	−0.16	0.45	−0.08	0.46	1.21	−2.20
SPAIN	−0.16	0.37	0.02	0.26	0.52	−1.33

Source: Own elaboration

3. The share of regional growth explained by the use of productive capital that is neither ICT nor infrastructures is positive and homogeneous among Spanish regions, with the exception of Cantabria and Extremadura. This result confirms that, in all regions, a significant and stable part of productivity growth is due to traditional firm investment in plant and equipment (non-ICT).
4. Additionally, it is worth noting that in many regions, the contribution of ICT capital is higher –and in some cases much higher – than that of infrastructures and the rest of capital. This higher contribution is still more significant if one compares the relative weight of ICT with respect to total capital. Thus, the new technologies associated to intensive ICT use are more favourable to improvements in labour productivity. Consequently, a constant effort in ICT investment should be reflected sooner or later in productivity gains (Mas and Quesada, 2005a, 2005b).

However, all these contributions, although positive, end up not being reflected in labour productivity gains. They are accompanied by generalised and almost always intensive falls of TFP. Thus we found – in the former section – a weak advance in labour productivity in all sectors of the regions. And now we see that given the improvements in the quantity and quality of factors used in the production function, there is also a loss in production efficiency in all regions. As mentioned before, this finding on the last decade is quite striking and requires a deeper explanation of its causes.

6.3 Regional Convergence

The neoclassical growth model[10] predicts productivity convergence among different territories if regions share production technology, savings and depreciation rates and employment creation. Thus, the confirmation of this prediction depends upon the accomplishment of the conditions of such parameters, something that should be validated empirically. One should expect the convergence result to be more likely among regions than between different countries, since regions share a common economic and institutional system.

In empirical tests of the convergence hypothesis, the literature has defined two basic concepts, σ-convergence and β-convergence. The first one analyses whether regions become more or less alike with the passing of time, for instance in productivity levels. To test for the presence of convergence, a measure of dispersion –like the coefficient of variation – is computed over time for the 17 regions and the two cities.

Over the last 20 years in Spain, we find a process of regional convergence in productivity levels (Fig. 6.7a). Regions are more alike in 2006 than they were in 1985.

It is equally interesting to check whether there exist regional differences in the productive resources that improve productivity over time. Over the last 21 years, we

---

[10] Solow (1956). Also the growth accounting methodology, used above by Solow (1957).

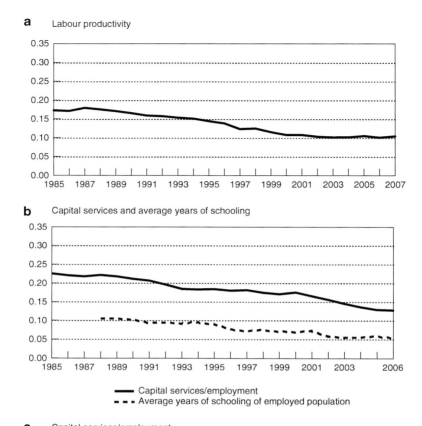
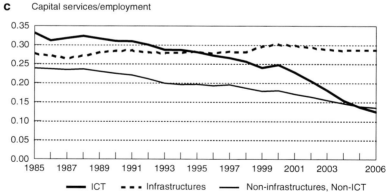

Fig. 6.7 σ-convergence (Coefficient of variation)
Source: Foundation BBVA-Ivie, INE and own elaboration

6 The Sources of Spanish Regional Growth

find a process of regional convergence both in total productive capital (excluding residential capital) per worker and in the level of qualification of the labour force (Fig. 6.7b). Thus, regions are more alike now than they were before in productive capital endowments, and also in the education, experience and productivity of their labour force. Notice that regional differences are smallest in the human capital variable.

Figure 6.7c complements the previous one. It verifies whether there is convergence in the endowments of each of the assets considered in the definition of capital: infrastructures, ICT capital and the rest. ICT capital endowments show the most intensive convergence process as reflected in a strong decrease of the coefficient of variation. While in non-infrastructures, non-ICT capital, the process of convergence is equally positive, it shows less intensity. By contrast, infrastructures do not show any sign of convergence between regions. Over the last two decades, the existing differences in infrastructures between regions have not disappeared. They are even greater (as seen previously in Fig. 6.4) in those regions with large territories, and low employment and production. Therefore, it is likely that there has not been much progress in gaining an equal endowment of resources by region, and particularly in those with high population density and activity levels which show congestion problems. However, one should bear in mind the different picture that one gets of regional endowments in infrastructures depending upon the indicator used. In this case, we use labour employment as a normalising variable, which is the relevant variable for *growth accounting*.

An alternative way of analysing regional convergence, complementary to σ-convergence, is β-convergence. This is a concept, which defines regional convergence whenever regions that are initially placed in an unfavourable position – with a lower initial level of the variable under investigation – show the highest rates of growth. If this is the case for a sufficiently long period of time, one should expect that the poorest regions will end up catching up with the richest ones. However, this result is not guaranteed if the initial differences are large enough and the differences in the growth rates are small.

Figure 6.8a shows the labour productivity level in 1985 on the horizontal axis and the annual growth rate over the period 1985–2006 on the vertical one. The resulting relation is a negative one, as shown by the adjusted regression line, which gives significant values for the explanatory power of the equation as well as for the confidence of the estimated parameter. The decreasing line indicates that the communities which were in the lower part of the set of Spanish regions in terms of labour productivity levels of the private sector, were those enjoying the highest growth rates of productivity. In other words, those regions in the worst positions at the beginning of the period were also the fastest improving regions. This is the case of Galicia, Extremadura and Castile-La Mancha. However, communities that initially were in better positions like the Balearic Islands, Madrid and the Basque Country are showing the lowest improvement. This analysis confirms the presence of a convergence process of productivity among Spanish regions.

Figure 6.8b presents a similar exercise carried out for capital endowments (excluding residential capital) per worker, that is to say, the capital labour ratio.

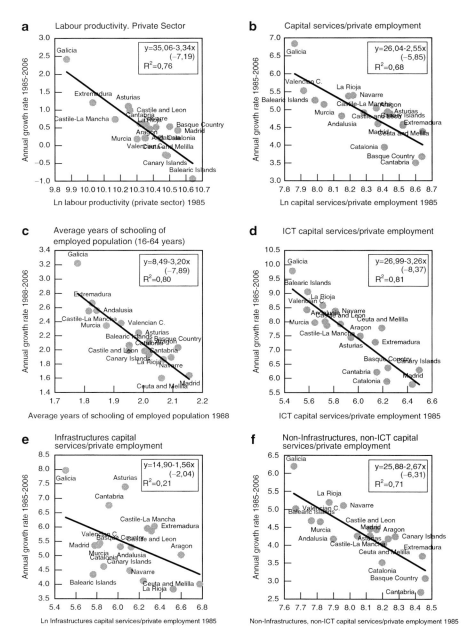

Fig. 6.8 β-convergence. *t*-stasistic in brackets
Source: Foundation BBVA-Ivie, INE and own elaboration

Again we obtain a negative and statistically significant relation. This result is replicated in the case of the labour force qualification, as measured by the years of schooling, a variable that has also shown a convergent trend as shown in Fig. 6.8c.

The remaining parts of Fig. 6.8 show the β-convergence analysis applied to the capital labour ratio defined for the three types of capital considered. First, we observe an intensive convergence process of the different ICT capital per hour worked (Fig. 6.8d). This confirms the σ-convergence result obtained above (Fig. 6.7c). Therefore, it seems that the convergence in the endowments of ICT capital is one of the determinant forces in the convergence of labour productivity in Spanish regions.

In infrastructures, we observe (Fig. 6.8e) a much weaker process of convergence than that of the other productive capital assets. The coefficient of determination and the value of the slope of the adjusted regression line tell us that the initial position does not explain a great deal of the variance, and that the dependency relation is not very strong. At any rate, this β-convergence has not been able to reduce the existing dispersion in endowments (σ-convergence).

Finally, we find convergence between the Spanish regions in terms of capital labour ratio when capital is formed by all capital assets that are not ICT or infrastructures (Fig. 6.8f). This relationship is decreasing and significant, and the coefficient of determination is high. Regions like Galicia, the Valencian Community and the Balearic Islands–initially in the lowest levels of endowments – are also the regions that improved more over the period, with rates of growth twice as large as those of the best situated regions.

6.4 Conclusions

Before the start of the current crisis, the performance of the Spanish economy was quite remarkable over the last 20 years, in terms of output growth and particularly outstanding in employment. This latter achievement brought to an end the extremely chronic problem of unemployment that started with the first energy crisis. Growth was general in all Spanish regions, although with different rates. Spain attracted migrating population flows from other countries, especially from Latin America and Eastern Europe. However, after the slow down of growth in 2007, unemployment has made a powerful return rising more than 50% in only one year.

Over these years, the darkest side of Spain was the overall presence of a very slow growth of productivity. Although the regions enjoy different levels of productivity, all of them share a slow progress of this variable; lower than the average of EU-15 and much lower than the United States. The slow gain in labour productivity is the result, in part at least, of a product specialisation biased towards activities with low added value. These are industries like *construction, hotel and restaurants* and *personal services*, three great reservoirs of jobs. However, given the intensity of the accumulation of productive capital in all activities and regions over these years, there also exists a problem of inefficiency in the use of resources, as shown by the reversion of labour productivity in many regions, and the persistence of a negative TFP in all of them. Growth has been more the result of the effort made in creating employment and keeping a high rate of capital accumulation – *transpiration* – than the outcome of *inspiration*. Until now, the externalities derived from the accumulation of physical and human capital have not emerged, technical progress has been very slow and the combination of the factors of production utilised has been hardly efficient.

There are two complementary explanations for this poor performance of productivity. First, as in many other European economies, some service industries have shown very weak productivity gains, in particular in comparison with the dynamism of the United States. In this country, the services of *Wholesale Trade, Transport* and *Business Services* have been the winners in productivity gains since the mid-nineties. An additional contributing factor to the dynamism of the United States was the fast development of the ICT production sectors.

As with the majority of countries, Spain and most of its regions do not have a powerful ICT producing sector. This is different from what we see in the United States, Sweden, Finland or the UK. Only in the region of Madrid does this ICT producing sector present a significant contribution. Furthermore, the construction sector –where productivity gains are very slow – stands for a very large weight in the GDP of many regions. This high contribution of the construction industry has contrasted with the negative effects on productivity, with significant negative growth rates in regions like Murcia. Finally, services industries –with the exception of *Financial Intermediation* – have shown slower advances in Spanish regions than in the EU-15, and in some regions they have contributed even negatively.

Secondly, growth accounting has allowed us to test that in all Spanish regions, without exception, TFP contribution has been negative. That is to say, the slow advances in labour productivity have taken place in spite of the intensive process of –physical and human – capital accumulation. This high rate of investment has not been accompanied by technical progress or efficiency improvements in the utilisation of factors. The improvements of the qualification of the labour force and the important accumulation of ICT capital have given rise to a contribution to labour productivity, which is larger than the productivity gain, without the effect of the negative contribution of the TFP. To the question of why we get this result, we propose, at least, two possible answers: first, knowledge investments are not worthwhile unless there is a strong specialisation of the economy in knowledge intensive industries; second, investments in knowledge mature very slowly.

Finally, the work has analysed regional convergence using the concepts of σ-and β-convergence. We have found that there is convergence in labour productivity among the Spanish regions. The most intensive convergence process takes place in ICT capital endowments, followed by the educational levels of the workers and by the rest of capital (non-infrastructures, non-ICT). In contrast, infrastructures endowments do not show a profile of convergence, a great discrepancy from the rest of the sources of growth.

References

Aschauer, D. A. (1989). Is public expenditure productive? *Journal of Monetary Economics, 23*, 177–200.

Basu, S., & Fernald, J. G. (1995). Are apparent productive spillover a figment of specification error? *Journal of Monetary Economics, 36*, 165–188.

Basu, S., & Fernald, J. G. (1997). Returns to Scale in US Production: Estimates and Implications. *Journal of Political Economy, 105*(2), 249–283.
Becker, G. (1964). *Human Capital*. Nueva York: Columbia University Press.
Cuadrado-Roura, J. R., Mancha, T., & Garrido, R. (1998). *Convergencia Regional en España. Hechos, tendencias y perspectivas*. Madrid: Fundación Argentaria.
Cuadrado-Roura, J. R., García-Greciano, B., & Raymond, J. L. (1999). Regional convergence in productivity and productive structure: the Spanish case. *International Regional Science Review, 22*(1), 35–53.
Cuadrado-Roura, J. R., & Parellada, M. (2002). *Regional convergence in the European regions: Facts, prospects and policies*. Berlin: Springer.
De La Fuente, A. (2001). Infraestructuras y política regional. In T. García-Milà (Ed.), *Nuevas fronteras de la política económica, 2001*. (pp. 18–55). Barcelona: Generalitat de Cataluña y Universidad Pompeu Fabra.
De la Fuente, A. (2008). Dinámica regional de la renta y la población. In Velarde Fuentes and J. Serrano Sanz (dirs) *La España del siglo XXI*, vol III (pp. 679–719). Madrid: La economía, Editorial Biblioteca Nueva.
De La Fuente, A. (2008). *Inversión en infraestructuras, crecimiento y convergencia regional*. Economic Reports 20-08, FEDEA
De La Fuente, A., & Doménech, R. (2006). Capital humano, crecimiento y desigualdad en las regiones españolas. *Moneda y Crédito, 222*, 13–56.
Dolado, J. J., González-Páramo, J. M., & Roldán, J. M. (1994). Convergencia entre las provincias españolas. Evidencia Empírica. *Moneda y Crédito, 198*.
Draper, M., & Herce, J. A. (1994). Infraestructuras y Crecimiento. Un Panorama. *Revista Economía Aplicada, 2*(6), Winter.
Garrido, R., Mancha, T., & Cuadrado, J. R. (2007). La Política Regional y de Cohesión en la Unión Europea: veinte años de avance y un futuro nuevo. *Investigaciones Regionales, 10*, 239–266.
Goerlich, F. J., & Mas, M. (2006). (Dirs.) *La Localización de la Población sobre el Territorio. Un siglo de cambios. Un estudio basado en series homogéneas 1900–2001* (536 páginas). Bilbao: Fundación BBVA. Includes CD with the database.
Goerlich, F. J., & Mas, M. (2008). Pautas de localización de la población a lo largo del siglo XX. *Investigaciones Regionales, 12*, 5–34.
Gordon, R. J. (1999). *Has the "new economy" rendered the productivity slowdown obsolete?* (mimeo). Chicago: Northwestern University.
Gordon, R. J. (2000). Does the new economy measure up to the great inventions of the past? *Journal of Economic Perspectives, 14*(4), 3–22.
Gordon, R. J. (2002). *Technology and economic performance in the American economy*, Working Paper no. 8771. Cambridge, MA: NBER.
Gordon, R. J. (2003). *High-tech innovation and productivity growth: does supply create its own demand*, Working Paper no. 9437. Cambridge, MA: NBER.
Jorgenson, D. W. (1999). Information technology and growth. *American Economic Review, Papers and proceedings, 89*(2), 109–115.
Jorgenson, D. W. (2000). *Information technology and the US economy*. Presidential Address to the American Economic Association, January, 2001.
Jorgenson, D. W. (2001). Information technology and the US economy. *American Economic Review, 91*(1), 249–280.
Jorgenson, D. W., Ho, M. S., & Stiroh, K. J. (2002). *Information technology, education, and the sources of economic growth across US industries*. USA: Federal Reserve System.
Jorgenson, D. W., & Stiroh, K. (2000). Raising the speedy limit: US economic growth in the information age. *Brookings Papers on Economic Activity, 1*, 125–211.
Maroto-Sánchez, & Cuadrado-Roura J. R. (2006). *La productividad en la Economía Española*. Madrid: Instituto de Estudios Económicos.

Mas, M. (2006) *Infrastructures and ICT: Measurement issues and impact on economic growth.* EUKLEMS Working Paper Series no 12, European Commission, 6th Framework Programme, (available in www.euklems.net).

Mas, M., Maudos, J., Pérez, F., & Uriel, E. (1995). Public capital and convergence in the Spanish regions. *Entrepreneurship and Regional Development, 7*(4), 309–327.

Mas, M., Maudos, J., Pérez, F., & Uriel, E. (1996). Infrastructures and productivity in the Spanish regions. *Regional Studies, 30*(7), 641–649.

Mas, M., Maudos, J., Pérez, F., & Uriel, E. (1998). Public capital, productive efficiency and convergence in the Spanish regions (1964–93). *The Review of Income and Wealth, 44*(3), 383–396.

Mas, M., Pérez, F., Serrano, L., & Uriel, E. (2002). *Capital humano. Metodología y series históricas 1964–2001* (297 pp). Valencia: Fundación Bancaja.

Mas, M., Pérez, F., & Uriel, E. (2006). Spanish new capital stock estimates. In M. Mas & P. Schreyer (Eds.), *Growth, capital and new technologies.* Bilbao: Fundación BBVA.

Mas, M., & Quesada J. (2005a). *Las Nuevas Tecnologías y el Crecimiento Económico en España* (pp. 384). Bilbao: Fundación BBVA.

Mas, M., & Quesada, J. (2005b). ICT and economic growth. A quantification of productivity growth in Spain. OECD Statistics Working Papers, Statistics Directorate, STD/DOC(2005)4. Paris: OECD.

Mas, M., Quesada, J., & Robledo, J. C. (2007a). In Reig, E. (Dir.) *Competitividad, Crecimiento y Capitalización en las Regiones Españolas* (pp. 371). Bilbao: Fundación BBVA.

Mas, M, Pérez, F. & Uriel, E. (2007b) of stock if los servicios del capital eu España if su distribución territorial (1964–2005). Neuva Metodología, Fundación BBVA, Bilbao

Mas, M, Pérez, F, Uriel, E, Serrano, L & Soler, A (2008) Series de capital humano (1964–2007) Fundación BANCAJA.

Mincer, J. (1958). Investment in human capital and personal income distribution. *The Journal of Political Economy, 66,* 281–320.

National Research Council. (2007). *Measuring and Sustaining the New Economy,* 5 vols. Washington: The National Academies Press.

OCDE. (2001). *Measuring productivity. Measurement of aggregate and industry-level productivity growth.* Paris: OCDE.

Pérez, F. (2006). Productividad, capitalización y especialización. *Información Comercial Española, 829,* 27–47.

Pérez, F. (2007). *Las claves del desarrollo a largo plazo de la economía española.* Fundación BBVA. pp. 221.

Pérez, F. (2008). La capitalización de la economía española y la mejora de la productividad. In Velarde Fuentes, and J. Serrano Sanz, J. Mª (dirs): *La España del siglo XXI,* volume III: (pp. 97–130). Madrid: La economía, Editorial Biblioteca Nueva.

Pérez, F., Maudos, J., Pastor, J. M., & Serrano, L. (2006). *Productividad e internacionalización. El crecimiento español ante los nuevos cambios estructurales* (pp. 289). Valencia: Fundación BBVA.

Pérez, F., & Serrano, L. (2000). Capital humano y patrón de crecimiento sectorial y territorial: España (1964–1998). *Papeles de Economía Española Capital Humano y Bienestar Económico, 6,* 20–40.

Pérez, F., & Serrano, L. (2008). Los inmigrantes y el mercado de trabajo español. Una aproximación económica. In J. García Roca, J. Lacomba (Eds.), *La inmigración en la sociedad española. Una radiografía multidisciplinar* (pp. 157–203). Spain: Edicions Bellaterrra.

Schultz, T. (1961). Investment in human capital. *American Economic Review, 51,* 1–17.

Solow, R. (1956). A contribution to the theory of economic growth. *Quarterly Journal of Economics, 70*(1), 65–94.

Solow, R. (1957). Technical change and the aggregate production function. *Review of Economics and Statistics, 39*(3), 312–320.

Stiroh, Kevin J. (2002). Information Technology and the U.S. productivity revival: What do the industry data say. *American Economic Review, 92*(5), 1559–1576.

Chapter 7
Regional Productivity Convergence and Changes in the Productive Structure

Juan R. Cuadrado-Roura and Andrés Maroto-Sánchez

7.1 Introduction: Approach and Research Hypothesis

The subject matter of economic convergence across countries and regions has played a significant role in economic literature for over two decades. Since the beginning of the 1990s, the comparison of countries about the existence or non-existence of economic convergence has been used as a possible test to choose between neoclassical and "new" endogenous growth models.[1] As it is known, the conventional neoclassical models support the idea that economic convergence would occur, sooner or later, based on the free mobility of inputs and diminishing returns to capital. This results in a higher productivity of this input in economies with a lower initial relative endowment and incites more balanced relative input prices and aggregate GDP per capita. The "new" economic growth models do not predict that a convergence process would necessarily occur, as the differences among different countries could remain stable over time and could even become increased. Underlying these theories, we find the thesis that technical progress is endogenously generated, while the role of other types of capital (human capital in particular) and of positive externalities is emphasized.

The issue of economic convergence across the regions of a country or across a group of countries involved in an integration process (such as the European Union, EU) has given rise to extensive and abundant literature in recent years.[2] However,

---

J.R. Cuadrado-Roura (✉)
Universidad de Alcalá, Departamento de Economía Aplicada, Pl. Victoria, 2, 28802 - Alcalá de Henares, Madrid, España
e-mail: jr.cuadrado@uah.es

[1] In fact, some researches aiming to reinforce the validity of some of the mentioned models used regional data as a statistical base, as this data offered sufficiently extensive series and referred to more homogeneous economies than the comparisons among countries of different continents.

[2] See the surveying article regarding the studies carried out by Eckey and Türck (2007) and their methodologies.

neither from a theoretical perspective nor as a topic of debate could we consider this to be a new topic in regional studies. During the first half of the 1960s, the evolution of interregional disparities was object of lively discussions between those supporting the thesis that the market and the free mobility of inputs would lead to a regional convergence in income per capita (from approaches based on the conventional neoclassical model[3]), and those denying this possibility as a con of the initial differences between the variety of the regions and the cumulative processes generated by the market forces themselves.[4]

From the mid-1980s onwards, the concern for interregional disparities and their evolution over time (convergence *versus* divergence) occupies an important place within regional economic literature.[5] In the case of the EU-15[6], this is due to a decrease in differences among countries and regions, leading to a consequent economic and social cohesion, which constitutes one of its principal objectives and is therefore allocated important amounts of funding. There are two reasons for this extensive literature on the Spanish case. The first is related to the European regional policy and the Community funds allocated to the country. The second is that the development of the "State of Autonomies" has intensified the need to understand the evolution of disparities among regions, designing policies aimed at reducing these disparities and their practical application and effects. Furthermore, it is worth mentioning, from a more academic viewpoint, the impetus of the analysis and debate regarding regional economic convergence on the basis of the contributions made by Barro y Sala-i-Martin[7] and all those authors discussing and debating their theses, either questioning trends towards convergence, the speed and terms of this process, or stating the existence of groups or "clubs" of regions (countries) which converge towards different stationary states.[8]

The main objective of this chapter is to provide some results and elements from an analysis of regional economic convergence in Spain taking into account the relationship between structural changes and productivity trends. A paper by

---

[3] Within this group, we can include, for example, the works by Easterlin (1960); Borts (1960); Borts and Stein (1964); and Siebert (1969), among others.

[4] The contributions made by Myrdal (1957) and Hirschman (1957), as well as others related to the development theories (dependence; unequal exchange) are included in this group. The contribution of Clark et al. (1969) should also be added, with the introduction of the concept of economic potential, which always favors the central regions.

[5] Generally speaking, from mid-1970s to mid-1980s, regional matters were abandoned in almost all countries. This was mainly due to the fact that the onset and negative effects of the international crisis made governments to focus on adjustments at a macroeconomic level (inflation, employment, external unbalances), sectoral problems linked to the crisis, the strong impact of energy costs in some industries, and the readjustment of the excess supply capacity existing in previous years.

[6] The EU has actually 27 country members. EU-15 corresponds to the countries being members until 2002.

[7] See Barro and Sala-i-Martín (1991); (1995).

[8] See, for example: Chaterji (1993); Dewhurst and Mutis-Gaitan (1995); Chaterji and Dewhurst (1996); Cheshire and Carbonaro (1995); Armstrong (1995); Quah (1993a, 1993b); Quah (1996a; 1996b); Cuadrado (2001); Cuadrado et al. (2002).

7 Regional Productivity Convergence and Changes in the Productive Structure

Cuadrado et al. (1999) provided empirical evidence regarding the apparent depletion of the convergence process among the Spanish regions. The conclusions specified that convergence in GDP per capita came to a halt in the first half of the 1980s and reasoning was given to consider that convergence in productivity (which boosted convergence in income per capita) could not remain in the future. The analysis confirmed that the main source of convergence in productivity observed between 1955 and 1995 was the convergence of regional productive structures (mainly due to the transfer of labor force from the agricultural sector to other sectors, more specifically in the case of less-developed regions), and that this source of convergence seemed to have been depleted by the end of the 1980s.

This chapter analyses the evolution of productivity and regional productive structures in Spain during the period 1955–2006, i.e. over a whole five decades. This time span allows us not only to approach the situation up to the current state, but also to obviate the problems that always seem to be present when considering short time spans when studying the interregional convergence. On the other hand, a significant reason to embark upon this analysis arose when an attempt was made to approach the evolution of the income per capita of the Spanish regions. Studying the evolution of income per capita of each region along the aforementioned five decades (1955–2006), the Spanish case shows quite an acceptable interregional economic convergence. This is due to the fact that many of the most underdeveloped regions in 1955 (Extremadura, Castile-La Mancha, Galicia or Murcia, for example) grew more rapidly than the most advanced regions in the same year (the Basque Country, Madrid, and Catalonia). However, if such a broad period is divided into two subperiods (1955–1987 and 1986–2006), the results obtained show a clear difference (see Figs. 7.1a,b).

During the first period, the behaviour pattern effectively responds to a more rapid growth of the most underdeveloped regions compared with the most advanced ones in 1955 (R^2 of 0.77). On the contrary, the process of regional convergence clearly slows down in the second period, and thus the data shows a much more disperse spectrum (R^2 of 0.33) from the end of the 1980s and the beginning of 1990s. Some developed regions (such as Madrid, Catalonia, and Navarre) have increased their income per capita to the same level as some of the lesser regions and, simultaneously, some underdeveloped regions (such as Andalusia, Galicia, and Murcia) register a relatively low growth of their income per capita. All this has slowed down the convergence process and has even opened up a stage of slight divergence in terms of income per head.

Taking the above indicated approach and the two previous figures as a departing point, the objective of this chapter is to analyze the existing relationship between the evolution of regional productive structures and the convergence or nonconvergence in productivity as a possible explanatory cause of what occurred and what is occurring in the Spanish case[9]. Therefore, the basic hypothesis is that convergence

---

[9] In the ERSA Congress held in Liverpool at the end of August, we submitted a paper Cuadrado and Maroto (2008) where the behavior of five countries of southern Europe were analyzed under this same perspective during the period between 1980 and 2006. Results reinforce the thesis, even showing some differences by countries.

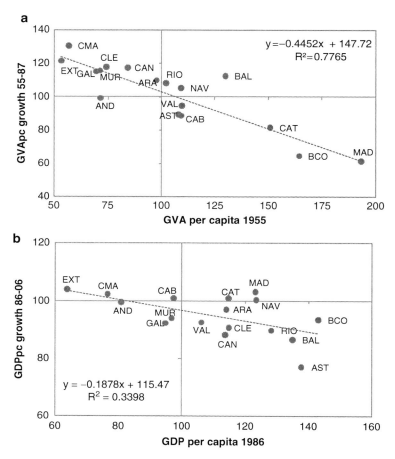

Fig. 7.1 (**a**) Relationship between initial level and growth of income per capita in the Spanish regions, 1955–1987 (100=total economy) (Source: Own elaboration from BBVA-Funcas). (**b**) Relationship between initial level and growth of income per capita in the Spanish regions, 1986–2006 (100=total economy)
Source: Own elaboration from INE

among regions is linked to the development of regional productive structures, as well as the evolution of employment per capita and labor productivity by regions.

Obviously, although the analysis carried on confirms, to a sufficient extent, the hypothesis set out, what is demonstrated cannot be identified as a complete explanation of convergence/nonconvergence among Spanish regions. As indicated in the text, the results must be taken as part of the "explanation." Quah (1992) highlighted some years ago that the regional growth (and also that of countries) is always a complex process, which is the result of various factors, and shows instability and cyclical fluctuations that must not be left aside.

The text is organised as follows. Section 2 analyses some aspects regarding the databases and methodology used for the empirical analysis. The main results obtained are shown in Sect. 3, explaining the difference between the evolution of σ-convergence in income per capita and its breakdown in productivity and employment per capita (Sect. 3.1), the estimation of σ-convergence in productivity (3.2) and, finally, the evolution of sectoral productivities and the tendency of homogenization of regional productive structures (3.3). The chapter concludes with some final remarks.

7.2 Data and Methodological Issues

The database used for the analysis comprises several time series regarding production, employment, and productivity for the 17 Spanish regions[10] and has been prepared mainly on the basis of two statistical sources. Firstly, data corresponding to the period from 1955 to 1987 were obtained from the statistical databases prepared jointly by the Fundación BBVA (BBVA Foundation) and FUNCAS (Foundation of Savings Banks). They include 2-year time series on income (in terms of production and added value at the cost of the factors), population, and employment at a regional level for four large economic sectors: primary, manufacturing, construction, and services. Due to the biennial nature of such series, we have opted to use the arithmetic average as an approach to the intermediate data. The selection of this statistical source is based on the broad historical coverage offered by it, which is an essential factor for this type of analysis.

However, the previous database does not contain data from after the mid-1990s[11], and this is the reason why we have completed the analysis with data offered by the *Instituto Nacional de Estadísti*ca or INE (Spanish National Statistics Institute) in the Spanish Regional Accountancy for the period 1987–2006. This source offers annual data in terms of GDP, population, and employment at a regional level for five economic sectors: primary, manufacturing, energy (finally included with manufacturing for coherence with the previous database), construction, and services. On the one hand, this data allow us to complete the aforementioned historical series and, on the other hand, provides official annual data regarding national income and its regional distribution throughout the Spanish regions.

Section 3 presents the main empirical results regarding regional convergence in Spain between 1955 and 2006, as well as some of its possible explanatory factors. GDP per capita has been used as an approximation of income per capita. Further on, income per capita has been broken down into two terms: employment per inhabitant and apparent labor productivity (measured using GDP per worker). Finally, changes

---

[10] In particular, the 17 Spanish autonomous regions, except for Ceuta and Melilla: Andalusia, Aragon, Asturias, the Balearics, the Canary Islands, Cantabria, Castile-La Mancha, Castile-Leon, Catalonia, the Valencian Community, Extremadura, Galicia, Madrid, Murcia, Navarre, the Basque Country, and La Rioja.

[11] FUNCAS has offered regional data referring to a new time series covering from 2000 to 2006. However, using this resulted in new problems of linkage with the previous series by BBVA-FUNCAS and, therefore, we preferred to use the regional accountancy database of the INE.

in productive structure, which would have a direct influence on the convergence or divergence of overall productivity, have been measured using productive inequality indices or industrial specialization indices.

In economic literature, the progressive reduction of regional disparities regarding income per capita over time is traditionally known as *sigma-convergence* (see Barro and Sala-i-Martín 1991; or Cuadrado et al. 1999, among others). This concept of convergence is frequently measured by examining the evolution of the standard deviation of any variable that approximates income per capita correctly. However, other dispersion indicators can be used to this end.[12] In order to analyse the evolution of regional inequality level in the Spanish regions chosen for the sample, the evolution of the following index is examined:

$$\sigma_t = \left[\frac{\sum_{i=1}^{N} (\ln Ypc_{it} - \ln Ypc_t)^2}{N} \right]^{1/2} \quad (7.1)$$

where $\ln Ypc_{it}$ is the logarithm of GDP per capita of the region i in the moment t; $\ln Ypc_t$ is the logarithm of GDP per capita of Spain in the moment t, and N corresponds to the number of regions under consideration (17 in this case). Results are shown in Sect. 3.1.

Among the factors that could explain convergence or divergence previously obtained, some authors (Cuadrado et al. 1999, Maroto and Cuadrado 2008) have emphasized the importance of the evolution of employment and its productivity at a regional level. To this effect, GDP per capita is broken down in employment per capita and apparent labor productivity. Following this decomposition, and using logarithms, the following expression has been obtained:

$$\ln Ypc_{it} = \ln Lpc_{it} + \ln \Pi_{it} \quad (7.2)$$

where Lpc_{it} is the number of workers per capita in the region i in the moment t, and Π_{it} is the GDP per worker in the same region and moment.

Finally, the value of overall productivity depends, on the one hand, on the productivity within each economic sector and, on the other hand, on the productive structure or how the labor factor is allocated in those productive sectors.[13] The

---

[12] Other dispersion measures used in literature on regional convergence are, for example, the variation coefficient or the Williamson index. Moreover, other interesting inequality indices to apply could be those developed by Gini, Atkinson or Theil Eckey and Türck (2007). All these indicators register a similar evolution over time, as can be seen, for the Spanish case, in the works carried out by Cuadrado (1988); Suárez and Cuadrado (1993); Esteban (1994); Villaverde (1996); Ezcurra (2001), among others.

[13] See, among others, Dollar and Wolff (1988); van Ark (1995); Peneder (2003); Fagerberg (2000); Timmer and Szirmai (2000); Cuadrado and Maroto (2008); and Maroto and Cuadrado (2006); Maroto and Cuadrado; (2007).

7 Regional Productivity Convergence and Changes in the Productive Structure

results of this breakdown become the core of Sect. 3.2 of the present analysis. In order to examine the possible role played by regional convergence in terms of productive or sectoral structure in the convergence of overall productivity, an inequality index is introduced to the productive structure, which is defined using the following expression:

$$ID = \frac{\sum_{i=1}^{N}\left[(\Pi_{Ait} - \Pi_{At})^2 + (\Pi_{Iit} - \Pi_{It})^2 + (\Pi_{Cit} - \Pi_{Ct})^2 + (\Pi_{Sit} - \Pi_{St})^2\right]}{N}$$

(7.3)

where Π_{Ait}, Π_{Iit}, Π_{Cit}, and Π_{Sit} are, respectively, the weights of agriculture, manufacturing, construction, and services sector in terms of employment in the region i and in the moment t; while Π_{At}, Π_{It}, Π_{Ct}, and Π_{St} correspond to the respective percentages for the whole country. The value of the previous index would be zero if productive structure was the same in the $N=17$ Spanish regions. Furthermore, this indicator can be broken down in the sum of inequality indices regarding agriculture, manufacturing, construction, and services.

7.3 Main Results

The empirical results of the analysis carried out are presented and discussed in this section, which is divided into three subsections. The first one examines the evolution of regional σ-convergence in terms of income per capita, as well as its decomposition into employment per capita and productivity (according to the previous section). In Subsect. 3.2, convergence or nonconvergence regarding overall productivity is analysed in depth. Finally, both factors of the evolution of aggregate productivity:sector productivities and changes in the productive structure are examined in Subsect. 3.3.

7.3.1 Regional Convergence in Terms of Income and Its Decomposition into Productivity and Employment Per Capita

The result of the estimation of σ-convergence in terms of regional income per capita for the period between 1955 and 2006 is the trend line shown in Fig. 7.2, where the values of σ-convergence of labor productivity and employment per capita referring to the Spanish regions as a whole have also been included.

The evolution of regional differences of income per capita in Spain allows us to differentiate two broad periods: from 1955 to 1978/1979 and from 1978/1979 onwards. During the first one, a rapid process of convergence occurred where the

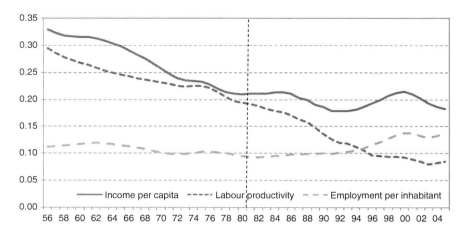

Fig. 7.2 Sigma-convergence at a regional level in Spain. Income per capita, productivity and employment per capita, 1955–2006
Source: Own elaboration from INE and BBVA-Funcas

differences in income per capita by autonomous regions were significantly reduced. Several studies[14] ascribe this process to the migratory flows registered in Spain during such period, which resulted of large population contingents moving from the less-developed regions to the most dynamic in the country and migration flows to other European countries. This modified significantly the denominator of income per capita of many regions.[15] However, as shown in Fig. 7.2, a factor that undoubtedly contributed to reducing regional disparities in terms of income per capita was also the evolution of the overall productivity by regions, which registers a notable process of convergence between 1955 and 1978/1979, almost in parallel with that observed regarding income per capita.

This trend, however, ceased from 1979/1980. The values of σ-convergence of regional levels of income per capita draw a fluctuating path from that date on, linking the stages of stagnation, convergence, and divergence. Thus, between 1979 and 1986/1987, convergence sharply comes to a halt, which coincides with the impact of the international economic crisis in the Spanish economy; with very low or even negative growth rates in the whole country and almost all the autonomous communities. After another brief period of convergence, regional levels of income per capita diverge (between 1991 and 2000), and converge again slightly from 2000 to 2006.

The explanation of these movements undoubtedly includes various factors. However, the decomposition of income per capita in productivity and employment per head offers some indication of what is underlying the movements registered during the period 1979–2006. As observed in Fig. 7.2, convergence of labor

---

[14] See for example: Alcaide (1988); Cuadrado-Roura (1988); Mas et al. (1995); Cuadrado- Roura and García Greciano (1995) and Cuadrado et al. (1998).

[15] Some estimations ascribe around 50% of the reduction of interregional differences regarding income per capita to this factor.

productivity by regions has followed an advancing path, although in the last years (1996–2006) this has virtually come to a standstill as the values are so reduced and therefore it is difficult to imagine new advances taking place – at least at an aggregate level – in terms of regional convergence in productivity. In parallel with the aforementioned, an opposite movement is registered in employment per capita, which had already been registering a slight trend towards regional divergence since the beginning of the 1980s. This trend then becomes more intense and the values of its σ-convergence increase significantly from the year 1991, and subsequently, it stabilizes in the last years of the decade, although at a comparatively higher level. This behavior of employment per capita has influenced the evolution of regional convergence regarding income per head.

The changes concerning the estimations of regional convergence of income and employment per capita in the last years (2000–2006) could be due to different reasons, and a future analysis will be significant when data referring to a broader time span is available. However, we believe that such changes are mostly due to the different variations experienced by population and employment in the diverse autonomous regions in the aforementioned period, which are, in turn, due to the immigration flows in Spain which have a different impact at a regional level.

Table 7.1 provides comparative data regarding the growth of the population and employment by autonomous regions in the period 2000–2006, and takes as a reference the growth of these variables between 1955 and 2000. The table shows the following: while some regions (in general, the richest ones) have registered much higher population growth rates than the Spanish average (the Balearics, the Canary Islands, Murcia, Madrid, and the Valencian Com., followed by La Rioja and Catalonia), others, which are mostly the least-developed regions, have registered increases much below the Spanish average (Aragon, Cantabria, the Basque Country, Extremadura, Galicia, Castile-Leon, and Asturias). This movement has promoted the convergence process of income per capita over the last years, where the contribution of productivity by regions has been scarce[16] and employment per head also shows clear discrepancies in its growth rates by autonomous regions. This, undoubtedly, demonstrates what is shown in Fig. 7.2 regarding the last years of the period under analysis.

7.3.2 Regional Convergence in Overall Labor Productivity

According to the previous section, the process of regional convergence in terms of income per capita occurred in Spain at the end of the 1980s had come to a halt, and even declined in some periods over the last 25 years. Among other explanatory

---

[16]The concentration in these years of new jobs in generally low-productive activities, such as construction and some services, would also explain why the aggregate labor productivity has shown very low and even negative increases in some years, which is also shown at a regional level. This will be analyzed in more depth in the following section.

Table 7.1 Growth of population and employment by regions in Spain (annual average rates, in %)

	Population			Employment	
	1955–2000	2000–2006		1955–2000	2000–2006
Regions with above-average growth rates			Regions with above-average growth rates		
Balearics	1.46	2.97	Murcia	1.14	4.38
Canary Islands	1.43	2.46	Balearics	2.77	4.21
Murcia	0.90	2.42	Madrid	2.47	4.15
Valencian Com.	1.02	2.33			
Madrid	1.62	2.13			
Regions with growth rates similar to the average			Regions with growth rates similar to the average		
La Rioja	0.30	1.84	Cantabria	0.68	3.97
Catalonia	1.06	1.73	Canary Islands	2.02	3.81
Castile-La Mancha	−0.20	1.45	Valencian Com.	1.22	3.73
Navarre	0.68	1.19	Catalonia	1.77	3.61
			Navarre	1.30	3.07
			Castile-La Mancha	0.09	3.00
			Basque Country	1.30	2.98
			La Rioja	0.59	2.95
Regions with below-average growth rates			Regions with below-average growth rates		
Aragon	0.15	0.81	Asturias	−0.12	2.68
Cantabria	0.45	0.78	Extremadura	−0.55	2.44
Basque Country	0.93	0.33	Galicia	−0.32	2.44
Extremadura	−0.49	0.19	Castile-Leon	−0.30	2.42
Galicia	0.00	0.18	Andalusia	0.78	1.39
Castile-Leon	−0.34	0.06	Aragon	0.46	0.59
Asturias	0.16	−0.10			
SPAIN	0.63	1.41	SPAIN	1.04	3.50

The regions registering growth rates similar to the average will be those within the range (Growth of Spain ±standard deviation); and those with higher or lower growth rates will be the regions above or below that range

Source: Own elaboration from INE and BBVA-Funcas

factors is the role played by employment per capita. Such a variable has had a clear divergent effect on regional convergence in Spain in this latter period, which slowed down the convergent process observed up until the final years of the 1980s decade, despite the role of convergence in terms of productivity in the years analyzed (see Fig. 7.2).

To contribute to the aforementioned debate on regional convergence in Spain, it is necessary to provide empirical evidence regarding sectoral data and some alternative explanations (complementary to those introduced in the previous section) regarding the mechanisms generating regional convergence and divergent processes in Spain. More specifically, this section focuses on the evolution of regional convergence in terms of overall productivity and changes in the productive structure of Spanish regions between 1955 and 2006.

Figure 7.3 shows that convergence in labor productivity of the Spanish exists along the whole period of 1955–2006.Those regions with the above-average initial productivity levels, such as Madrid, the Basque Country, the Balearics, Catalonia, and Asturias, registered lower growth rates from then up to date. On the contrary,

7 Regional Productivity Convergence and Changes in the Productive Structure 159

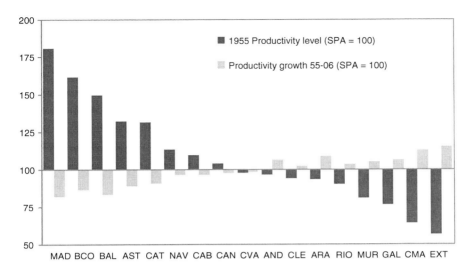

Fig. 7.3 Regional convergence regarding productivity per worker in Spain, 1955–2006
Source: Own elaboration from the INE and BBVA-Funcas

the average annual productivity growth is clearly above the Spanish average growth in regions such as Extremadura, Castile-La Mancha, Galicia, or Murcia, which started with lower initial levels in the mid-1950s. However, as observed in Fig. 7.2, although such convergence was significant in the mid-1990s, afterwards this convergence clearly slowed down.[17]

This fact, principally, demonstrates a phenomenon broadly examined in economic literature: the decline observed in European countries regarding productivity compared to other countries, mainly the United States, since the mid-1990s.[18] Data demonstrates the poor evolution of the average productivity of European countries from 1995 to date.[19] A significant point for the subject under analysis in this chapter is that Spanish productivity performance has been even poorer than that of other European countries.[20] Such a negative evolution of overall productivity in Spain

---

[17] The coefficient of typical deviation in the year 1955 in terms of regional productivity in Spain was 0.306. In 1995, this decreased by 0.098 (an annual average fall of 0.0052 from the mid-1950s until the mid-1990s), while in 2006 it decreased by 0.089 (an annual average fall of just 0.0008 since 1995).

[18] See European Commission (2004); Van Ark (2006); Timmer et al. (2007); O'Mahony and van Ark (2003); OCDE (2005); Maroto and Rubalcaba (2008) or Rubalcaba and Maroto (2007), among others.

[19] Despite the recovery observed in recent years, while productivity by employed person in the European Union (EU-15) increased at an annual average rate of 1.04% between 1995 and 2006, productivity in the United States during such period registered an increase of the annual average rate of 1.95% (European Commission 2007a).

[20] See European Commission (2007b and c), Maroto and Cuadrado (2006), 2008); Pérez (2006); Segura (2006); among others.

has been reflected in most of the Spanish regions, which could have exerted a negative impact on convergence regarding productivity.

On the other hand, the patterns observed regarding productivity differ significantly from one region to another. In 2006, the highest levels of productivity per worker were registered in Aragon (18.4 points above the Spanish average), Andalusia (15.1), the Basque Country (12.5), and Madrid (10.3). In regions such as Navarre, Catalonia, Cantabria, Castile-Leon, La Rioja, Asturias, and the Canary Islands, productivity is close to the national average, while in the others, this level is clearly below such average (5.7 points in the Balearics; 6.5 in the Valencian Community; 7.2 in Murcia; 9.4 in Galicia; 9.6 in Castile-La Mancha; and 14.6 in Extremadura). Nevertheless, a convergence process in terms of labor productivity among the Spanish regions has obviously occurred, although this process seems to have slowed down since the mid-1990s.

Following on from this, the evolution of productivity in Spain predominantly reflects the performance of the employment variable (Maroto and Cuadrado 2006). For this reason, and regardless of other explanatory factors discussed in the present chapter, the evolution of productivity in the Spanish economy is directly linked to that of employment. Generally speaking, the reduction of regional disparities regarding occupation also boosts the processes of convergence in productivity. Figure 7.4 shows this relationship between productivity and employment for the Spanish regions, and also demonstrates that those regions whose productivity increased above the country average (Castile-La Mancha, Galicia, Andalusia, and La Rioja) experienced increases in employment appreciably below the average aggregate growth. Some regions have even shown a decline in employment (for example, Extremadura and Castile-Leon). On the contrary, the regions registering

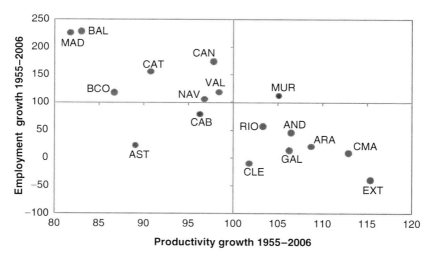

Fig. 7.4 Relationship between productivity and employment among the Spanish regions (Spanish average growth = 100)
Source: Own elaboration from the INE and BBVA-Funcas

a lower growth in productivity between 1955 and 2006 (Madrid, the Balearics, the Basque Country, Catalonia, the Canary Islands, Navarre, and the Valencian Community) were those where the absorption of employment was considerably higher than the Spanish average in those years. Just three regions were not affected by this general trend: while Murcia achieved relatively high increases in productivity and employment, Cantabria, and, especially, Asturias, did not show an increase in productivity despite the low levels of employment created in the period analyzed.

In this section, we have thoroughly examined the regional convergence of labor productivity in Spain between 1955 and 2006. Some authors state that the convergence processes in terms of productivity could be the consequence of technological or organizational imitation in less-developed regions implying lower costs than carrying out innovation or invention processes. However, there are other mechanisms that could generate processes of regional convergence in productivity. As we will see in the next section, it is possible to explain such convergence using two factors: convergence of sector productivities and changes in the productive structure.

7.3.3 Convergence in Intrasectoral Productivity and Productive Structure

As demonstrated in this work, productivity per worker has undergone a clear and sustained process of regional convergence in Spain from 1955 to the mid-1990s. However, this process seems to have slowed down from that latter date onwards. The value of aggregate productivity of an economy depends, in turn, on two factors: on the one hand, the internal productivities of each economic sector comprising such economy and, on the other hand, how economic resources are distributed among these sectors. If the productivity is higher in industry or services than in agriculture, for example, a transfer of resources from the primary sector to other sectors could explain a convergence in aggregate productivity, which would not be necessarily so at an individual level in productive sectors. For this reason, this section provides a detailed analysis of regional disparities regarding these two factors. The main conclusion obtained is that the role played by each of these two economic spheres varied considerably during the period under consideration. As we will see further on, both spheres exchange their possible convergent effects during the period covering up until the end of the 1980s and since then to date.

Figure 7.5 shows the results of σ-convergence of productivity considering the four large economic sectors. As already mentioned, appreciable differences are observed within two periods of time. Until the final years of the 1980s decade, interregional differences in terms of productivities remained stable, although with only minor differences among the sectors. In the agricultural sector, a slight divergent tendency is observed. The reasons explaining these are based on its strong random behavior, which is linked to its dependence on weather conditions, which characterizes these types of activities creating differences in regional

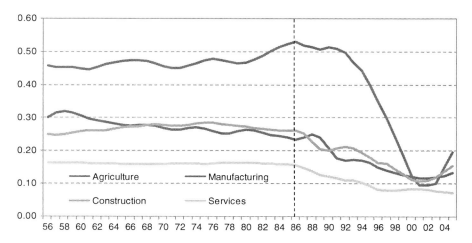

Fig. 7.5 Sigma-convergence at a regional level in Spain Productivity by large sectors, 1955–2006 (three-year mobile averages)
Source: Own elaboration from the INE and BBVA-Funcas

productivity. The opposite process is observed in the manufacturing sector, where Fig. 7.5 illustrates a slight process of σ-convergence between 1955 and the end of the 1990s. Finally, the other two sectors (construction and services) show no convergence or divergence processes along that same period, with the interregional productivity differences remaining stable.

Therefore, despite the convergence process regarding overall productivity registered between 1955 and the end of the 1980s in Spain, this process was not based on the convergence in within sector productivities, whose differences remained virtually stable in that mentioned period. On the contrary, and as we will examine in more depth further on, the most important factor in the convergence of aggregate productivity involved the changes in productive structure Cuadrado et al. (1999). However, from this time, a convergence process in intrasectoral productivities is observed (particularly in the primary sector). This reduction in interregional differences at a sectoral level could be mainly due to the poor performance of Spanish productivity, as previously mentioned. Additionally, various notable factors played an essential role in this process. Firstly, Spain was joining the EU and the effects of cohesion policies regarding productivity in the less-developed regions. On the other hand, the significant processes of population and employment absorption in certain regions, which originated from migratory flows in recent years, could also explain such behavior.[21] And the last factor affecting this process is the apparent weakening role of structural change since the end of the 1990s (see Fig. 7.6) regarding productive convergence.

---

[21] Due, on the one hand, to the direct influence of the employment variable on productivity (defined as GDP per worker) in Spain and, on the other hand, to the changes registered in statistical sources from the year 2000, which resulted in the emergence of population and employment.

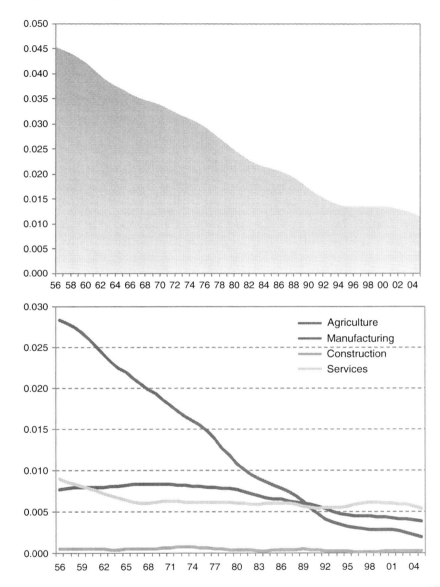

Fig. 7.6 Index of productive inequality at a regional level in Spain, 1955–2006 (three-year mobile averages)
Source: Own elaboration from BBVA-Funcas

Another explanatory factor of the evolution of aggregate productivity is the changes carried out regarding the allocation of resources among the different economic sectors or convergence in terms of productive structure. Until the end of the 1980s, a clear tendency towards regional convergence was seen in Spain regarding overall productivity, despite the fact that such convergence was not observed intrasectorally. Thus, the issue would be how to combine the existence of such aggregate convergence and lack of within sector productivity convergence. Regardless of the existence of other possible explanatory factors, the previous phenomenon could be caused by on the one hand, variations in the weight of each sector and its interrelationship with the overall productivity levels[22], and secondly, if the shift of employment from the primary sector to more productive sectors occurs to a larger extent in the less-developed regions, processes of σ-convergence could arise regarding aggregate productivity, even if these do not exist in the sectoral productivities.

The aforementioned approach suggests that the convergence in productive structures across the Spanish regions could have been an important source of productivity convergence – at least, until the end of the 1980s, when such capacity seems to have ceased. In order to analyze this hypothesis, we use the productive inequality index[23] described in the second section. Figure 7.6 shows the results of such indicator. The left-hand Fig. 7 shows that, in terms of employment, the productive structure of the Spanish regions becomes progressively more homogeneous until the end of the 1980s. The right-hand figure shows, however, that the reason for this convergence is mainly based on the notable loss of weight of the primary sector in the poorest regions. In line with what has been already stated, this fact helps us to explain σ-convergence in terms of total productivity and, therefore, of income per capita from the mid-1950s to the end of the 1980s.

However, after the 1990s, convergence in productive structure considerably slowed down, as the minor interregional differences in manufacturing and services, which were low from the 1950s, the virtually nonexistent differences in the construction sector and the reduction in the primary sector registered as from this date. The result is that the differences in recent years have remained quite low (around 0.005),

---

[22] For example, if the services sector has a higher weight in rich regions, which are also characterized by a higher productivity, and if the growth of productivity in such a sector is lower than in other sectors, a similar growth of sectoral productivities in the different regions would be compatible with a higher growth of total productivity in the less-developed regions. This would result in a convergence process in aggregate productivity (Cuadrado et al. 1999; Cuadrado and Maroto 2006; Maroto 2009)

[23] A similar analysis has been carried out on the basis of the specialization index of each Spanish region, defined with the following expression:

$$IE_{ij} = \frac{E_{ij}/\sum_i E_{ij}}{\sum_j E_{ij}/\sum_i \sum_j E_{ij}} = \frac{E_{ij}/\sum_j E_{ij}}{\sum_i E_{ij}/\sum_i \sum_j E_{ij}}$$

where Eij is employment of sector i (with $i=1,\ldots,4$) in the region j (with $j=1,\ldots,17$).

The results obtained using this specialisation index corroborate the conclusions reached in the case of sigma-convergence in productive structure. A convergence process is observed in regional productive specialisation, as the less-specialised regions in 1955 were those relatively increasing their specialisation to the largest extent between that year and 2006 (see Annex 1) and therefore the margin of possible future positive effects seems to be scarcely probable.

7.4 Final Remarks

The aim of this chapter has been to explore the evolution of regional economic convergence throughout a five-decade period (1955–2006). The research hypothesis was that the evolution of productivity, employment per capita, and sectoral productive structures of Spanish regions provides an explanation of the changes undergone, although other influencing factors could exist.

The analysis carried out provides highly acceptable empirical evidence regarding the aforementioned hypothesis. Firstly, σ-convergence in terms of income per capita of Spanish autonomous communities leads us to differentiate between two subperiods. In the first of these subperiods (from 1955 to 1978–1979), regional disparities of income per capita registered a rapid convergence, where the migratory flows occurring in Spain over this period had an unquestionable influence. However, convergence in regional productivity per worker also contributed significantly, which relates to the remarkable approach registered in the sectoral composition of the productive bases of Spanish regions. This result coincides with that obtained some years ago by Cuadrado et al. (1999).

The second subperiod (1979–2006) shows quite a different evolution of σ-convergence. During the first years, convergence ceased completely and then further consecutive periods of slight convergence, divergence and, again, slight convergence, were registered. This study demonstrates some of the facts explaining these changes. In the first place, regional convergence in productivity remained until the mid-1990s although towards the end at a very low level and almost coming to a standstill until the year 2006. Secondly, a process of divergence in employment per capita was registered, which undoubtedly influenced the income-related convergence and even the divergence variations. And finally, data regarding population and employment in the period 2000–2006 also played a significant role in the recent evolution of regional disparities due to the increases registered by both variables being distributed very unevenly in the regions, as illustrated in Table 7.1.

The fact that the convergence of productivity by regions has come to a halt in recent years is clearly related to the disappearance of a factor boosting such convergence for many years: the approaching process of regional productive structures. It is obvious that, in this way, no new boosts to regional convergence are registered, both regarding overall productivity and income per capita. On the contrary, although regional divergence of employment per capita was not very remarkable, it contributed to the slowing down of convergence in income per capita and even promoted a divergence process between 1993 and 2000.

ANNEX: Regional Convergence in Spain: Specialisation Index

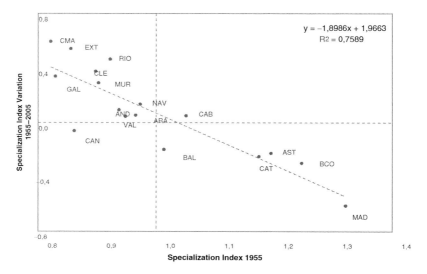

Fig. 7.A1 Regional convergence in the global specialisation index in Spain, 1955–2005

7 Regional Productivity Convergence and Changes in the Productive Structure

Table 7.A1 Indices of productive specialisation by Spanish regions

	Primary sector			Manufacturing and energy			Construction			Services		
	1955	2005	CREC	1955	2005	CREC	1955	2005	CREC	1955	2005	CREC
Andalusia	1.21	1.18	−0.03	0.64	0.72	0.08	1.01	1.20	0.19	0.89	1.02	0.13
Aragon	1.11	0.80	−0.31	0.89	1.42	0.53	0.96	0.92	−0.03	0.90	0.93	0.02
Asturias	0.88	0.78	−0.10	1.46	1.05	−0.41	1.68	1.04	−0.65	0.75	1.00	0.24
Balearics	0.87	0.39	−0.48	1.02	0.44	−0.58	0.96	1.28	0.32	1.20	1.13	−0.07
Canary Islands	1.28	0.44	−0.85	0.36	0.38	0.02	0.81	1.22	0.41	0.99	1.15	0.17
Cantabria	0.90	1.28	0.38	1.36	1.01	−0.36	1.01	1.16	0.15	0.94	0.95	0.01
Castile-La Mancha	1.45	2.62	1.17	0.56	1.12	0.56	0.63	1.09	0.46	0.65	0.83	0.18
Castile-Leon	1.28	2.13	0.85	0.69	1.03	0.34	0.84	1.05	0.21	0.78	0.90	0.11
Catalonia	0.44	0.52	0.08	2.02	1.35	−0.67	0.98	0.82	−0.16	1.26	0.98	−0.27
Valencian Com.	1.02	0.67	−0.35	1.14	1.24	0.10	0.68	1.10	0.41	0.95	0.95	0.00
Extremadura	1.51	2.97	1.46	0.33	0.54	0.21	0.97	1.14	0.18	0.62	0.94	0.31
Galicia	1.45	1.67	0.22	0.48	1.09	0.61	0.71	0.97	0.26	0.67	0.93	0.26
Madrid	0.17	0.09	−0.08	1.02	0.68	−0.35	2.03	0.89	−1.14	2.06	1.17	−0.89
Murcia	1.15	1.66	0.51	0.90	1.01	0.12	0.67	1.19	0.52	0.89	0.91	0.02
Navarre	1.09	1.00	−0.10	0.95	1.57	0.63	0.96	1.00	0.04	0.89	0.86	−0.03
Basque country	0.39	0.51	0.12	2.06	1.57	−0.49	1.30	0.76	−0.53	1.24	0.94	−0.30
La Rioja	1.16	2.22	1.06	1.01	1.54	0.53	0.72	1.01	0.29	0.80	0.77	−0.03
Average	1.02	1.23	0.21	0.99	1.05	0.05	1.00	1.05	0.05	0.97	0.96	−0.01
Typical deviation	0.38	0.85	0.63	0.51	0.39	0.45	0.37	0.15	0.45	0.34	0.11	0.28
Upper limit	1.40	2.08	0.83	1.50	1.43	0.50	1.37	1.19	0.50	1.31	1.07	0.27
Lower limit	0.64	0.38	−0.42	0.49	0.66	−0.40	0.62	0.90	−0.39	0.63	0.85	−0.29

Those indices below the lower limit (average minus standard dev.) are marked in *red*, and those above the upper limit appear in *blue* (average plus standard deviation). Shaded in *blue* are those growths below the lower limit growth and, shaded in *yellow*, those above the upper limit growth

Source: Own elaboration

References

Alcaide, J. (1988). Las cuatro Españas económicas y la solidaridad regional. *Papeles de Economía Española, 34*, 62–81.

Armstrong, H. W. (1995). Convergence among regions of the European Union, 1950–1990. *Papers in Regional Science, 74*, 143–152.

Barro, R., & Sala-i-Martín, X. (1991). Convergence across states and regions. *Brooking Papers on Economic Activity, 1*, 107–182.

Barro, R., & Sala-i-Martín, X. (1995) Economic growth. McGraw Hill. New York.

Borts, G. H. (1960). The equalisation of returns and regional economic growth. *American Economic Review, 50*, 319–347.

Borts, G. H., & Stein, J. L. (1964). *Economic growth in the free market*. Nueva York: Columbia University Press.

Comisión Europea (2007b). Raising productivity growth: key messages from the European competitiveness report 2007. Communication from the Commission, COM(2007)666. Bruselas: Comisión Europea.

Chaterji, M. (1993). Convergence clubs and endogenous growth. *Oxford Review of Economics, 8*, 57–69.

Chaterji, M., & Dewhurst, J. H. (1996). Convergence clubs and relative economic performance in Great Britain 1977–1991. *Regional Studies, 30*(1), 31–40.

Cheshire, P., & Carbonaro, G. (1995). Convergence-divergence in regional growth rates: An empty black box? In H.W. Armstrong, R.W. Vickerman (eds.), Convergence and divergence among European regions (pp. 89–111). London: Pion.

Clark, C., Bradley, J., & Wilson, G. (1969). Industrial location and economic potential in Western Europe. *Regional Studies, 3*, 18–76.

Cuadrado, J. R. (1988). Tendencias económico-regionales antes y después de la crisis en España. *Papeles de Economía Española, 34*, 17–60.

Cuadrado, J. R. (2001). Regional convergence in the EU. From hypothesis to the actual trends. *Annals of Regional Science, 35*, 333–356.

Cuadrado-Roura, J,R., & García, G.B. (1995). Las diferencias interregionales en España. Evolución y perspectivas. In: Martin P (ed), La economía española en un escenario abierto. Edit. Visor y F. Argentaria, pp. 151–196

Cuadrado, J. R., García, B., & Raymond, J. L. (1999). Regional convergence in productivity and productive structure: the Spanish case. *International Regional Science Review, 22*(1), 35–53.

Cuadrado, J.R., Mancha, T., & Garrido, R. (2002). Regional dynamics in the European Union: winners and losers. In J.R. Cuadrado-Roura, M. Parellada. Regional convergence in the European Union (pp. 23–52). Springer: Berlin.

Cuadrado JR, Maroto A (2008) Regional convergence in productivity and productive structure. Presentado en el 48th Congress of ERSA, Liverpool, August, polic.

Dewhurst, J., & Mutis-Gaitan, H. (1995). Varying speeds of regional GDP per capita convergence in the European Union, 1981-91. In H.W. Armstrong, R.W. Vickerman (eds.), Convergence and divergence among European regions (pp. 22–39). London: Pion.

Dollar, D., & Wolff, E. N. (1988). Convergence of industry labour productivity among advanced economies, 1963–1982. *The Review of Economics and Statistics, 70*(4)), 549–558.

Easterlin, R. A. (1960). Interregional differences in per capita income, populations and total income, 1840–1950. *Trends in the American Economy in the Nineteenth Century. A Report of the NBER*. NY: Princeton University Press.

Eckey, H.-F., & Türck, M. (2007). Convergence of EU regions. A literature report. *Investigaciones Regionales, 10*, 5–32.

Esteban, J.M. (1994). La desigualdad interregional en Europa y en España: descripción y análisis. In J.M. Esteban, J. Vives (dir.), Crecimiento y convergencia regional en España y en Europa, (vol. II, pp. 13–84). Barcelona: Instituto de Análisis Económico.

Ezcurra, R. (2001). Convergencia y cambio estructural en la Unión Europea, *Documento de Trabajo*, 111. Departamento de Economía, Universidad Pública de Navarra

Fagerberg, J. (2000). Technological progress, structural change and productivity growth: A comparative study. *Structural Change and Economic Dynamics, 11*, 393–411.

Hirschman, A. O. (1958). *The Strategy of Economic Development*. New Haven: Yale University Press.

Maroto, A. (2009). *La productividad en los servicios en España, Colección Economía y Empresa*. Madrid: Marcial Pons.

Maroto, A., & Cuadrado, J. R. (2006). *La productividad en la economía española, colección estudios*. Madrid: Instituto de Estudios Económicos.

Maroto, A., & Cuadrado, J. R. (2007). El crecimiento de los servicios: Obstáculo o impulsor del crecimiento de la productividad? Un análisis comparado. *Series Working Papers* 04–07. Alcalá: Instituto de Análisis Económico y Social.

Maroto, A., & Cuadrado, J. R. (2008). Evolución de la productividad en España. Un análisis sectorial, 1980–2006. *Economía Industrial, 367*, 15–34.

Maroto, A., & Rubalcaba, L. (2008). Services productivity revisited. *International Services Industries Journal, 28*(3), 337–353.

Mas, M., Maudos, J., Pérez, F., Uriel, E. (1995). Growth and convergence in the Spanish provinces. In H. Armstrong, R. W. Vickerman (Eds.), *Convergence and divergence among European regions*. London: Pion.

Myrdal, G. (1957). *Economic Theory and underdeveloped regions*. Londres: Duckworth.

OCDE (2005). *Growth in services. Fostering employment, productivity and innovation*. París: OCDE.

O'Mahony, M., & van Ark, B. (2003). *EU productivity and competitiveness: An industry perspective. Can Europe resume the catching-up process?*. Bruselas: Comisión Europea.

Peneder, M. (2003). Industrial structure and aggregate growth. *Structural Change and Cyclical Dynamics, 14*, 427–448.

Pérez, F. et al. (2006). *Productividad e internacionalización: el crecimiento español ante los nuevos cambios estructurales*. Madrid: Fund. BBVA.

Quah, D. (1992). *Empirical Cross-Section Dynamics in Economic Growth. FMG Discussion Papers, dp 154*. London: London School of Economics and Political Science.

Quah, D. (1993a). Empirical cross-section dynamics in economic growth. *European Economic Review, 37*, 426–434.

Quah, D. (1993b). Galton's fallacy and the test of the convergence hypothesis. *Scandinavian Journal of Economics, 95*(4), 427–443.

Quah, D. (1996a). Regional convergence clusters across Europe. *European Economic Review, 40*, 951–958.

Quah, D. (1996b). Empirics for economic growth and convergence. *European Economic Review, 40*, 1353–1375.

Rubalcaba, L., & Maroto, A. (2007). Productivity in European services. In L. Rubalcaba (Eds.), *Services in European economy: Challenges and policy implications* (pp. 81–99). Londres: Edward Elgar.

Segura, J. et al. (2006). *La productividad en la economía española*. Madrid: Fund. Areces.

Suárez, L., & Cuadrado, J. R. (1993). Thirty years of Spanish regional change: Interregional dynamics and sectoral transformation. *International Regional Science Review, 15*, 121–156.

Timmer, M., O'Mahony, M., & van Ark, B. (2007). EUKLEMS growth and productivity accounts: An overview. *International Productivity Monitor, 14*, 71–85.

Timmer, M., & Szirmai, A. (2000). Productivity growth in Asian manufacturing: The structural bonus hypothesis examined. *Structural Change and Cyclical Dynamics, 11*, 371–392.

Van Ark, B. (1995). Sectoral growth and structural change in post-war Europe. Research memorandum GD-23. Groningen Growth and Development Centre, Groningen.

Van Ark, B. (2006). Productivity in the European Union: A comparative industry approach update on the EUKLEMS project. Presentado en el *OECD workshop on productivity analysis and measurement*, Berna, Octubre, 16–18.

Villaverde, J. (1996). Desigualdades provinciales en España, 1955–1991. *Revista de Estudios Regionales, 45*, 89–108.

Chapter 8
Infrastructure Investment, Growth, and Regional Convergence in Spain

Angel de la Fuente*

8.1 Introduction

This chapter presents estimates of the contribution of infrastructure investment to the growth of output and employment in Spain and its regions and analyzes the impact of this factor on the process of regional convergence. These estimates are obtained using a simple supply-side model estimated with a panel of Spanish regional data. The model has two key ingredients. The first one is an aggregate production function that relates regional output to the level of employment and the stocks of productive factors (infrastructure, other non-residential physical capital and the average level of schooling of the adult population). The second one is an employment equation that describes the evolution of this variable as a function of observed changes in factor stocks and in wage levels, allowing for the inertia that arises from the existence of adjustment costs.

The remainder of the chapter is divided into five sections. Section 2 briefly describes the evolution of aggregate investment in productive infrastructure and its distribution by region. Section 3 sketches an econometric model of growth that is used in Sects. 4 and 5 to quantify the impact of infrastructure investment on regional and national growth and its contribution to convergence in income per capita. Section 6 concludes this chapter.

A. de la Fuente
Instituto de Análisis Económico, CSIC. Universidad Autónoma de Barcelona, 08193, Bellaterra – Barcelona, Spain
e-mail: Angel.Delafuente@uab.es

*This paper was originally published in Spanish (de la Fuente, 2008a) and it is included here with permission from *Papeles de Economía Española*. It is part of a project cofinanced by the ERDF and Fundación Caixa Galicia. Financial support from the Spanish Ministry of Science under grant n. ECO2008-04837/ECON is also gratefully acknowledged.

8.2 Infrastructure Investment in Spain

This section analyzes the evolution of infrastructure investment in Spain and its regions between 1964 and 2004. The data I have used are taken from the last available version of the database on investment flows and regional capital stocks that has been constructed by the Instituto Valenciano de Investigaciones Económicas (IVIE, Mas et al., 2007). This source provides series of infrastructure investment (transport networks, water works, and urban structures financed by the different Spanish administrations, some public enterprises, and private toll road operators) valued at current and constant prices (of the year 2000). Accumulating these investment flows, the IVIE constructs different capital aggregates. The one I will use is the so-called *net capital stock*, which is closest to the data used to estimate the econometric model that underlies the impact estimates. Data on regional output and population are taken from de la Fuente (2008b) and are constructed (essentially) by linking the historical series on GVA, employment and population constructed by Fundación BBVA (several years) with those available in the Regional Accounts of the National Statistical Institute (Contabilidad Regional de España, base 2000) from 1995 onward.

Figures 8.1 and 8.2 show the time path of aggregate investment in infrastructures between 1964 and 2004. On average over the entire period, infrastructure investment absorbed 2.35% of aggregate Spanish output (measured by gross value added, GVA) and 12.7% of total non-residential investment. The investment rate, measured as a fraction of aggregate GVA, displays a downward trend until 1979, showing a sharp decline during the first years of the transition from Franco's regime to democracy. After this year, the trend becomes positive although still subject to sharp fluctuations (see Fig. 8.1). A similar, although less marked, pattern is also found in the time path of the share of infrastructures in total nonresidential investment (Fig. 8.2).

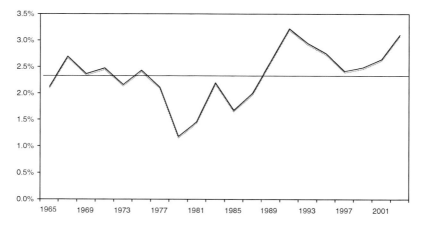

Fig. 8.1 Infrastructure investment in Spain as a percentage of aggregate gross value added

8 Infrastructure Investment, Growth, and Regional Convergence in Spain

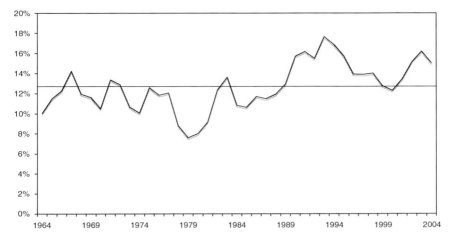

Fig. 8.2 Infrastructures as a percentage of total non-residential investment in Spain

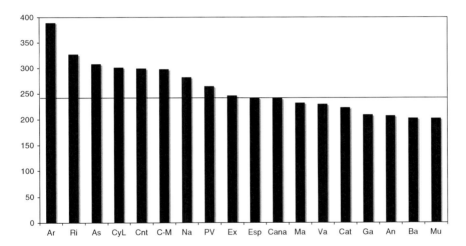

Fig. 8.3 Average investment per person and year between 1965 and 2004 measured in euros of 2000. Ar = Aragón; Ri = Rioja; As = Asturias; CyL = Castilla y León; Cnt = Cantabria; $C\text{-}M$ = Castilla la Mancha; Na = Navarra; PV = País Vasco; Ex = Extremadura; Esp = Spain (excluding Ceuta and Melilla); $Cana$ = Canarias; Ma = Madrid; Va = Valencia; Cat = Cataluña; Ga = Galicia; An = Andalucía; Ba = Baleares; Mu = Murcia

The regional distribution of infrastructure investment has been rather uneven. Figure 8.3 shows a first indicator of average investment intensity during the period 1964–2004: average investment per person and year measured at constant prices of 2000. In terms of this variable, the most favored regions have been Aragón, la Rioja, and Asturias, with per capita annual investment levels above 300 euros, and the least favored ones have been Murcia, Baleares, and Andalucía, with only a bit over 200 euros per person and year.

Figures 8.4 and 8.5 summarize the relationship between investment intensity and initial income per capita (in 1965) with both variables measured in deviations from

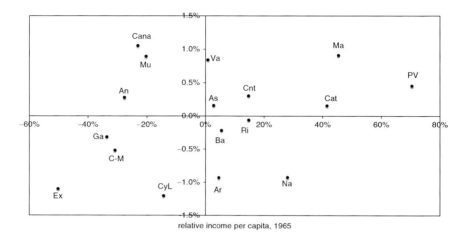

Fig. 8.4 Average annual growth rate of the total stock of infrastructures vs. per capita income in 1965. *Note:* In both figures, all variables are measured in deviations from the national average. Income per capita is GVA per capita at current prices in 1965. Ex = Extremadura; Ga = Galicia; C-M = Castilla la Mancha; An = Andalucía; Mu = Murcia; $Cana$ = Canarias; CyL = Castilla y León; Va = Valencia; As = Asturias; Ba = Baleares; Ar = Aragón; Ri = Rioja; Cnt = Cantabria; Na = Navarra; Cat = Cataluña; Ma = Madrid; PV = País Vasco

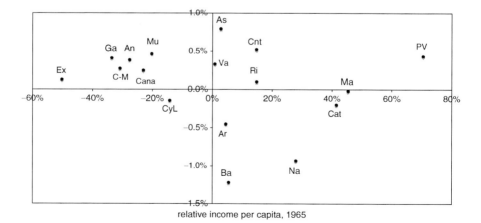

Fig. 8.5 Average annual growth rate of the per capita stock of infrastructures versus income per capita in 1965

8 Infrastructure Investment, Growth, and Regional Convergence in Spain

the national average. Investment intensity is now measured by the average annual rate of growth of the stock of infrastructures, which is the direct determinant of this factor's contribution to output growth. The measures of investment intensity used in Figs. 8.4 and 8.5 are slightly different: in the first case, I have used the growth rate of the *total* stock of infrastructures, while in the second, I have worked with the growth rate of the *per capita* stock. It is interesting to note that the correlation between investment intensity and initial income is positive (0.27) when the first variable is measured through the growth of the total stock of infrastructures and negative (−0.21) when we switch to the per capita stock. This result tells us that even though total investment has generally been greater in initially rich regions, these territories have tended to lose ground in terms of per capita stocks due to the rapid growth of their population. In a latter section, I will analyze in greater detail the redistributive impact of public investment policy.

To conclude, Fig. 8.6 shows the relative per capita endowment of infrastructure of each of the Spanish regions in 1965 and 2004. It should be noted that the per capita stock of infrastructures is not necessarily a good measure of the effective endowment of a given territory, because it does not take into account things like its land area or the nature of its terrain that can have a very significant impact on its need for certain types of networks or installations and on their cost. At any rate, the figure suggests that there has been a tendency towards the gradual equalization of per capita infrastructure stocks. The coefficient of variation of this variable went down by 24% between 1965 and 2004. The only exceptions to the general pattern of convergence to the mean have been the Cantabric communities (with the exception of Galicia) and Extremadura, which have improved their already favorable initial positions, and Baleares, whose distance to the mean has changed sign and become significantly greater during the period.

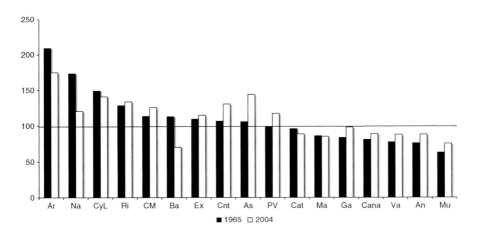

Fig. 8.6 Relative endowment infrastructures per capita (Spain = 100)

8.3 A Model of Growth and Employment

This section sketches the model I will use to construct the impact estimates that will be presented below. The model has two equations: a regional production function and an equation that describes the evolution of employment taking into account the delays that arise in the presence of adjustment costs.

The production function is Cobb–Douglas with constant returns to scale in labor, infrastructure and other capital for a given level of educational attainment. It adopts the following form

$$Y_{it} = K_{it}^{\theta_k} P_{it}^{\theta_p} (A_{it}L_{it})^{\theta_l} H_{it}^{\theta_h} \tag{8.1}$$

where the constant returns assumption implies that

$$\theta_l = 1 - \theta_k - \theta_p \tag{8.2}$$

In (1), Y_{it} is the output of region i at time t, L the level of employment, K and P the stocks of physical capital and productive infrastructures, H a measure of average school attainment and A an index of technical efficiency or total factor productivity (TFP). The parameters θ_i (with $i = l, k, h$ and p) measure the elasticity of aggregate output with respect to the stocks of the different productive factors. An increase of 1% in the stock of infrastructures, for instance, will increase output by θ_p%, holding constant the volume of other input and the level of technical efficiency.

Taking logs and time differences in (1), we obtain a relation between the growth rate of regional output on one hand and the growth rates of factor stocks, employment and TFP on the other hand,

$$\Delta y_{it} = \theta_l \Delta a_{it} + \theta_k \Delta k_{it} + \theta_l \Delta l_{it} + \theta_h \Delta h_{it} + \theta_p \Delta p_{it}, \tag{8.3}$$

where lower-case letters indicate that we are working with logs and the symbol "Δ" denotes time differences.

Differentiating (1) with respect to the level of employment to obtain the marginal product of labor, setting it equal to the real wage and rearranging, we obtain a conditional labor demand of the form

$$l_{it}^* = \frac{1}{1-\theta_l} \left(\ln \theta_l + \theta_l a_{it} + \theta_k k_{it} + \theta_h h_{it} + \theta_p p_{it} - w_{it} \right), \tag{8.4}$$

where w is the logarithm of the real wage. This function describes the aggregate demand for labor under the assumptions of perfect competition in product and factor markets and no adjustment costs. Since this last assumption is clearly inappropriate in Spain, I will interpret (4) as a long-term demand function and assume that employment adjusts gradually towards the level that would be optimal in the absence of adjustment costs. In particular, I will assume that the growth rate of observed employment, Δl_t, depends on the growth rate of long-term labor demand and on the difference between optimal and observed employment as described in the following expression (5)

$$\Delta l_{it} = -d + \gamma_1 \Delta l_{it}^* + \gamma_2 (l_{it}^* - l_{it}), \qquad (8.5)$$

where d is the (exogenous) rate of job destruction.

Combining (4) and (5), the short-term elasticity of employment with respect to the stock of infrastructures will be given by

$$\lambda_p = \frac{\gamma_1 \theta_p}{1 - \theta_l} \qquad (8.6)$$

My estimates of the impact of public investment on employment will be obtained by multiplying the observed increase in the (log of the) regional stock of infrastructures by the elasticity given in (6). Hence, they must be interpreted as short-term estimates that will not pick up all the effects of public investment on employment growth. It is also important to note that my calculations implicitly assume that public investment has no effect on real wages. Otherwise, the estimate would have to be corrected to take into account the loss of employment due to the increase in real wages induced by the programs we are analyzing.

Introducing some additional assumptions regarding the determinants of the growth of TFP, de la Fuente (2003a) estimates the system formed by (3) and (5) using a panel of Spanish regional data that covers the period 1964–1993 with the results shown in the first column of Table 8.1. De la Fuente and Doménech (2006) reestimate the regional production function using a somewhat longer sample, updated series of capital stocks, and a new and improved series of average school attainment (column 2 of Table 8.1). As can be seen in the table, the reestimation of the model yields noticeable changes in the coefficients of human capital (which goes up) and the stocks of infrastructures and other capital (which go down).

Table 8.1 Estimated values of the main parameters of the model

Parameter	de la Fuente (2003a)		de la Fuente and Doménech (2006)	
	Coeff.	(t)	Coeff.	(t)
θ_k	0.297	(5.73)	0.171	(3.27)
θ_p	0.106	(2.14)	**0.0567**	(3.25)
θ_h	0.286	(7.30)	0.835	(2.04)
θ_l	0.597		**0.772**	
γ_1	**0.181**	(6.47)		
γ_2	0.040	(5.21)		

Note: t statistics in parentheses next to each coefficient. The coefficient of employment, θ_l, is not estimated directly but recovered using the assumption of constant returns to scale in capital, infrastructures and labor, that is, $\theta_l = 1 - \theta_k - \theta_p$. For further details, see de la Fuente (2003a). The coefficients shown in bold type are the ones used to produce the estimates reported below

Since the estimate of the infrastructures parameter, θ_p, obtained by de la Fuente and Doménech (2006) seems in principle the more reliable one (due to the use of a longer sample and a considerable improvement in the human capital variable) and is, in any event, the more conservative one, it is the one I will use in the present chapter. However, given that the reestimation of the complete model is not feasible in the short-term (due to the lack of a homogeneous wage series for the entire sample), I have kept the values of the employment adjustment parameters estimated by de la Fuente (2003a).

8.4 The Contribution of Infrastructure Investment to Output and Employment Growth

According to the model developed in the previous section, infrastructure investment contributes to output growth through two different channels. An increase in the stock of this factor has a direct impact on output through the production function. In addition, it also generates an increase in employment that results in further output growth.

In the notation of the previous section, the direct contribution to output growth of a given increase in the stock of infrastructures in region i, Δp_{it}, will be given by

$$\theta_p \Delta p_{it} \tag{8.7}$$

Taking into account only the short-term effect of investment on employment, the increase in this variable induced by Δp_{it} will be equal to

$$\Delta l_{it}^p = \lambda_p \Delta p_{it} = \frac{\gamma_1 \theta_p}{1 - \theta_l} \Delta p_{it} \tag{8.8}$$

and the total contribution to output growth will be

$$\Delta y_{it}^p = \theta_p \Delta p_{it} + \theta_l \Delta l_{it}^p = (\theta_p + \theta_l \lambda_p) \Delta p_{it}. \tag{8.9}$$

Using (8) and (9) and the data described in Sect. 2, I have calculated the contribution of infrastructure investment to output and employment growth in Spain and its regions during different periods between 1965 and 2004. The aggregate results are summarized in Fig. 8.7. During the first half of the sample period, infrastructure's contribution to Spanish growth displays a downward trend that reflects both the decrease in the level of investment (measured as a fraction of GVA) and the existence of decreasing returns to this factor (which reduces the return to successive projects). Starting in the 1980s, however, the trend is reversed as the increase in the investment rate more than compensates for the second factor.

8 Infrastructure Investment, Growth, and Regional Convergence in Spain

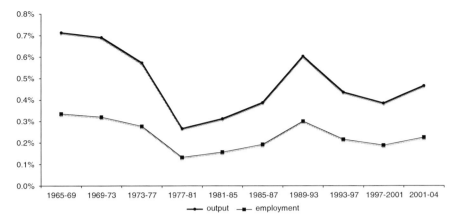

Fig. 8.7 Infrastructure investment's contribution to the growth of aggregate output and employment in Spain
Note: Weighted average of infrastructure's contributions to output and employment growth in the Spanish regions

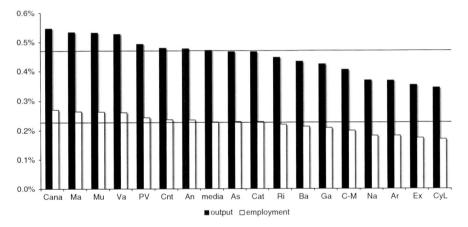

Fig. 8.8 Average annual contribution of infrastructure investment to the growth of regional output and employment, 1965–2004

On average over the entire sample period, infrastructure investment contributed 0.47 points per year to the growth of Spanish aggregate output (excluding Ceuta and Melilla) and 0.23 points to the growth of employment. These figures represent, respectively, 14.6% and 24.9% of the observed growth of these magnitudes.

Figure 8.8 shows the average contribution of infrastructure investment to the growth of the variables of interest in each autonomous community during the sample period. The estimated effects range from 0.35% to 0.55% points per year in the case of output and between 0.17 and 0.27 points in the case of employment.

Detailed results for the different regions are given in the Appendix (see Tables A.1 and A.2).

8.5 Infrastructure Investment and the Distribution of Income Across Regions

What has been the effect of infrastructure investment on regional income disparities? To answer this question, in this section, I will estimate the contribution of this variable to the rate of *beta convergence* in income per capita across the Spanish regions.

The rate of beta convergence (Barro and Sala-i-Martin, 1990) is a measure of the average speed at which regional disparities decrease over time. This coefficient is obtained by regressing the rate of growth of income per capita on the initial level of the same variable and measures the fraction of the income per capita differential relative to the national average that is eliminated each year in a hypothetical average region. Starting from a model of the determinants of income per capita (or its growth over time), the rate of beta convergence can be written as the sum of a series of components that capture the contributions of each of the relevant variables to the convergence process. These terms are obtained from a series of "partial convergence" equations, in which the dependent variable is the growth of per capita income induced by each of the factors included in the model and the independent variable is the initial level of income per capita, as in the original convergence equation.[1]

My decomposition of the rate of regional convergence will be based on the model developed in Sect. 3. Starting from the aggregate production function given in (1), grouping the terms that include A and H (which will not be used in what follows) together into a single term that I will call B and dividing through by regional population, N, regional income per capita, Q, can be written as a function of the per capita stocks of productive factors and the employment rate of the population:

$$Q_{it} = \frac{Y_{it}}{N_{it}} = B_{it}\left(\frac{K_{it}}{N_{it}}\right)^{\theta_k}\left(\frac{P_{it}}{N_{it}}\right)^{\theta_p}\left(\frac{L_{it}}{N_{it}}\right)^{1-\theta_k-\theta_p} \qquad (8.10)$$

Taking logs and time differences in (10), we obtain an equation,

$$\Delta q_{it} = \Delta b_{it} + \theta_k(\Delta k_{it} - \Delta n_{it}) + \theta_p(\Delta p_{it} - \Delta n_{it}) + (1 - \theta_k - \theta_p)\Delta(l_{it} - n_{it}) \quad (8.11)$$

that will allow us to quantify the (direct) contribution of infrastructure investment to the growth of income per capita in each region under two alternative assumptions about the evolution of its population. The increase in income per capita induced by

---
[1] For additional details, see de la Fuente (2003b).

the observed investment in infrastructure, Δp, *holding regional population constant* (cp) will be given by

$$\Delta q_{it}^{cp} = \theta_p \Delta p_{it}, \qquad (8.12)$$

whereas the same magnitude, calculated with "variable population" (vp) will be

$$\Delta q_{it}^{vp} = \theta_p (\Delta p_{it} - \Delta n_{it}), \qquad (8.13)$$

where Δn is the observed growth rate of population.

To obtain the indicator we seek, we estimate a partial convergence equation of the form

$$\Delta q_{it}^j - \overline{\Delta q_t^j} = -b_{jt}(q_{it} - \bar{q}_t), \qquad (8.14)$$

where $j =$ cp or vp, the bars indicate (unweighted) sample averages and q_{it} is (log) income per capita at current prices at the beginning of the subperiod that starts in t. The coefficient b in this regression will measure the contribution of infrastructure investment to regional convergence or, more precisely, the speed of income convergence (or divergence if $b < 0$) induced by the observed evolution of the stock of infrastructure holding constant the remaining determinants of income per capita.

Depending on the assumption we make about the evolution of population, we will obtain two alternative estimates of the rate of convergence induced by infrastructures. The first one ($j =$ cp) measures the redistributive impact that public investment would have had if the regional distribution of the population had

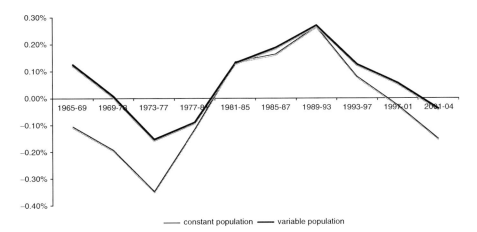

Fig. 8.9 Rate of beta convergence in income per capita induced by infrastructure investment
Note: The contribution of infrastructures to output growth that is used to calculate its redistributive impact only includes the direct effect of this factor and does not take into account its indirect effect via employment

remained constant, and the second one ($j = vp$) takes into account the observed evolution of the population, holding constant the employment rate in each region.

Figure 8.9 shows the estimated values of both partial convergence indicators in different subperiods. Given that the regional distribution of the Spanish population remained basically unchanged during the 1980s and the first half of the 1990s, the values of both indicators are very similar during this period. In the initial and final years of the sample, however, there are significant differences between them. Since richer regions have generally gained demographic weight over time (as a result of internal migration flows during the first part of the sample period and of external ones in its final years), infrastructure investment in these regions has been diluted by rapid population growth. As a result, the redistributive impact of public investment is always greater when the calculation is made under the variable population assumption. The difference is particularly important during the early years of the sample period.

Regardless of the demographic assumption we choose, the figure reveals a strong increase in the redistributive impact of infrastructure investment between the mid-1970s and the mid-1990s, followed by a gradual reduction in the final part of the sample period. Somewhat surprisingly, I find that the decentralization process that starts following the end of Franco's regime has been characterized by a clearly redistributive pattern of public investment that has contributed to the reduction of income differences across regions or at least has limited the negative impact of other factors. The considerable flow of investment resources to poorer regions through EU cohesion policies has certainly played an important role in this change of orientation. The redistributive bias in public investment, however, becomes apparent even before Spain's accession to the EU. Likewise, the reversal of this pattern starts in the mid-1990s, precisely at the time when EU aid reaches its maximum intensity. Hence, the gradual decline in the redistribution indicator we observe in these years is not the result of the reduction in EU aid, but of a change in the investment priorities of the different Spanish administrations, which was sufficiently marked so as to prevail over the strong redistributive bias of Community cohesion policy.

One thing that should be kept in mind when evaluating the changes in the orientation of Spanish public investment policy I have documented or making policy recommendations for the future is that redistribution via infrastructure investment can have a significant opportunity cost in terms of aggregate growth, because in our country the returns to such investment tend to be lower in relatively backward regions. Figure 8.10 displays the time path of the correlation between an indicator of investment intensity (average annual investment per capita measured at constant prices) and the expected return to infrastructure investment (calculated using the estimated production function and the underlying data on output levels and factor stocks). A striking result that should give us some food for thought is that this correlation has been negative during practically the entire sample period – a finding which suggests that the regional distribution of public investment leaves considerable room for improvement from the point of view of efficiency. A second result of interest is that this coefficient and the measure of redistributive impact shown in Fig. 8.9 almost always moves in opposite directions. Hence, there exists a

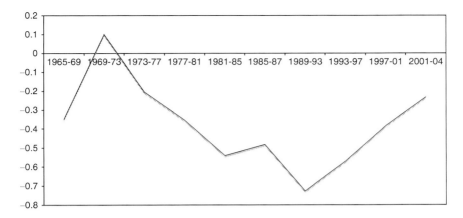

Fig. 8.10 Correlation between average investment per capita at constant prices and the expected return to infrastructure investment

clear trade-off between redistribution and efficiency that should at least be taken into account in the design of public investment policy.[2]

8.6 Conclusion

In this chapter, I have used a simple growth model to quantify the contribution of infrastructure investment to regional and national growth. I extract two main conclusions from the analysis. The first one is that infrastructure investment has had a significant positive impact on output and employment, both at the regional and at the aggregate level. On average during the sample period, this factor has contributed almost half a point per year to the growth of Spanish output and close to a quarter of a point to the growth of employment. The second conclusion is that public investment has been used as an instrument for regional redistribution during most of the period we have studied. As such, it has contributed significantly to income convergence across regions, particularly during the decade following Spain's accession to the EU. Redistribution, however, has had a significant efficiency cost.

---

[2] See de la Fuente (2001, 2004) for a more detailed analysis of this issue, including an estimate of the opportunity cost of a redistributive public investment policy and some policy recommendations.

Appendix: Detailed Results

Table 8.A.1 Infrastructure investment's contribution to the growth of regional and national output

	1965–1969 (%)	1969–1973 (%)	1973–1977 (%)	1977–1981 (%)	1981–1985 (%)	1985–1987 (%)	1989–1993 (%)	1993–1997 (%)	1997–2001 (%)	2001–2004 (%)
And	0.70	0.70	0.45	0.24	0.39	0.54	0.85	0.39	0.29	0.30
Ara	0.57	0.27	0.71	0.18	0.21	0.24	0.34	0.28	0.52	0.50
Ast	0.78	0.50	0.46	0.28	0.46	0.34	0.55	0.47	0.45	0.50
Bal	0.50	0.53	0.43	0.18	0.38	0.52	0.48	0.53	0.41	0.48
Cana	1.05	0.79	0.71	0.41	0.31	0.40	0.58	0.42	0.53	0.36
Cant	0.41	0.40	0.48	0.32	0.42	0.58	0.76	0.59	0.46	0.49
CyL	0.50	0.34	0.35	0.17	0.30	0.31	0.46	0.34	0.39	0.40
C-M	0.42	0.59	0.42	0.16	0.28	0.53	0.76	0.37	0.28	0.35
Cat	0.86	0.89	0.57	0.15	0.25	0.30	0.56	0.43	0.30	0.49
Val	0.78	0.91	0.79	0.24	0.40	0.38	0.65	0.50	0.38	0.34
Ext	0.55	0.30	0.21	0.15	0.34	0.45	0.69	0.40	0.25	0.26
Gal	0.43	0.27	0.46	0.44	0.34	0.36	0.59	0.62	0.42	0.43
Mad	0.83	0.84	0.54	0.30	0.23	0.37	0.56	0.46	0.58	0.85
Mur	0.45	0.44	0.99	0.50	0.55	0.66	0.71	0.48	0.33	0.29
Nav	0.33	0.14	1.39	0.31	0.07	0.25	0.51	0.35	0.19	0.22
PV	0.84	0.91	0.67	0.39	0.35	0.37	0.53	0.42	0.26	0.27
Rio	0.56	0.38	1.24	1.40	0.09	0.13	0.23	0.10	0.16	0.25
Tot ccaa	0.71	0.69	0.57	0.27	0.31	0.39	0.60	0.44	0.38	0.47

Note: Includes indirect effects via employment creation

Table 8.A.2 Infrastructure investment's contribution to the growth of regional and national employment

	1965–1969 (%)	1969–1973 (%)	1973–1977 (%)	1977–1981 (%)	1981–1985 (%)	1985–1987 (%)	1989–1993 (%)	1993–1997 (%)	1997–2001 (%)	2001–2004 (%)
And	0.34	0.35	0.22	0.12	0.19	0.27	0.42	0.19	0.15	0.15
Ara	0.28	0.13	0.35	0.09	0.10	0.12	0.17	0.14	0.25	0.25
Ast	0.38	0.25	0.23	0.14	0.23	0.17	0.27	0.23	0.22	0.24
Bal	0.25	0.26	0.21	0.09	0.19	0.26	0.24	0.26	0.20	0.23
Cana	0.51	0.39	0.35	0.20	0.15	0.20	0.29	0.21	0.26	0.18
Cant	0.20	0.20	0.24	0.16	0.21	0.29	0.38	0.29	0.23	0.24
CyL	0.24	0.17	0.17	0.08	0.15	0.16	0.23	0.17	0.19	0.19
C-M	0.21	0.29	0.21	0.08	0.14	0.26	0.37	0.18	0.14	0.17
Cat	0.42	0.44	0.28	0.07	0.13	0.15	0.27	0.21	0.15	0.24
Val	0.38	0.45	0.39	0.12	0.19	0.19	0.32	0.25	0.19	0.17
Ext	0.27	0.15	0.10	0.07	0.17	0.22	0.34	0.20	0.12	0.13
Gal	0.21	0.13	0.23	0.22	0.17	0.17	0.29	0.30	0.21	0.21
Mad	0.41	0.41	0.27	0.15	0.11	0.18	0.28	0.22	0.29	0.42
Mur	0.22	0.22	0.49	0.25	0.27	0.32	0.35	0.24	0.16	0.14
Nav	0.16	0.07	0.68	0.15	0.04	0.12	0.25	0.17	0.09	0.11
PV	0.41	0.45	0.33	0.19	0.17	0.18	0.26	0.21	0.13	0.13
Rio	0.27	0.19	0.61	0.69	0.05	0.06	0.11	0.05	0.08	0.12
Tot ccaa	0.33	0.32	0.28	0.13	0.16	0.19	0.30	0.22	0.19	0.22

References

Barro, R., & Sala-i-Martin, X. (1990). *Economic growth and convergence across the United States*. NBER Working Paper no. 3419.

de la Fuente, A. (2001). Infraestructuras y política regional. In T. García-Milà (Ed.), *Nuevas fronteras de la política económica, 2001* (pp. 18–55). Barcelona: Generalitat de Cataluña y Universidad Pompeu Fabra.

de la Fuente, A. (2003a). *The effect of Structural Fund spending on the Spanish regions: an assessment of the 1994-99 Objective 1 CSF*. Documento de trabajo D-2003-02. Madrid: Dirección General de Presupuestos, Ministerio de Economía y Hacienda.

de la Fuente, A. (2003b). Convergence equations and income dynamics: the sources of OECD convergence, 1970–95. *Economica, 70*(280), 655–671.

de la Fuente, A. (2004). Second-best redistribution through public investment: a characterization, an empirical test and an application to the case of Spain. *Regional Science and Urban Economics, 34*, 489–503.

de la Fuente, A. (2008a). Inversión en infraestructuras, crecimiento y convergencia regional. *Papeles de Economía Española, 118*, 15–26.

de la Fuente, A. (2008b). *La evolución de algunos agregados económicos regionales entre 1995 y 2005: comparación de diversas fuentes y un intento de homogeneización. Versión 1.0.* (Mimeo). Barcelona: Instituto de Análisis Económico (CSIC).

de la Fuente, A., & Doménech, R. (2006). Capital humano, crecimiento y desigualdad en las regiones españolas. *Moneda y Crédito, 222*, 13–56.

Fundación BBV. (1998). *El stock de capital en España y sus comunidades autónomas*. Bilbao: Fundación BBV.

Instituto Nacional de Estadística (INE). (2008). Contabilidad Regional de España. In *electronic database INEbase*. Madrid: Economía Cuentas Económicas. http://www.ine.es/inebase/cgi/um?M=%2Ft35%2Fp010&O=inebase&N=&L=.

Mas, M., Pérez, F., & Uriel, E. (2002). *El stock de capital en España y su distribución territorial*. Bilbao: Fundación BBVA.

Mas, M., Pérez, F., Uriel, E., Cucarella, V., Robledo, J. C., & Serrano, L. (2007). *El stock y los servicios del capital en España y su distribución territorial (1964–2005), Nueva metodología*. Bilbao: Fundación BBVA.

Fundación BBVA. (several years). *Renta nacional de España y su distribución provincia*l. Bilbao: Fundación BBVA.

Chapter 9
Public Capital Effects and Regional Spillover in Spain

Oriol Roca-Sagalés and Hector Sala

9.1 Introduction

Public investment, and thus public capital accumulation, is a key determinant of the macroeconomic performance at a regional level. This chapter evaluates to what extent Spain as a whole and each of its regions individually respond to the economic stimulus provided by this investment.

The economic impact of public capital has been the subject of growing attention in the literature since Aschauer (1989). In his seminal contribution, Aschauer showed the crucial role of public capital to understand the size and evolution of the total factor productivity (TFP). The TFP was defined by Solow (1956) as the part of the production which cannot be explained by the accrual of the production factors. Since then, it was also known as the Solow residual and was subsequently the object of attention in the macroeconomic literature. For example, Arrow (1962), Romer (1986, 1990), and Mankiw et al. (1992), among many others, searched for the main determining factors of the TFP and focussed on the role of technology and the human capital stock.

It is in this context that Aschauer (1989, 2000) and Barro (1990) showed that public capital stock is essential to explain economic growth. In particular, an insufficiency in the provision of public capital can lead to substantial inefficiencies in the private sector and reduce the possibilities of economic progress.

Following the contributions of Aschauer and Barro, the 1990s produced numerous studies on the impact of public capital stock on economic growth and the TFP. Especially prolific in this context was the research conducted on the Spanish and U.S. economies, as these were the ones with the best and most accessible data on public capital stock. An illustrative example is the special issue of the journal

---

O. Roca-Sagalés (✉)
Universitat Autonoma de Barcelona, Departament d'Economia Aplicada, Campus de Bellaterra. Edifici B, 08193 Bellaterra – Barcelona, spain.
e-mail: Oriol.Roca@uab.es

Moneda y Crédito,[1] in which the economic effects of public capital were analysed from several perspectives. Apart from the evidence on the U.S. and Spain, in those first years, Lynde and Richmond (1993) published an international analysis on the connection between public capital and the TFP. In Sect. 2 of this chapter, we briefly survey the literature in this field, which now includes two decades of relevant contributions.

Despite this lengthy process, this area of research is still alive and highly interesting for various reasons. First, because of the wider historical perspective and enhanced accuracy of new databases; second, because of the continuous progress in the quantitative techniques, which allow the obtainment of new and more precise results; and third, because of the current constraints that affect the conduction of economic policy. We must recall, in particular, that European governments are subject to the restrictions imposed by the Stability and Growth Pact as regards deficit and public debt. At the same time, Spain is involved in an intense discussion on the decentralisation of public expenditure and on how the different Autonomous Communities (*Comunidades Autónomas*) have to be financed. In this context, guaranteeing an efficient allocation of public resources (i.e. productive investment) is one of the aspects which must be given priority. This guarantee applies to the efficiency of public expenditures in areas where these resources will be truly productive, and should also aim at fostering competitiveness through suitable investment in communication and transport infrastructures. In fact, the essential purpose of this chapter is to provide an updated estimation of the regional effects of public investment and, thereby, contribute to the existing debate on such important issues.

We refer to an updated estimation, since this research is a continuation and improvement over our past work in Roca-Sagalés and Sala (2006). In that article, we assessed the magnitude of the spillover effects generated by public investment in Spain and its regions. More precisely, for years 1970–1998, we aimed at quantifying the extent to which output in a particular region benefited from investment in infrastructures in other regions of the country. In this chapter, we contrast the robustness of those results with a new analysis in which: (1) we extend the period under scrutiny to 2004; (2) we rely on new capital stock series, since the database has undergone methodological changes (see Mas et al., 2007); (3) the employment database is different as we now take data from the Spanish Regional Accounts (*Contabilidad Regional de España*); and (4) we estimate the long-term elasticity of output with respect to the public capital stock with a new procedure, which provides very similar results for the Spanish economy as a whole (see Sect. 4). There are also two main elements in common with Roca-Sagalés and Sala (2006). The first one is the estimation of 18 independent vector autoregressive (VAR) models, one for each Autonomous Community and one for Spain as a whole (Ceuta and Melilla are excluded from the analysis). The second one is the classification of public capital stock in two components, one corresponding to the region itself and another one

---

[1] See Moneda y Crédito, number 198, year 1994.

which is external to the region and corresponds to the rest of Spain. This distinction allows the evaluation of regional spillover effects stemming from public investment. It should be pointed out that no differentiation is made on how geographically close is the stock of external public capital with respect to the particular region being analysed. This is not a serious drawback for two reasons. First, because Spain is not a large country (as would be the case of the U.S.) and has no isolated regions. Second, because we focus on evaluating the impact of public infrastructures, and it is reasonable to assume that any part of the network of infrastructures is interconnected with the rest.

Regarding the empirical methodology, we use the VAR approach; in particular, the application for the U.S. developed by Pereira and Flores (1999), and Pereira (2000, 2001).[2] This methodology allows us to address three fundamental aspects of the impact of public capital, which first studies on this issue did not take into account. First, the public capital stock (in our case defined as the communications and transport infrastructures) can be treated as an endogenous variable. Second, it enables the assessment of the impact of public capital on employment and private capital stock, beyond the traditional evaluation of its effects on production. Third, it allows the computation of the feedback effects among all considered variables in response to changes (or shocks) in public capital stock.

The empirical results are based on the impulse–response functions (IRFs) associated to the VARs estimated for Spain as a whole and for each of its Autonomous Communities. We consider the responses, or part of the responses that are statistically significant, which we determine following the standard practise in the empirical literature using VAR models. In particular, we consider a response or part of the response as statistically significant if its error band does not include the value zero. And we choose an error band of one standard deviation delimited by the 16% and the 80%, which entails working with a confidence interval of 68%, instead of 95%. As explained by Sims and Zha (1999), this is more adequate because it provides a more precise estimate of the effective IRFs' statistical significance.

Regarding the empirical results, the fundamental contribution of Roca-Sagalés and Sala (2006) consisted in outlining and quantifying the relevance of the spillover effects in Spain. Specifically, the direct aggregate impact of public infrastructures on output accounted only for two-thirds of the total effects, while the spillover effects (that is, those deriving from the public capital stock located in other regions) reached the remaining third and appeared as fundamental to explain the whole economic impact of public investment in infrastructures. This main result revealed a geographical pattern. In the geographically central regions, the direct effects of public investment were relatively more important, while the spillover effects were relatively more intense in the peripheral regions.

Among the main results of this chapter is the confirmation, first of all, that the Spanish economy taken as a whole reacts positively to increases in public capital stock. This is so both in terms of output and employment, and there is no evidence

---

[2]This literature is analysed in Kamps (2005).

of crowding-out effects concerning private capital stock. Second, with regard to output and employment, we confirm the existence of significant spillover effects of public investment throughout the Spanish regions. Third, our results uncover a new dimension of the regional economic impact of public capital. Specifically, the regional results are clearly conditioned by the regional endowment of public capital. In the Autonomous Communities with public capital under-endowment (understood as a provision which is clearly below the Spanish average), additional investment in infrastructures has a strong repercussion on GDP and private capital, as well as on employment. However, in the Autonomous Communities with a relative provision of public capital far above the average, these effects are clearly lower and, in some cases, negative. Finally, a new result brought by our analysis concerns the crowding-out effect of public investment on private investment at the regional level. Indeed, this crowding-out effect is only detected in the Autonomous Communities with a relative over-provision of public capital.

These results lead to the conclusion that public investment in infrastructures should be closely connected to economic activity. Of course, public investment is in itself a promoter of economic activity, but to take optimum advantage of infrastructures the necessary condition is that an already existing demand for these is satisfied.

The rest of the chapter is structured as follows. In the second section, we briefly revise some relevant literature on the economic effects of public capital. In the third section, we present the data and the main regional features of the Spanish economy regarding the distribution of GDP, employment and capital stock. In the fourth section, we present the estimation of the VAR models for Spain as a whole and for its 17 Autonomous Communities. In the fifth section, we evaluate the results obtained from the point of view of the elasticities of GDP, employment and private capital with respect to public capital. Section six concludes this chapter.

9.2 The Effects of Public Capital in the Literature

The seminal contribution of Aschauer (1989) showed that public capital stock is an essential factor to understand the TFP. In particular, Aschauer argues that the TFP fall in the U.S. in the 1970s can only be understood when considering the impact of the reduction in public investment and the subsequent deficit of public capital. The contribution of Barro (1990) is even more forceful as it establishes that sustained economic growth is only possible with an adequate provision of public capital. Lacking this, economic activity will face productive bottlenecks, which deteriorate the productivity of the traditional production factors, such as employment and private capital.

One of the fundamental contributions of Aschauer (2000) was the classification of public capital stock according to how productive its components are. Among the most productive ones are communications and transport infrastructures, which are the hardcore of the stock of productive capital due to their greater impact on the

TFP. Among the less productive components is the rest of public capital, in particular, health care, education, culture and research centres, which have less impact on the TFP. Our research focuses on the first of these two components and its economic incidence.

One of the reasons why the Spanish and U.S. economies are the most studied cases is the historical availability of long time series for public capital stock. Nevertheless, the literature in this area includes a variety of international results which go from Lynde and Richmond (1993) up to the recent review of results for the OECD economies by Kamps (2005). These studies are generally based on two types of methodological strategies, the first one being the estimation of production functions, and the second one the estimation of cost–benefit functions.

Our analysis follows the first type of strategy and thus differs from relevant contributions in the field, such as that of Demetriades and Mamuneas (2000) for 12 OECD economies, and that of Avilés et al. (2003) for Spain. In this latter case, the assessment of the impact of public infrastructures on private activity is based on cost functions estimates for the industry and construction sectors. Avilés et al. (2003) document a significant impact and important spillover effects whose magnitude varies depending on how these are estimated.

The evaluation of the economic impact of public capital has traditionally been based on the estimation of production functions, in most cases of the Cobb–Douglas type, but also of the constant elasticity of substitution (CES) type. In both cases, the production function is usually linearized so that a Solow decomposition can be carried so as to quantify the TFP. Once the TFP is computed, a regression can be made in order to (1) relate the TFP with different measurements of public capital stock and (2) infer its final incidence on the GDP through the estimated impact of public capital on the TFP (see Raurich and Sala, 2006). This strategy, however, has two important limitations as regards the analysis we intend to perform. On the one hand, the estimated causal relationships are one directional and do not permit any kind of feedback effects. This is so because public capital stock is added as an extra production factor (besides the standard ones, private capital stock and employment) and it either affects output directly as explanatory variable, or indirectly by entering a TFP equation. It seems reasonable to expect, however, that changes in private capital will lead to changes in employment and vice versa, which would indirectly entail modifications in the desired level of public capital stock. The analysis based on the estimation of structural equations does not usually evaluate these interactions or feedback effects. On the other hand, there is the limitation of disregarding the possibility of regional spillover effects of public capital, which cannot be addressed either with the estimation of structural equations. As explained in Sect. 4.1, these limitations can be overcome by the use of the VAR methodology.

The prolific literature on the economic impact of public capital in Spain has involved several perspectives including aggregate, sector and geographical ones. For example, the works of Flores de Frutos et al. (1998), Pereira and Roca-Sagalés (2001), Boscá et al. (2002), Fernández and Montuenga (2003), and Raurich et al. (2009) take an aggregate perspective. On the contrary, Mas et al. (1996), Moreno et al. (1997), Pereira and Roca-Sagalés (1999), Cantos et al. (2005), Roca-Sagalés and Sala (2006), as well as Moreno and López-Bazo (2007) take a regional perspective. Avilés et al. (2003) combine the regional perspective with sector disaggregation.

This regional dimension is precisely what allows the evaluation of the spillover effects stemming from public investment. As noted, this question has already been addressed in other papers with different data and methodologies. However, the available empirical evidence is far from yielding a uniform picture. While some studies suggest a positive relationship between the spillover effects of infrastructures and economic growth (Moreno et al., 1997; Cantos et al., 2005; Pereira and Roca-Sagalés, 2003), others condition these effects to factors linked to the level of urbanisation of the areas studied (Boarnet, 1998) or to their geographical location (Roca-Sagalés and Sala, 2006). In this last context, the impact of the infrastructures located in regions which are economically contiguous (but, of course, not necessarily linked from a geographical point of view) can even be negative in terms of regional output and/or private investment (Kelejian and Robinson, 1997; Chandra and Thompson, 2000; Martínez López, 2006; Moreno and López-Bazo, 2007).

9.3 Regional Data and Analysis of the main Macroeconomic Figures

9.3.1 Data

The data used is taken from two sources. Data on public and private capital stock are taken from the Fundación Banco de Bilbao Vizcaya Argentaria (FBBVA) and the Instituto Valenciano de Investigaciones Económicas (IVIE), and correspond to the latest updating of this traditional dataset in the Spanish statistical panorama. This database incorporates important methodological changes whose explanation can be found in Mas et al. (2007). We consider as public capital stock all items corresponding to infrastructures, which include those related to roads, ports, airports and railways, as well as urban and hydraulic infrastructures, regardless of whether these belong to the central, regional (Autonomous Community) or local public administrations. Each Autonomous Community is assigned the public capital stock located in its domain.

GDP and employment data are obtained from the *Contabilidad Regional de España* (CRE) published by the *Instituto Nacional de Estadística*. It should be pointed out that the CRE does not provide long homogeneous time series. Due to methodological changes, these are splitted into several series with three bases, 1980, 1986 and 1995. Our analysis is carried out on the linked series, which in the GDP case is expressed in constant thousands of euros (for each Autonomous Community) corresponding to year 2000. This is ALS. the reference year for the capital stock series.

Therefore, the database underlying our empirical analysis includes: (1) variables for public capital stock, private capital stock, GDP and employment, all of which are used in logarithmic form; (2) the 1970–2004 period; and (3) Spain as a whole, as well as its 17 Autonomous Communities (Andalusia, Aragon, Asturias, the Balearic Islands, the Canary Islands, Cantabria, Castile-Leon, Castile-La Mancha, Catalonia, the Community of Valencia, Extremadura, Galicia, the Community of Madrid, Murcia, Navarre, the Basque Country and Rioja).

9.3.2 Regional Analysis of the Evolution of GDP, Employment and Capital Stock

Table 9.1 provides information on the regional distribution, in percentage points, of the main macroeconomic figures under study. This distribution is based on the yearly average of a full decade (from 1995 to 2004) in order to reflect the recent structural situation of the Autonomous Communities. In this way, we prevent potential biases stemming from an evaluation of the situation based on a single year.

As we can see, five Autonomous Communities (Andalusia, Catalonia, the Community of Valencia, the Community of Madrid and the Basque Country) concentrate two-thirds of the total production in Spain. It thus follows that the aggregate results will be largely affected by the estimates obtained for these regions. In addition, it should be stressed that their share in terms of employment is slightly lower than two-thirds, which reflects their above-average productivity levels.

Table 9.1 Regional distribution of GDP, employment, and public and private capital stock. 1995–2004. Percentages

	GDP	Employment	Private capital	Public capital
Andalusia	14.0	14.9	13.1	16.0
Aragon	3.1	3.2	2.7	4.7
Asturias	2.1	2.4	1.9	3.4
Balearic Islands	2.3	2.1	3.2	1.5
Canary Islands	3.9	4.1	3.5	3.8
Cantabria	1.3	1.2	1.2	1.6
Castile-Leon	5.5	5.9	5.2	8.0
Castile-La Mancha	3.5	3.9	3.5	5.5
Catalonia	18.0	17.4	19.4	13.5
Community of Valencia	9.9	10.6	12.3	9.1
Extremadura	1.8	2.2	1.4	3.0
Galicia	5.3	6.7	4.5	6.0
Community of Madrid	17.6	14.6	18.0	9.8
Murcia	2.5	2.7	2.6	2.3
Navarre	1.7	1.5	1.5	1.7
Basque Country	6.5	5.5	5.0	5.9
Rioja	0.7	0.7	0.7	1.0
Spain	100.0	100.0	100.0	100.0

Source: own drafting from data obtained from FBBVA-IVIE and from CRE

These aggregate figures, however, conceal substantial disparities among these five regions, insofar as the Community of Madrid is the Autonomous Community with greater productivity levels in Spain (its GDP share is 3% points above its employment share), while Andalusia is the second Autonomous Community, after Galicia, with the lowest relative productivity level (with a GDP share almost 1% point below the employment share). The Basque Country and Catalonia come just behind the Community of Madrid, with differentials in their GDP and employment shares amounting to 1 and 0.6% points respectively, while the Community of Valencia lies just after Andalusia with an employment weight, which is 0.7% points above the GDP one.

The Community of Madrid and Catalonia stand out as they concentrate 37.5% of total private capital stock, a figure which practically amounts to 50%, if the Community of Valencia is incorporated. In these three regions, the share in terms of private capital stock surpasses the GDP and employment ones. The opposite occurs in Andalusia, with a share of 13.1% of the private capital stock, and in the Basque Country, where it is also lower.

In the context of this research, it is crucial to remark that Andalusia, in clear contrast with the above figures, is the Autonomous Community with the greatest share of public capital stock in Spain, which amounted to an average of 16.0% between 1995 and 2004. Note that this value surpasses this region's shares on GDP, employment and private capital stock. On the contrary, the other four Autonomous Communities are undersupplied with public capital. The clearest cases are those of Catalonia and the Community of Madrid, in which the weight of public capital is 4.5 and 7.7% points below their GDP weights respectively. These two are followed by the Community of Valencia, the Basque Country and the Balearic Islands. It turns out that the differential in the Balearic Islands amounts to 0.8% points despite the fact that its GDP share only reaches 2.3%.

The ratio of GDP over public capital stock, presented in Fig. 9.1, illustrates which Autonomous Communities are oversupplied and undersupplied in terms of public capital stock in Spain. This ratio takes a value of 2.48 for the whole country, indicated by the horizontal line. As can be seen, the Community of Madrid, the

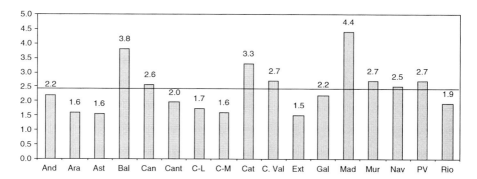

Fig. 9.1 Ratio of GDP over public capital stock. 1995–2004

9 Public Capital Effects and Regional Spillover in Spain   195

Balearic Islands, Catalonia, the Community of Valencia and the Basque Country are the Autonomous Communities with a GDP ratio over public capital greater than the Spanish average. These are thus the regions where public capital stock is underendowed relative to the Spanish average. On the contrary, Aragon, Asturias, Castile-La Mancha, Castile-Leon, Extremadura and Rioja are the regions with a greater relative endowment of public capital. These are followed by Cantabria, Galicia and Andalusia, where public capital stock is mildly over-endowed relative to the Spanish average.

As a complementary exercise, we conducted the same analysis by taking as relevant indicators the ratios of employment and private capital stock (rather than the GDP, as before) over public capital stock. We classified again the regions and found that the resulting grouping reinforces the one obtained when GDP is taken as a reference. Hence, the overall picture classifies the Autonomous Communities in three groups: a group of four with clear under-endowment of public capital stock (the Balearic Islands, Catalonia, the Community of Valencia, and the Community of Madrid); a group of eight Autonomous Communities with clear over-endowment (Andalusia, Aragon, Asturias, Cantabria, Castile-La Mancha, Castile-Leon, Extremadura and Rioja); and, finally, five Autonomous Communities in a situation close to the average which, depending on the specific variable taken as reference (GDP, employment or private capital), would appear slightly above or below the average (the Canary Islands, Galicia, Murcia, Navarre and the Basque Country).

9.4 Empirical Methodology and Econometric Estimation

9.4.1 The VAR Methodology

Our empirical analysis on the impact of public capital is based on the VAR methodology. The choice of this technique derives from the theoretical approach developed by Pereira and Roca-Sagalés (2003). These authors start off from a dynamic production function whose technology is based on private capital, employment and public capital as the main inputs in the generation of production. One of the particularities of this approach is that it allows to evaluate whether the economic impact of public capital spills over economically (but maybe not geographically) adjacent regions. In other words, public investment may not only impact economic activity in the area where this investment takes place, but it may also benefit other areas that are economically interrelated. If we find that the existence of such spillover effects depends on the economic situation of each region, this would suggest that there is an endogenous and optimum level of public investment which must be determined in each case depending on the specific economic impact of public investment in each region.

In addition, the use of the VAR methodology allows to consider the response of each dependent variable (in our case, GDP, employment, private and public capital stock) to changes in any of these variables. This would not be possible in the event that these variables were to be considered exogenous, which is frequent in the estimation of structural models. The inclusion of the feedback effects generated by any shock on the variables of the model is one of the main advantages of the VAR methodology.

In the particular case of a shock on public capital stock, the evaluation of the feedback effects is especially important as it allows to quantify whether greater public investment is detrimental of private investment or, on the contrary, there is complementarity. The first case, in which a substitution takes place, would indicate the well-known crowding-out effect of public over private investment.

Of course, the estimation and evaluation of the elasticities is also different from the case of a structural model. As explained in next section, we compute the long-term GDP, employment and private capital responses to changes in public capital stock in two different ways. In the first place, through the long-term accumulation of the responses of these variables to a one-off shock, as we already did (Roca-Sagalés and Sala, 2006). In the second place, through the accumulation of only the yearly statistically significant responses. If the results from both calculations do not diverge excessively, then we will be assured on the robustness of the estimates.

9.4.2 Estimation of the Aggregate VAR Model

One of the crucial aspects of the VAR methodology is to establish the order of the integration of the variables included in the analysis, that is, GDP, employment, private and public capital stock of Spain as a whole, as well as the corresponding regional series. To do so, we use the ADF (Augmented Dickey-Fuller) unit roots test, in which (1) the number of lags included in the test regression is determined by the Bayesian Information Criterion (BIC); and (2) the deterministic components (constant and trend) are included whenever they are statistically significant.

The results of the ADF test are diverse. The clearest picture is obtained for the GDP and employment series, which can be safely classified as I(1) variables because once differentiated their tendency component is suppressed. This holds in all cases, both for the aggregated series and for their regional counterparts. The study of the public and private capital stock series is conducted following the procedure of Pereira and Flores (1999), in which their ratios over GDP, and not their levels, are analysed. In case that the ADF tests reveal a non-stationary behaviour, the variables in the ratios can be interpreted as first-order integrated variables. This is indeed the general conclusion we obtain from the results of the ADF tests on the ratio of private capital stock over GDP. The results on the ratio of public capital stock over GDP are less clear and, in some cases, not fully conclusive on the possibility of a first- or a second-order degree of integration. Nevertheless, given the existing empirical evidence concerning this question, considering that our time series hardly include four decades, and taking into account the well-known robustness problems of the ADF test, we decide to treat all series as I(1).

Table 9.2 The aggregate VAR model for the Spanish economy[a]

	ΔY	ΔL	ΔK	ΔPK
Constant	0.070	0.014	0.006	0.010
	(0.027)	(0.016)	(0.004)	(0.010)
Trend	−0.001	0.001	−0.001	−0.001
	(0.000)	(0.001)	(0.000)	(0.000)
$\Delta Y(-1)$	−0.260	0.062	0.023	0.087
	(0.211)	(0.124)	(0.032)	(0.075)
$\Delta L(-1)$	0.915	0.813	0.110	0.070
	(0.290)	(0.172)	(0.045)	(0.104)
$\Delta K(-1)$	−0.332	−0.331	0.864	−0.002
	(0.445)	(0.263)	(0.068)	(0.159)
$\Delta PK(-1)$	0.106	−0.101	−0.043	0.712
	(0.326)	(0.192)	(0.050)	(0.116)
Adjusted R^2	0.29	0.63	0.91	0.68

Note: Standard errors in brackets.
[a] For the sake of brevity, we omit the specific results for each of the 17 Autonomous Communities. These are available upon request.

Next, we consider all series in their logarithmic form and specify the variables in first differences. This allows us (1) to work with stationary variables and, thus, ignore co-integration issues; and (2) to interpret the dependent variables in the VAR models as growth rates. To sum up, in all this process, we follow the standard procedure in the literature.

The specification of the estimated models (the one for Spain, but also the seventeen regional models presented in the following section) follows several criteria. First, the inclusion of deterministic components, such as constant and trend is considered in the case that these are statistically significant. Second, the number of lags is chosen according to the significance of the coefficient attached to those lags in the equation where public capital is the dependent variable.

Regarding the specification of the aggregate VAR model, following these criteria and the Bayesian Information Criterion (BIC), we chose a first-order model with constant and trend, whose estimated coefficients are shown in Table 9.2.

9.4.3 Impulse–Response Functions

In order to assess the economic impact of the public capital stock, we use the IRFs associated to the estimated VAR models. The order in which the variables are considered is important, as this influences the results. Accordingly, we assume that, at the aggregate level, the government does not have contemporary information regarding the evolution of the rest of the economic variables, which is equivalent to assume that changes in these variables (GDP, employment and private capital) do not affect public investment contemporaneously. In other words, public capital reacts with a delay of 1 year to changes in the rest of the variables. This implies that the order of the variables is headed by public capital and, as a consequence, we are considering a case in which changes in public capital affect the rest of the variables contemporaneously (while the inverse is not true). The reason for this assumption is twofold. First, it seems reasonable to assume that the government is not able to adjust its decisions on public investment in response to changes in the GDP, employment and private investment before a year has elapsed. This is a plausible assumption because of the delay in gathering the information on the evolution of the economic variables, and also because of the time it takes for the economic policy decisions (definition and execution of the budgets, for example) to be implemented. Second, it also seems reasonable to assume that GDP, employment and private capital will be immediately influenced by changes in public capital stock. For example, a rise in public investment enhances the hiring of workers and increases output in the short-term.

The same assumptions and justification apply to the regional models, where there is an extra decision to be taken. In particular, given that most of the decisions concerning public investment are actually taken by the central government, we assume that the order is headed by the public capital located in the rest of the country, followed by the regional public capital. This is justified by the fact that the percentage of public capital located in any of the regions is relatively small compared with the public capital located in the rest of the country. Therefore, in the regional analysis, we work with the hypothesis that the central government does not react to changes in any of the regional variables contemporaneously (that is, before a year has elapsed), while all regional variables react contemporaneously to changes in public capital investment taking place in the rest of the country. Overall, these identification assumptions allow us to define a benchmark case where there is no contemporary relation between the regional and the extra-regional components of public capital.

Next step is the estimation of the IRFs, whose trajectory is plotted in Figs. 9.2–9.4. These figures show the accumulated impact and the yearly evolution of GDP, employment and private capital in response to a one-off shock in public capital.

Figure 9.2 plots the GDP performance, which initially responds positively and intensely, and subsequently reduces its sensitivity until it stabilises as from the eighth period. As Fig. 9.2 illustrate, the accumulated GDP effect after 20 years is positive and statistically significant, while just the first and second annual responses are statistically different from zero.

The effects on employment follow the same pattern although taking substantially lower values (see Fig. 9.3). In this case, the accumulated effects after 20 years are not statistically different from zero (taking into account one standard error bands), while, similarly to the GDP case, the first and second annual responses are statistically different from zero.

Regarding the private capital stock, the reaction is much slower and less intense than in the previous cases (see Fig. 9.4). Thus, none of the annual impacts and neither the cumulative effect are statistically different from zero. In other words, the evolution of private capital is not sensitive to temporary shocks in public capital.

a Accumulated Responses

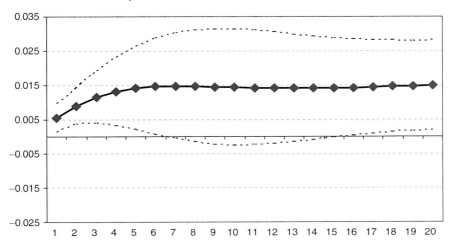

b Non-accumulated Responses

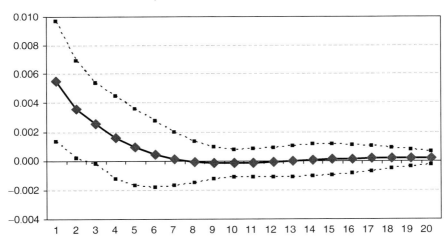

Fig. 9.2 GDP impulse–response functions to a one-off shock in public capital stock (the bands at both sides of the IRF correspond to one S.E.)

When evaluating the IRFs, so as to compute the corresponding long-term responses or elasticities, it is crucial to determine the significance of the effects. The long-term is determined by the time horizon at the end of which the effects of the shock vanish, which occurs when the IRFs converge to zero. For example, in the GDP case, this occurs in the eighth period. However, we consider a horizon of twenty periods in order to be more precise in the computation of all elasticities. Recall, also, that the long-term elasticity provides the percentage of variation of a

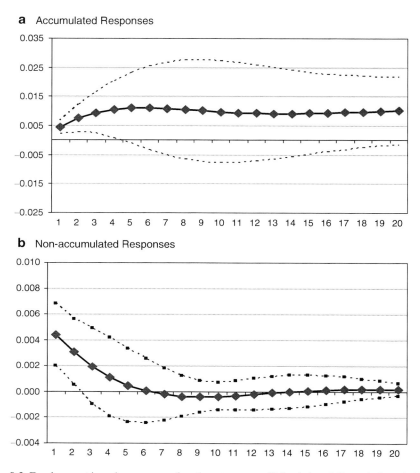

Fig. 9.3 Employment impulse–response functions to a one-off shock in public capital stock (the bands at both sides of the IRF correspond to one S.E.)

variable in response to an increase of 1% in the public capital stock. Through the VAR model approach, this response includes all feedback effects.

To determine how significant the responses are, we rely on the error bands. Traditionally, these bands were determined by adding and subtracting twice the standard error of each response, which established a confidence interval of 95%. However, since Sims and Zha (1999), the standard practise in the VAR literature is the establishment of error bands which add and subtract just one standard error, which yields confidence intervals of 68%. The underlying justification is the greater likelihood provided by these intervals as regards the evaluation of the results. Therefore, following Sims and Zha (1999), in next section we take as statistically significant responses those based on one standard error bands.

a Accumulated Responses

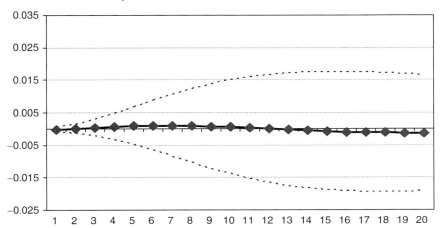

b Non-accumulated Responses

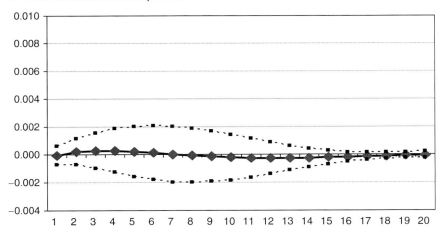

Fig. 9.4 Private capital impulse–response functions to a one-off shock in public capital stock (the bands at both sides of the IRF correspond to one S.E.)

9.5 Results

Next, we present the empirical results obtained for Spain as a whole, which are followed by a detailed regional analysis based on the estimation of 17 VAR models corresponding to the Spanish Autonomous Communities.

9.5.1 Aggregate Results

Table 9.3 provides the values resulting from accumulating the GDP, employment and private capital responses (shown in Figs. 9.2, 9.3 and 9.4) to a one-off shock on public capital stock. Plain addition of the GDP responses yield an elasticity of 0.408. In turn, when only the statistically significant yearly responses are added up, this elasticity is reduced to 0.291. Regarding employment, the computed elasticity is extremely robust to the method used, as it takes values respectively of 0.247 and 0.241. However, in the first case, the accumulated effect is not statistically different from zero. Finally, the private capital elasticity is slightly negative in the first case (and as before not statistically different from zero), whereas it is virtually null in the second case. This leads us to the conclusion that there are no significant effects on private investment and, therefore, there is no significant crowding-out of public investment on private investment.

Comparing these results with existing estimations in the literature is not an easy task. First, due to the variety of econometric techniques used in the computation of the elasticities. Second, due to the definition of fundamental concepts, such as elasticity, which does not always coincide. Despite the difficulty involved in making comparisons, there is a range of values providing what appears to be a reasonable order of magnitude. Regarding the GDP elasticity with respect to public capital stock in Spain, De la Fuente (1996) places this range between 0.19 and 0.71 and thus, our calculation fits perfectly into this interval. In this context, recall that in Roca-Sagalés and Sala (2006) this value is placed at 0.26, somewhat lower than the 0.29 resulting from this update.[3] In addition, the positive effects of public infrastructures on employment are consistent with the evidence provided by Demetriades and Mamuneas (2000) for a group of OECD countries, by Aschauer (2001) for the U.S. and by Pereira and Roca-Sagalés (2001) and Roca-Sagalés and Sala (2006) for Spain. Finally, the absence of the crowding-out effect is difficult to interpret to the extent that the evidence available for the Spanish case is mixed. Furthermore, the aggregate result in our case conceals substantial regional disparities. These disparities are the subject of analysis in the following section.

Table 9.3 Aggregate elasticities. Comparison of results

Spain	Cumulated responses up to $t=20$	Significant cumulated responses
GDP	0.408*	0.291*
Employment	0.247	0.241*
Private capital	−0.035	−0.002*

*Indicates that 0 is not within the one standard error bands

---

[3] Recall that this update not only extends the sample size from 1998 to 2004, but also that data is obtained from different databases (in the case of employment) or incorporates substantial methodological changes (in the case of capital stock).

9.5.2 Results by Autonomous Community

Next, we estimate VAR models for each one of the 17 Autonomous Communities. These include the same four endogenous variables than the aggregate model: output (GDP), employment, private and public capital stock as variables, with the particularity that public capital stock is divided in two components. One corresponds to the public capital located in the region itself, and the other one to the public capital located elsewhere in the country. The specification of the regional VAR models follows the one selected for the aggregate model, and we thus run first-order models with constant and trend in all cases.

Column (1) in Table 9.4 shows the GDP impact of public capital on output, which is diverse across Autonomous Communities. By itself, of course, this diversity is not especially relevant. However, it uncovers a specific regional pattern related to the regional endowment of public capital stock. This pattern allows us to classify the Autonomous Communities in three groups according to the intensity of the public capital economic impact.

The first group includes the Autonomous Communities with a high elasticity and, therefore, a relatively high impact of public investment on economic growth. These elasticities range from 0.48 in the Community of Valencia to 0.89 in the Basque Country, while it stands at 0.57 in the Community of Madrid, 0.59 in the Balearic Islands and 0.75 in Catalonia. It should be noted that, with the exception of the Basque Country, these Autonomous Communities compose the group with the lowest endowment of public capital relative to their economic activity. The second group includes the regions were the impact of new public investment is virtually null. This includes the Autonomous Communities with a zero elasticity (Andalusia, Aragon, the Canary Islands and Extremadura) or negative, but very close to zero elasticities (Cantabria with -0.07; Navarre with -0.08; and Rioja with -0.04). Finally, the third group includes Asturias, Galicia and Murcia where these elasticities are clearly negative. In Asturias and Galicia, these negative effects could be associated to the structural crisis which has dragged these Autonomous Communities down for decades. Even in the recent booming years (from 1995 to 2004 in our sample period), they have not benefited as much as the rest of Spain. Although with differences, the employment elasticity with regard to public capital stock – in column (3) – displays a similar pattern in which the Autonomous Communities of the first group are the most sensitive, while those with public capital over-endowment have again a value close to zero.

Our analysis does not allow the establishment of threshold values from which additional public investment would yield extra profits. However, it is possible to identify a negative correlation across regions between the economic impact of public capital and the relative degree of public capital endowment. This correlation is shown in Fig. 9.5, where the dotted lines indicate the average situation of Spain. Note that the most responsive group to public investment is the one in the upper right-hand box, while the group with virtually null effects appears in the bottom left-hand box.

Table 9.4 Aggregate and regional elasticities of output, employment and private capital with respect to public capital*

	GDP elasticity with respect to		Employment elasticity with respect to		Private capital elasticity with respect to	
	Public capital in the region (1)	Public capital in the rest of the country (2)	Public capital in the region (3)	Public capital in the rest of the country (4)	Public capital in the region (5)	Public capital in the rest of the country (6)
Spain	0.291		0.241		−0.002	
1. Andalusia	0	0.234	0.096	0	0.006	0
2. Aragon	0	0.153	0.094	0.517	0.087	0
3. Asturias	−1.436	0	−1.659	0.236	0	0
4. Balearic Islands	0.594	0.175	−1.399	0	2.330	0
5. Canary Islands	0	0	0	0.543	0	0.122
6. Cantabria	−0.068	0	−0.536	0.272	−0.744	0
7. Castile-León	0	0.235	−0.533	0.180	−0.870	−0.032
8. Castile–La Mancha	0.281	0	0.196	0.302	0	0.585
9. Catalonia	0.747	0.101	0.649	0	0.845	0
10. C. of Valencia	0.478	0	0	0.195	1.243	0.052
11. Extremadura	0	−0.402	0	0.356	0	−0.562
12. Galicia	−0.997	0.314	−0.535	0.199	0	−0.137
13. C. of Madrid	0.568	0.182	0.544	0.607	0.582	0.347
14. Murcia	−0.879	0.378	−0.410	0.666	−0.749	0.064
15. Navarre	−0.081	0	−0.057	0.195	0	0
16. Basque Country	0.887	0.346	0.960	0.610	3.770	0
17. Rioja	−0.040	0.174	0.111	0.601	−0.012	0

*Indicates that 0 is not within the one standard error bands

9 Public Capital Effects and Regional Spillover in Spain

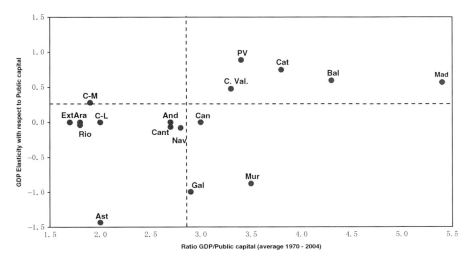

Fig. 9.5 GDP elasticity with respect to public capital vs. ratio GDP/Public capital

Regarding the crowding-out effect, the aggregate elasticity of private capital with respect to the public capital stock is almost zero. This implies the absence of private investment substitution by public investment, which is in line with part of the literature. And only with part of it, because the literature in this area is far from achieving a consensus on the magnitude of the crowding-out effect. For example, studies such as Aschauer (1989), Argimón et al. (1997) and Pereira (2001), to name some, find a positive relation between public capital stock and private capital stock. On the contrary, Pradhan et al. (1990), Ghali (1998) and Voss (2002), to name some other ones with the opposite view, deny that this complementariness occurs. In the specific case of Spain, there is evidence in favour provided by Flores de Frutos et al. (1998), Pereira and Roca-Sagalés (2001), Roca-Sagalés and Sala (2006) and Martínez López (2006).

What matters from the point of view of our analysis is that this aggregate elasticity is a black box concealing a diversity of regional situations. Column (5) in Table 9.4 displays the corresponding elasticities and reflects a wide heterogeneity in the regional magnitude of the crowding-out effect. This diversity, which is along the lines of the results shown by Roca-Sagalés and Sala (2006), reveals also a regional pattern in which the size of these elasticities is related to the relative endowment of public capital stock. Indeed, in the Autonomous Communities with public capital stock under-endowment, in particular, the Balearic Islands, the Community of Valencia, Catalonia and the Community of Madrid, which follow the Basque Country, public and private capital stock complementarities are very important. On the contrary, there is no sign of a significant impact of public on private capital stock in Andalusia, Aragon, Asturias, the Canary Islands, Castile-La Mancha, Extremadura, Galicia, Navarre and even Rioja. And it turns out that the majority of these Autonomous Communities are relatively oversupplied in terms of public capital. Finally, a significant crowding-out effect of public investment over private investment is identified in Castile-Leon (−0.87), Murcia (−0.75) and Cantabria (−0.74).

Concerning the economic incidence of the spillover effects resulting from public investment, our results uncover their positive incidence on output and employment of economically interrelated regions. It is thus clear that the expected benefit of public investment is not restricted to the area where this is undertaken: it further acts as an economic catalyser in other interrelated areas. It should be stressed that this link does not necessarily involve geographical proximity, what matters is the economic relationships across regions. In columns 2, 4 and 6 of Table 9.4, it can be seen in more detail that this conclusion is valid for all Autonomous Communities except for Extremadura.

In this context, it is important to point out that our results are in consonance with the literature that has recently dealt with this question for the Spanish case (Pereira and Roca-Sagalés 2001; Avilés et al. 2003; Cantos et al., 2005; Martínez López, 2006; Roca-Sagalés and Sala, 2006). These papers argue that the economic impact of public capital can only be precisely evaluated when the spillover effects are taken into account. In this regard, the contribution of our analysis goes beyond this confirmation and highlights two important facts. First, the incidence of investment in public capital in a particular region benefits all the Autonomous Communities. This takes place through various channels (employment, output and/or private investment) by which the spillover effects spread through to other regions the positive impact of public capital. Second, the crucial link between these regions does not need to be geographical, what is relevant is their economic connection. Third, the overall impact of public capital is negatively correlated with the relative endowment of public capital in each particular region.

9.6 Conclusions

This chapter has showed that public capital stock is an important determinant of both regional economic growth and the performance of the labour market at a regional level. This is so through the direct influence of public investment in any region itself, and through the indirect impact stemming from the resulting spillover effects in economically interrelated regions. In short, a comprehensive assessment of the total economic impact of public investment can only be achieved if both its direct and indirect effects (spillovers) are evaluated.

Concerning specifically the direct effects of public capital stock, we have identified a substantial degree of regional heterogeneity. Within this heterogeneity, our research uncovered a clear regional pattern according to which the direct effects in terms of output, employment and private capital stock exhibit a strong correlation with the regional endowment of public capital. Therefore, we have identified a relationship where the Autonomous Communities with relative public capital under-endowment are more sensitive to the output and employment effects of public investment. Moreover, in these Autonomous Communities, there is a greater complementarity between public and private capital stock. In contrast, in those communities with public capital stock over-endowment either this relationship does not hold or, in some particular cases, it is negative.

Regarding the indirect or spillover effects of the infrastructures, we find them relevant in all Autonomous Communities. Furthermore, they do not seem to be especially sensitive to the geographical situation of the region, nor to the relative regional endowment of public capital stock.

One of the conclusions stemming from these results is that public investment is not equally efficient in all Autonomous Communities. Rather, it is clearly more productive in regions where public capital relative to GDP, employment and private capital is lower. That is, from an efficient point of view, congestion of public infrastructures calls for further public investment.

Our results confer this research area a renewed interest in several dimensions. First of all, determination of the optimum location of public investment projects seems to be a crucial issue. However, our research does not provide an unambiguous response to this matter. Although we have documented a greater impact of the public capital direct effects in regions with congested infrastructures, our analysis is not enough to enlighten the location where the spillover effects originate and, therefore, to identify in which regions further public investment would have a greater impact. We have evaluated the Autonomous Communities which benefit from the spillover effects, but not those that generate these effects nor the extent to which they do so. As a consequence, further research ventures should focus on the generation of the spillover effects and contribute to answer the following important question: Which regions are able to boost macroeconomic activity to a greater extent in their economically interrelated regions? Apart from being interesting in itself, the answer to this question would contribute to improve the allocation of public resources to investment in infrastructures.

References

Argimón, I., González-Páramo, J. M., & Roldán, J. M. (1997). Evidence of public spending crowding-out from a panel of OECD countries. *Applied Economics, 29*, 1001–1010.
Arrow, K. J. (1962). The economic implications of learning by doing. *Review of Economic Studies, 29*, 155–173.
Aschauer, D. (1989). Is public expenditure productive? *Journal of Monetary Economics, 23*, 177–200.
Aschauer, D. (2000). Public capital and economic growth: issues of quantity, finance and efficiency. *Economic Development and Cultural Change, 3*, 391–406.
Aschauer, D. (2001). Output and employment effects of public capital. *Public Finance and Management, 1*(2), 135–160.
Avilés, A., Gómez, R., & Sánchez, J. (2003). Capital pública, actividad económica privada y efectos desbordamiento: Un análisis por Comunidades Autónomas de los sectores Industria y Construcción en España. *Hacienda Pública Española/ Revista de Economía Pública, 165*, 25–51.

Barro, R. (1990). Government spending in a simple model of endogenous growth. *Journal of Political Economy, 98*, 103–125.

Boarnet, M. G. (1998). Spillovers and the locational effects of public infrastructure. *Journal of Regional Science, 38*(3), 381–400.

Boscá, J. E., Escribá, J., & Murgui, M. (2002). The effects of public infrastructres on the private productive sector of Spanish regions. *Journal of Regional Science, 42*(2), 301–326.

Cantos, P., Gumbau, M., & Maudós, J. (2005). Transport infrastructures, spillover effects and regional growth: Evidence of the Spanish case. *Transport Reviews, 25*(1), 25–50.

Chandra, A., & Thompson, E. (2000). Does public infrastructure affect economic activity? Evidence from the rural interstate highway system. *Regional Science and Urban Economics, 30*, 457–90.

De la Fuente A. (1996). Infraestructuras y Productividad: Un Panorama de la Evidencia Empírica. *Información Comercial Española, 757*, 25–40.

Demetriades, P. O., & Mamuneas, T. F. (2000). Intertemporal output and employment effects of public infrastructure capital: Evidence from 12 OECD economies. *Economic Journal, 110*, 687–712.

Fernández, M., & Montuenga, V. (2003). The effects of public capital on the Spanish productivity growth. *Contemporary Economic Policy, 21*(3), 383–393.

Flores de Frutos, R., Gracia-Díez, M., & Pérez-Amaral, T. (1998). Public capital stock and economic growth: an analysis of the Spanish economy. *Applied Economics, 30*, 985–994.

Ghali, K. H. (1998). Public investment and private capital formation in a vector error-correction model of growth. *Applied Economics, 30*, 837–844.

Lynde, C., & Richmond, J. (1993). Public capital and total factor productivity. *International Economic Review, 34*, 401–414.

Kamps, C. (2005). The dynamic effects of public capital: VAR evidence for 22 OECD countries. *International Tax and Public Finance, 12*, 533–558.

Kelejian, H. H., & Robinson, D. P. (1997). Infrastructure productivity estimation and its underlying econometric specifications: A sensitivity analysis. *Papers in Regional Science, 76*, 115–131.

Mankiw, G., Romer, D., & Weil, D. (1992). A contribution to the empirics of economic growth. *Quarterly Journal of Economics, 107*, 407–437.

Martínez López, D. (2006). Linking public investment to private investment. The case of Spanish regions. *International Review of Applied Economics, 20*(4), 411–423.

Mas, M., Maudos, J., Pérez, F., & Uriel, E. (1996). Infrastructures and productivity in the Spanish regions. *Regional Studies, 30*(7), 641–649.

Mas, M., Pérez, F., & Uriel, E. (2007). *El stock de capital y los servicios del capital en España y su distribución territorial (1964–2005)*. Bilbao: Fundación BBVA.

Moreno, R., Artís, M., López-Bazo, E., & Suriñach, J. (1997). Evidence on the complex link between infrastructure and regional growth. *International Journal of Development Planning Literature, 12*(1–2), 81–108.

Moreno, R., & López-Bazo, E. (2007). Returns to local and transport infrastructure under regional spillovers. *International Regional Science Review, 30*(1), 47–71.

Pereira, A. (2000). Is all public capital created equal? *Review of Economics and Statistics, 82*, 513–518.

Pereira, A. (2001). Public capital formation and private investment: What crowds in what? *Public Finance Review, 29*, 3–25.

Pereira, A. M., & Flores, R. (1999). Public capital and private-sector performance in the United States. *Journal of Urban Economics, 46*, 300–322.

Pereira, A. M., & Roca-Sagalés, O. (1999). Public capital formation and regional development in Spain. *Review of Development Economics, 3*(3), 281–294.

Pereira, A. M., & Roca-Sagalés, O. (2001). Infrastructures and private sector performance in Spain. *Journal of Policy Modelling, 23*, 371–384.

Pereira, A. M., & Roca-Sagalés, O. (2003). Spillover effects of public capital formation: evidence from the Spanish regions. *Journal of Urban Economics, 53*, 238–256.

Pradhan, I., Ratha, D. K., & Sarma, A. (1990). Complementary between public and private investment in India. *Journal of Development Economics, 33*(1), 101–116.

Raurich, X., & Sala, H. (2006). L'impacte econòmic de la inversió pública a Catalunya: una aproximació desagregada. *Nota d'Economia, 83*(84), 9–29.

Raurich, X., Sala, H., & Sorolla, V. (2009). Labour market effects of public capital stock: Evidence for the spanish private sector. *International Review of Applied Economics, 23*(1), 1–18.

Roca-Sagalés, O., & Sala, H. (2006). Efectos desbordamiento de la inversión en infraestructuras en las regiones españolas. *Investigaciones Regionales, 8*, 143–161.

Romer, P. (1986). Increasing returns and long run growth. *Journal of Political Economy, 94*, 1002–1037.

Romer, P. (1990). Endogenous technological change. *Journal of Political Economy, 98*, S71–S102.

Sims, C. A., & Zha, T. (1999). Error bands for impulse responses. *Econometrica, 67*(5), 1113–1155.

Solow, R. (1956). A contribution to the theory of economic growth. *Quarterly Journal of Economics, 70*(1), 65–94.

Voss, G. M. (2002). Public and private investment in the United States and Canada. *Economic Modelling, 19*, 641–664.

Chapter 10
Supply and Use of Human Capital in the Spanish Regions

José Manuel Pastor, Josep Lluis Raymond, José Luis Roig, and Lorenzo Serrano

10.1 Introduction

Besides enrichment at personal level entailed by the increase in the cognitive and intellectual levels of the person associated with education, a large number of studies have verified the greater the human capital of a person, the greater is his employability, his participation in the labour market, his functional and geographical mobility and, thereby, his productivity. This results in higher wages and less likelihood of unemployment for individuals with more schooling. From the social point of view, the accumulation of resources associated to higher educational attainment levels permits societies to make sustained progress towards higher levels of welfare. It makes possible to adapt to globalised environments, which are progressively changing and specialise more rapidly and less traumatically in the more productive sectors. The industries which grow faster and create more added value are precisely the most intensive as regards human capital.

In recent decades, Spanish society has undergone substantial transformations. Attention is usually drawn to the important political and economic transformations. However, we must not forget other areas where Spanish society has made important progress, such as the improvements in education. It is true that this progress is the direct consequence of the economic and social progress of the country, but it is also true that the improvements in education has been one of the factors which has promoted this social and economic progress.

Naturally, to a large extent, these improvements are the combined result of the decisions of the families and the efforts made by them in this area. However, the education policies laid down throughout recent decades by the national and regional governments in this area have also been decisive.

L. Serrano (✉)
Universitat de Valencia, Departament D'analisi Econòmica, Edifici Departamental Oriental, Campus dels Tarongers, Avda. dels Tarongers s/n 46022 - Valencia, España
e-mail: lorenzo.serrano@uv.es

The accumulation of human capital and its progressively more extended use are among the basic features of the recent evolution of Spain. Likewise, they are among the key factors of the development of its regions and the inequalities that continue to subsist between them.

Our objective is to go over the achievements of Spanish society as regards improvements in the per capita endowments of human capital (Sect. 2), the degree of use of this potential human capital in the productive process (Sect. 3) and the returns obtained from human capital, which is finally used (Sect. 4). To achieve this, we will analyse the evolution of Spain and its regions during the 1977–2007 period.

10.2 Human Capital in Spain and Its Regions

Before beginning the presentation of the results obtained, it is pertinent to examine the concept of human capital. Any empirical analysis of human capital is a particularly complex task due to the difficulty involved in measuring it adequately. The concept of human capital includes aspects, such as the education received, work experience and the mental and physical ability. The difficulty involved in quantifying these aspects is evident: it would be necessary to evaluate not only the knowledge acquired by each person and his capacity to apply this knowledge, but also the capacity to acquire and apply new knowledge in the future. This should be calculated as it constitutes the whole of the resources a person has, and resources which condition his present and future productivity.

The estimation of human capital through educational data is the usual option and, in addition, in some cases, this is the only possible option. Since the objective of education is to provide knowledge, it is reasonable to suppose that higher levels of education will provide more knowledge and, therefore, more human capital. Moreover, the educational process does not only provide more specific knowledge, but it also facilitates subsequent learning and the generation and absorption of future knowledge once the person leaves the educational system. This also entails more human capital.

For the reasons explained, it should not be surprising that almost all the measurements made of the aggregate supply of human capital of an economy are based, to a greater or lesser extent, on educational data. A synthetic indicator of per capita human capital normally used in the literature is the average number of years of schooling. This is also the basic indicator, which we will apply in the subsequent analyses. To do so, we will use the data on educational attainment and the years of schooling completed provided with territorial disaggregation by the Series of Human capital of the Fundación Bancaja IVIE (2008).

Figure 10.1 presents the synthetic indicator of average years of schooling of the population for the 1977–2007 period, calculated by distinguishing between the population at working age, active, unemployed and employed. As can be seen, the improvements in education of the Spanish population over the last three decades

10 Supply and Use of Human Capital in the Spanish Regions 213

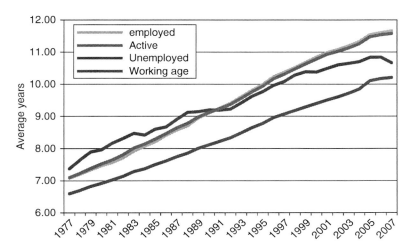

Fig. 10.1 Average years of schooling. Spain 1997–2007
Source: Fundación Bancaja-Ivie (2008)

have been substantial as regards all the groups. The years of education of the population at working age has increased by 3.6 years, those of the active and employed population by approximately 4.5 years and those of the unemployed population by 3.3 years. Of the four groups taken into consideration, those employed are the ones with more human capital (11.7 years of study in 2007), as compared with those active (11.6), the unemployed (10.7) and the group at working age (10.2).

The greater human capital of the active population as compared to the population at working age reflects the fact that the readiness of persons to participate in the job market is greater when human capital is greater. Likewise, the fact that the average years of schooling of the employed population is higher than the unemployed population reflects that the higher the human capital, the higher is the employability and, therefore, the higher the probability to be employed.[1]

However, the growth of a synthetic indicator, such as the average years of schooling of the population is the result of the variations in the composition of this group. Specifically, the increases in the average years of study is due to a relative increase in the number of persons with higher educational levels and the relative reduction of the persons with lower educational levels. Figure 10.2 represents the composition by educational attainment levels of the working age population and we can observe a continual reduction in the percentage of persons with primary studies and the important progress made by persons with intermediate studies and especially by those with higher (university) studies.

Specifically, we should point out the substantial growth in the percentage of people with university degree, which has multiplied by 3.3, and has gone from 3.7% in 1977 to 15.9% in 2007. In addition, the participation of the group with

---
[1] See Pastor et al. (2007).

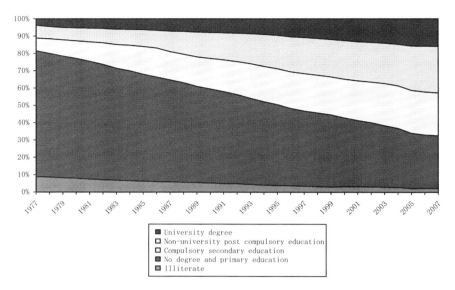

Fig. 10.2 Percentage of the population by educational levels. Population at working age, Spain
Source: Fundación Bancaja-Ivie

non-university post-compulsory education studies in 2007 is 2.6 times the figure for 1977. Thus, in 1977, only 7.4% of the working age population held non-university post-compulsory degree whereas in 2007, these accounted for 26.7%. Moreover, it can be seen that there is considerable growth in the number of persons who have completed compulsory secondary education, which had increased 2.4 times (from 7.3% to 24.8%).

Behind this aggregated evolution of the whole of Spain, there are very particular situations in each of the Spanish regions. In order to make an in-depth regional analysis, we will look at Spanish regions, both as regards human capital endowments and their evolution.

Table 10.1 offers the information regarding the average years of study of the population at working age in the regions. As can be seen, growth is the basic feature. The supply of human capital per capita increases in all the regions throughout the period. This was already happening before Spain entered the EU in 1986 and this trend was maintained in the following years.

In terms of differences, the first conclusion is that the endowments of human capital per capita are very dissimilar among regions. In 2007, between the region with more human capital per capita (Madrid) and the one with the lowest human capital (Ceuta), there is a difference of 2.3 years of schooling, with a variation range of 25.3%. The average years of study in Spain of the population at working age are 10.2. Madrid, the Basque Country and Navarre are the regions with higher levels of human capital (11.2, 11 and 10.9 average years of study respectively). However, Ceuta, Castile-La Mancha and Extremadura are the regions whose resident populations have less years of study (9.0, 9.4 and 9.5 years respectively).

Table 10.1 Average years of education. Population at working age

	1977	1986	1996	2007
Andalusia	5.81	6.89	8.37	9.69
Aragon	6.65	7.72	9.04	10.32
Asturias	6.95	7.85	8.94	10.02
Balearic Islands	6.38	7.49	9.01	10.04
Canary Islands	6.29	7.43	8.73	9.73
Cantabria	7.08	8.05	9.32	10.38
Castile – Leon	6.71	7.65	8.87	9.95
Castile – La Mancha	5.76	6.84	8.01	9.42
Catalonia	6.86	7.92	9.35	10.22
Community of Valencia	6.42	7.43	8.82	10.29
Extremadura	5.78	6.55	7.85	9.51
Galicia	6.33	7.22	8.50	9.85
Madrid	7.68	8.71	9.91	11.28
Murcia	6.18	7.05	8.73	9.88
Navarre	7.37	8.08	9.58	10.87
Basque Country	7.21	8.40	9.73	10.97
La Rioja	6.66	7.67	8.81	10.27
Ceuta	n.a	n.a	8.67	9.00
Melilla	n.a	n.a	9.19	9.65
Spain	6.60	7.61	8.96	10.21
Coefficient of Variation	0.085	0.075	0.060	0.055
Relative range of variation	1.332	1.330	1.263	1.253

Source: Fundación Bancaja-Ivie (2008) and own elaboration

If this situation is compared with the supply in 1977, it can be seen that the territorial pattern is similar. In 1977, Madrid, Navarre and the Basque Country were the regions with more human capital per capita (7.7, 7.4 and 7.1 average years of study respectively). However, Castile-La Mancha and Extremadura had the lowest supplies (5.8 years in both cases).

It should be pointed out that this territorial pattern means that the wealthier regions are those which have higher levels of per capita human capital, while in the less developed areas, the endowments of human capital are lower. Therefore, this involves a situation, which will contribute to inequalities in productivity and per capita income. In 2007, the regional coefficient of correlation between average years of schooling and per capita GDP is 0.821.

In short, in recent decades there has been substantial progress in educational attainment in Spain, but substantial regional differences remain. The next step in the analysis is to ask whether the tendency in the educational attainment levels has resulted in an approximation among regions or whether the regional differences in human capital have increased. In order to achieve this, we will use the traditional instruments of σ-convergence and β-convergence in order to analyse the convergence in human capital in the Spanish regions.

Figure 10.3 shows the evolution of the coefficient of the variation of the average years of study of the population at working age in the Spanish regions. The interpretation of this indicator is very simple. For example, a situation in which

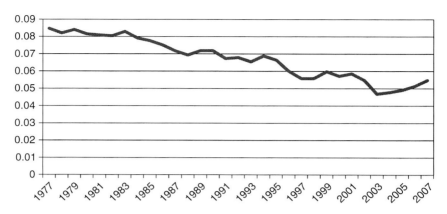

Fig. 10.3 σ-convergence in human capital. Spanish Regions
Source: Fundación Bancaja-Ivie (2008) and own elaboration

half the regions have 50% more human capital than the average for Spain and the other half 50% less than the average would generate a variation coefficient of 0.5. A higher figure would, naturally, reflect a higher level of inequality.

After a period of relative stability of the variation coefficient, which ended at the beginning of the 1980s, it can be seen that there was a prolonged reduction of inequality. In recent years, however, the variation coefficient has risen slightly. The inequality at the beginning of the period stood at approximately 8.5% and fell to 5.5% at the end of the period. Consequently, it is clear that there is a reduction in inequality in human capital between the Spanish regions, in other words, σ-convergence in per capita human capital.

This gradual reduction of inequalities between regions is due to an increase of the educational levels of the regions with less human capital with respect to those with higher endowments. This situation, in which the regions that grow most are those that start with lower initial levels is known as β-convergence. Figure 10.4 shows the initial values of the logarithm of the average years of study in the initial year 1977 as regards the rate of annual growth between 1977 and 2007. As can be seen, there is a clearly negative and statistically significant relation between the initial levels of average years of study of the regions and the growth in the years of study in each region, therefore, there is β-convergence in per capita human capital in the Spanish regions. That is, to say, the regions with lower levels of education (Castile La Mancha, Extremadura and Andalusia) are those that have grown in the period under analysis with annual rates of 1.65%, 1.67% and 1.7% respectively. On the contrary, Madrid, the Community with more years of study, had a lower rate of growth (1.28%).

This behaviour should have contributed to the reduction of regional inequality as regards levels of income. With more similar endowments of per capita human capital, the regional levels of labour productivity (and per capita income also) would tend to converge ceteris paribus.

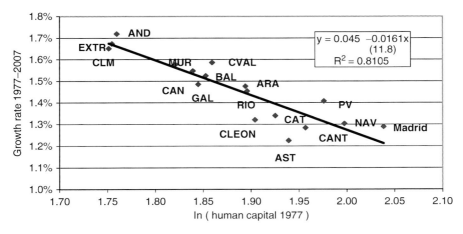

Fig. 10.4 β-convergence in human capital. Spanish regions. Growth rate 1997–2000
Source: Fundación Bancaja-Ivie (2008) and own elaboration

10.3 Degree of Use of Human Capital

The human capital available in a territory is one of the basic sources of its development. However, if its benefits are to materialise, it is necessary to use this human capital properly and there is nothing to guarantee this. Firstly, human capital needs to be used. But, secondly, it should be used efficiently. In this section, we will deal with the first question, and will leave the analysis of the second question for the next section.

Evidently, if human capital is not used, it cannot contribute to the production of goods and services. This may happen due to two reasons. In the first place, the persons at working age in a region can decide not to participate in the labour market, remaining outside the active population. In the second place, part of the people who offer their human capital in the job market might not find jobs and become part of the unemployed population.

Thus, only a part of the potential human capital of a region, one that corresponds to the employed population, ends up contributing to the production of that territory.

The equivalence with the usual statistics of the labour market is immediate. The regions have a potential human capital, that of their populations at working age. However, only a part is supplied to the labour market, that of the active population. Finally, only a part of this is used in the productive process, the human capital of the employed population.

By analogy with the labour market indicators, it is possible to elaborate several indicators of the degree of use of the human capital. In the first place, we define the rate of activity of human capital as a ratio of schooling years of the active population to the schooling years of the working age population. This indicator measures the part of the potential human capital, which reaches the labour market.

In the second place, the rate of unemployment of human capital is a quotient of the years of study of the unemployed population and the years of study of the active population. This indicator shows us the part of the human capital supplied to the labour market, which is not employed.

Finally, there is the rate of employment of human capital as a quotient between the years of study of the employed populations and the years of study of the population at working age. This indicator is the result of the previous two and informs us about the share of the potential human capital of a territory, which is used in the production of goods and services.

Figure 10.5 shows the evolution of these indicators for the whole of Spain throughout the 1977–2007 period. At the beginning of the period, only 53% of the potential human capital was used due to the fact that only 56% of this capital was supplied to the labour market and 5% of this 56% remained unemployed. The data shows a progressive deterioration in the capacity of the Spanish economy to use its human capital until mid-1980s. In 1986, when Spain entered the European Union, the rate of employment of human capital amounted to 43%, ten points less than 10 years previously. The main reason lays in the high rate of unemployment of human capital which grew to 21% as the rate of activity of human capital continued to be approximately 55% throughout the whole period. From this time onwards, there was a considerable increase in the level of use of human capital in Spain, which was only reduced during the economic crisis of the 1990s. After this pause, the improvement process accelerated. The result was that, in 2007, Spain used 62% of its potential human capital, a rate of employment, which entailed the maximum of the period under consideration. This favourable evolution was due to a substantial fall in the rate of unemployment of human capital. It was only 7% in 2007, when it had reached

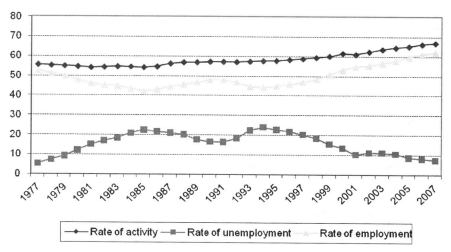

Fig. 10.5 Degree of use of human capital in Spain (%)
Source: Fundación Bancaja-Ivie (2008) and own elaboration

24% in the middle of the 1990s. In addition, the rate of activity of the human capital grew to its historical maximum to reach 67% in 2007, 11% points more than in 1977.

In short, after Spain entered the European Union, and especially since the middle of the 1990s, Spain not only increased its supply of human capital, but was able to use this factor to a greater extent. This contributed to boosting sustained economic growth as well as being facilitated by this growth, which generated a very positive virtuous circle for the development of the country.

The degree of use of human capital in the Spanish regions is an essential component for the analysis of this productive factor as a source of territorial inequality or as a convergence engine. In the previous section, we have seen the significant differences between regions as regards the supply of human capital. The regions with less human capital could use their lower potential human capital to a greater extent than the rest. In this case, the unequal supply of per capita human capital would be compensated by the varying degree of use. Of course, the contrary may occur, in which case, the territorial inequalities would be exacerbated. Therefore, it would be advisable to analyse the current situation and the evolution of the Spanish regions in this area in detail. The period under consideration will be 1977–2007 with special attention paid to periods which, as we have seen in the previous graph, mark different phases as regards the use of human capital. These periods include 1986, which coincided with the accession of Spain to the European Union, and 1996, which coincided with a change in economic policy in order to qualify to join the euro and when a phase of sustained growth began that continued up to a short time ago.

Table 10.2 shows the rates of activity of human capital of the Spanish regions. Except for scarce and insignificant exceptions, the Spanish regions have continued to evolve in a similar way to the nation as a whole: Slight drops between 1977 and 1986, followed by subsequent growth which became more intense as from 1996. Furthermore, the data show the existence of substantial differences between the Spanish regions. Thus, in 2007, the rates varied from 71.8% in the Balearic Islands and 59.2% in Asturias. This supposes a relative variation range of 1.214, that is to say, if Asturias had the rate of the Balearic Islands, it could increase the human capital supplied to the labour market by 21.4% with the consequent impact on its GDP. The communities with more rate of activity of human capital tend to be the more developed regions. The Balearic Islands, Catalonia, Madrid, Navarre are above 68%. The coefficient variation, whose value is 0.052, confirms the degree of relative inequality.

The indicators of inequality throughout the period show that there was a slight increase in this inequality. The variation coefficients and the variation ranges grew slightly throughout the whole period, especially as from 1986. Moreover, it should be pointed out that there have been substantial changes. Thus, in 1977, Galicia, a relatively underdeveloped region, had the highest rate (61.7%). Madrid and Navarre were located in the national average of 55%. Throughout the last three decades, the regions have shown differing capacities in their efforts to increase the degree of use of their human capital. It is also remarkable that these changes were concentrated after the accession of the country to the European Union with all that this entailed as regards institutional reforms and the opening of the Spanish economy.

Table 10.2 Rates of activity of the human capital (%)

	1977	1986	1996	2007
Andalusia	52.3	51.5	56.9	64.0
Aragon	54.5	53.4	57.1	68.2
Asturias	53.6	51.8	51.4	59.2
Balearic Islands	58.0	55.0	62.4	71.8
Canary Islands	55.8	57.1	58.8	68.4
Cantabria	52.6	51.6	53.8	64.2
Castile y León	52.2	50.9	54.3	62.0
Castile-La Mancha	53.6	51.6	55.2	64.8
Catalonia	57.5	56.9	61.6	70.2
Community of Valencia	56.5	55.6	59.1	66.9
Extremadura	51.9	51.0	57.0	61.3
Galicia	61.7	58.5	56.1	63.7
Madrid	55.8	56.0	59.9	70.6
Murcia	58.4	54.8	58.3	67.5
Navarre	55.2	55.1	58.2	68.3
Basque Country	55.8	55.2	58.8	66.0
La Rioja	56.8	51.5	54.9	66.2
Ceuta			58.3	60.4
Melilla			61.4	63.4
SPAIN	55.6	54.6	58.2	66.8
Variation coefficient	0.047	0.046	0.049	0.052
Relative range of variation	1.188	1.150	1.213	1.214

Source: Fundación Bancaja-Ivie (2008) and own elaboration
Note: Rate of activity of the human capital as a quotient of the years of education of the active population and the years of education of the population at working age

Table 10.3 shows the results obtained in terms of unemployment rates of human capital. Again we find common patterns, such as the growth of this rate between 1977 and 1986 and a sharp decrease between 1996 and 2007. However, this final decrease is not sufficient to compensate the previous growth. Except in the case of Murcia, all the regions had higher rates in 2007 than in 1977. Between 1986 and 1996, the evolution is less similar. Again the accession to the European Union and the following years were a crucial period in the subsequent evolution of the regions.

In terms of human capital supplied to the labour market and which is not used by the employers, the inequality is much higher than that observed in terms of rates of activity of the human capital. In 2007, the rates of unemployment of the human capital oscillated from the values of the autonomous cities of Ceuta and Melilla (16.7% and 17.3% respectively) to those of Andalucia (11%) and Rioja (4.5%). The coefficient of variation of human capital unemployment 0.295, increases by six times the regional coefficient of variation of human capital participation rate.

The relative inequality in 2007 is much smaller than that registered in 1977 (a variation coefficient of 0.450), but it is 50% greater than that estimated for 1986 (a variation coefficient of 0.200). Therefore, this is an important component of the final use of human capital which, as we have just seen, has potential to give rise to substantial and changing differences as regards the use of human capital.

Table 10.3 Rates of unemployment of human capital (%)

	1977	1986	1996	2007
Andalusia	10.9	29.3	30.7	11.0
Aragon	3.6	17.9	15.9	4.8
Asturias	4.6	21.1	21.8	8.7
Balearic Islands	4.2	14.3	13.1	5.1
Canary Islands	8.3	25.4	21.4	9.3
Cantabria	3.9	19.3	24.5	6.1
Castile y León	5.3	19.9	20.9	7.0
Castile-La Mancha	4.7	16.1	19.1	7.3
Catalonia	3.8	21.4	18.3	5.5
Community of Valencia	4.1	20.0	21.4	8.2
Extremadura	8.2	26.7	28.8	10.9
Galicia	2.4	15.7	19.6	7.3
Madrid	5.4	19.2	19.8	5.7
Murcia	5.9	20.7	23.4	5.9
Navarre	3.7	19.2	12.7	4.9
Basque Country	4.7	24.8	20.8	5.7
La Rioja	1.8	16.9	14.9	4.5
Ceuta			26.3	16.7
Melilla			23.7	17.3
SPAIN	5.4	21.5	21.6	7.3
Variation coefficient	0.450	0.200	0.238	0.295
Relative range of variation	6.048	2.052	2.416	2.448

Source: Fundación Bancaja-Ivie (2008) and own elaboration
Note: Rate of unemployment of human capital as a quotient between the years of study of the unemployed population and the years of study of the active population

The final regional differentials concerning the degree of use of human capital are more or less important depending on whether inequality in participation and unemployment rates reinforce or offset each other. If only small amounts of human capital entered the market that would make easier their employment, reducing employment rate differentials. A higher employment probability, in turn, could lead to a supply increase, rising human capital employment rate differentials.

Table 10.4 shows the rates of employment of human capital obtained for the Spanish regions. General reductions can be observed between 1977 and 1986, general increases were common between 1996 and 2007, and there was an uneven evolution between 1986 and 1996. At the present time, the rates oscillate between 68.2% in the Balearic Islands and 50.2% in Ceuta. These are substantial differences. Extremadura, with the human capital which its population at working age already has, could use 25% more human capital, if it had a rate like that of the Balearic Islands. This would suppose a very considerable increase in its per capita GDP. Thus, it is particularly significant that the wealthier regions are situated above the national average in this regard. The Balearic Islands, Madrid and Catalonia are all over 66%, while Ceuta, Extremadura and Andalusia do not reach 57%.

The variation coefficient was 0.067 in 2007, a value which is 28% above that registered in rates of activity of the human capital (0.052). This shows that the differences in rates of unemployment are increasing the inequality in rates of activity.

Table 10.4 Rates of employment of the human capital (%)

	1977	1986	1996	2007
Andalusia	46.6	36.4	39.4	56.9
Aragon	52.6	43.8	48.0	64.9
Asturias	51.1	40.9	40.2	54.0
Balearic Islands	55.6	47.1	54.2	68.2
Canary Islands	51.1	42.6	46.2	62.1
Cantabria	50.5	41.7	40.6	60.3
Castile y León	49.5	40.7	42.9	57.6
Castile-La Mancha	51.1	43.3	44.6	60.1
Catalonia	55.3	44.7	50.3	66.3
Community of Valencia	54.2	44.4	46.5	61.4
Extremadura	47.7	37.4	40.6	54.6
Galicia	60.2	49.3	45.1	59.0
Madrid	52.8	45.3	48.0	66.5
Murcia	55.0	43.5	44.6	63.5
Navarre	53.1	44.5	50.8	65.0
Basque Country	53.2	41.5	46.5	62.2
La Rioja	55.8	42.8	46.8	63.3
Ceuta			42.9	50.3
Melilla			46.8	52.4
SPAIN	52.6	42.8	45.6	61.9
Variation coefficient	0.063	0.073	0.089	0.067
Relative range of variation	1.291	1.354	1.374	1.262

Source: Fundación Bancaja-Ivie (2008) and own elaboration
Note: rate of employment of human capital as a quotient between the years of study of the employed population and the years of study of the population at working age

Mostly, the regions with higher human capital participation rates also tend to show a lower human capital unemployment rate. In 2007, the coefficient of correlation between rates of activity and unemployment of human capital is -0.590, which shows this strong correspondence. The relationship between both the variables became especially intense during the last decade, as in 1996 the coefficient of correlation was negative, but stood only at -0.175.

The inequality recorded in 2007 is significant, but moderate in historical terms. It lays only somewhat above the levels of 1977 (0.063) and quite far below those of 1986 (0.073) and 1996 (0.089). After achieving record levels in the second half of the 1990s, the regional inequality in the level of use of human capital has been substantially reduced (25% since 1996), although it continues to be a factor of territorial imbalance to be taken into account.

Analyses carried out for the Spanish case (Pastor et al. 2007) show that personal characteristics, such as age, gender and educational level are significant determinants both as regards the decision to participate in the labour market and in the probability of employment. In particular, ceteris paribus, the likelihood of being active increases with the level of educational attainment of the person and the likelihood of being unemployed is reduced. Higher human capital increases the opportunity cost of not working (fostering efforts in the search for work) and makes the candidate more employable (greater likelihood of being hired by a firm).

For these reasons, the regions with larger stocks of human capital per capita are those which use this capital to a wider extent. This will have evident consequences in terms of wider regional inequality. The coefficient of regional correlation between the supply of human capital per capita (average years of education of the population at working age) and the degree of use of the human capital (rate of employment of the human capital) was 0.684 in 2007. This result confirms the positive relationship in Spain between having more human capital and using a greater percentage of it. Figure 10.6 illustrates this relationship, in which a key component for favouring greater use of the existing human capital is to have a population well endowed with this factor.

In Spain, the less developed regions have less human capital and are also, partly for this reason, able to use a smaller proportion of this capital. This tends to make the differences in development greater and more persistent. However, it can be expected that the convergence in the stocks of human capital will generate a faster convergence process through its additional effect on the level of use of this factor.

Therefore, the different levels of use of human capital are generating a greater regional inequality. We will explicitly analyse the relationship between the level of use and the regional GDP per capita. To do so, we will make use of the estimation of the GDP per capita by Autonomous Community in 2007 from the Spanish Regional Accounts elaborated by the National Institute of Statistics (INE). Table 10.5 provides these estimations which confirm the existence of a marked degree of inequality. The GDP per capita of the Basque Country is 30.8% greater than the national average, while that of Extremadura is 31.3% below this average. In short, the GDP per capita in some regions is 90% higher than in others. The variation coefficient is 0.1797, a value which would also be obtained if half the regions had a GDP per capita 17.97% greater than the average and the other half a GDP per capita 17.97 % below the average.

The coefficient of correlation between the rates of employment of human capital which we have estimated for 2007 and the GDP per capita is 0.609. Clearly, the wealthiest regions tend to be the same ones that make a better use of their human capital. In part, this is due to the fact that these are the regions with more human capital. The coefficient of correlation between the rates of activity of human capital and the GDP per capita was 0.572 in 2007. The fact that these tend to be the regions where a smaller part of the human capital supplied remains unemployed is a contributing factor. The regional coefficient of correlation between the rate of unemployment of human capital and the GDP per capita is -0.494.

In order to gain an idea of the impact of the differences in the use of human capital in terms of regional inequality, we will carry out a simple and illustrative counterfactual exercise. We will suppose that all the regions could maintain their productivity per unit of human capital employed although they use different amounts of this factor. We will also suppose that all regions have the same degree of use of human capital (for example, without the loss of generality, 61.9% which was the average national value in 2007). In this case, the GDP per capita estimated for each region would be given by the values in column 2 of Table 10.5. The Basque Country would continue to have the highest GDP per capita and Extremadura the lowest, but now the difference between both regions would only be 67% instead of

Table 10.5 GDP Per capita (€) and level of use of human capital 2007

	PIBpc	Spain=100	Counterfactual PIBpc	Spain=100
Andalusia	18,298	78.2	19,893	85.0
Aragon	25,361	108.4	24,176	103.3
Asturias	21,200	90.6	24,277	103.8
Balearic Islands	25,238	107.9	22,910	97.9
Canary Islands	21,004	89.8	20,945	89.5
Cantabria	23,377	99.9	24,007	102.6
Castile y León	22,589	96.6	24,253	103.7
Castile-La Mancha	18,564	79.3	19,122	81.7
Catalonia	27,445	117.3	25,622	109.5
Community of Valencia	21,239	90.8	21,404	91.5
Extremadura	16,080	68.7	18,223	77.9
Galicia	19,800	84.6	20,754	88.7
Madrid	29,965	128.1	27,861	119.1
Murcia	19,574	83.7	19,071	81.5
Navarre	29,483	126.0	28,072	120.0
Basque Country	30,599	130.8	30,431	130.1
La Rioja	24,717	105.6	24,179	103.3
Ceuta	21,994	94.0	27,078	115.7
Melilla	21,089	90.1	24,905	106.5
SPAIN	23,396	100.0	23,396	100.0
Variationcoefficient	0.180		0.144	
Relative range of variation	1.903		1.670	

Source: Fundación Bancaja-Ivie (2008) and own drafting
Note: Counterfactual PIBpc is PIBpc in the case that all the regions have a rate of employment of human capital like that of the whole of Spain

90%. Furthermore, the regional variation coefficient of the counterfactual regional GDP is 0.1444, clearly less than the actual figure of 0.1797. The existence of differences in the degree of use of human capital would increase GDP per capita in Spain by 25%. In other words, this would account for fifth part of the total inequality as regards GDP per capita.

The effect of the lack of use of human capital is especially marked in some of the less developed regions. Extremadura and Andalusia are the regions with less GDP per capita and they have rates of employment of human capital among the lowest, below 57%.

It is clearly disheartening that the regions which are less developed and have less human capital are those which have a greater percentage of this human capital unused. As we have seen, this paradox is, up to certain point, only apparent. Part of the difficulty involved in exploiting a greater proportion of the scarce human capital in these regions is associated precisely to their low endowments of per capita human capital.

10.4 Returns to Human Capital

The analysis of the returns to human capital supposes the consideration that the acquisition of human capital, in particular through education, is an investment process and as such is subject to costs and benefits. The most widely used

10 Supply and Use of Human Capital in the Spanish Regions 225

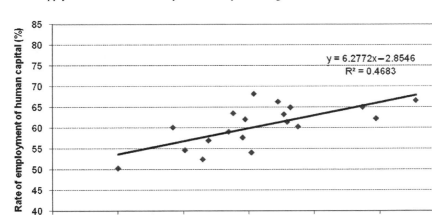

Fig. 10.6 Regional degree of use of human capital (2007)
Source: Fundación Bancaja-Ivie (2008) and own elaboration. Note: Rate of employment of human capital as a quotient of the years of study of the employed population and the years of study of the population at working age

instrument for measuring the returns to education is the one developed by Mincer (1974), the "Mincerian Wage Equation". This equation has the following form:

$$\ln w_i = \alpha + \beta \cdot s_i + \theta \cdot \text{Expe}_i + \gamma \cdot \text{Expe}_i^2 + \varepsilon_i$$

where $\ln w_i$ is the logarithm of the wage of the person i,[2] s_i are the years off education of the person,[3] Exp e_i and Exp e_i^2 are the work experience of the person and its square, respectively.[4]

In this equation, the β coefficient is interpreted as the percentage increase in the wage derived from each additional year of education, which approximates the return from each additional year of education. Alternatively, education in the equation can be specified in the form of dummy variables which show the educational level achieved by the person. These dummy variables make it possible to relax the implicit assumption in the continuous variable of equal return to each additional year of education regardless of the years of education already accumulated.

---

[2] Usually defined as hourly wage.

[3] When the number of years a person has dedicated to education is not available, the variable s is an imputation of the years legally required to obtain the level of education declared by the person.

[4] Unless sufficiently detailed data on the periods of employment and unemployment of the persons is available, the variable used is the potential experience, which is usually defined as Exp= Age–s–6.

As regards the quadratic specification of the experience, this picks up the accumulation effect of human capital linked to the experience on the job. However, the quadratic term incorporates the possibility of obsolescence and depreciation of the human capital in the later stages of the life cycle of the person. Thus, the expected signs of the θ and γ coefficients, respectively, are positive and negative.

The Wage Structure Survey corresponding to 1995 and 2002 is the largest microdatabase currently available in Spain with a sample size of about 200,000 wage-earners. The population from which the sample is drawn is that of establishments with ten or more workers. It includes all manufacturing and service industries, except for Public Administrations.[5] The educational levels taken into consideration and the years assigned (within brackets) are the following: no degree (2.5), primary (5), compulsory secondary (8), post-compulsory secondary (11.5), tertiary short cycle (15.5), tertiary long cycle (18), vocational training first level (10) and vocational training second level (13).[6]

The returns to education obtained from the estimation of a simple Mincerian equation using years of education for the total and gender segmented samples, corresponding to the years 1995 and 2002, appear in Table 10.6. The comparison of the returns between both years shows a slight fall in 2002. However, the results by gender show that the fall of the returns was deeper for female workers.[7] It should be mentioned that these results are not very different from those obtained by Harmon et al. (2001) for Spain in 1994, by using the EUHP.

In Table 10.7, the returns are those corresponding to the estimations with education dummy variables. The educational level of reference is primary, so that

Table 10.6 Returns to education (%)

	1995	2002
Men	8.62	8.00
Women	8.73	7.34
Total	8.66	7.86

Source: Wage Structure Survey 1995 and 2002 and own elaboration

---

[5]The sample corresponding to 1995 does not include education, health care and community and personal services.

[6]See Pastor et al. (2007) for more detailed information.

[7]A question which is repeatedly asked in the literature on returns to education is that concerning the potential endogenous nature of education. As a first approximation, it may be thought that the more capable persons are those who study longer so that the estimated "β" coefficient expressing the return to education shows an upward bias due to the correlation between the non-observable innate ability and years of education. Other authors as well as most of the empirical literature, nevertheless, justify a negative bias. By using data from the 2005 Survey of Living Conditions, the estimation by OLS of a Mincerian equation offers an average return of the equation amounting to 7.2%. When this same equation is estimated by Instrumental Variables using the number of years of education of parents as an instrument of years of education, the estimated return to education increases to 9.8% (See Raymond, Roig and Gómez (2009)). These results are in line with the literature on the subject which suggests a potential underestiamtion of the return to education when estimated by OLS.

10 Supply and Use of Human Capital in the Spanish Regions

Table 10.7 Returns to education (%). Results by educational levels. Estimates with dummy variables of educational levels

	1995			2002		
	Total	Men	Women	Total	Men	Women
Obligatory secondary education	4.10	3.89	4.76	2.92	2.81	2.88
Post-obligatory secondary education	8.40	8.21	8.76	6.65	6.68	6.20
Short tertiary cycle	7.97	8.11	7.41	7.37	7.66	6.49
Long tertiary cycle	9.03	9.08	8.86	8.00	8.21	7.41
Vocational training level I	7.45	7.30	7.85	6.64	6.70	6.12
Vocational training level II	6.95	6.91	7.07	6.22	6.27	5.89

Note: Returns as regards passing from primary studies to the corresponding level

Table 10.8 Comparison of returns with and without control of the sector of activity

	Return to education (%)	Return controlling for sector (%)	Percentage difference
Andalusia	7.49	6.62	−11.64
Aragon	6.81	5.93	−12.94
Asturias	6.48	5.71	−11.96
Balearic Islands	7.93	6.49	−18.20
Canary Islands	8.48	6.89	−18.69
Cantabria	6.37	5.53	−13.20
Castile-La Mancha	7.89	5.99	−24.13
Castile and León	6.77	5.49	−18.92
Catalonia	7.72	7.52	−2.63
Community of Valencia	6.99	6.02	−13.87
Extremadura	8.37	5.49	−34.42
Galicia	7.75	6.51	−16.08
Madrid	9.17	8.92	−2.72
Murcia	6.96	5.50	−20.92
Navarre	6.70	6.02	−10.19
Basque Country	6.83	6.40	−6.32
Rioja	6.44	5.59	−13.24

Source: Wage Structure Survey 2002 and own drafting

the returns show the return per additional year of education which implies each educational level with respect to primary. The returns by educational level capture the previous fall between both years and the larger reduction in women's returns. The reduction affects all educational levels, but it is larger in obligatory secondary education and in post-obligatory education.

The returns to education by autonomous communities (Table 10.8) show up substantial differences. Madrid is the autonomous community with the highest return at 9.2%, while Cantabria and La Rioja obtain a return of 6.4%. The correlation between returns to education and the average number of years of education by region is 0.23. If Madrid is eliminated from the sample, the correlation coefficient becomes negative, but low to –0.25. These results do not make it possible to point to any robust relationship between returns and average years of education.

However, when estimating Mincerian equations for each autonomous community including industry dummy variables, a different result is obtained. In introducing industry variables, the estimated returns are conditioned to the industry where the worker job belongs to. As human capital requirements differ by industry, we should expect workers sector choice to be conditioned to their education level, at least at the medium and long run. We allow the relationship between education and wages to follow two different paths: on the one hand, the direct relationship education $\rightarrow$ productivity $\rightarrow$ wage, and on the other hand, an indirect path education $\rightarrow$ industry $\rightarrow$ productivity $\rightarrow$ wage. As a result, some of the direct effect, captured by the coefficient on years of education, is absorbed by the indirect effect through the relation between education and sector choice. The size of the effect of introducing sector controls can be appreciated in Table 10.8, where both returns with and without sector controls are compared. The largest differences can be found in the cases of Extremadura, Castile La-Mancha and Murcia. On the contrary, the sector control has more reduced effects in Madrid, Catalonia and the Basque Country. As can be easily deduced, the choice of sector conditions the return to education to a greater extent in economies with little diversification and with economic development below the average. This last has to do with the concentration of wage-earners with higher education in a reduced number of sectors in these economies. Once controlled by sector, there is a positive correlation of 0.468 between return to education and GDP per capita. The more developed regions have somewhat higher rates of return to education.

The foregoing discussion shows that the choice of sector is a way to benefit from the investment in education. This previous analysis was carried out without explicitly considering in the estimation of returns that workers make a choice of sector and the result of this choice is related to the level of education of the individual. Consequently, it would seem adequate to estimate the regional returns to education by explicitly taking into account the effect of the choice of sector by wage-earners.

Considering the complexity entailed by the endogenisation of the choice of sector, a route was followed which simulated the effect that the increase of 1 year of education for each worker would have on the average wage growth of each autonomous community. The increase in 1 year of education of the wage-earners will have two effects:

1. It will affect the choice of sector. Consequently, the sector structure of employment will differ from that of the baseline situation.
2. An additional year of education will increase the wage of workers according to the returns to education in each sector.

The combination of both effects will lead to a new average regional wage as a weighted average of the new (and increased) regional sectorial wages weighted by the new sector structure of employment of each region.

In turn, the average regional real wage is the weighted average of regional sector wages weighted by the actual sector structure of employment.

The percentage difference between both average wages approximates the growth in the average regional wage due to an additional year of education of the workers in the region, that is, the rate of return to education.

10 Supply and Use of Human Capital in the Spanish Regions

Our starting point is the estimation of probit models of choice of sector as a function of age, years of education and gender of the individuals. The predicted probabilities by the models (one per sector-region) reproduce the sector structure of the wage-earners in our sample. A second step is the simulation of an increase in 1 year of education for all individuals in the sample from each autonomous community and forecasting the probabilities of sector membership due to the education increase. These probabilities allow to introduce the effect that education has on sector choice. Moreover, the estimation of sector returns to education with an equation that uses interactions between years of education and industry dummies in each autonomous community makes it possible to calculate the wage growth due to an additional year of education of the wage-earners in each sector.

That wage growth is weighted by the sector structure resulting from the simulation of increase in 1 year of education in the sample individuals. The growth rate of the average wage with respect to the real average wage applying the weights corresponding to the current sector structure, approximates the wage growth associated to an additional year of education incorporating the effect of sector change due to the increased education. As a result, we compare the return to education linked to a fixed sector structure with the return when the sector structure is allowed to vary with the changes in the education level of the workers.

The results are shown in Table 10.9. The return to education as average growth due to the simulated increase in education appears in column 1, while the return in column 2 is the average weighted return when using the actual sector structure. The difference (column 3) approximates the effect that the choice of sector has as a way to benefit from the investment in education. As can be seen, in line with the

Table 10.9 Growth in average wage and average sector performance

	Average salary growth (%) (1)	Average return obtained as an average of sector returns (%) (2)	Difference (%) (3)
Andalusia	8.3	6.5	1.8
Aragon	7.5	5.8	1.7
Asturias	7.9	5.9	2.0
Balearic Islands	8.7	6.1	2.6
Canary Islands	10.1	6.9	3.2
Cantabria	7.7	5.7	2.0
Castile-La Mancha	9.2	5.8	3.4
Castile-León	7.8	5.5	2.3
Catalonia	8.6	7.6	1.0
Community of Valencia	7.9	6.0	1.9
Extremadura	10.3	5.2	5.1
Galicia	9.0	6.4	2.6
Madrid	10.1	8.8	1.3
Murcia	8.4	5.5	2.9
Navarre	7.4	5.8	1.6
Basque Country	7.4	6.5	0.9
La Rioja	7.8	5.8	2.0

Source: Wage structure Survey 2002 and own elaboration

previous results, Extremadura, Castile La-Mancha and Murcia are the regions where the choice of sector plays a more relevant role as regards the total returns, while Madrid, Catalonia and the Basque Country are in the opposite situation. Given the actual industrial structure of the Spanish regions, there is a positive correlation of 0.500 between the GDP per capita and the return to human capital. Furthermore, education implies an additional advantage for the persons educated in regions, such as Extremadura, Castile-La Mancha and Murcia as it enables them to access more productive sectors to a greater extent than in other more developed regions. In addition, an improvement in per capita human capital in these regions would facilitate the structural change towards more productive industries.

10.5 Conclusions

The supply of human capital of the Spanish regions has undergone a sustained generalised growth. This is due to the increase in human capital per capita of their populations, boosted by the development of the educational system, promoted by the public policies and taking advantage of the efforts made by the house holds.

There have been and continue to be substantial differences between the regions as regards the human capital per capita of their inhabitants. The more developed regions have more human capital per capita. This inequality of human capital is a consequence of the differentials in human capital per capita between territories, but it also contributes to these inequalities. However, throughout the period a sustained convergence process can be observed, so that the degree of relative inequality of the supply of human capital per capita is reduced by a third.

It is necessary to add the notable inequality in the degree of use of human capital in the Spanish regions to these differences in the endowments of human capital. It can be observed that there is a common temporal pattern of falls in the degree of use of the potential human capital until the middle of the 1980s, a subsequent recovery from the time Spain joined the European Union, another slight fall during the crisis at the beginning of the 1990s and a sustained recovery from the middle of the 1990s up to the present time. The result at national level is an increase of more than 9% points in the degree of use of human capital in Spain. This has contributed to the growth undergone by the Spanish regions throughout the period.

However, the regional inequality is also notable in this area and grows substantially until the middle of the 1990s. It began to decrease from then until the present time. The result is that the inequality in this area in 2007 is very similar to that of 1977. Moreover, the regions with more human capital per capita are those which have a higher level of use of such of capital, while the contrary occurs in those which have less. Therefore, this differing ability to use human capital would contribute substantially to generating regional inequality in income per capita.

The returns to schooling are high for the whole of Spain despite the existence of some over-education and the mismatch in some cases between educational curricula and social needs. Furthermore, there are substantial differences in the return to education by regions, associated to a large extent to the sector composition of each economy. Madrid is the region with the highest return to education despite its high stock of human capital per capita.

The real challenge of higher education is to achieve educational contents in accordance with social needs. At the present time, doubts occasionally arise concerning whether such harmonisation is adequate, and, despite this, education shows high rates of return. If returns to education are high even though a certain degree of mismatch exists, its reduction should be shown in a still higher profitability from the investment in education.

In short, the improvements in accumulation of human capital and in its degree of use, together with the efficiency with which it is used have been important factors in the growth of the Spanish regions. Moreover, the differences between the regions in these three areas are substantial and constitute in themselves one of the aspects of regional inequality. They also contribute considerably to the differences in per capita income between the Spanish regions. However, the regional stock of per capita human capital has converged continually during the period under analysis. This contributes to reducing regional inequality. Less satisfactory are the results in terms of degree of use as the inequality in this variable increased slightly during the last 30 years. In addition, once the sector structure of each region is considered, the returns to education are somewhat greater in the more developed regions.

The future development of Spain and its regions will depend on its ability to accumulate more human capital, to use a greater percentage of it and to do so more efficiently. This process is compatible with a greater territorial balance that will depend to a large extent on achieving a reduction in the notable differences, which continue to exist between the Spanish regions as regards these questions.

References

Fundación Bancaja-Ivie (2008). *Series de capital humano*. Valencia: Fundación Bancaja-Ivie, http://www.ivie.es/banco/capital.php?idioma=EN

Harmon, C., Walker, I., & Westergaard-Nielsen, N. (2001). *Education and Earnings in Europe: A Cross-country Analysis of the Returns to Education*. Cheltenham, U.K: Edward Elgar.

Mincer, J. (1974). *Schooling, Experience and Earnings*. Nueva York: NBER.

Pastor, J. M., Raymond J. L., Roig J. L., & Serrano J. L. (2007). *El rendimiento del capital humano en España*. Valencia: Fundación Bancaja.

Raymond, J.L., Roig, J.L. and Gomez, L. (2009). "*Rendimientos de la educación en España y movilidad intergeneracional*" in: Papeles de Economía Española, 119, pp. 188–205.

Chapter 11
Inequality and Welfare in Intra-Territorial Income Distribution

Luis Ayala, Antonio Jurado, and Francisco Pedraja

11.1 Introduction

Among the different perspectives making up the analysis of the income distribution, the study of intra-territorial distribution of personal income is frequently omitted from the main lines of research. The juxtaposition of abundant change factors when forming the regional distributive process, the theoretical difficulties of integrating, in a unique analysis framework, the connections and contradictions between the personal and territorial distribution of income and the lack of databases with information that is sufficiently representative of the territorial singularities are the main reasons for the relatively low attention paid to intra-territorial distribution compared with other dimensions concerning inequality.

However, in the Spanish case, there are several reasons justifying the detailed study of the differences regarding the distribution of income across the different geographical areas. Firstly, the territorial division of Spain is one of the key factors of the current economic and social organisation model, and its results and possible reforms play a principal role in the public debate. Secondly, the advances made in the process of decentralisation of central government functions to the autonomous regions have been translated into an increasing decentralisation of some of the most important redistributive instruments, such as health, education or housing policies. A precise analysis of the results of such processes in terms of social welfare would seem necessary. Thirdly, there is plenty of empirical evidence on the truncated trend towards a reduction of regional economic disparities in the last decade, measured considering the gross added value per capita. Contrary to the intense process of regional convergence, which occurred in the 1960s and 1970s, the differences among the Spanish autonomous regions intensified in the first half of

---

F. Pedraja (✉)
Universidad de Extremadura, Facultad de Ciencias Económicas y Empresariales, Departamento de Economía, Avda. de Elvas, 06071 - Badajoz, España
e-mail: pedraja@unex.es

the 1980s, moderated in the following years and experienced a considerable increase from the mid-1990s onwards.[1] There is also a need to consider whether the evolution of differences in inequality levels within each autonomous region has followed this same pattern.

It is also worth mentioning the importance of the supranational policies which aim to improve the income levels of the poorest regions. The large transfers of European Funds for regional development should have been used, a priori, to mitigate the dispersion of welfare differences across the autonomous regions. Finally, there is increasing theoretical and empirical literature in other countries which places the territorial perspective as an important part of the explanation for the changes in inequality and the trends in welfare levels.[2] In the Spanish case, the excessive distant publishing dates for the Encuesta de Presupuestos Familiares (Household Budget Survey) and the lack of sufficient representative information at a territorial level in the Encuestas Continuas (Continuous Surveys) have, in the past, hindered the in-depth analysis, regionally speaking, of those factors determining the distributive process.

The aim of this chapter is to assess the variations in the differences regarding inequality and welfare levels across the Spanish autonomous regions, using a broad time span as a reference. In order to do so, a wide variety of inequality and welfare indicators are estimated on the basis of the information provided by the Family Budget Survey of 1973/74, 1980/81, 1990/91 and 2006 and the Encuesta Continua of the year 2000 (longitudinal file annualised by the INE –Spanish National Statistics Institute). The consideration of such a broad time perspective allows us to study the evolution of the differences among the autonomous regions using the convergence analysis, for which instruments from the theories on economic growth are used. Additionally, using different decomposition exercises, this research attempts to contrast the existence of possible changes in the inequality structure over time.

This chapter is organised as follows: The data and the main methodological decisions taken are explained in the first section. The second section presents the analysis of differences in the inequality levels within each autonomous region and the assessment of their changes over time, as well as the changes that occur in the structure of inequality using a decomposition exercise which employs the autonomous regions as divisions of population. In the following section, we contrast whether the changes over time regarding internal inequalities have or have not resulted in convergence. The fourth section is dedicated to analyse the main differences in the welfare levels on the basis of the estimation of a group of summarised functions of social welfare. Finally, the chapter ends with some brief conclusions.

---

[1] The researches corroborating the change of tendency in regional convergence are varied, including those by Cuadrado-Roura et al. (1998), Mella (1998), Villaverde (1999), Raymond (2002) and Goerlich et al. (2002).

[2] For further information, see Bishop et al. (1994), Moffitt and Gottschalk (2002) and Heshmati (2004), among others.

11.2 Data and Methodological Decisions

11.2.1 Territorial Information in the Encuestas de Presupuestos Familiares

The analysis of the intra-territorial distribution of income has been traditionally carried out in Spain using microdata from the Encuestas de Presupuestos Familiares (EPF). The almost 10-year surveys between 1973/74 and 1990/91 offered information with sufficient territorial de-aggregation by autonomous regions, offering the possibility of extending the analysis to a provincial level, although this was conditioned by the decrease in the sample representativeness.

In a pioneering work, Ruiz-Castillo (1987), using data on income and consumption in Spanish households, outlined the first pattern of inequality within each region on the basis of the EPF 1980/81. The results obtained revealed a relative inequality considerably higher in some of the autonomous regions (Andalusia, the Canary Islands, Cantabria and Extremadura) than in others (La Rioja, the Basque Country, Navarre and Catalonia). Although their main focus was on poverty, the research carried out by the Grupo de Economía del Bienestar Grupo de Economía del Bienestar of the University of Málaga also served to sketch the first map of poverty in the Spanish territory, using the province, not the region, as the unit of reference.[3] Martín-Guzmán (1996) extended previous works (Bosch et al., 1989; Martín Reyes et al., 1989; García Lizana and Martín Reyes, 1994) by exploiting the EPFs dated 1973/74, 1980/81 and 1990/91. The results obtained demonstrated an inequality pattern in the autonomous regions, which was quite similar over three decades to the results obtained by Ruiz-Castillo (1987), with minor changes in regional indicators between 1973/74 and 1980/81 and a significant fall, almost without exceptions, between 1980/81 and 1990/91. In line with this, but using the province as the reference unit, Goerlich and Mas (2001) analysed the extent of the differences regarding intra-provincial income disparities, finding a certain convergence process between 1973 and 1990.

Aside from the aforementioned researches, which are of a general nature, there were various others which, from diverse perspectives, tried to analyse the changes in the intra-territorial distribution of income in the 1980s by using the Encuestas de Presupuestos Familiares (EPF).[4] However, the possibility of expanding outcomes to include what happened in the following decade has been rendered impossible, as the Encuesta de Presupuestos Familiares disappeared. The decision to not carry out a new 10-year survey caused a severe limitation in the long-term distributive

---

[3] See García Lizana et al. (1989), Martín Reyes et al. (1989) and García Lizana and Martín Reyes (1994).

[4] Ruiz-Huerta et al. (1995), for example, attempted to analyse the relationships between the correction of disparities in the personal distribution of income and the changes in spatial distribution. Gradín (2000) used, among other criteria, the regional dimension to assess the polarisation level of income distribution throughout Spain.

analysis in Spain, which resulted in the need to find other sources in order to reconstruct the changes over time.

Until the recent publication of a new EPF including data corresponding to 2006, the only existing source of territorial information at a regional level regarding income and expenditure of households was the Encuesta Continua de Presupuestos Familiares. This survey, which was established in the mid-1980s, underwent a significant methodological variation from 1997 onwards. Among other consequences, the quarterly edition, which was not until this date representative at a regional level, was expanded to 8,000 households. Its design as a rotary panel enables to annualise the survey, reaching almost 10,000 observations. This figure, although more than thrice that of the previous Encuesta Continua, is considerably lower than the 10-year EPFs. This could give rise to some homogeneity problems in inter-temporal comparisons.[5]

If we compare the sample size of the Encuesta Básica de Presupuestos Familiares (Basic Household Budget Survey) of 1990/91 with that of the Encuesta Continua, a slightly greater reduction by over half of the number of observations can be appreciated (Table 11.1). This sample is also considerably lower than that of the EPF 2006, with almost 20,000 observations. According to statistical logic, the reduction is proportionally lower in less-populated regions. The new design of the sample also considers the changes registered in type of urban settlements, with an acceleration in the decade of intra-regional migrations towards urban areas (Bover and Arellano 2002).

A simple procedure to verify the possibilities and limits from comparing the surveys with a different sample could include paying attention to the differences in the orders of autonomous regions according to their relative income or expenditure. The results obtained from the ECPF and the EPF 2006 do not offer important discontinuities with respect to those shown by the previous Encuestas de Presupuestos Familiares. Moreover, the order of the autonomous regions does not differ from that resulting from other sources, which also offer data on household income in each autonomous region.

Furthermore, regarding the differences in the positions of each autonomous region with respect to the national average income and expenditure, if these were abnormally high according to the results of the basic surveys, this could indicate possible anomalies in the information of the ECPF due to the sample size. However, such differences are not higher in the ECPF 2000 than in the other surveys. Even in the case of regions with smaller samples, such as Cantabria, Navarre and La Rioja, no significant variations are appreciated in the differences among positions regarding income or expenditure, although a larger break in the temporary pattern is significant in the EPF 1990/91 with respect to the previous surveys and in the ECPF. Nevertheless, the possible estimations of income distribution within each of the regions should be interpreted with caution. Despite the apparent robustness of the

---

[5] Some works have used the ECPF in order to analyse intra-territorial income distribution, although with different methodological options to those used in this study (Goerlich et al., 2002).

11 Inequality and Welfare in Intra-Territorial Income Distribution

Table 11.1 Sample size, relative average income and expenditure

	1973/74 Obsv.	1973/74 Avg. income	1973/74 Avg. Expenditure	1980/81 Obsv.	1980/81 Avg. income	1980/81 Avg. Expenditure	1990/91 Obsv.	1990/91 Avg. income	1990/91 Avg. Expenditure	2000 Obsv.	2000 Avg. income	2000 Avg. Expenditure	2006 Obsv.	2006 Avg. income	2006 Avg. Expenditure
Andalusia	4,486	79.6	80.4	4,414	80.2	86.4	3,674	84.4	86.9	1,164	87.1	88.6	2,106	86.7	96.8
Aragon	1,221	102.7	98.8	1,301	99.8	101.1	1,105	100.7	91.6	479	98.6	102.2	850	97.8	101.4
Asturias	728	98.2	94.4	691	104.9	93.5	443	102.8	105.4	433	106.6	102.1	649	107.3	101.1
Balearics	455	110.9	96.6	478	105.2	106.9	429	108.0	104.2	357	107.9	100.8	793	117.3	109.5
Canary Islands	942	99.8	105.7	866	84.3	88.9	772	87.1	92.0	463	89.2	92.3	907	95.8	94.7
Cantabria	479	98.6	115.3	528	108.1	120.1	362	100.7	96.6	218	98.0	116.0	531	104.0	94.5
Castile-Leon	2,856	82.6	80.3	3,340	90.2	90.4	3,162	94.3	88.4	718	92.7	84.8	1,376	97.2	92.8
Castile-La Mancha	1,804	75.8	76.9	1,805	71.5	74.7	1,694	86.2	86.5	479	87.7	85.9	1,160	88.8	84.4
Catalonia	2,477	124.8	118.3	2,368	123.6	109.1	1,644	118.7	118.9	1,132	114.1	111.9	1,949	110.9	117.9
Valencian C.	1,912	93.2	95.3	1,768	98.8	100.7	1,706	95.4	90.0	836	99.9	94.7	1,564	98.6	100.1
Extremadura	1,027	72.8	67.1	931	64.3	68.2	830	72.1	71.9	353	74.5	71.9	902	77.1	82.9
Galicia	1,727	78.1	82.9	1,580	81.2	90.3	1,739	93.2	92.8	736	90.1	96.8	1,311	90.3	98.2
Madrid	1,421	129.9	136.6	1,269	126.7	125.8	764	114.6	121.2	808	117.2	117.6	1,172	120.1	117.1
Murcia	564	83.7	79.6	456	81.9	93.7	526	91.9	93.2	367	82.8	99.7	874	86.3	93.7
Navarre	398	104.4	110.4	364	119.3	123.0	367	108.6	124.2	225	113.0	110.3	676	117.4	113.7
Basque Country	1,322	123.9	123.6	1,204	116.4	117.5	1,360	113.5	111.2	500	109.7	113.7	1,783	112.3	114.4
Rioja	332	101.4	101.9	344	96.8	97.1	357	117.8	94.9	241	96.0	103.2	623	92.2	86.9
Spain	24,151	100.0	100.0	23,971	100.0	100.0	21,155	100.0	100.0	9,631	100.0	100.0	19,435	100.0	100.0

Source: Own elaboration from the Encuesta de Presupuestos Familiares or ECPF (Households' Budget Survey) 1973/74, 1980/81,1990/91, 2006 and ECPF 2000

average aggregate indicators, the comparison of inequality indicators over time could be affected by the differences in the number of observations. It is advisable to complement the absolute interpretations with the elaboration of relative comparisons. Under the restrictive supposition that each survey reflects, in a proportional way, the problems of statistical representativeness of each region, the use of differences with respect to the average could contribute to partly solve the aforementioned difficulties.

11.2.2 Methodological Options

As in any study measuring distributive results, the methodological options used for an adequate assessment of intra-territorial distribution of income includes selecting the correct reference variable, a homogeneous treatment of households of different sizes and characteristics and selecting a robust system of inequality indicators.

Choosing the reference variable means facing the dilemma of whether the most representative indicator of a household's welfare is their expenditure or their income. This recurrent topic in distributive analysis it is particularly relevant when a spatial dimension is added. The disaggregated analysis of inequality by population sub-groups has traditionally demonstrated that their classification in terms of welfare in each territory shows a high sensitivity to the chosen variable. For example, the fact that, generally speaking, the elderly register higher poverty rates regarding expenditure than regarding income, where a more pronounced risk aversion has a significant influence, indicates that opting for expenditure could have a negative effect on those autonomous regions with older populations. However, the well-known underestimation of income is particularly significant in smaller autonomous regions to the extent that the sample shortage particularly fuels the difficulties concerning the appropriate collection of household income data in these areas. Nevertheless, as previously indicated, the differences in the relative situation of each autonomous region depending on their average expenditure or income do not seem to be particularly pronounced in those regions with lower population rates and higher apparent problems of sample representativeness.

As the limitations of the two options are considerable, these could be related however to the ultimate objectives of each distributive analysis and, more specifically, to their theoretical bases. In a context of increasing de-centralisation of the main social welfare services, it seems logical to analyse income distribution from a spatial perspective taking into consideration the idea of a minimum level of resources in each territory. This invokes, in any analysis regarding empirical tests of poverty or inequality, a link between income and the concept of a minimum amount of resources as a necessary, although not sufficient, requirement for social welfare (Atkinson, 1989). However, both the ECPF and the EPF-2006 provide limited information on income, with no de-aggregation by sources to date, with some problems in quality. Apart from the traditional problem of the underestimation of income, which is frequent in the Household Budget Surveys, we have to add to this the manner in which the data is collected in such surveys. The persons being interviewed can either record their exact amount of income or just specify the interval within which it is included. The INE makes amendments in order to correct the possible bias implied by the second option, although its complete rectification is unlikely. Yet, it is not clear whether these limitations of a statistical nature are more relevant than the inevitable influence of lifestyle on a household's expenditure. With the necessary caution, income will be the reference variable in our empirical analyses, although the results are subjected to a sensitivity analysis with the figures corresponding to expenditure.

The choice of income does not close the door to other alternatives. In the case of the ECPF, the INE offers the direct information from quarterly surveys as well as annual longitudinal files created on the basis of data provided by such surveys. In the present work, we have opted for using the annualised data. Although there are some disadvantages, such as the elimination of certain observations in order to create the longitudinal file, the calculations made with quarterly surveys present time sequences for the highly unstable inequality indicators. Also, there is the great advantage of structural similarity with the previous basic surveys. The first estimates, which try to compile the different sources of information regarding household's income seem to demonstrate a significant similarity with the results previously obtained from the Encuestas Continuas, rather than with the Encuestas Básicas or the European Community Household Panel (Ayala et al., 2004). The estimates of severe poverty, for example, offer much lower indicators than those of the ECHP.[6]

The variable that we will take as the basis for the analysis is the total net monetary income of each household, thus excluding salaries in kind or imputed rents. The calculations using the income variable also exclude these non-monetary components. The adjustment of the households' incomes in each territory taking into consideration the different needs of each type of household requires the use of equivalence scales. In our study, we use the most frequent three: OECD, OECD modified version and a parametric scale, although in order to simplify, we will focus on the latter.[7] Following the methodology suggested by Buhmann et al. (1988), who counts the number of equivalent adults raising the size of the household to a parameter between 0 and 1:

$$e_h = n_h^\phi, \quad 0 \leq \phi \leq 1.$$

In our estimates, we will use $\phi = 0.5$.

---

[6] Our preliminary calculations in this research also demonstrate important differences in the order of the autonomous regions by inequality levels depending on whether the ECHP or the ECPF is considered.

[7] For more detailed information about the origin of these concepts of equivalence scales and their relationship with inequality matters, see Jenkins (2000).

The last methodological decision concerns the use of inequality indicators, which allow us to obtain a general picture of the distributive process in each autonomous region. Given the well-known sensitivity of the indicators chosen, affected by different value judgements, we estimate a wide range of indicators, including the Gini index, the generalised entropy indices and the Atkinson index with diverse inequality aversion parameters:

$$\text{Gini} = [1/(2n^2\mu)]\Sigma_i^n \Sigma_j^n |y_i - y_j|,$$

$$\text{GE}(c) = (1/c(c-1))\{[(1/n)\Sigma_i^n (y_i/\mu)^c] - 1\}, \neq 0, c \neq 1,$$

$$\text{GE}(1) = (1/n)\Sigma_i^n (y_i/\mu)\log(y_i/\mu), \ c = 1,$$

$$\text{GE}(0) = (1/n)\Sigma \log(\mu/y_i), \ c = 0,$$

$$\text{Atk}(e) = 1 - [(1/n)\Sigma_i^n (y_i/\mu)^{1-e}]^{1/(1-e)}, e \geq 0, \ e \neq 1,$$

$$\text{Atk}(e) = 1 - \exp[(1/n)\Sigma_i^n \text{Ln}(y_i/\mu)^e], e = 1,$$

where y_i represents the equivalent income corresponding to each individual $i=1 \ldots n$, y_j is the income of the following individual, and μ corresponds to the average population income. As is known, the Theil indices are based on the loss of entropy derived from the fact that the distribution is not perfectly egalitarian with the possibility of assigning different weightings to income movements. As these are additively decomposable indices, we will use them in the analysis of inequality sources. In turn, the group of Atkinson indices allows us to incorporate inequality aversion judgements, whose implementation will be particularly necessary in the construction of the functions of social welfare of each territory.

11.3 Inequality in Intra-Territorial Income Distribution

The application of the wide array of indicators suggested in the previous section to the data from the Encuestas de Presupuestos Familiares and the ECPF allows us to obtain a relatively updated view of the differences in distributive results within each autonomous region. The estimated indicators, with the indicated limitations, could be useful in order to reconstruct the series regarding the intra-territorial income distribution until the first half of the twenty-first century.

The estimation of internal inequalities for the year 2006, approximated by the Gini index, offers a quite heterogeneous chart of territorial realities (Table 11.2). A group of autonomous regions (Navarre, the Basque Country, La Rioja, Aragon, Asturias and the Balearics) stands out registering significantly lower inequality

Table 11.2 Inequality indicators by autonomous regions (2006) (net income by equivalent adult, $\phi=0.5$)

	Gini	Gini (relative)	Confidence interval (Gini)*	GE ($c=0$)	GE ($c=1$)	GE ($c=2$)	ATK ($\varepsilon=1$)	ATK ($\varepsilon=2$)
Andalusia	0.313	103.2	0.296–0.330	0.164	0.174	0.246	0.152	0.276
Aragon	0.274	90.3	0.245–0.302	0.127	0.126	0.147	0.119	0.23
Asturias	0.277	91.4	0.244–0.310	0.132	0.129	0.149	0.123	0.24
Balearics	0.279	92.1	0.251– 0.307	0.133	0.130	0.147	0.125	0.244
Canary Isl.	0.315	103.8	0.290–0.339	0.166	0.164	0.194	0.153	0.286
Cantabria	0.283	93.5	0.244–0.323	0.137	0.151	0.232	0.128	0.233
Castile-Leon	0.284	93.5	0.262–0.305	0.133	0.133	0.155	0.124	0.235
Castile-L.M.	0.292	96.4	0.268–0.316	0.142	0.137	0.149	0.132	0.254
Catalonia	0.284	93.5	0.266–0.301	0.136	0.132	0.147	0.127	0.245
Valencian C.	0.293	96.8	0.274–0.313	0.145	0.148	0.189	0.135	0.255
Extremadura	0.308	101.7	0.284–0.333	0.153	0.155	0.179	0.142	0.258
Galicia	0.284	93.8	0.263–0.305	0.134	0.136	0.16	0.126	0.235
Madrid	0.314	103.6	0.293–0.336	0.164	0.168	0.209	0.151	0.275
Murcia	0.313	103.3	0.288–0.338	0.163	0.176	0.236	0.15	0.266
Navarre	0.276	91.0	0.244–0.308	0.129	0.126	0.142	0.121	0.233
Basque C.	0.272	89.7	0.254–0.290	0.123	0.121	0.133	0.116	0.224
Rioja	0.254	83.9	0.220–0.289	0.109	0.105	0.112	0.103	0.203
SPAIN	0.303	100	0.297–0.309	0.154	0.155	0.191	0.143	0.267

*95%
Source: Own elaboration from the Encuesta de Presupuestos Familiares 2006

levels than the national total. On the contrary, in other regions (Andalusia, the Canary Islands, Murcia and Madrid), the internal distributive process has resulted in inequality levels exceeding the national average.

A first inference drawn from the estimated inequality levels in the different regions of the territory is the apparent non-existence of a close link between the average income level and the concentration of its distribution. Both in the group with the highest equi-distribution and in that with the highest income dispersion, the autonomous regions comprising such groups have very different positions in the national classification by average income.

However, precautions should be applied to the comparisons as imposed by the characteristics of the databases. As already indicated, the problems of sampling de-aggregation could introduce some biases not only in the indices' levels, but also in the subsequent order of the respective autonomous regions. In fact, the estimation of confidence levels and standard errors of the regional indices reveals the presence of important limitations for obtaining statistically significant differences among autonomous regions.

The problems in obtaining robust orders oblige us to, at least, complete the table with estimations of the rest of indices suggested. The results hardly undergo any changes after the introduction of alternative measures of inequality. The most inegalitarian autonomous regions, according to the Gini index, remains so in the rest of the indicators. The order continues to be quite stable when modifying the values of c and so does, therefore, the sensitivity of the estimated inequality to the differences between the different distribution strata, or when the level of inequality aversion is increased, through ε Among the autonomous regions with the highest levels of internal inequality, The Canary Islands and Madrid become the least egalitarian regions –changing position with Andalusia– as these show an increase in inequality aversion. Among the autonomous regions with the highest levels of equality, the order is particularly robust and includes La Rioja, Navarre and the Basque Country as the most egalitarian regions.

The final chart of results offers significant similarities to those obtained by other authors in previous decades. According to the data by Ruiz-Castillo (1987), Cantabria, the Canary Islands and Andalusia were already those regions with the most concentrated intra-territorial distribution of income at the beginning of the 1980s. On the opposite pole in this respect were, as at present, the Basque Country and Navarre. One of the main changes is the inclusion of Madrid among the less egalitarian regions. As already mentioned, some of the differences observed could be related to the cited sampling problems, which are more frequent in the one-province and smallest regions. Nevertheless, the differences seem to be also due to the natural limitations arising when trying to compare the results from works based on highly different methodologies. Despite the inevitable problems resulting from comparing sources with different sample sizes, the only homogeneous possible comparison is to replicate the methodological options applied in the case of the new EPF with the previous Encuestas de Presupuestos Familiares.[8]

The results from such an exercise are shown in Table 11.3. Firstly, it is worth mentioning a general structure of inequality relatively similar in the different surveys. The variation range is no higher in the new surveys than in the former EPF, and the maximum and minimum inequality levels are relatively similar. This is compatible, however, with various changes in the inequality values, where some kind of statistical procedure would be recommended to analyse the existence or non-existence of convergence in inequality levels.

A natural way to examine the possible re-orderings of the autonomous regions is the estimation of the differences with respect to the whole nation (Fig. 11.1). The most revealing aspect is probably the apparent consistency over time of the territorial pattern of internal inequalities. An extensive group of autonomous regions has historically registered more equitative distributive processes. This is the case of La Rioja, the Basque Country –with the emergence of income inequalities only in the 1980s, linked to the difficult process of industrial adjustment– Asturias –where inequality shows a strong dependence on transfers from the Social Security–, Navarre, the Balearics and the Valencian Community.

---

[8] A similar exercise is included in the work carried out by Goerlich et al. (2002), who use the ECPF-99 to compare the variation of inequality in each autonomous region from the 1970s. Unlike our results, their estimations show an increase in inequality in the majority of autonomous regions since 1990. These differences could be partly due to the use of different methodological criteria, as they opted for expenditure instead of income, for the year 1999 instead of 2000 and 2006 and the expenditure per capita, without adjustments using equivalence scales.

11 Inequality and Welfare in Intra-Territorial Income Distribution   243

Table 11.3 Inequality indicators by autonomous regions (1973–2006) (net income by equivalent adult, $\phi = 0.5$)

	Gini							GE ($c=1$)						
	1973		1980		1990		2000		2006		1973	1980	1990	2000	2006
Andalusia	0.336	95.2	0.326	98.0	0.319	100.9	0.295	104.6	0.313	103.2	0.194 86.4	0.186 93.5	0.191 103.7	0.152 116.0	0.174 111.9
Aragon	0.356	100.7	0.33	99.3	0.287	90.7	0.279	98.9	0.274	90.3	0.220 98.1	0.197 99.0	0.146 78.9	0.127 96.9	0.126 80.9
Asturias	0.353	99.9	0.301	90.4	0.257	81.3	0.266	94.3	0.277	91.4	0.221 98.7	0.151 76.1	0.115 62.5	0.121 92.3	0.129 82.8
Balearics	0.349	98.8	0.318	95.5	0.296	93.6	0.258	91.5	0.279	92.1	0.274 122.0	0.171 85.8	0.146 79.2	0.110 84.0	0.130 83.4
Canary I.	0.338	95.7	0.336	101.1	0.326	102.9	0.286	101.4	0.315	103.8	0.200 89.3	0.204 102.6	0.177 95.8	0.132 101.1	0.164 105.8
Cantabria	0.348	98.5	0.306	91.9	0.284	89.8	0.284	100.7	0.283	93.5	0.208 92.8	0.186 93.4	0.133 72.0	0.135 103.1	0.151 97.3
C.-Leon	0.378	107.0	0.335	100.7	0.312	98.5	0.283	100.4	0.284	93.5	0.264 117.8	0.195 97.8	0.168 91.1	0.131 100.0	0.133 85.4
C.-Mancha	0.350	99.1	0.314	94.4	0.315	99.6	0.230	81.6	0.292	96.4	0.227 101.2	0.172 86.4	0.224 121.7	0.087 66.3	0.137 87.9
Catalonia	0.365	103.2	0.302	90.8	0.305	96.2	0.265	94.0	0.284	93.5	0.237 105.5	0.199 100.1	0.158 85.7	0.115 87.8	0.132 84.8
Valencian C.	0.330	93.5	0.291	87.6	0.285	90.0	0.266	94.3	0.293	96.8	0.191 85.2	0.145 72.6	0.140 76.0	0.115 88.0	0.148 95.2
Extremadura	0.356	100.8	0.318	95.7	0.310	97.9	0.268	95.0	0.308	101.7	0.212 94.5	0.182 91.6	0.165 89.3	0.121 92.3	0.155 99.8
Galicia	0.325	92.1	0.347	104.2	0.310	97.8	0.261	92.6	0.284	93.8	0.194 86.3	0.211 106.0	0.173 94.0	0.114 86.7	0.136 87.5
Madrid	0.365	103.1	0.33	99.3	0.320	101.1	0.286	101.4	0.314	103.6	0.264 117.5	0.185 93.0	0.224 121.6	0.134 102.1	0.168 108.2
Murcia	0.308	87.2	0.299	89.8	0.339	107.1	0.240	85.1	0.313	103.3	0.172 76.6	0.148 74.4	0.223 121.1	0.095 72.6	0.176 113.3
Navarre	0.294	83.1	0.318	95.5	0.263	82.9	0.253	89.7	0.276	91	0.187 83.5	0.180 90.4	0.112 60.5	0.103 78.6	0.126 81.0
Basque C.	0.327	92.6	0.271	81.4	0.307	97.0	0.246	87.2	0.272	89.7	0.202 90.2	0.122 61.4	0.170 92.4	0.095 72.8	0.121 77.7
Rioja	0.310	87.8	0.26	78.3	0.320	101.2	0.258	91.5	0.254	83.9	0.191 85.2	0.109 54.9	0.191 103.4	0.109 83.3	0.105 67.5
SPAIN	0.353	100.0	0.333	100.0	0.317	100.0	0.282	100.0	0.303	100	0.224 100.0	0.199 100.0	0.184 100.0	0.131 100.0	0.155 100.0

Source: Own elaboration from the Encuesta de Presupuestos Familiares 1973/74, 1980/81, 1990/91, 2006 and the Encuesta Continua de Presupuestos Familiares 2000

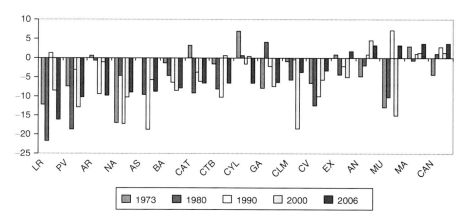

Fig. 11.1 Evolution of relative differences regarding inequality compared to the national total (Gini index)
Source: Own elaboration from the Encuesta de Presupuestos Familiares, 1973/74, 1980/81,1990/91, 2006 and the Encuesta Continua de Presupuestos Familiares, 2000

Other autonomous regions find themselves in the opposite situation, where inequality seems to be more entrenched than in the rest of the Spanish territory. This is the case of the Canary Islands, whose distributive process is marked by its peculiar model of economic growth and demographical structure, or Madrid, where most of the social tensions related to the new process of economic modernisation crystallyse, such as the changes in labour relations and the atypical employment relationships, the modifications in household structure or a higher incidence of immigration than in other areas. It is of significance that the results corresponding to the same estimation year as in the work by Ruiz-Castillo (1987) offer certain dissimilarities with those obtained in such a study, although these seem to be consistent with the time sequence of our estimations. In Andalusia, in turn, the below-average inequality indicators until the 1980s turned into the opposite trend from that date onwards. A possible influential factor is the reinforcement of provincial asymmetries.

The results do not register significant changes with the use of alternative inequality indicators (Table 11.3). The estimation of the Theil index ($c=1$) corroborates this, with only specific exceptions. Such is the case, among others, of the higher growth of inequality with this indicator in Andalusia and Madrid compared to the national average and the relative improvements in terms of intra-territorial equity of Catalonia and the Balearics.

An interesting aspect of inequality measurement is identifying the relative contribution of each territorial unit to general inequality. In order to obtain this, we could use the index, which combines the properties that can be required from the additively decomposable indices (Shorrocks, 1980), such as the generalised entropy index, with $c=0$.

Table 11.4 Contribution to inequality by autonomous regions

	1973 %	1980 %	1990 %	2000 %	2006 %	% Contribution / % Population				
						1973	1980	1990	2000	2006
Andalusia	15.3	15.2	17	18.9	17.8	0.96	0.95	1.03	1.09	1.07
Aragon	3.6	3.5	2.8	3.2	2.5	0.98	1.00	0.81	1.01	0.82
Asturias	2.7	2.7	1.9	2.5	2.2	0.92	0.83	0.64	0.93	0.85
Balearics	1.4	1.8	1.6	1.9	2	0.70	0.86	0.87	0.87	0.86
Canary Islands	2.9	3.2	3.7	3.9	4.6	0.94	1.01	1.07	1.03	1.07
Cantabria	1.0	1.2	1.1	1.4	1.1	0.71	0.85	0.81	1.06	0.89
Castile-Leon	9.1	7.3	6.7	6.8	5.1	1.20	1.00	0.95	1.00	0.86
Castile-L.M.	5.1	4.0	4.4	2.8	3.9	1.06	0.89	0.98	0.66	0.92
Catalonia	10.9	13.6	14.4	14.2	14.5	0.67	0.83	0.90	0.88	0.88
Valencian Com.	7.7	7.5	8.0	9.2	10.4	0.78	0.74	0.80	0.89	0.94
Extremadura	3.3	2.6	2.9	2.4	2.4	1.04	0.90	0.99	0.87	0.99
Galicia	8.6	8.4	6.8	5.5	5.3	1.17	1.16	0.98	0.85	0.87
Madrid	11.1	11.6	12.9	13.4	14.2	0.91	0.95	1.03	1.04	1.06
Murcia	1.9	2.0	2.9	2.0	3.0	0.82	0.82	1.15	0.73	1.05
Navarre	1.1	1.2	0.9	1.1	1.1	0.83	0.90	0.70	0.81	0.83
Basque Country	4.0	3.6	5.3	3.8	4.1	0.73	0.65	0.98	0.75	0.80
La Rioja	0.6	0.4	0.7	0.5	0.5	0.81	0.57	1.02	0.83	0.71
SPAIN	100	100	100	100	100	1.00	1.00	1.00	1.00	1.00
Inter-reg. inequality	10.25	9.69	5.44	6.17	4.9	–	–	–	–	–

Source: Own elaboration from the EPFs 1973/74, 1980/81, 1990/91, 2006 and the ECPF 2000

The development of this decomposition exercise seems to confirm that the differences in the average income of each autonomous region (inter-territorial inequality) do not contribute greatly to inequality in Spain (Table 11.4). However, this result should not be interpreted as a highly limited explanatory capacity of the territorial variable. The logic of the decomposition method establishes that a relatively limited percentage of total inequality corresponds to any a priori significant variable. Changes over time are more significant, this component becoming less determining in the most recent period than two or three decades ago. The arrival of investments and transfers to the regions with the lowest income levels may have had an influence on this evolution, as anticipated in diverse researches focussed on the convergence of the disposable per capita income.

The most remarkable aspect is the high contribution made by Andalusia, Catalonia and Madrid. These three autonomous regions contribute to half of total inequality (2006). Nevertheless, there are significant differences among the three situations, given that, as already mentioned in the previous section, the relative situation of inequality varies considerably among them. More specifically, Madrid and Andalusia proportionally contribute through relative inequality to a greater extent than through demographical weight. Both register, together with the Canary Islands, the highest relationship between the relative contribution to inequality and to total population. On the opposite side, we find those autonomous regions where inequality is less intense and population volume is reduced, including Navarre, the Basque Country and La Rioja, among others.

11.4 Convergence in Inequality Levels

In the two previous sections, we have highlighted the changes in internal inequalities over time. Undoubtedly, a key question is to understand whether the differences across autonomous regions have remained stable or, to the contrary, have increased or decreased. In order to prove this, the convergence process must be examined. The lack of sufficiently long enough series prevents the analysis of temporal series, or even of panel data, which are frequently used when studying these processes. However, available data allows us to replicate, although with the natural limitations, some of the standard techniques of convergence measurement.

In the field of regional analysis, the research on long-term convergence across the different territories has been a subject of increasing interest, including the concepts of β-convergence and σ-convergence. The first of such processes is verified when poor regions register a higher increase than the rich ones in an approaching process (Barro and Sala-i-Martin, 1992). σ-convergence refers to the evolution of dispersion over time of the reference variable chosen.

The notion of β-convergence can be summarised as follows:

$$\frac{1}{T}\left[\text{Ln}\left(\frac{Y_{i,t}}{Y_{i,t-T}}\right)\right] = a - b\left[\frac{\text{Ln}(Y_{i,t-T})}{T}\right] + u_t^i, \tag{11.1}$$

where sub-indices i ($i = 1, 2, ..., G$) and t ($t = 1, 2, ..., T$) refer to territories and moments in time, respectively. In this expression, b represents the effect of initial income over the average variation rate of the period. The annual average convergence rate is obtained as follows:

$$\beta = -T^{-1}\text{Ln}(1-b). \tag{11.2}$$

If $0 < b < 1$, $\beta > 0$, which allows us to confirm that convergence exists in the period under analysis, where β indicates the annual convergence speed. However, β was not defined for values higher than one, avoiding the possibility of "systematic overtaking" among countries (Sala-i-Martin, 1994).

In addition, using σ-convergence, the dispersion of the reference variable is analysed over time, with the frequent use of statistical dispersion indicators, such as the coefficient of variation. As demonstrated by Quah (1993) and Sala-i-Martin (1994), β-convergence is necessary, but not sufficient in order for σ-convergence to occur, while σ-convergence is sufficient, but not necessary for β-convergence to exist.

The use of both approaches has been standard since the beginning of the 1990s. Nevertheless, these have been the object of significant criticism, such as those made by Friedman (1992) and Quah (1993). This latter author contributed to the development of the well-known "twin peaks" literature, which focuses on aspects regarding the global distribution of income beyond the variance analysis. More specifically, Quah (1996) attempted to demonstrate the bimodal nature of such distribution by using Markovian transition matrices in order to explain the re-orderings of countries. In a similar way and in order to solve some gaps in the previous approaches, Boyle and McCarthy (1997, 1999) suggest the γ-convergence alternative. This approach provides other nuances to the idea of convergence on the basis of Kendall's W coefficient of rank concordance. More specifically, γ-convergence can clarify situations where the two previous approaches give rise to ambiguous situations, adding the concept of re-rankings to the study of convergence.

The main added value of the contribution by Boyle and McCarthy (1997, 1999) is the development of a type of β-convergence analysis that reflects the extent of mobility within the income distribution during a specific period of time. By using γ- and σ-convergence together, the nature of β-convergence can be identified, with a measure of the distribution dynamics among territories. The idea of the resulting convergence is similar to an image of the ordinal ranking evolution throughout a certain period.

Therefore, while σ-convergence can be estimated from a dispersion statistic, γ-convergence can be contrasted by focussing on the dispersion of territorial re-orderings:

$$\sigma = \left(\frac{\text{var}(D_{ti})/\text{media}(D_{ti})}{\text{var}(D_{t0})/\text{media}(D_{t0})} \right), \quad (11.3)$$

$$\gamma = \left(\frac{\text{var}(R_{ti} + R_{t0})}{\text{var}(R_{t0} * 2)} \right), \quad (11.4)$$

where var(D) is the variance of an inequality index of the different autonomous regions, var(R) is the variance of the orderings according to the inequality indices, t_i indicates the moment in which inequality was measured and t_0 refers to the year of reference, 1973 in this case, which is the year of the first Encuesta de Presupuestos Familiares available.

In order to check the statistical significance, we use the expression $T(N-1)W$, approximately distributed as a χ^2 with $n-1$ degrees of freedom. In the estimates carried out, the null hypothesis that the T years are not related is rejected in all cases. Although the R-squared of some estimates of β-convergence does not seem high, the adjustment obtained is generally acceptable (Table 11.5).

In all the estimates, the b coefficients are positive. Therefore, the negative value $-b$ indicates that the higher the initial inequality, the lower its increase or the higher its decrease. According to the limitations established by the possible heterogeneity from the sampling differences of the surveys, a convergence process could be possible in the internal inequality levels of the autonomous regions. More specifically, if we take the Gini index and the idea of β-convergence as a reference, the decade registering the highest approaching level to the initial situation was the 1980s, although the values for the following decade are quite similar.

Table 11.5 Convergence of intra-territorial inequality

	1973–1980	1973–1990	1973–2000	1973–2006	1980–1990	1980–2000	1980–2006	1990–2000	1990–2006
β-Convergence (Gini index)									
R^2	0.23	0.43	0.27	0.46	0.39	0.22	0.20	0.38	0.19
$-b$ coefficient	−0.566**	−0.961***	−0.553**	−0.832***	−0.855***	−0.500**	−0.462*	−0.761***	−0.383*
β-convergence (Theil index, $c=0$)									
R^2	0.16	0.41	0.22	0.46	0.42	0.23	0.24	0.35	0.19
$-b$ coefficient	−0.553	−1.003***	−0.533**	−0.817***	−0.850***	−0.522**	−0.499**	−0.752***	−0.379*
β-convergence (Theil index, $c=1$)									
R^2	0.15	0.28	0.33	0.53	0.43	0.32	0.34	0.61	0.45
$-b$ coefficient	−0.547	−0.986**	−0.759***	−1.136***	−1.050***	−0.571***	−0.618***	−0.975***	−0.634***
β-convergence (Theil index, $c=2$)									
R^2	0.40	0.18	0.76	0.77	0.43	0.71	0.62	0.90	0.82
$-b$ coefficient	−1.007***	−0.871*	−1.097***	−1.316***	−1.283***	−0.809***	−0.838***	−1.063***	−0.917***

	γ-Conv.		σ-Conv.			% var. previous year (γ)		% var. previous year (σ)	
1980	0.668		1.140						
1990	0.461		1.060			−33.2%		14.0%	
2000	0.734		0.801			−31.0%		−7.0%	
2006	0.576		0.733			59.3%		−24.4%	
						−21.5%		−8.4%	
	γ-Conv.		σ-Conv.						
Average Var.	−1.66%		−0.94%						
γ- and σ-convergence (Theil index, $c=0$)									
1980	0.662		1.390						
1990	0.452		1.086			−33.8%		39.0%	
2000	0.717		0.722			−31.8%		−21.9%	
2006	0.572		0.618			58.8%		−33.5%	
						−20.2%		−14.5%	
Average Var.	−1.68%		−1.45%						
γ- and σ-convergence (Theil index, $c=1$)									
1980	0.631		1.180						
1990	0.487		1.793			−36.9%		18.0%	
						−22.9%		52.0%	

2000	0.639	0.596	31.3%	−66.8%
2006	0.456	0.712	−28.7%	19.4%
Average Var.	−2.36%	−1.03%		
γ- and σ-convergence (Theil index, $c=2$)				
1980	0.483	1.037	−51.72%	3.7%
1990	0.472	4.492	−2.28%	333.3%
2000	0.390	0.131	−17.43%	−97.1%
2006	0.197	0.279	−49.35%	113.6%
Average Var.	−4.8%	−3.8%		

(*), (**), (***) indicate statistical significance at 10%, 5% and 1%, respectively.

Source: Own elaboration from the EPFs 1973/74, 1980/81, 1990/91, 2006 and ECPF 2000

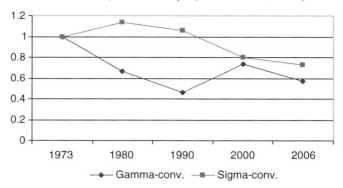

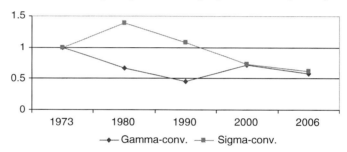

Fig. 11.2 γ-convergence and σ-convergence of intra-territorial inequality

Concerning the other types of convergence and also taking into consideration the Gini index, the process seems to be more moderate, with a slight annual σ- (1.66%) and γ-convergence (0.94%).[9] It is worth mentioning that the 1980s was the period where the approaching was clearer. In fact, it is one of the few time spans when γ- and σ-convergence coexist. In the 1970s, the dispersion was not reduced, but mobility was intense. These changes are clearly shown in Fig. 11.2.

The use of other indicators, such as those comprising the generalised entropy family, does not significantly alter the results. Again, it is confirmed that the 1980s was the decade with the highest convergence, from a β-convergence perspective and maintaining the idea of reducing the differences regarding long-term

---

[9]The results obtained must be interpreted taking into consideration that simple σ-convergence statistics are used, while the inequality indicators are mainly weighted.

11 Inequality and Welfare in Intra-Territorial Income Distribution 251

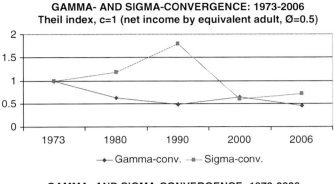

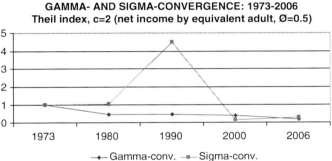

Fig. 11.2 (Continued)

intra-territorial inequality. However, when parameter c is assigned a higher value, the 1990s becomes the decade with the highest convergence level. The analysis of γ- and σ-convergence offers different outcomes depending on the value of c. With $c = 0$, the two types of convergence are observed in the 1980s and in 2000–06, with $c = 1$, γ-convergence exists in the 1980s (with sigma-divergence) and in 2000–2006, and σ-convergence in the 1990s (with gamma-divergence); and with $c = 2$, the 1990s is the only decade where both types of convergence coexist.

According to the indicators chosen, it is possible to confirm the existence of a convergence process of internal income differences in each autonomous region between 1973 and 2006. This process seems to have been more intense in the 1980s than in the previous and following decades. However, the prominence of the 1990s as the main period in which regions corrected intra-territorial differences as a higher value is assigned to c demonstrates that, if we focus on what occurs in households with the highest income level, a clearer convergence can be seen in the most recent period.

11.5 Regional Differences in Social Welfare

So far, we have observed the differences regarding unequal income distribution within each autonomous region, their changes over time and the contribution of each territory to overall inequality. Now, a final question to complete the picture of intra-territorial distribution of income is to identify the possible differences concerning social welfare[10] on the basis of the inequalities observed. A common procedure to make comparisons regarding social welfare from the personal income distribution is to integrate different representative arguments of average income and its distribution in the same function. These abbreviated functions of social welfare, using the terminology suggested by Cowell (1999), allow us to assess the achievements made in welfare, qualifying average income according to equity criteria. Given an income distribution y, social welfare can be summarised as:

$$W(y) \equiv \omega[\mu(y), I(y)], \tag{11.5}$$

where $\mu(y)$ represents the average income and $I(y)$ is an indicator of inequality. Therefore, welfare would increase, ceteris paribus, if average income increased or inequality decreased:

$$\frac{dW(y)}{d\mu(y)} > 0, \quad \frac{dW(y)}{dI(y)} < 0. \tag{11.6}$$

The main advantage of these abbreviated functions of social welfare is that they offer a simple criterion to compare implicit welfare in a distribution according to two easily estimatable parameters. Specialised literature suggests various alternatives in order to specify the possible form of these social welfare functions. One which is usually used expresses social welfare as a multiplicative trade-off between both components:

$$W(y) = \mu(y)(1 - I(y)). \tag{11.7}$$

This specification requires the use of adequate inequality indicators. Dutta and Esteban (1992) suggest various conditions to be fulfilled by the inequality indicator used as an argument of the function.[11] In practise, some of the inequality indicators normally estimated do not comply with the required properties. However, the

---

[10] The concept of welfare used herein is subject to the parameters provided by the income distribution in each territory (average income and inequality). As stated by Osberg and Sharpe (2005), a more general notion of welfare should include not only the distributive aspects, but also the different access to preferential goods by the citizens of each region.

[11] The suggestions are: S-concavity, continuity, invariance with respect to population replications, weak homotheticity, and monotonicity along rays from the origin in the relative case or weak translability and monotonicity along rays parallel to the line of equality in the absolute case.

indicator suggested by Atkinson (1970) does fulfil these requirements. The Atkinson family of indices allows us to incorporate social welfare criteria in the inequality measurement through the imposition of restrictions in the form of income utility:

$$U_\varepsilon(y) = a + b\frac{y^{1-\varepsilon}}{1-\varepsilon}, \quad \text{for } \varepsilon > 0, \varepsilon \neq 1, \tag{11.8}$$

$$U_\varepsilon(y) = a + b \ln y^{1-\varepsilon}, \quad \text{for } \varepsilon = 1,$$

where a and b are constants and ε is an inequality aversion parameter. From such expressions, we can infer the Atkinson family of inequality measures, already mentioned in the first section of this chapter.

The consideration of the Atkinson index allows us to define a social welfare function as the product of average income and an inequality indicator whose values depend on the degree of inequality aversion:

$$W_e = \mu \left[\frac{1}{n} \sum_{i=1}^{n} \left(\frac{y}{\mu}\right)^{1-e} \right]^{\frac{1}{1-e}} \quad W_e = \mu \left[\exp\left(\frac{1}{n} \sum_{i=1}^{n} \text{Ln}\left(\frac{y}{\mu}\right)\right) \right] \tag{11.9}$$

for $\varepsilon \geq 0$, $\varepsilon \neq 1$

for $\varepsilon = 1$.

The inclusion of ε enables us to incorporate highly different value judgements with respect to the weighting of the equity component in the representation of social welfare. The lower the value adopted for ε, the lesser the weight of inequality in the assessment of social welfare. In the extreme case of $\varepsilon = 0$, inequality does not have any weight as a welfare component. When the ε values are higher than zero, this implies positive weightings of inequality, reaching its maximum weighting when $\varepsilon \to \infty$.

The availability of disaggregated data by autonomous regions in the Encuestas de Presupuestos Familiares leads us to estimate the extent of the regional differences in social welfare. Such data provides a definition of the double component of average income [$\mu(y_i)$] and inequality [$I(y_i)$] for each region i. The Atkinson index is estimated taking two different inequality aversion parameters as a reference ($\varepsilon=1$, $\varepsilon=2$). In order to check the possible sensitivity of the results to the adjustment of the household income depending on whether scale economies are or are not taken into consideration, the welfare functions have been estimated considering the double criteria of income per capita ($\phi=1$) and equivalent household income ($\phi=0.5$).[12]

---

[12] The comparisons made concerning welfare are not corrected regional purchasing power parities, given the limits in the availability of homogeneous series covering the whole period analysed. Its consideration could obviously alter the orders obtained. Previous works using instruments for the adjustment of regional purchasing power have demonstrated the existence of significant differences regarding the orders obtained through nominal indicators (Ayala et al., 2002).

Table 11.6 Differences of social welfare by autonomous regions, 2006

	Average income		Inequality		Social welfare			
	$\mu(y)$ [$\phi = 0.5$]	$\mu(y)$[$\phi = 1$]	Atk($\varepsilon = 1$)	Atk($\varepsilon = 2$)	$W(\phi = 0.5, \varepsilon = 1)$	$W(\phi = 0.5, \varepsilon = 2)$	$W(\phi = 1, \varepsilon = 1)$	$W(\phi = 1, \varepsilon = 2)$
Andalusia	0.86	0.84	1.06	1.03	0.85	0.85	0.83	0.83
Aragon	0.97	0.98	0.83	0.86	0.99	1.02	1.01	1.03
Asturias	1.06	1.08	0.86	0.90	1.09	1.10	1.11	1.12
Balearics	1.16	1.18	0.87	0.91	1.18	1.20	1.21	1.22
Canary Islands	0.95	0.93	1.07	1.07	0.94	0.92	0.92	0.91
Cantabria	1.03	1.03	0.90	0.87	1.05	1.08	1.05	1.08
Castile-Leon	0.96	0.98	0.87	0.88	0.98	1.00	1.00	1.02
Castile-La Mancha	0.88	0.85	0.92	0.95	0.89	0.89	0.86	0.86
Catalonia	1.10	1.10	0.89	0.92	1.12	1.13	1.12	1.14
Valencian C.	0.97	0.98	0.94	0.96	0.98	0.99	0.99	1.00
Extremadura	0.76	0.75	0.99	0.97	0.76	0.77	0.75	0.76
Galicia	0.89	0.88	0.88	0.88	0.91	0.93	0.90	0.92
Madrid	1.19	1.19	1.06	1.03	1.18	1.17	1.18	1.18
Murcia	0.85	0.83	1.05	1.00	0.85	0.85	0.82	0.83
Navarre	1.16	1.16	0.85	0.87	1.19	1.21	1.19	1.21
Basque Country	1.11	1.14	0.81	0.84	1.15	1.18	1.17	1.20
La Rioja	0.91	0.92	0.72	0.76	0.95	0.99	0.97	1.01
TOTAL	1.00	1.00	1.00	1.00	1.00	1.00	1.00	1.00

Source: Own elaboration from the Encuesta Continua de Presupuestos Familiares, 2006

The construction of the social welfare index for each autonomous region offers a wide variety of experiences (Table 11.6). A common pattern does not seem to exist in the different regions with respect to the possible linearity between both components: efficiency and equity. While some regions with an average income above the national average present inequality indicators below such average (Navarre, the Basque Country, Asturias, Catalonia and the Valencian Community), the region with the highest average income (Madrid) registers a higher inequality, as aforementioned, than the national total. Heterogeneity is higher in regions with lower incomes, with inequality experiences that can be lower (Castile-La Mancha, Castile-Leon, Extremadura, Galicia and La Rioja) or higher than the national total (Andalusia, Murcia and the Canary Islands).

The combination of income levels higher than the average and inequality levels generally lower than the national average suggests, a priori, that the richer regions should register higher welfare indicators than the rest. The individual order depends, however, on the weighting assigned to inequality. In regions with similar income levels, such as Aragon and the Valencian Community, the higher the level of aversion to inequality, the higher the differences observed in the levels of social welfare.

In some cases, the different values adopted by the welfare indicator, whether $\varepsilon = 1$ or $\varepsilon = 2$ are taken as a reference, hinder the possibility of referring to complete dominance. Nevertheless, there are some sufficiently clear differences across regions. If we take ($\phi = 1$) and the two parameters of ε as a reference, there are two regions which undoubtedly register a higher level of social welfare than the rest, and these are the Balearics and Navarre. These are followed by Madrid and the Basque Country, where the results do not show which dominates the other, given the change of order occurring when $\varepsilon = 1$ turns into $\varepsilon = 2$, and then by Catalonia and Asturias. The last positions of the ranking are occupied by six autonomous regions where dominance criteria can be established in the rank of ε values used for those regions with the lowest levels of welfare, i.e. Extremadura and Murcia. Andalusia, Castile-La Mancha, Galicia and the Canary Islands are also included in the same group.

The use of the Encuestas de Presupuestos Familiares corresponding to the previous decades enables us to reconstruct the paths of social welfare in each autonomous region (Table 11.7). From this data, a certain reduction of differences can be inferred, in line with the aforementioned double process of improvement in convergence of long-term regional average incomes, and also a reduction of differences regarding the levels of internal inequality across the autonomous regions.

Although there are some gaps in the temporal trend, the systematic improvement of some autonomous regions stands out. This is the case for Asturias, Castile-Leon and Galicia, among others, which are mainly boosted by the ageing of the population, which is compensated by the development of income transfer programs. Castile-La Mancha is another example, where the significant improvement registered in the levels of social welfare is explained by the advances made both in efficiency and equity. The opposite experience is that of the Canary Islands, where, as mentioned, significant problems for improving convergence in income

Table 11.7 Differences of social welfare by autonomous regions, 1973–2006

	$\mu(y)$ [$\phi = 0.5$], Atk($\varepsilon = 1$)					$\mu(y)$ [$\phi = 0.5$], Atk($\varepsilon = 2$)				
	1973	1980	1990	2000	2006	1973	1980	1990	2000	2006
Andalusia	0.81	0.81	0.84	0.86	0.85	0.83	0.83	0.83	0.86	0.85
Aragon	1.03	1.00	1.04	0.99	0.99	1.04	0.99	1.11	0.97	1.02
Asturias	0.98	1.09	1.09	1.07	1.09	1.00	1.13	1.21	1.07	1.10
Balearics	1.12	1.08	1.11	1.10	1.18	1.20	1.17	1.14	1.11	1.20
Canary Islands	1.01	0.85	0.86	0.89	0.94	1.00	0.86	0.83	0.88	0.92
Cantabria	0.99	1.11	1.05	0.97	1.05	1.00	1.16	1.09	0.95	1.08
Castile-Leon	0.81	0.90	0.95	0.93	0.98	0.83	0.90	0.98	0.93	1.00
Castile-La Mancha	0.76	0.73	0.86	0.92	0.89	0.73	0.68	0.91	0.96	0.89
Catalonia	1.22	1.28	1.21	1.16	1.12	1.17	1.38	1.26	1.18	1.13
Valencian C.	0.95	1.04	0.99	1.02	0.98	0.97	1.13	1.04	1.03	0.99
Extremadura	0.73	0.65	0.72	0.76	0.76	0.73	0.70	0.58	0.78	0.77
Galicia	0.81	0.79	0.93	0.92	0.91	0.82	0.72	0.93	0.94	0.93
Madrid	1.28	1.28	1.14	1.17	1.18	1.30	1.35	1.21	1.16	1.17
Murcia	0.88	0.85	0.90	0.86	0.85	0.92	0.75	0.91	0.89	0.85
Navarre	1.12	1.22	1.14	1.16	1.19	1.25	1.28	1.16	1.18	1.21
Basque Country	1.27	1.24	1.14	1.13	1.15	1.31	1.37	1.07	1.16	1.18
Rioja	1.07	1.05	1.17	0.98	0.95	1.16	1.20	1.11	1.01	0.99
Spain	1.00	1.00	1.00	1.00	1.00	1.00	1.00	1.00	1.00	1.00

Source: Own elaboration from the Encuesta de Presupuestos Familiares 1973/74, 1980/81, 1990/91, 2006 and the Encuesta Continua de Presupuestos Familiares, 2000

per capita and the increase in inequality levels coexist. However, its relative situation has improved in recent years.

Within the wide variety of experiences, some peculiarities must be highlighted, such as the continuance of Aragon and the Valencian Community in levels around the national average during the whole period, or the problems in Extremadura and Andalusia. In Extremadura, the slowing down of inequality has not been sufficient to compensate the much slower advances in convergence regarding income per capita, which are determinants of its systematic last position in the ranking of relative welfare. In Andalusia, an important part of the slowing down originates from the difficulties of reducing inequality and the continuance of distances concerning the average income.

Generally speaking, changes have been more intense in the bottom part of the ranking of autonomous regions than in the other extreme. A group of autonomous regions, including Madrid, Catalonia, Navarre, the Basque Country and the Balearics, has registered the highest welfare levels from the beginning of the 1970s. However, different behaviours have occurred in the last three decades, which do not allow us to demonstrate convergent paths. Madrid is the main example to be highlighted, because, although it remains as one of the autonomous regions with the highest level of relative welfare, it experienced a certain deterioration due to a higher increase in inequality than in other regions. Catalonia has also registered a certain worsening in the long-term relative welfare levels due to a lesser income growth than in other autonomous regions comprising the group of the highest average wealth.

11.6 Conclusions

The analysis of inter-territorial income distribution has become of increasing interest in the Spanish case. Several reasons justify the analysis of internal inequalities in each autonomous region. These reasons range from the mere diagnosis of the extent of differences in the levels of inequality and social welfare to the possible assessment of results of the decentralisation process of an important part of public intervention for equity reasons.

In an attempt to overcome the traditional statistical restriction in the long-term reconstruction of the inter-territorial distributive process, the present work has focussed on the analysis of data from the Encuestas de Presupuestos Familiares. However, the reconstruction of long-term trends is partly limited by difficulties in sampling heterogeneity and design of surveys due to the changes that have occurred over time. This analysis, although limited by the restrictions imposed, allows us to obtain some relevant conclusions.

Firstly, all the results obtained delimit specific typologies of autonomous regions according to their levels of internal inequality. Therefore, regardless of the indicator chosen, there is a clear territorial differentiation concerning the level of income concentration. The same occurs in the analysis of trends over time.

Secondly, it is worth highlighting the limited weight acquired by inter-territorial inequalities in Spain to explain global inequality in personal distribution. Internal differences in each autonomous region are virtually the only explanatory factors of inequality. Therefore, the results obtained have facilitated the identification of the higher contribution of some regions, which is mainly linked to their greater populations, although this effect is not strictly proportional.

Thirdly, a triple focus of convergence analysis has been developed, where the concept of γ-convergence has been added to the traditional concepts of σ-convergence and β-convergence. This has added a measure of the re-orderings according to the levels of intra-territorial inequality and has allowed us to verify the existence, in the long-term, of an approaching process among territories. Nevertheless, this effect has not been constant during the three decades under analysis, the reduction of differences being concentrated from the 1980s onwards.

Finally, the analysis of social welfare in each autonomous region reveals the importance of inequality reduction for its improvement. It is also worth mentioning how significant differences have become entrenched in territorial social welfare. In the long term, the levels of social welfare of some autonomous regions have remained considerably higher than the average.

From the whole range of results obtained, significant political implications are derived. Although almost no doubt exists regarding the real extent of the intra-territorial distributive convergence process, there are still some considerable differences. For this reason, we should observe with uncertainty the possible effect of the territorial decentralisation process in the long run of certain basic services of social welfare. If the objective of maintaining such differences in a relatively narrow variation range is accepted, it seems to be necessary to coordinate the design of mechanisms to correct intra-territorial inequalities. Likewise, the specific instruments to correct the problems related to inter-territorial inequity should be reinforced.

References

Atkinson, A. B. (1970). On the measurement of inequality. *Journal of Economic Theory, 2*, 244–263.
Atkinson, A. B. (1989). *Poverty and Social Security*. Hertfordshire: Harvester Wheatsheaf.
Ayala, L., Martínez, R., & Ruiz-Huerta, J. (2001). *La descentralización territorial de las prestaciones asistenciales: efectos sobre la igualdad*. Instituto de Estudios Fiscales. P.T.2001/16.
Ayala, L., Martínez, R., Sastre, M., & Ruiz-Huerta, J. (2002). *Perfil de la población española en pobreza y riesgo social: situación y tendencias a partir del Panel de Hogares de la Unión Europea (1993-1997) y la Encuesta Continua de Presupuestos Familiares* (Mimeo). Madrid: Ministerio de Trabajo y Asuntos Sociales.
Ayala, L., Navarro, C., & Sastre, M. (2004). *El Panel de Hogares de la Unión Europea: posibilidades y límites para el análisis dinámico*. (Mimeo).
Barro, R. J. (1991). Economic Growth in a cross-section of countries. *Quarterly Journal of Economics, 106*, 407–443.
Barro, R. J., & Sala-i-Martin, X. (1992). Convergence. *Journal of Political Economy, 100*, 223–251.
Barro, R. J., & Sala-i-Martin, X. (2003). *Economic Growth*. Massachusetts: MIT.
Bishop, J. A., Formby, J. P., & Thistle, P. D. (1994). Convergence and divergence of regional income distributions and welfare. *The Review of Economics and Statistics, 79*, 228–235.
Bosch, A., Escribano, C., & Sánchez, I. (1989). *Evolución de la pobreza y la desigualdad en España: Estudio basado en las Encuestas de Presupuestos Familiares 1973-74 y 1980-81*. Madrid: Instituto Nacional de Estadística.
Bover, O., & Arellano, M. (2002). Learning about migration decisions from the migrants: Using complementary datasets to model intra-regional migrations in Spain. *Journal of Population Economics, 15*, 331–355.
Boyle, G. E., & McCarthy, T. G. (1997). A simple measure of β-convergence. *Oxford Bulletin of Statistics, 59*, 257–264.
Boyle, G. E., & McCarthy, T. G. (1999). Simple measures of convergence in per capita GDP: A note on some further international evidence. *Applied Economics Letters, 6*, 343–347.
Buhmann, B., Rainwater, L., Schmaus L., & Smeeding T. (1988). *Equivalence scales, well-being, inequality, and poverty: Sensitivity estimates across ten countries using the Luxembourg Income Study (LIS) database*. Review of Income and Wealth, 34, 115–142.
Cowell, F. (1999). Measurement of Inequality. In A.B. Atkinson and F. Bourguignon (Eds.), *Handbook of Income Distribution*. Amsterdam: North-Holland.
Cuadrado-Roura, J. R., Mancha, T., & Garrido, R. (1998). *Convergencia regional en España*. Madrid: F. Argentaria/Visor.
Cuadrado-Roura, J. R., Mancha, T., & Garrido, R. (2002). Regional Dynamics in the European Union: Winners and Losers. In J. R. Cuadrado-Roura and M. Parellada (Eds.), *Regional Convergence in the European Union* (pp. 23–52). Berlin: Springer.
Dutta, B., & Esteban, J. M. (1992). Social welfare and equality. *Social Choice and Welfare, 50*, 49–68.
Friedman, M. J. (1992). Do old fallacies ever die? *Journal of Economic Literature, 30*, 2129–2132.
García Lizana, A., & Martín Reyes, G. (1994). La pobreza y su distribución territorial. In M. Juárez (Ed.), *V Informe Sociológico sobre la Situación Social en España*. Madrid: Fundación FOESSA.

García Lizana, A. et al. (1989). La riqueza y la pobreza bajo una perspectiva regional. *Documentación Social, 76*, 101–124.
Goerlich, F., & Mas, M. (2001). Inequality in Spain, 1973-91: Contribution to a regional database. *Review of Income and Wealth, 47*, 361–378.
Goerlich, F., Mas, M., & Pérez, F. (2002). Concentración, convergencia y desigualdad regional en España. *Papeles de Economía Española, 93*, 17–36.
Gradín, C. (2000). Polarization by sub-populations in Spain. *Journal of Population Economics, 13*, 529–567.
Heshmati, A. (2004). Regional income inequality in selected large countries. *IZA Discussion Paper 1307*.
Jenkins, S. P. (2000). *Modelling Household Income Dynamics*. Essex: Institute for Social and Economic Research, University of Essex, ESRC Working Paper no. 99-9.
Martín Reyes, G., García Lizana, A., & Fernández Morales, A. (1989). La distribución territorial de la pobreza en España. In *VI Jornadas de Estudio del Comité Español para el Bienestar Social : La pobreza en la España de los ochenta*. Madrid: Editorial Acebo.
Martín-Guzmán, P. (1996). *Encuesta de Presupuestos Familiares. Desigualdad y pobreza en España*. Madrid: Instituto Nacional de Estadística.
Mella, J. M. (1998). (coord.) *Economía y política regional en España ante la Europa del siglo XXI*. Madrid: Akal.
Moffitt, R., & Gottschalk, P. (2002). Trends in the Transitory Variance of Earnings in the United States. *Economic Journal, 112*, 68–73.
Osberg, L., & Sharpe, A. (2005). How should we measure the "economic" aspects of well-being. *Review of Income and Wealth, 51*, 311–336.
Quah, D. T. (1993). Galton's fallacy and tests of the convergence hypothesis. *The Scandinavian Journal of Economics, 95*, 427–443.
Quah, D. T. (1996). Twin peaks: Growth and convergence in models of distribution dynamics. *Economic Journal, 106*, 1045–1055.
Raymond, J. L. (2002). Convergencia real de las regiones españolas y capital humano. *Papeles de Economía Española 93*, 109–121.
Ruiz-Castillo, J. (1987). La medición de la pobreza y la desigualdad en España, Banco de España (no 42). Madrid: Estudios Económicos.
Ruiz-Huerta, J., López Laborda, J., Ayala, L., & Martínez, R. (1995). Relaciones y contradicciones entre la distribución personal y la distribución espacial de la renta. *Hacienda Pública Española, 134*, 153–190.
Sala-i-Martin, X. (1994). *Regional Cohesion: Evidence and Theories of Regional Growth and Convergence*. Discussion Paper no 1075, Centre for Economic Policy Research.
Shorrocks, A. (1980). The class of additively decomposable inequality measures. *Econometrica, 48*, 613–625.
Villaverde, J. (1999). *Diferencias regionales en España y Unión Monetaria Europea*. Madrid: Pirámide.

Chapter 12
The Competiveness of the Spanish Regions[1]

Ernest Reig-Martínez

12.1 What Does Competitiveness Mean?

Competitiveness is a widely popular concept, which has saved in practise, to denote efficient economic behaviour. The wide dissemination of the *competitiveness ranking* of countries published annually by the *World Economic Forum* of Davos (Switzerland), or the fact that the European Union defines some of the global problems, which affect the countries of the EU in terms of the *competitiveness gap,* have footered the use of this expression in the media. The use of the term to denominate some of the objectives of the European Regional policy has also contributed to extending the use of the expression, as well as the work of prestigious consultants, such as Michael Porter, in influential works, such as *The Competitive Advantage of Nations* (1990). This expansion has been to the detriment of conceptual clarity. While the expression *competitiveness* was limited to business economics, its meaning remained relatively well determined: the capacity of a company to be competitive can be placed in relation with the possibilities it has to maintain or increase the returns from its assets in the prevailing conditions in open markets. The fact that a company gains a market share at the cost of the other companies which operate in the same sector has served to establish a strong link between the idea of business competitiveness and the idea of *rivalry*.

E. Reig-Martinez
Universidad de Valencia. Facultad de CC. Económicas y Empresariales, DEPARTMENT d' ESTRUCTURA ECONÒMICA, Edifici Departmental Oriental, Avda. dels Tarongers, S/N (4P15) 46022 - València, España
e-mail: Ernest.Reig@uv.es

[1]This chapter brings together the main ideas expressed in the first two chapters of the book entitled Competitividad, crecimiento y capitalización de las regiones españolas, written by the author of this chapter and published in 2007 by the Fundación BBVA and also in Cuaderno No 8 of the Fundación BBVA 'Capital y Crecimiento' Project, published in 2008 under title of Competitividad y crecimiento: una perspectiva regional, of the same author.

The growing application of the concept of competitiveness, not to specific companies, but to regions or countries, entails a change of scale, which involves important risks from the analytical point of view. This is due, in the first place, to the fact that, at national or regional level, there is nothing equivalent to business bankruptcy. In the second place, the red numbers in the trade balance of a country or region are not equivalent to the losses reported on the financial statement of a company. Instead of constituting an unarguable symptom of competitive failure, they constitute an indicator of the temporary existence of a macroeconomic imbalance between domestic expenditures and internal production. The conceptual ambiguity also persists when other indicators related to foreign trade are used. Thus, if the improvements in competitiveness are linked to the gains in the relative market share of the exports of a country in the international market, then it must be acknowledged that this does not guarantee an improvement of national welfare. Actually, its significance in this area will depend on the reasons which gave rise to the improvements. This will not have the same connotation in terms of welfare if it responds to the capacity of the domestic companies to supply highly differentiated products, which are attractive for the consumers from other countries, than if it is the temporary fruit of a recession in the domestic market accompanied by the depreciation of the national currency. Something similar occurs with the adoption of the real exchange rate as an indicator of competitiveness (Cellini and Soci, 2002), as the temporary stability of the real exchange rate can conceal an important loss of profitability in the exporting companies when these cannot transfer their increases in costs per unit of the product to their foreign customers. In this case, it would be difficult to maintain that domestic exports remained competitive, even though this is the impression conveyed by the observed trend in the real exchange rate.

The differences between what is understood by the competitiveness of a company and that of a country have been highlighted by outstanding economists, such as Paul Krugman (1994), who labelled the tendency to consider international economic relations in the light of business-type competitive rivalry "a dangerous obsession". Krugman intended to point out that the main impulse for improving the standard of living in each country is found in national factors, and that countries do not compete with each other in the same way as companies do as the interdependence between countries is much richer and varied, and the mutual interest in accessing each others' markets is a good example of this. The economic history of the second half of the twentieth century generally backs up the thesis of prosperity shared through trade as the decadence of protectionism in the decades which followed World War II coincided with a period of intense economic growth. The scepticism of Krugman as regards "competitiveness" as a useful concept at territorial level is, however, much less at regional level than at national level. He admits the importance of regional differences in efficiency and productivity when attractive perspectives are offered in terms of returns capable of attracting capital and labour from other regions and boosting economic growth (Krugman, 2003).

The verification of the risks involved in mechanically transferring the vision of competitiveness in the business world to territorial units, such as countries or region's has led to the search for variables, which might be associated to the idea of competitiveness and might have an unmistakable meaning in terms of welfare. Thus, attention has been diverted towards a view of competitiveness, which is closely linked to economic growth and, in particular, to one of its key variables: labour's productivity. It is a fact that the improvements in the productivity of labour not only contribute to enhance economic well-being by raising real wages or shortening the working day, but also create resources available for investment and offer a sound basis in the long term for an increase in the supply of public goods. However, the determinants of productivity gains are mainly national. Therefore, contrary to what is sometimes taken for granted, the improvements in productivity recorded in other national economies do not, in themselves, damage the country which falls behind. These only make it possible to verify that economic performance is deficient in relative terms. Probably for these reasons, certain supra-national institutions and entities have decided to choose productivity as a reference when offering its own vision of the meaning of competitiveness.

The European Commission (1999) in its *Sixth Periodic Report on the Social and Economic Situation and Development of Regions in the European Union*, defined competitiveness, following the approaches previously adopted by the OECD such as:

"the ability of companies, industries, regions, nations and supra-national regions to generate, while being exposed to international competition, relatively high income and employment levels" (p. 75).

12.2 Two Approaches to Competitiveness: Prices and Costs Versus Productivity

It can be deduced from what has been explained above that it is common to consider the competitiveness of a national or regional economy from two different perspectives. The first is usually termed *external competitiveness* and is based on analysing the capacity of this economy to sustain or increase its presence in the national and international markets of the goods and services it produces. This is a type of competitiveness analysis oriented mainly to external trade, regardless of whether this is international or interregional. Within this conceptual framework, it is normal to pay special attention to relative prices and costs. The second perspective, known as *aggregate competitiveness* corresponds to a macroeconomic vision of competitiveness and centres its attention on the gross domestic product (GDP) per inhabitant and on labour productivity. This chapter adopts this second approach.

We should begin by establishing a basic distinction between what could be called *indicators of results*, which, as the name indicates, show the situation of an economy in terms of competitiveness through variables associated to its consequences, and *indicators of causal factors*, which address the determinants of competitiveness. Bearing this distinction in mind, the most relevant indicators of results of external competitiveness would be the evolution of the exports and imports of a country or region in relation to the world total or to a specific economic area, the trade balance, the degree of import penetration in the domestic market and the behaviour of several indicators of revealed comparative advantage. As determining factors in this case, it should be pointed to the evolution of the nominal exchange rate, the basic deflators of the economy and the price indexes of tradable goods, particularly the prices of manufactured goods. Together with these, it is also possible to use indicators of the profitability achieved in the sectors which produce tradable goods. Structural factors, related to the endowment of physical, technological and human capital, innovative capacity or the productive specialisation profile, may complete the range of explanatory elements to be considered.

On the contrary, the macroeconomic vision centres its attention on the capacity of a country or a region to achieve positive results in terms of growth of income and well-being per inhabitant, operating in the context of an open economy. Its main indicator of results is the growth of the GDP per inhabitant, as a variable representative of the evolution of the average income of the population. Labour productivity and the employment rate can also be considered as results, although they are also the fundamental cause for the changes in the average level of income per inhabitant (European Commission, 2003). As regards the determining factors, mention should be made of all those influencing workers' productivity, such as the various types of capital endowments per worker, the skills of the work force, the infrastructures, the orientation of the companies as regards innovation, the public and private efforts made as regards R&D, and all the aspects which influence the ability of a territory to support economic activity (geographical location, industrial relations, the quality of public institutions, the fiscal system, etc.). One way to systematise these determining factors is to distinguish between those which correspond to the "fundamentals", that is to say, to aspects, such as the educational level, the existing business culture, natural resources, the quality of the infrastructures and the public policies, and the "external economies", which follow from the agglomeration and the diversification of economic activity (Krugman, 2003).

The two perspectives mentioned, – the price-competitiveness perspective and the macroeconomic perspective – have many points in common. Productivity at sector level has a decisive influence on the evolution of cost and price indexes of the goods which a country or a region can supply to external markets. However, within the framework of a regional economy, the second perspective seems to show greater potential to capture the competitiveness factors, which appear to be more closely linked to the territory.

Therefore, the evolution of the competitiveness of a region can be measured by its GDP per inhabitant on condition that it is borne in mind that this can be broken down into three components which, together, determine its level: labour productivity, the employment rate and the age structure of the population. Discarding this last aspect, which can hardly constitute an objective for regional economic policy, attention can be focussed on the comparison of regions in terms of their capacity to raise labour productivity, and, simultaneously, to increase the proportion of their potentially active population in employment. This must take place within a context of external openness which makes it possible to achieve efficiency gains arising from competitive pressure in the marketplace.

12.3 Regions and Competitiveness

Transferring the ideas which have just been mentioned to the field of regional economics, it is evident that the balance between exports and imports does not constitute the most relevant aspect to assess the competitiveness of a region. In fact, the transitory imbalances in the interim balances, which make up the balance of payments of a region, such as the trade balance, can be compensated with balances of an opposing type in other components of the balance of payments, due to public transfers or the interregional mobility of private capital. In addition, within an integrated national financial system, the monetary flows deriving from a hypothetical deficit of the regional balance of payments regional do not necessarily restrict the volume of bank credit the region can dispose of, as this is granted by regional affiliates of nationwide banks. Consequently, the balance between exports and imports of goods and services does not constitute a suitable indicator of the competitiveness of a region in the short- and medium-term, if we wish to establish a link with economic growth and improvements in the well-being of the population.

Productivity, as mentioned before, is the key variable in the long run to determine a population's standard of living. And it is even more relevant on a regional scale as a determinant of comparative advantages than on a national scale. This is due to the fact that absolute differences in productivity play a much more important role in interregional trade than in international trade. While in international trade, governed by the principle of comparative advantage, absolute differences in country costs can be neutralised by modifying the exchange rate or making wages more flexible, such differences at regional level can be much more difficult to correct. If the wages which are paid in one region evolve in a similar way to that of the neighbouring regions, but productivity falls behind, then the situation will probably have to be corrected by means of migration or perhaps through compensatory income transfers, neither of these two options being favourable if they persist in the long-term. Labour mobility, which is much more intense at interregional than at international level, is one of the reasons that makes it difficult for the local cost of production factors to adjust to productivity lags. Apart from this, if a region's productivity is lagging behind the national average due to structural causes, such as deficient infrastructure, then it is even more unlikely that low relative productivity will lead local workers to the acceptance of lower monetary wages than the national average, as it is always a feasible option for workers to migrate to other more prosperous regions within the country. And, logically, the exchange rate is not available as a policy tool to redress regional economic imbalances.

Since a loss of competitiveness by a region, measured in terms of absolute production costs, will not usually be solved through wage flexibility it will result in job losses. The answer will frequently consist in public transfers from the national

Government – unemployment benefits – and private transfers – migrant remittances –, or in the sale of regional assets which will become the property of non-residents. In the long-term, this adjustment could also occur through further migration, which if is persistent, will gradually weaken the economic possibilities of the region through its negative impact on the size of the domestic regional market.

What has been explained above means that regions operate in a scenario where factors are mobile and it is impossible to adjust the exchange rate, which has forced some researchers to qualify the way Krugman and other authors see things: absolute differences in regional productivity are extremely important when it comes to explaining interregional trade and the law of comparative advantage does not provide a sufficiently satisfactory answer at regional level, although it does for larger political and territorial units (Camagni, 2002).

The main characteristic of the analyses carried out on regional competitiveness is the strong emphasis placed on the territory as a source of comparative advantages. The aim is to ascertain which production factors are relatively immobile and linked to specific geographical regions – infrastructures, business culture, social capital, human capital endowments – thus, helping to establish policies leading to the creation of a more favourable environment for the localisation of capital and labour. Nowadays, with increasingly global economies, regional and also city competitiveness depends on their capacity to foster knowledge and develop close-knit relationships between people and firms that allow the dissemination and adaptation of new technologies, and the exchange of information (Kitson et al., 2004).

In order to provide empirical content to the macroeconomic vision of competitiveness and apply it to Spanish regions, two main blocks of competitiveness indicators have been calculated in this chapter. The first belongs to the group termed indicators of results and the second to the group of indicators of causal factors:

1. Indicators based on a multiplicative decomposition of GDP per inhabitant at regional level.
2. Indicators based on the aggregation of a set of representative variables selected for each of the following structural determinants of competitiveness: infrastructures and accessibility, human resources, technological innovation and production environment.

12.4 Indicators of Regional Competitiveness Based on Results

Gross Domestic Product per capita (GDPpc) summarises the results of economic activity and is a good indication of the level of income and, indirectly, of the wellbeing of the inhabitants of regions, in this case in Spain. At the same time, the level and rate of growth in GDPpc is determined by two main driving forces; one that increases labour productivity and other that incorporates an increasing number of people into the labour market. Therefore, one way of explaining the differences in GDPpc across Spanish regions – Comunidades Autónomas in Spanish – is by decomposing this variable into its multiplicative factors: labour productivity (GDP/Employment), the proportion of the total labour force in employment, the overall activity rate – economically active population as a percentage of the working age population, aged between 16 and 64 years – and the weighting of the working age population in relation to total population. This type of analysis is common in comparative studies of regions and has been used, for example, by Gardiner et al. (2004). Tables 12.1 and 12.2 present the results of this decomposition for each of the Spanish regions, together with the autonomous cities of Ceuta and Melilla, at two different times, the first when Spain became a member of the European Communities and the second closer to the present day. In both cases, data are expressed in constant 2000 prices.

Table 12.1 Main factors explaining GDP per capita of spanish regions (1985–1986)

	GDP per capita (Year 2000 Euros per capita)	GDP/ Employment (Year 2000 euros per person employed)	Employment/ labour force (in %)	Labour force/ Working age population (in %)	Working age population/ total population (in %)
Andalusia	7.550	33.822	69.81	52.33	61.11
Aragon	10.465	34.093	82.29	57.96	64.36
Asturias (Principality of)	9.216	30.005	81.03	58.04	65.31
Balearic Islands	13.567	40.708	86.51	60.03	64.17
Canary Islands	10.242	38.368	73.40	58.69	61.97
Cantabria	9.773	31.520	83.34	58.73	63.35
Castile and Leon	9.578	32.738	81.74	57.61	62.13
Castile-La Mancha	8.027	27.759	83.82	55.28	62.40
Catalonia	11.655	38.401	77.93	60.52	64.36
Ceuta and Melilla	8.623	35.495	71.54	49.56	68.52
Valencia Region	9.943	34.414	80.11	58.83	61.31
Extremadura	6.142	25.214	71.92	54.10	62.60
Galicia	8.465	23.400	86.17	67.22	62.45
Madrid	13.275	46.930	79.04	57.05	62.73
Murcia	9.136	33.330	80.66	56.13	60.54
Navarra	12.890	40.482	80.57	60.87	64.92
Basque Country	12.824	43.402	76.45	57.99	66.65
Rioja (La)	10.829	35.640	83.07	58.09	62.97
Spain	10.138	35.583	78.39	57.85	62.83
Coefficient of Variation	0.2072	0.1856	0.0621	0.0649	0.0256

Source: Fundación BBVA, INE and own elaboration

Table 12.2 Main Factors Explaining GDP per Capita in Spanish Regions (2006–2007)

	GDP per capita (Year 2000 euros per capita)	GDP/ Employment (Year 2000 euros per person employed)	Employment/ labour force (in %)	Labour force/ working age population (in %)	Working age population/ total population (in %)
Andalusia	13.443	33.809	87.23	67.27	67.76
Aragon	19.123	41.385	94.58	74.45	65.62
Asturias (Principality of)	15.799	39.330	91.06	65.61	67.23
Balearic Islands	18.572	37.779	93.24	75.98	69.39
Canary Islands	15.783	35.407	88.87	70.93	70.71
Cantabria	17.269	38.597	93.73	70.06	68.14
Castile and Leon	17.193	40.627	92.31	70.68	64.86
Castile-La Mancha	13.867	32.826	91.76	70.34	65.45
Catalonia	20.770	42.795	93.39	76.75	67.72
Ceuta and Melilla	16.182	49.349	81.57	61.85	65.00
Valencia	15.942	34.911	91.39	73.17	68.29
Extremadura	12.320	32.894	86.70	66.56	64.90
Galicia	14.704	34.382	91.88	70.24	66.27
Madrid	23.153	46.865	93.62	76.32	69.15
Murcia	14.290	32.022	92.27	71.30	67.83
Navarra	22.598	47.369	94.93	75.52	66.55
Basque Country	22.949	49.654	93.42	72.90	67.86
La Rioja	19.086	40.701	94.04	74.28	67.13
Spain	17.616	39.356	91.57	72.26	67.65
Coefficient of variation	0.2074	0.1405	0.0272	0.0508	0.0207

Source: Fundación BBVA, INE and own elaboration

As can be observed, the Balearic Islands and Extremadura were top and bottom of the ranking respectively in terms of GDP per inhabitant in 1985/86, whereas in 2006/7, these positions were held by Madrid and once again by Extremadura. In the time elapsed between both points in time, the distance in relative terms between the first and last position changed, the multiple separating them dropping from 2.2 to 1.8. The top ranked group of regions includes, both in 1985/6 and 2006/7, Madrid, Navarra, the Basque Country, Catalonia, La Rioja and Aragon, despite the Balearic Islands ranking first in the first 2-year period and several places lower in the second. Extremadura, Andalusia and Castile La Mancha were the lowest ranked regions in both 1985/6 and 2006/7. It is worth highlighting how stable the coefficient of variation of GDPpc was between the two 2-year periods. In contrast, this ratio dropped markedly in the case of labour productivity and the proportion of the economically active population that was employed.

In order to better illustrate just how much each of the multiplicative components of GDPpc contributes to interregional inequality, it is worth using one of the Theil indexes ($T(0)$), which enables us to decompose this variable additively (Goerlich, 2001):

$$T(0) = -\sum_k \left[\sum_i p_i \log(k_i/k)\right].$$

In the formula above, *pi* is the weighting of region *i* in the Spanish population and *k* denotes each of the variables into which GDPpc is decomposed. Therefore, if *ki* represents, for example, productivity per person employed in region *i*, *k* would represent productivity per person employed in Spain as a whole. Hence, it is possible to ascertain to what degree the global inequality observed, $T(0)$, in GDPpc is due to regional imbalances in each of the following ratios: labour productivity (GDP/Employment), people in employment as a percentage of the regional labour force, activity rate, and working population as a percentage of the total population.

As can be observed in Table 12.3, the global index of GDPpc inequality has decreased slightly between the two points in time under consideration. In both cases, most of this inequality is due to differences in labour productivity, which accounted for 61% of the total in 1985/6 and 83% in 2006/7. The second most important factor in 1985/6 and the third most important in 2006/7 was people in employment as a percentage of the economically active population. This factor explains 24% of GDPpc inequality in 1985/6, but only 7.5% in 2006/7. The decrease in importance is primarily due to the remarkable decrease in unemployment recorded throughout these two decades, particularly from 1995 to the end of 2007, which saw the situation in the different regional labour market converge substantially.

These results coincide with those obtained with the same type of decomposition by Esteban and Vives (1994). Using a sample of nine European Union countries over the period dating from 1986 to 1989, these authors found that labour productivity was responsible for around 70% of regional inequality in per capita income, whereas employment as a percentage of the economically active population and the latter as a percentage of the total population each accounted for approximately 15%.

Table 12.3 Global index of inequality in GDP per capita

	1985–1986	2006–2007
GDP/Employment	0.01362	0.01782
Employment/Labour force	0.00547	0.00160
Labour force/Working age population	0.00267	0.00166
Working age population/Total population	0.00032	0.00021
GDP per capita	0.02208	0.02130

Source: Own elaboration

Labour productivity (GDP/Employment) is, therefore, the main reason behind regional inequality in income per capita. The regions that recorded the highest levels of labour productivity in 2006/7, and therefore, the regions that can be considered the most competitive according to this indicator, were the Basque Country, Navarra, Madrid and Catalonia, while the lowest levels were observed in Murcia, Extremadura, Castile-La Mancha and Andalusia. The high score recorded by the autonomous cities of Ceuta and Melilla is not significant due to statistical problems related to their small size.

Table 12.4 presents the growth rates for GDP per capita, employment and labour productivity between 1985/86 and 2006/7. Ceuta, Melilla and Extremadura registered the highest growth rates in GDP per capita, which is highly positive in the interest of convergence with other more developed regions. Generally speaking, the increases in income per capita over this period were based on gains in employment, which exceeded an annual 3% in quite a few regions, particularly in the two island regions, Murcia and Madrid. In contrast, gains in productivity were generally modest, with even negative growth rates being recorded in some regions where economic growth was higher. This must be interpreted bearing in mind the changes in production specialisation in Spain throughout this period, which increased the relative weighting of employment in construction, a sector that is characterised by low average levels of labour productivity.

Table 12.4 Growth rates between 1985–1986 and 2006–2007 (Percentages)

	GDP per capita	Employment	GDP / Employment
Andalusia	2.79	3.59	0.00
Aragon	2.91	2.26	0.93
Asturias (Principality of)	2.60	1.01	1.30
Balearic Islands	1.51	3.91	−0.35
Canary Islands	2.08	4.12	−0.38
Cantabria	2.75	2.11	0.97
Castile and Leon	2.83	1.56	1.03
Castile-La Mancha	2.64	2.53	0.80
Catalonia	2.79	3.06	0.52
Ceuta and Melilla	3.04	2.11	1.58
Valencia	2.27	3.35	0.07
Extremadura	3.37	2.06	1.27
Galicia	2.66	0.68	1.85
Madrid	2.68	3.79	−0.01
Murcia	2.15	3.87	−0.19
Navarra	2.71	2.63	0.75
Basque Country	2.81	2.09	0.64
La Rioja	2.74	2.86	0.63
Spain	2.67	2.88	0.48

Source: Fundación BBVA, INE and own elaboration

Table 12.5 Index of competitiveness 1 (1985–1986) standardised data

	GDP/ Employment	Employment/ Labour force	Labour force/ Working age population	Index of competitiveness 1
Andalusia	0.443	0.000	0.157	0.200
Aragon	0.454	0.747	0.476	0.559
Asturias	0.281	0.672	0.480	0.478
Balearic Islands	0.736	1.000	0.593	0.776
Canary Islands	0.636	0.215	0.517	0.456
Cantabria	0.345	0.810	0.519	0.558
Castile and Leon	0.397	0.714	0.455	0.522
Castile-La Mancha	0.185	0.839	0.324	0.449
Catalonia	0.638	0.486	0.620	0.581
Ceuta and Melilla	0.514	0.104	0.000	0.206
Valencia	0.468	0.617	0.525	0.536
Extremadura	0.077	0.126	0.257	0.153
Galicia	0.000	0.980	1.000	0.660
Madrid	1.000	0.553	0.424	0.659
Murcia	0.422	0.650	0.372	0.481
Navarra	0.726	0.645	0.640	0.670
Basque Country	0.850	0.397	0.477	0.575
La Rioja	0.520	0.794	0.483	0.599

Source: own elaboration

The result indicators of competitiveness, which appear in Tables 12.5 and 12.6, are based on the following breakdown of the GDP per inhabitant:

$$\text{PIB}_{pc} = \frac{\text{PIB}}{\text{Employment}} \times \frac{\text{Employment}}{\text{Active population}} \times \frac{\text{Active population}}{\text{Population}_{16-64}}.$$

The arithmetic average of the three variables situated at the right of the equal sign has been calculated in order to obtain the *Index 1 of Competitiveness* for the two periods and for each of the Autonomous Communities (Ceuta and Melilla are treated together). Subsequently, the growth rates in GDPpc, employment and GDP/Employment between 1985/6 and 2006/7 were calculated. The Competitiveness Index 2 was computed as the arithmetic average of these three growth rates and of the variables contained in Index 1. Before computing the arithmetic averages, all the variables were standardised in accordance with the following formula:

$$E_{ij} = (S_{ji} - \min_i S_{ji}) / (\max_i S_{ji} - \min_i S_{ji}),$$

where E_{ji} is the standardised value, which corresponds to the criteria or variable i for region j, and S_{ji} is the value corresponding to the initial, not standardised, data, while $\min_i$ and $\max_i$ correspond respectively to the minimum and maximum regional values at each point in time for variable i.

Table 12.6 Index of competitiveness (2006–2007) based on standardised data

	GDP/ Employment	Employment/ Labour force	Labour force/ Working age population	Index of competitiveness 1	Growth in employment (1985–1986 to 2006–2007)	Growth in labour productivity (1985–1986 to 2006–2007)	Index of competitiveness 2
Andalusia	0.101	0.424	0.364	0.296	0.845	0.170	0.381
Aragon	0.531	0.974	0.846	0.784	0.460	0.587	0.679
Asturias	0.414	0.711	0.252	0.459	0.095	0.753	0.445
Balearic Islands	0.326	0.874	0.948	0.716	0.938	0.012	0.620
Canary Islands	0.192	0.547	0.609	0.449	1.000	0.000	0.470
Cantabria	0.373	0.910	0.551	0.611	0.414	0.606	0.571
Castile and Leon	0.488	0.804	0.593	0.628	0.257	0.634	0.555
Castile-La Mancha	0.046	0.763	0.570	0.459	0.538	0.530	0.489
Catalonia	0.611	0.885	1.000	0.832	0.692	0.403	0.718
Ceuta and Melilla	0.983	0.000	0.000	0.328	0.414	0.880	0.455
Valencia	0.164	0.735	0.760	0.553	0.776	0.202	0.527
Extremadura	0.049	0.384	0.316	0.250	0.401	0.742	0.379
Galicia	0.134	0.772	0.563	0.490	0.000	1.000	0.494
Madrid	0.842	0.902	0.971	0.905	0.904	0.168	0.757
Murcia	0.000	0.801	0.634	0.479	0.926	0.086	0.489
Navarra	0.870	0.917	1.000	0.929	0.566	0.508	0.772
Basque Country	1.000	0.887	0.742	0.876	0.411	0.459	0.700
La Rioja	0.492	0.933	0.835	0.753	0.635	0.455	0.670

Source: own elaboration

The regional ranking stemming from *Index 1* is basically similar to the ordering based on the per capita GDP. Thus, in 1985/86, the Balearic Islands and Navarre top the list, followed by Madrid and Galicia, while Extremadura, Andalusia, and Ceuta and Melilla come last, while in 2006/7, the first places correspond to Navarre, Madrid, the Basque Country and Catalonia, and the last to Extremadura, Andalusia, and Ceuta and Melilla. The anomaly of finding Galicia, a region with a relatively low level of development, among the first places in 1985/86 was due to the way *Index 1 of Competitiveness* was constructed, which eliminates the influence deriving from the differences in the measurement units. This makes it possible to grant the same relative weight to all three variables that make up the GDP per capita, which does not occur when the ranking is based directly on the GDP per capita itself. Thus, the good relative position of Galicia in 1985/86 in relation to the labour market, having the second lowest rate of unemployment and the highest rate of activity, compensated its bad position in terms of labour productivity.

As regards the *Index of Competitiveness 2*, the best positions correspond to Navarre, Madrid, Catalonia and the Basque Country, and the worst to Extremadura, Andalusia, Asturias and Ceuta and Melilla. The appearance of Asturias in the last positions in the table is due to the fact that the *Index of Competitiveness 2* includes two dynamic variables, the rate of growth of employment and the rate of growth of productivity between the two points in time involved, and in the first of these, Asturias appears in the second worst position. Table 12.7 makes it possible to

Table 12.7 Regional ranking

	GDP per capita 2006–2007	Index of Competitiveness 1 1985–1986	Index of Competitiveness 1 2006–2007	Index of Competitiveness 2 2006–2007
Madrid	1	4	2	2
Basque Country	2	7	3	4
Navarra	3	2	1	1
Catalonia	4	6	4	3
Aragon	5	8	5	5
La Rioja	6	5	6	6
Balearic Islands	7	1	7	7
Cantabria	8	9	9	8
Castile and Leon	9	11	8	9
Ceuta and Melilla	10	16	16	15
Valencia	11	10	10	10
Asturias (Principality of)	12	13	14	16
Canary Islands	13	14	15	14
Galicia	14	3	11	11
Murcia	15	12	12	12
Castile-La Mancha	16	15	13	13
Andalusia	17	17	17	17
Extremadura	18	18	18	18

Source: own elaboration

compare the position of each region in the rankings, which have been described in this section, and verify the existence of a high degree of coincidence between the order of the regions in 2006/7 according to GDP per capita, and according to the indices of competitiveness calculated for that year.

12.5 Indicators of Competitiveness Based on Causal Factors

Several proposals can be found in the literature (for example, the European Commission, 2003) in relation to the group of variables which must be taken into account when selecting those that exercise a greater influence on the competitiveness of the regions. Here, the factors deemed determinants of competitiveness of the Spanish regions mainly through their effect on productivity, have been grouped in four large blocks:

1. Infrastructure and Accessibility

Three basic indicators have been taken into account for 1985/86: Capital endowments for transport infrastructure (roads, railways, ports and airports) in thousands of euros per km^2, capital endowments in urban structures in euros per inhabitant and the number of telephone lines per 1,000 inhabitants. A fourth indicator, the percentage of households in each region with an internet connection, has been added for the second point in time.

2. Human Resources

The indicators of regional human resource endowment are as follows: the proportion of the working age population with post-compulsory education, the average number of years of schooling of the working age population, university students as a percentage of the population aged 18–25 years and human capital stock-wealth per capita[2] in thousands of euros per capita as of 1995 prices.

3. Technological Innovation

As regards technological innovation, the following indicators have been used: technological capital per worker[3] in year 2000s constant price euros, government investment in R&D as a percentage of regional gross value added (GVA), private

---

[2] Human capital wealth jointly represents individuals' current and future productive capacity and is measured by means of the present value of the future wages to be received by an individual throughout his/her life. The main simplifying assumption is that the 1995 relative wage structure is maintained over time. Once calculations have been made accordingly for each type of individual, bearing in mind his education, age and gender in the base year, the estimates are applied to the economically active population in each region (Serrano and Pastor, 2002).

[3] Technological capital stock is obtained from the accumulation of real investment in R&D made in each region. Investment is assumed to accumulate in accordance with the permanent inventory method. The result is divided by the number of people in employment in each region (Gumbau and Maudos, 2006).

sector investment in R&D as a percentage of regional GVA, proportion of employment in R&D activities over the economically active population and applications to register patents per one million inhabitants. Two additional indicators have been added for 2003/4. The first measures scientific publications in international journals (ISI database), while the second registers the proportion of regional households with an Internet connection.

4. Economic and Social Environment

A wide-range of indicators have been chosen to capture aspects of the regional socioeconomic environment that can initially be considered relevant when it comes to positively influencing labour productivity, the location of firms and GDP per capita. Indicators are as follows: population density, in inhabitants per km^2, private non residential capital per km^2 in 1,000s of euros of 1,990 per km^2, industry diversification[4], proportion of employment in manufacturing industries and market services as a percentage of total employment, the proportion of employment in business services as a percentage of total employment, the proportion of exports plus imports over regional GDP, companies constituted per 1,000 inhabitants, the regional Human Development Index (HDI)[5], the index of social capital services per capita[6] and private non-residential capital per worker in the private sector. Due to more recent information being available, we have been able to include an additional indicator that measures GVA in activities with a high content of information and communication technologies (ICT) as a proportion of regional GVA.[7]

---

[4]The diversification ratio employed is calculated using the following formula:
Region i diversification ratio:

$$CD_i = \frac{\left(\sum_{j=1}^{L} Y_{ij}\right)^2}{L \sum_{j=1}^{L} Y_{ij}^2}, \; i = 1,...,N; j = 1,...,L; \; \frac{1}{L} \leq CD_i \leq 1$$

$$CD_i^* = \frac{L}{L-1}\left(CD_i - \frac{1}{L}\right); \; 0 \leq CD_i^* \leq 1,$$

Where Y_{ij} = value of output in region i of sector j

[5]This is a measurement of the level of wellbeing in a society, elaborated by the United Nations since 1990. It is calculated as the arithmetic average of three indicators: life expectancy, education and GDP per capita. In order to measure education, the index takes into account both the adult literacy rate and the gross rate of combined enrolment in primary school, secondary school and university (Herrero et al., 2004; Herrero and Soler, 2005).

[6]Pérez (2005, 2006) develops a measure of social capital and analyses its effects on economic growth.

[7]Mas and Quesada (2005) classify different branches of industry according to how much they use ICT in the Spanish economy as a whole. In our case, this national classification is applied to regional data and we have calculated the share of activities with high ICT content in each region's GVA.

The partial indicators (variables) included in the four groups detailed above are intended to capture the contribution made by the factors that exert a greater influence on decision making with regards to the localisation of mobile production factors, such as private capital and skilled labour.

After selecting the partial indicators, the next step was to cluster them into four higher level indicators, one per group. In order to do so, we made use of multi-variant analysis through a procedure known as principal component analysis (PCA). In this case, the objective was to non-arbitrarily generate aggregate variables for each of the four sub-groups of initial variables. As a result, only the first principal component has been considered, which expresses the maximum possible discrimination among regions in relation to the corresponding sub-group of variables. The numerical values of the characteristic vector for this first component have been used to weight each of the original variables. By multiplying them by the standardised values of these variables, we can obtain the aggregate indicator we are looking for and establish the subsequent regional ranking[8].

The results confirm, broadly speaking, the regional ranking based on GDPpc and its breakdown, but provide a more in-depth view of the strong and weak points of each region in a whole series of aspects related to their capacity to achieve a high level of labour productivity. It is worth pointing out that the scores of the four groups of factors obtained in the aggregate indexes illustrate a wider range of regional situations in "technological innovation" and "production environment" than in the case of "human resources" and above all "infrastructure and accessibility". The distance separating the most competitive from the least competitive regions is greater in the case of the first two, whereas the widespread improvement in terms of infrastructure that has taken place over the last 25 years in Spain as a whole and the increase in the average level of education has resulted in these two indicators reporting more uniform results.

By region, it is worth mentioning that out of the eight rankings that are included in Table 12.8, seven are topped by Madrid, while the Basque Country was at the top of the remaining ranking. In 1985/86, Madrid and the Basque Country were ranked in the top two positions by all indicators, while Catalonia, Navarra and the Balearic Islands alternated in the third place. The situation illustrated by the indicators calculated for the last point in time is somewhat different. In the first place, because Madrid undoubtedly confirms its supremacy in terms of competitiveness and, in the second place, because the Balearic Islands drop out of the top positions, although this region does remain well ranked considering Spain as a whole. Catalonia drops behind other highly developed regions in terms of human resources, whereas Aragon and Castile and Leon are well placed. As regards infrastructure and accessibility, Madrid, the Basque Country, the Balearic Islands and Catalonia are the four top-ranked regions in both points in time.

---

[8] Standardisation consists of subtracting the average and dividing by the standard deviation in order to prevent the variables with the greatest variance from dominating results.

Table 12.8 Regional indicators of competitiveness based on principal component analysis

(a) 1985–1986

(1) Infrastructure and accessibility		(2) Human resources		(3) Technological innovation		(4) Productive environment	
Basque Country	2.88	Madrid	4.47	Madrid	6.65	Madrid	5.76
Madrid	2.47	Basque Country	2.52	Basque Country	2.00	Basque Country	3.39
Balearic Islands	0.99	Navarra	1.14	Catalonia	1.66	Catalonia	2.66
Catalonia	0.97	Cantabria	1.02	Aragon	0.34	Valencia	0.96
La Rioja	0.61	Aragon	0.90	Navarra	0.19	Navarra	0.55
Aragon	0.47	Asturias	0.82	Asturias	−0.29	Aragon	0.46
Canary Islands	0.10	Catalonia	0.61	Cantabria	−0.32	Balearic Islands	0.40
Valencia	0.05	La Rioja	0.39	Murcia	−0.50	Cantabria	0.00
Asturias	0.02	Castile and Leon	0.37	Castile and Leon	−0.52	Canary Islands	−0.36
Cantabria	−0.22	Valencia	−0.69	Andalusia	−0.52	Asturias	−0.76
Castile and Leon	−0.52	Canary Islands	−0.74	Valencia	−0.57	Murcia	−1.09
Navarra	−0.59	Murcia	−1.22	Extremadura	−1.07	La Rioja	−1.14
Castile-La Mancha	−1.21	Balearic Islands	−1.25	Galicia	−1.20	Castile and Leon	−1.41
Galicia	−1.26	Andalusia	−1.49	Canary Islands	−1.27	Galicia	−1.48
Murcia	−1.29	Galicia	−1.83	Balearic Islands	−1.50	Andalusia	−1.63
Andalusia	−1.45	Extremadura	−2.46	La Rioja	−1.54	Castile-La Mancha	−2.53
Extremadura	−2.02	Castile-La Mancha	−2.59	Castile-La Mancha	−1.54	Extremadura	−3.78

(b) 2003–2004

Madrid	2.55	Madrid	3.70	Madrid	5.09	Madrid	7.20
Basque Country	2.45	Basque Country	2.94	Navarra	3.79	Catalonia	2.93
Catalonia	2.40	Navarra	1.78	Catalonia	2.90	Basque Country	1.94
Balearic Islands	1.18	Aragon	1.08	Basque Country	2.35	Balearic Islands	1.12
Navarra	1.05	Castile and Leon	0.93	Aragon	0.84	Valencia	0.86
Aragon	1.04	Catalonia	0.44	Valencia	0.14	Navarra	0.71
Canary Islands	0.31	Asturias	0.43	Asturias	−0.44	Aragon	0.61
La Rioja	0.02	Cantabria	0.26	Castile and Leon	−0.70	Canary Islands	−0.53
Valencia	−0.20	Valencia	−0.17	Galicia	−0.99	La Rioja	−0.73
Castile and Leon	−0.40	La Rioja	−0.19	La Rioja	−1.02	Cantabria	−0.91

(continued)

Table 12.8 (continued)

(1) Infrastructure and accessibility		(2) Human resources		(3) Technological innovation		(4) Productive environment	
Asturias	−0.55	Murcia	−0.76	Andalusia	−1.08	Murcia	−1.06
Cantabria	−0.77	Galicia	−0.89	Murcia	−1.11	Galicia	−1.14
Castile-La Mancha	−1.37	Canary Islands	−1.19	Cantabria	−1.27	Castile and Leon	−1.45
Andalusia	−1.61	Andalusia	−1.56	Canary Islands	−1.37	Asturias	−1.49
Galicia	−1.94	Balearic Islands	−1.76	Balearic Islands	−2.04	Andalusia	−1.98
Murcia	−1.97	Extremadura	−2.38	Extremadura	−2.43	Castile-La Mancha	−2.30
Extremadura	−2.18	Castile-La Mancha	−2.65	Castile-La Mancha	−2.67	Extremadura	−3.79

Source: own elaboration

The innovation indicator records one of the largest gaps between the most and least advanced regions. The most outstanding regions in the more recent cut-off point were Madrid, Navarra, Catalonia and the Basque Country. It is also worth highlighting the progress made by Navarra, which has risen up the ladder from fifth to second place. Finally, as far as the more or less favourable socioeconomic conditions are concerned, related to a regional economy's degree of external openness, the density of social capital it enjoys, how abundant in relative terms business initiatives are, and other aspects, the top positions are held by Madrid, the Basque Country, Catalonia, Valencia and the Balearic Islands. Leaving aside the exceptional case of Ceuta and Melilla (due to their small economic and demographic size), the strong relative position of Madrid is based especially on its density of productive (non-residential) capital per square kilometre, the high proportion of employment in services to businesses and the weighting of industries with a high content of information and communication technologies within total output, along with a strong endowment of social capital per inhabitant.

The lowest scores in the different indexes were normally recorded in Extremadura and Castile La Mancha, although it is worth mentioning the fact that a region, such as the Balearic Islands, where income per inhabitant is well above the national average, was scored quite low by the human resources and innovation indicators. This is more than likely related to the nature of the region's industrial structure in which services, such as catering and accommodation, which on average do not requires highly skilled workers, figure prominently. Furthermore, some regions have moved up the rankings between the two cut-off points, the clearest case being Galicia, which has risen three places in the human resources ranking and four in technological innovation.

12.6 The Spanish Regions and the Labour Market

One of the characteristics of macroeconomic definitions of regional competitiveness is that they refer to a region's ability to create jobs for a high share of its population. Indeed, productivity and the employment rate are both a part of what has been called "revealed competitiveness" (Gardiner et al., 2004) and are basic components in a region's economic performance. European policymakers are aware that Europe's gap in terms of competitiveness with other regions in the developed world is to a great extent due to a lesser degree of participation in the labour market and the poor trend in employment. For this reason, since the European Council held in Lisbon in 2000, the European Union has been discussing how to improve the employment situation, along with economic reform and social cohesion, as its strategic objectives towards achieving a competitive and knowledge-based society. Accordingly, the EU proceeded to set quantitative goals for employment to be accomplished by 2005 and 2010, referring to the working age population as a whole and also to specific social groups, such as women and the oldest workers. The economic situation in the European Union in 2007 meant that the targets set for 2005, in terms of the global

Table 12.9 Global employment rate (15–64 years)[a], Female employment rate (15–64 years)[a] and Employment rate for workers aged 55–64 years (2007) (percentages)

	Global employment rate	Female employment rate	Employment rate for workers aged 55–64 years
Andalucía	59.1	45.6	35.8
Aragon	71.8	61.6	47.6
Asturias (Principality of)	60.4	51.2	38.4
Balearic Islands	70.7	60.7	50.1
Canary Islands	63.5	53.2	42.5
Cantabria	66.4	55.7	44.4
Castile and Leon	65.9	53.6	44.4
Castile-La Mancha	65.4	49.6	43.2
Catalonia	71.9	62.3	51.7
Ceuta and Melilla	49.9	33.3	36.8
Valencia	67.0	55.7	44.7
Extremadura	58.5	44.6	39.6
Galicia	65.3	56.2	42.9
Madrid	71.7	62.8	48.9
Murcia	66.5	52.9	42.7
Navarra	72.0	61.0	49.4
Basque Country	68.3	58.8	44.2
La Rioja	69.6	56.6	45.7
Spain	66.6	55.5	44.6
EU-25	65.8	58.6	44.9
EU-27	65.4	58.3	44.7
Lisbon 2005 Strategy Objectives	67.0	57.0	–
Lisbon 2010 Strategy Objectives	70.0	60.0	50.0

[a]16–64 years for Spain and the Spanish regions
Source: Eurostat, INE and own elaboration

employment rate, had still not been reached. In Spain, however, job creation has been much more favourable in recent years, until the outbreak in 2007 of the current economic and financial crisis, than in the European Union as a whole. As can be observed in Table 12.9, some Spanish regions, namely Aragon, the Balearic Islands, Catalonia, Madrid and Navarra, had managed by 2007 to achieve or exceed the employment objectives set for 2010, both in terms of the general population and of women in particular. The goal for older workers, aged between 55 and 64 years, had only been achieved at this time in the Balearic Islands and Catalonia, although Navarra was also close to reach this target. It is worth highlighting the overall similarity between the rankings based on the competitiveness indicators outlined in previous sections and those based on the performance of regions in terms of employment.

Although there have traditionally been many shortfalls in terms of the behaviour of the Spanish economy, where employment is concerned, the increase in employment throughout the last economic cycle has been the mainstay of economic growth. This boom in employment was boosted by a decrease in real interest rates and intense immigration that has given rise to significant demographic growth and also had a remarkable impact in terms of wage moderation. The population aged between 16 and 64 years increased by 4.7 million people between 1994 and 2007, whereas 8.1 million people within that same age group found jobs. As a result, the employment rate of people of a working age, between 16 and 64 years, rose from 46.1% in 1994 to 66.6% in 2007. This substantial increase saw Spain surpass the average for the European Union. The activity rate was also improved, due to the rise in traditionally low female activity rates, and the unemployment rate dropped markedly to around the average for European Union in 2007, a situation unheard for decades. In 2008, however, the labour market started to display a negative trend, mainly due to job losses in the building industry, and the unemployment rate rose well and truly above the average for Europe.

On a regional scale, there are a wide variety of situations in Spain where the labour market is concerned. Table 12.10 describes the situation in 1985 and 2007. In 1985, the regions with the highest activity rates were Galicia, Navarra, the Balearic Islands and Catalonia, while those with the lowest were the autonomous cities of Ceuta and Melilla, Andalusia, Extremadura and Castile la Mancha. In 2007, the most favourable situations – as far as this indicator is concerned – were observed in Catalonia, Madrid, the Balearic Islands, Aragon and Navarra and the least favourable in Ceuta and Melilla, Asturias, Extremadura and Andalusia. Galicia, where many women worked on small family-run farms in 1985, is a special case. The highest unemployment rates in 1985 were registered in Andalusia, Extremadura and Ceuta and Melilla and 22 years later, these same regions still

Table 12.10 Activity and unemployment rates in Spanish regions (Percentages)

	Activity rate		Unemployment rate	
	1985	2007	1985	2007
Andalusia	52.02	67.80	30.24	12.81
Aragon	57.25	75.83	18.54	5.26
Asturias (Principality of)	58.79	66.03	18.96	8.53
Balearic Islands	60.72	75.96	13.44	6.99
Canary Islands	58.75	70.94	26.83	10.52
Cantabria	59.41	70.56	15.12	5.94
Castile and Leon	57.39	70.99	18.38	7.22
Castile-La Mancha	55.45	70.82	17.03	7.65
Catalonia	60.25	76.99	22.76	6.58
Ceuta y Melilla	49.32	61.92	28.51	19.37
Valencia	58.74	73.43	20.37	8.80
Extremadura	54.63	67.28	27.87	13.11
Galicia	67.73	70.72	13.33	7.70
Madrid	56.13	76.56	21.55	6.35
Murcia	56.25	71.99	20.58	7.58
Navarra	61.21	75.61	20.57	4.80
Basque Country	58.00	72.76	23.02	6.15
La Rioja	58.18	73.85	17.17	5.70
Spain	57.72	72.61	21.85	8.31
Coefficient of Variation	0.0682	0.0493	0.2241	0.3056

Source: Fundación BBVA, INE and own elaboration

displayed the highest rates among the Spanish regions, but at a considerably lower absolute level than in the 1980s.

The unemployment rate varies considerably from one region to another. There is almost a 10 point difference between the minimum and maximum unemployment rates across Spanish regions, which reveals a high degree of regional labour market segmentation. Such large differences in regional unemployment levels are consistent with low interregional labour force mobility. It is true that in the 1980s, the fact that high unemployment rates were widespread did slow down migratory flows substantially, but the fact that such large differences have persisted, even when some regions have recorded what is conventionally known as full employment, indicates that, in spatial terms, the labour market remains remarkably rigid. However, it must be taken into account that not even the relatively small wage gap that exists across Spanish regions should be interpreted entirely as an incentive for interregional labour mobility. In fact, wage differences are more than likely largely due to the differences in average human capital endowment in different regions (Pérez and Serrano, 1998). It seems that what is really important when deciding to move from one region to another is the remuneration per year of study. If this is the case, the persistence of regional differences in wage levels, linked to the lack of sufficiently intense migratory flows, does not necessarily mean that labour resources are not being assigned efficiently from a territorial viewpoint (Serrano, 2002). This is due to the fact that while part of the differences in wages is undoubtedly the result of the differences in interregional unemployment rates, or in the endowment of physical capital per person in employment, the other part reflects the differences in education and professional training that exist at territorial level and correcting them is a relatively long process in which education policy must play a leading role.

12.7 Conclusions

The usefulness of the concept "competitiveness" when applied at territorial level, particularly in relation to countries, has been the subject of much debate. Some research workers even deny that "competitiveness", with its strong rivalry overtones stemming from business-focused literature, can be meaningfully applied to national economies. In contrast, at regional level, there is widespread agreement in recognising that the competitive capacity of a region does not merely lie in the sum of the competitiveness of the firms operating there. The territory of a given region can display a series of aspects that favour improvements in efficiency and productivity, thus putting it in a particularly favourable situation to attract mobile factors of production. However, a lack of policy tools to make economic adjustments at regional level – exchange rate, wage differentiation according to productivity – which are normally available in the case of international relations among countries makes the differences in absolute costs and productivity enormously important to explain interregional trade flows.

In this chapter, regional competitiveness indicators have been built up using a macroeconomic approach as a basis, with labour productivity being the primary point of reference. This approach was applied to Spanish regions in two stages. In the first stage, a decomposition of GDP per capita in a series of multiplicative factors was achieved, while in the second stage, PCA was employed in order to obtain, from a large number of variables, several aggregate indicators of competitiveness. More specifically, four aggregate indicators have been built, referring to infrastructure and accessibility, human resources, technological innovation and production environment. The regional ranking derived from the competitiveness indexes based on the decomposition of GDP was quite similar to that obtained from applying PCA. In this last case, it is worth mentioning that the differences between the most and least competitive regions are larger where technological innovation and the existence of a favourable productive environment are involved than with relation to the other two aspects. This is due to significant government spending on infrastructure and education over the last few decades, which has managed to reduce regional differences with regards to infrastructure and human resources sub-indicators. The top-ranked regions, according to the various indicators that have been calculated, were usually Madrid, the Basque Country, Navarra and Catalonia. In this sense, it is worth mentioning that this coincides with the results of other studies that, employing a different methodology, identified the above regions as "winners" at European level, detecting for them an upward trend in the regional ranking, which in the case of Madrid and Navarra was highly pronounced (Cuadrado-Roura et al., 2002).

A "revealed competitiveness" approach (Gardiner et al., 2004), such as that contemplated in this chapter should also consider developments in regional labour markets. In this sense, we found large and persistent differences in regional unemployment rates. Moreover, marked regional differences exist concerning the progress that Spanish regions have made towards achieving the employment targets established by the Lisbon Strategy for European Union member States. Finally, substantial coincidences are observed between the highest ranked regions in terms of competitiveness and those which in 2007 recorded the highest activity rates and, albeit to a lesser extent, the lowest unemployment rates.

References

Camagni, R. (2002). On the concept of Territorial competitiveness: Sound or misleading? *Urban Studies, 39*, 2395–2411.

Cellini, R., & Soci, A. (2002). Pop competitiveness. *Banca Nazionale del Lavoro Quarterly Review, 220*, 71–101.

Cuadrado-Roura, J. R., Mancha-Navarro, T., & Garrido-Yserte, R. (2002). Regional Dynamics in the European Union: Winners and Losers. In J. R. Cuadrado-Roura and M. Parellada (Eds.), *Regional Convergence in the European Union. Facts, Prospects and Policies* (pp. 23–52). Berlin: Springer.

Esteban, J. M. (1994). La desigualdad interregional en Europa y en España: descripción y análisis. In J. M. Esteban and X. Vives (Dirs.) *Crecimiento y convergencia regional en España y Europa, vol. II. Instituto de Análisis Económico* (pp. 13–84). Madrid: Consejo Superior de Investigaciones Científicas.

European Commission. (1999). *Sixth Periodic Report on the Social and Economic Situation and Development of Regions in the European Union.* European Communities.

European Commission. (2003). *A Study on the Factors of Regional Competitiveness.* A draft final report for The European Commission Directorate-General Regional Policy. Bruselas: Cambridge Econometrics, Ecorys-Nei, University of Cambridge.

Gardiner, B., Martin, R., & Tyler, P. (2004) Competitiveness, productivity and economic growth across the European regions. *Regional Studies, 38*(9), 1045–1067.

Goerlich, F. J. (2001). On factor decomposition of cross-country income inequality: Some extensions and qualifications. *Economics Letters, 70*, 303–309.

Gumbau, M., & Maudos, J. (2006). Technological activity and productivity in the Spanish regions. *The Annals of Regional Science, 40*(1), 55–80.

Herrero, C., & Soler, A. (2005). *Renda i desenvolupament humà.* Informe econòmico i social de les Illes Balears, 37. Caixa de Balears.

Herrero, C., Soler, A., & Villar, A. (2004). *Capital humano y desarrollo humano en España, sus Comunidades Autónomas y Provincias 1980-2000.* Madrid: Fundación Bancaja.

Kitson, M., Martin, R., & Tyler, P. (2004). Regional competitiveness: An elusive yet key concept? *Regional Studies, 38*(9), 991–999.

Krugman, P. (1994). Competitiveness: a dangerous obsession. *Foreign Affairs, 73*(2), 28–44.

Krugman, P. (2003). *Growth on the Periphery: Second Wind for Industrial Regions? The Allander Series.* Scotland: Fraser Allander Institute.

Mas, M., & Quesada, J. (2005). *ICT and Economic Growth. A quantification of productivity growth in Spain.* OECD Statistics Working Papers, Statistics Directorate, STD/DOC(2005)4. Paris: OECD.

Pérez, F. (Director) (2006). *La medición del capital social: Una aproximación económica. Actualización y mejoras en la base de datos.* Bilbao: Fundación BBVA.

Pérez, F. (Director) (2005). La medición del capital social: Una aproximación económica. Bilbao: Fundación BBVA.

Pérez, F., & Serrano, L. (1998). *Capital humano, Crecimiento económico y desarrollo regional en España (1964 – 1997).* Madrid: Fundación Bancaja.

Porter, M. A. (1990). *The Competitive Advantage of Nations.* Mankato: Free.

Serrano, L. (2002). Salarios regionales y dotaciones de capital humano. *Revista de Economía Aplicada, 10*(28), 23–38.

Serrano, L., & Pastor, J. M. (2002). El valor económico del capital humano en España. In *Capital humano y actividad económica.* Madrid: Fundación Bancaja.

Chapter 13
Regional Growth and Regional Policies: Lessons from the Spanish Experience

Juan R. Cuadrado-Roura

Regional studies and research have a long record in Spain, which in the last three decades has been significantly enriched thanks to the contributions made by researchers from different fields, particularly by economists.[1] The main result is that a large base of analytical works have been produced, carried out using rigorous approaches and methods, and which have shed new light on many of the country's regional problems and their future prospects.

Within this framework, however, it seems necessary to make a systematic study of the regional policies applied in Spain; supplemented by further works which assessed both their achievements and their limitations. This is precisely what gave rise to the design of this volume and the selection of the works which make it up. Of course, the book does not cover all issues which might be considered, but the contributions included analyze a set of issues which provides a wide and up-to-date view of the Spanish case.

The starting point has been a review of the regional policies applied in Spain since the middle of the 1960s up to the present, with some previous issues which we thought should be known. Then, an assessment is made of factors which explain regional growth, the progress made towards reaching convergence, both with the EU and within Spain, the impact of the investments in infrastructures and human capital at regional level, the behavior of productivity and the analysis of the position of regional competitiveness.

The aim of this final chapter is very clear. It would not be prudent to establish "conclusions", since in Social Sciences these tend to be quite debatable, and generally, they are also rather vulnerable in the course of time. Besides, each of

---

J.R. Cuadrado-Roura
Universidad de Alcalá, Departamento de Economía Aplicada, Pl. Victoria, 2, 28802 - Alcalá de Henares, Madrid, España
e-mail: jr.cuadrado@uah.es

[1] An analysis of the progression of the studies about Regional Economy in Spain can be found in Cuadrado-Roura (2002).

the chapters already provides its own conclusions. However, what does seem interesting is the possibility of extracting some "lessons" from the experience studied, as well as some of the findings and suggestions provided by the studies carried out. Thus, the main objective of this chapter is "to learn" both the positive and the negative lessons that the Spanish case provides, which perhaps might be useful for studying other cases in different countries.

The organization of this chapter does not follow in a correlative way the order of the 12 previous chapters. On the contrary, I am going to adopt a structure which will cover in a more interrelated way the issues dealt and the main lessons which, in my opinion, can be drawn. Obviously, a number of questions which not necessarily have always a clear answer will arise, and which as a result, we will be forced to leave unanswered for future research works. Taking into account all these caveats, the sections which make up the chapter are the following. In the first section, a review is made of the regional policies in the country with the purpose of drawing some lessons or guidelines of a more general nature. Section 13.2 is focused on the lessons that can be drawn from the factors of regional growth and productivity, on the basis of the Spanish case. Section 13.3 is focused on whether convergence has been achieved or not, both with the EU and within the country, including a very interesting foray into intraregional income disparities. The role played by the infrastructures and their contribution to the achievement of a new regional balance, as well as the spillover effects, will be dealt with in Sect. 13.4, while the following section draws some lessons from the efforts, progress and resistances met in the improvement of human capital. Finally, Sect. 13.6 highlights some features and results from the analysis of the competitiveness at regional level, and the chapter closes with a few comments on the new scenario, which the current crisis is provoking and its potential implications.

13.1 About the Regional Policies Applied: From Diversity and Variability to a More Clear Ranking of Objectives, Tools and Policies

As pointed out in Chap. 1, Spain constitutes a very interesting case-study of regional problems, in general, and regional development policies, in particular. Not only from the point of view of the economy, of course, but also from a political, social and institutional point of view.

Spain's History, as that of other European States, is a complex one. For more than five centuries, it has been possible to distinguish a dialectic that confronts, almost on a permanent basis, the *centralist* (or centralizing) ideas with those in favor of a high degree of devolution, or *autonomy*, which some historic regions have demanded. Of course, the debates raised by this question have also to do with the evolution of national economy and with regional disparities which resulted from Spain's economic development. In the first chapter, the most significant features which Spanish History offers on these problems have been briefly outlined.

The goal sought was just to help *to understand why* in the twentieth century were once again raised a number of economic, political and institutional problems, and how they were dealt with in the early 1960s, the starting point for the application of the regional policies as they are actually understood.

The above does not imply that before that dates a number of programs and projects whose features might very well be identified with what nowadays is understood as "regional policies" and of "territory organizing" had already been put forward. As a way of example, suffice to mention the process for colonizing Sierra Morena and other areas in Andalusia during the second half of the eighteenth century, the creation of state enterprises for promoting the production of a number of manufactured goods, and how their location was chosen, or the set up of the hydrographical confederations, during the 1920s, which have been seen as pioneering projects for territorial organization due to their comprehensive development of a number of Spanish river valleys. In this sense, during the rule of General Primo de Rivera (1923–1930), as well as during the Second Republic (1931–1939), and the first phase of Franco's regime (1939–1959/60), there are too a number of actions, which had an impact on the territory, although they cannot be included under the heading of properly said "regional policies." Strictly speaking these correspond to the policies applied during the period object of our in-depth analysis: 1960–2008.

13.1.1 A Regional Policy "from the Center": 1964–1975

During the 1950s, a number of Western European countries had already carried out actions whose purpose was to correct the regional imbalances within the country (Italy), or the organization of its territory (France), besides the long tradition regarding local development which existed in other countries (i.e., the United Kingdom). Besides, the literature about the relationships between the market and regional imbalances (from Myrdal and Hirschman up to the first Neoliberalism followers) supplied arguments favoring the awareness that every development process should include actions oriented at extending its benefits to the least developed regions in each country.

In the Spanish case, the introduction of an indicative economic planning system based on the French model was the opportunity to introduce also this idea, although with its own features. The three Development Plans (which covered the period from 1964 to 1975) included diagnostics, objectives, and chapters specifically designed for the criteria and actions which the State intended to promote under the heading of "regional development policy."

Figure 13.1 seeks to summarize how these policies were set out. As happens with any outline or diagram, it is not easy to include in it all features and changes of the regional policy followed during the period 1964–1975. However, this figure offers an indicative synthesis of the objectives, strategies, and main tools used, which allows us to comment its most significant features.

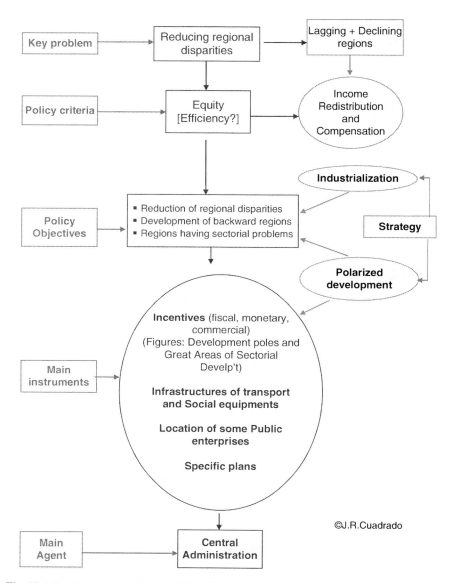

Fig. 13.1 Spanish Regional Policy, 1964–1975: A synthesis

The first question to be highlighted is that during all this period the leading role in regional policy always corresponded, as the main agent and practically the only one, to the *Central Administration*. The "regions" were not recognized by then as such, and it was the Central Government, in keeping with that seen in dictatorial regimes, which took decisions and ruled from the "Center" a country made up by provinces, at whose head was a Governor appointed by the Central Government.

However, the main characteristics of the regional policies applied during this period were the following: (1) the clear priority given to *"industrializing"* the least developed regions as the way for their development and trying to *reindustrializing* those regions with specific sectorial problems; (2) this did not prevent that some attention was also paid to develop the tourism potential, and to some agrarian areas in the country; (3) the key role played by the *polos de desarrollo* (development poles) as an instrumental tool based, in the end, in the grant of incentives (latter extended to *Grandes Áreas*, i.e., extended areas to be industrialized) for attracting enterprises to them, especially manufacturing ones; (4) the preference given to *sectorial* criteria at national level, above those properly regional ones; (5) the location of some state-owned enterprises (SOEs) in backward or problematic areas, although without a dominant criterion and only in specific cases; and (6) the so-called "special plans" were relegated to a secondary position; these were started for some agrarian areas (for instance, for Tierra de Campos), and there was almost no continuity for the old "plans," which already existed for the provinces of Badajoz and Jaén.

From the analysis of the policies really implemented between 1964 and 1975 (see Chap. 2), some *interesting lessons can be drawn.*

The first is that the "regional policy" of this long period was only, and to a large extent, a supplementary item of the general economic development policy which the government wanted to carry out. In a way, it was even an "embellishment," although this term can seem a bit exaggerated, since the actions carried out meant the use of rather important financial and human resources.

The second is that, contrary to that stipulated by official rules, the policies applied *were not continued*, and in quite a few cases, they were started in a *rather uncoordinated* way, if not with a significant improvisation due to political reasons. As an example of the latter, we can mention some of the "poles" chosen for purely political (Grenade, Córdoba, Villagarcía de Arosa), or those which were officially started including incentives for the companies which were to locate there without having solved before the communications, infrastructure, etc. problems, or doing it with long delays (Valladolid, Logroño, Oviedo...). As a result, in several cases, the success of some decisions and projects was very limited or nonexistent, while in others, it was necessary to extend the advantages and aids for some of the "development poles," as it was not possible to achieve effective results in the short-term. Regional development policies must be always for the long-term, and *cannot be subject to decisions basically based on political advantages.*

Finally, a *further lesson,* but a very important one and related to some extent with the previous one. Although the responsibility for regional policy fell on the *Comisaría del Plan,* which was attached to the President's Office, this department did not really enjoy enough authority and coordination with other Ministries, which continued carrying out their own plans (that was the case of the Departments of Public Works, Agriculture and Interior, for instance).

Does the above mean that regional policy during the period 1964–1975 did not reach any result? Obviously, no. A number of the "development poles" became significant industrial centers (Zaragoza, Huelva, Burgos, Vigo), although in varying degrees. Equally, some of the actions for the development of tourist and rural areas achieved very acceptable results. However, the strong expansion recorded by the Spanish economy since 1962 (with an average growth of the GDP of more than 5% in real terms at the end of the period mentioned) generated wealth, jobs, and a significant growth of the production activity. This helped to reinforce the migratory processes from the most backward regions to the most dynamic ones, which resulted, together with the economic growth itself, in a convergence process of the income interregional differences. Available estimates ascribe to this demographic process over 50% of the reduction in the interregional imbalances in income per head which took place during this period. But, what all this hided was a larger concentration in production, employment, and population in a few of the country's areas: Madrid, the Basque Country, Catalonia and, to a lesser extent, the Valencian Community.

13.1.2 Regional Policy Since 1977: A Turning Point Towards a New Way of Doing Regional Policy

Franco's death (1975) and the strong impact of the international economic crisis on Spain meant a clear break in the application of regional policies in the country. In theory, some of the projects and actions started in the previous period stayed alive. But in practice, the economic policy of the first democratic governments (since 1977 to the second half of the eighties) had to face, above all, the serious macroeconomic imbalances which affected the country (inflation, external deficit, high unemployment, public deficit, etc.), and the need of carrying out a strong and long delayed industrial reorganization, which affected a large number of basic industries (iron and steel, shipbuilding, chemistry, etc.) as well as some other manufacturing activities (textile, wood, metallic manufactures, etc.).

The economic crisis entailed two kinds of consequences at the regional level. First, some of the regions which had up to then been regarded as "wealthy" or dynamic (the Basque Country, Madrid, Catalonia...) became *problematic regions*,[2] sharing the need of receiving the potential support with the least developed, which had been the only beneficiaries of aids in the past. This support had a more *sectorial* profile (aids to the industries and enterprises in crisis) *than regional*. The second consequence of the crisis was that some of the factories which had been located in the least industrialized regions during the Development Plans, *were also in crisis* and suffered the effects of the need to be reorganized or closed, dashing the expectations which they had generated as engines for the local and regional development. What happened in the area of Campo de Gibraltar, in Sagunto (Valencia), or in Asturias, constitute good examples of this.

The period during which regional development policies were paralyzed in practice began to change in a significant way since 1986, when Spain became a full member of

---

[2] See: Cuadrado-Roura (1988), Alcaide et al. (1990), and Cuadrado-Roura (1991).

the European Union. This made possible two very important changes: on the one hand, Spain started to receive funds from the European Community earmarked for regional development; and, on the other hand, an important change in the way actions were implemented at regional level.

In fact, since its accession to the Community, Spain gained access to the European Structural Funds, although these were not yet very large. But, just 2 years later, the EU agreed to give an important boost to regional policy, as part of the agreements for promoting the Single Act as well as a consequence of the applications of the solidarity principle. The above meant the large *quantitative* and *qualitative* jump which took place in 1988, when it was decided to increase twofold the assets earmarked to the *Structural Funds* and promote the cohesion policies. Later, in Maastricht (1992), with the start of the process towards the European Monetary Union and the set up of the Euro, Spain could benefit besides from the new *Cohesion Fund,* which meant adding new financial resources for the country's development.

Thus began a long period during which Spain, with the help of the EU Structural Funds, started a *"new" regional policy*, which was completely in line with the European guidelines. In total, between 1989 and 2006, it is estimated that Spain received funds amounting to €105,495 million (as of 2000 prices). It is necessary to clarify that, in terms of aid per head, Spain received clearly less aid than Ireland, Portugal, or Greece and, on the other hand, the country have also contributed financially to the EU in keeping with established budgetary criteria. Actually, in 2006, the net financial balance of Spain with the EU amounted to just €2,359 million, and in 2007, to €2,168 million, according to the official estimations.

Spain's adaptation to the guidelines of the EU regional policy, and to the administrative system set up for having access to the structural funds' resources was very fast and efficient. The same happened when later some changes were introduced in that policy regarding its application. This is why it is possible to say that the regional policy applied in Spain since its accession to the EU experienced a very important turn. A turn which can be described with the following five points:

1. To have access to *large further resources* from Brussels and the capacity of the Spanish Administration (Central, regional and local) to provide its share of the funds required to cofinancing the programs and projects.
2. To apply a regional policy with *medium- and long-term objectives*, subject to the programming periods of the EU and thus, out of reach of the arbitrary behavior of the past as a result of the internal political changes, or the arbitrary adoption of new criteria.
3. *Regional policy* has been applied *"with" the regions as joint actors*. The fact that the Constitution of 1978 in Spain gave place to the creation of autonomous regions granted to these a clear role in the definition of their own development programs and, also in part, in those at national level.
4. To force the Spanish Administration (Central, regional and/or local) to adopt a *much clearer "discipline" in the management of the assets*, the execution of the projects, and in the assessment of their results.

5. Finally, the Spanish regional policy has had to attend the basic principles and criteria approved by the EU. That is, the well-known principles of *concentration, programming, joint participation, and additionality*.

To sum up, the regional policy implemented in Spain during the last 20 years has shown rather different features than those described for 1964–1975. Figure 13.2 seeks to synthesize the objectives, the strategy, and the main tools used, for the period 2000–2006, although they were similar to those for the programming period 1994–1999.

The *lessons from the experience*, which can be drawn from the above can be summarily described in the following points:

(1) EU contributions to Spain through the structural funds, together with the joint financing which the Spanish Administration (Central, autonomous regions and local entities) was required to provide *made possible to carry out quite large investments and activities*. It can be said that Spain took advantage of its opportunity

(2) In the distribution of the resources between 1989 and 2006, Spain – contrary to other EU countries – gave a clear preference to investments in *Infrastructures* (46%) and *Social Facilities* (24.7%), which together represent 70% of the total. But, attention has also been paid to the direct incentives and support to *productive activity* (9.6%) and those for *economic environment* (19.4%, including actions for entrepreneurial promotion and for unemployed training, as well as those activities carried out within the framework of the Community's special programs, such as Interreg, Urban, Leader and others); other activities absorbed the rest (0.3%)

(3) The results which have been obtained from the implementation of a regional policy linked to the EU can be assessed in two ways: the *quantitative* criteria and the *qualitative* criteria. According to the *quantitative view*, during the period 1989–2006, the structural and cohesion funds contributed to *the capitalization of the Spanish economy and that the income per head grew at least on average 0.4 points more than it would have done without those resources*. From a dynamic point of view, the *convergence towards the European average* would have progressed much more slowly without the Community funds. The simulations made point to the fact that the difference in *relative income* (PPP adjusted, EU-15=100) in those scenarios with aid and without aid amount to 1.33, 4.01 and 5.76% points for the periods 1989–1993, 1994–1999 and 2000–2006, respectively. The above means that real convergence has progressed in 2.44% points between the first and the second period, and in 8.98% points between the first and the third

(4) However, as it will be later pointed out, *the progresses made in terms of convergence* by the regions towards the EU have not been uniform, although all of them have progressed. This last fact had the consequence that some autonomous regions stopped being eligible for the maximum aids for convergence ("Objective 1" regions), as their income per head surpassed the threshold of 75% of the European average stipulated, even after taking into account the so-

13 Regional Growth and Regional Policies: Lessons from the Spanish Experience

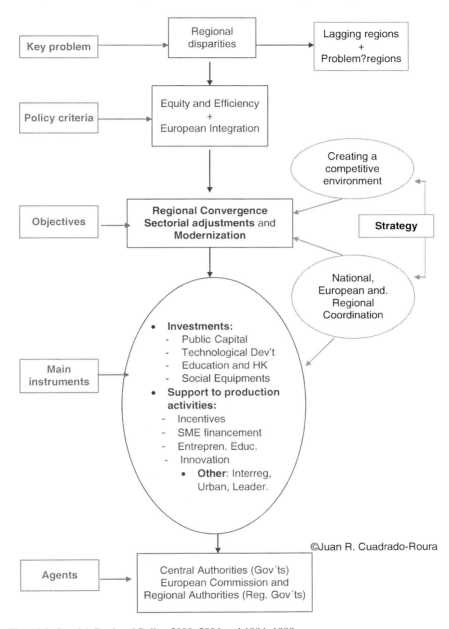

Fig. 13.2 Spanish Regional Policy 2000–2006 and 1994–1999

called "statistical effect" resulting from the extension of the EU to 27 Member States

(5) Nor the convergence among the regions within Spain has progressed at the same pace, as we shall also see. Intraregional differences in terms of income per capita continue to be remarkable. But it must be taking into account that in the process, which has resulted in the reduction of intraregional and interregional imbalances in welfare in Spain have also played a role: the "Fondo de Compensación Interterritorial" (the Interregional Compensation Fund set up in the Constitution) and the fact that Spanish Social Security System pools all its resources together, as well as the taxation and expenses and public investment system, which is not linked to the Community regional policy

(6) From the point of view of the *qualitative advantages*, it is possible to draw *lessons from the Spanish experience*, some of which have already been mentioned, thanks to the application of a regional policy linked to the EU criteria and norms:

   (a) The first is that Spain was able to start having, again, a regional development policy, which during the period 1975–1985 had virtually disappeared

   (b) Second, the new regional policy 1989–2006, as is also happening during the programming period 2007–2013, has had to adjust to *more sensible criteria* than those in the past regarding the medium and long-term programs, which had to be submitted both for the "Objective 1" and "Objective 2" regions and for the remaining projects financed with structural funds

   (c) Third, a higher level of *financial discipline and control* has been introduced, as the Spanish authorities must submit the actions with a financing framework programmed by years and with commitments made by all and each of those involved, and

   (d) Finally, the *philosophy of policy "evaluation"* (ex ante, on going and ex post) has been progressively introduced within the Spanish Administration, something which did not appear in its rule-book in the past

13.2 The Factors of Regional Growth and of Productivity: Some Lessons to be Drawn from the Spanish Experience

The preoccupation about regional growth and the analysis of factors which contributed to it and to promote the convergence processes have been issues of particular interest for regional economists, especially since the 1990s. A number of works included in this volume make reference to this issue and allow to make some reflections and to draw some interesting lessons.

If we exclude the brief downfall in 1993–1994, the Spanish economy has recorded during the last 20 years a sustained economic growth process, which has been brusquely interrupted by the crisis that started in the middle of 2007. This growth (an average rate of 2.7% in real terms between 1990 and 1998, and of 3.7% in 1999–2007) has taken place together with an intense growth in employment, with an increase in the employment level (from 58.5% in 1989 to 65.6% in 2007), increase of the participation level (from 58.2% to 71.6%, respectively in the years mentioned above), unemployment reduction (from 17.3% to 8.3%), a large inflow of foreign immigrants (which is estimated at about 5 million persons), and a high effort in capital accumulation.

13.2.1 The Evolution of Productivity and the Factors of Regional Growth

The panorama which we have just described has always presented a *very weak point*: Spanish labor productivity has recorded since the middle of the 1990s, very low growth rates, clearly below those of the US and of a number of European countries, but also below the EU average.[3] The causes of this situation are varied, but they are due, first, to the country's specialization in very labor-intensive activities and with a low added value and, second, to the inefficient use of the main production factors, capital, labor, and technology, all of which has been hidden by an expansive situation in which were present some speculative bubbles, as the real estate and the financial.

In terms of capital accumulation, the investment effort (ratio between the gross capital formation and the GDP) has been one of the highest in the EU. A very significant part of that effort was absorbed by the construction industry (especially the residential), but, in real terms, the part of that accumulation allocated to productive capital (including facilities, machinery, transport material and ICT) was also rather significant. Although with cyclical oscillations, the average growth rate of the nonresidential working capital for the period 1985–2007 reached 5.44%. The net nonresidential capital stock at the closing of 2007 has been estimated to be made up by 20.34% in infrastructures, 4.31% in ICT (a really low figure), and 75.35% of capital which does not correspond to either infrastructures or to ICT.

When we estimate the sources of labor productivity increase in the private sector (which has been estimated in 1.87% between 1985 and 1995, but which is negative between 1995 and 2000, and barely positive between 2000 and 2006, with an average of 0.8% for the whole period), it is possible to conclude that the contribution of the infrastructures was always low, and that the qualification of the workforce has been the most positive components (although lower than in other countries), together with the ICT capital and the capital which does not correspond to either infrastructures or to ICT (see Chap. 6). What is really worrying is that the total

---
[3] See: Maroto and Cuadrado-Roura (2006). See Chap. 6 in this book.

factors productivity has recorded practically always negative values, which means that the Spanish productive system suffers from problems in terms of technology, organization, innovation, as well as from other components of the residue.

From the regional point of view, productivity evolution shows important differences. Several backward regions show a very low labor productivity (Extremadura, Castile-La Mancha and Murcia); other hover around Spain's average (Andalusia, the Canary Islands, Valencia Comm. and the Balearic Islands.), and two regions reach the highest productivity level: the Basque Country and the region of Madrid. Although from a dynamic point of view, some regions recorded rates of change of the productivity clearly above Spain's average between 1985 and 2007 (Galicia, Extremadura, Castile-León and Castile-La Mancha); the main cause of this was the low growth of their populations and not a high growth of their output. On the contrary, in some tourist regions (Valencian Community, Andalusia and Murcia), the productivity recorded an average change in the rate below 0.5%, which was even of zero (the Canary Islands) or negative (the Balearic Islands).

The question, and in part the *lesson which can be drawn from these data*, is, on the one hand, *the Spanish economy has hidden a very low productivity* (negative in TFP), which has been compatible with a high growth of GDP and employment and, second, that this general trend shows a *high dispersion by autonomous regions*. Between 2000 and 2005, no Spanish region reached the average increase rate of the productivity of the EU-15 (which actually was rather below half that of the US). On the other hand, *regional differences* are worrying in the case of the ICT-producing industries, in Manufacturing (excluding electricity) and in practically all services (although there are some branches, such as Finance and Business Services, which are spared). And which is very clear is that the specialization of each region in different economic branches determines to a large extent its results in terms of labor productivity, and that the future improvements must come from efforts to promote changes within each industry, that is, in the internal composition of the main production branches, reinforcing those which can really reach higher productivity levels. The *conclusion* is that regional policy must give priority to these *productivity and efficiency problems. The regions and their enterprises must be competitive*, and this must be the priority objective of any regional policy.

13.2.2 The Exhaustion of the Structural Changes as the Source for Improving Productivity and Convergence

The increases in productivity of countries and regions depend, as it is known, on many factors. In many economies, one of them has resulted without any doubt from the evolution of the productive structure. That is, from the transfer of the labor factor from those industries whose productivity was lower towards those in which it was or is higher. Besides, it must be taken into account that the evolution of regional productivity is related with the possibility of achieving a higher convergence in terms of GDP per head.

From the analysis made on the Spanish case, it is possible to draw also a *lesson from experience* which seems particularly interesting, since it was obtained from a very long period: 1955–2006.

The results are clear: between 1955 and 1978/79, there was a rather fast regional convergence process, in which the differences in income per head among the autonomous regions significantly decreased. As it has already been mentioned, the migratory movements which took place explain at least 50% of this convergence. But a factor which undoubtedly contributed to reducing regional disparities was the evolution of aggregated productivity by regions, which records also a very important convergence process during that period. However, this convergence trend in income per head was brusquely interrupted since 1979/80, in large part, due to the impact of the international economic crisis, and what can be seen later is that the convergence practically stopped since then, although with some fluctuations (see Fig. 7.13) and a short trend to converge again between 2000 and 2006.

The breakdown of the income per head in its components of productivity and employment per head shows that although labor productivity keeps converging until 1996, when it practically stops, there is a movement in the opposite direction regarding the employment per capita, which records a regional divergence since 1990. The latter has a clear influence on the evolution of regional convergence in income per head, since the progresses recorded in productivity are offset by the divergence in terms of employment per capita.

These facts demand an explanation of the reasons which are behind the coming to a halt of the convergence of regional productivities. The analysis of the evolution of regional productive structures provides part of the answer to this fact. The gradual coming to a halt of the convergence in productivity by regions which took place in the last few years is clearly related with the *almost total exhaustion* of the process by which the productive regional structures by industries became more similar.

The *main lesson which can be drawn* is that it cannot be expected any additional regional convergence through this way in the future, both in productivity and in income per head. And, at the same time, the regional divergence in employment per capita, which has been taking place, contributed, and will continue doing so, to slowing down regional convergence in income per head in Spain.

On the other hand, an *additional lesson which can be drawn from all the above* is that the regions of an already mature country, as is Spain, where the large structural changes are almost exhausted, must make a larger effort in improving their labor productivity and the TFP, which are key factors for progressing towards income convergence. Of course, the achievement of those improvements is related with their sectorial specialization, but also with increases in productivity within each industry, with the use of skilled labor factor, with innovation, the use of more advanced technologies, and the correction of those factors that check the improvement of their TFP, which in Spain has shown in the last years negative values in almost all the autonomous regions.

13.3 There is Convergence, but Towards Where? And, How?

The analysis of the economic convergence of the Spanish regions has been object of a rather large literature. The contributions selected in this volume also study this issue and provide new results and reflections.

13.3.1 A Clear Economic and Regional Convergence Towards the European Community

As has already been mentioned, the average growth rate of the Spanish economy has been rather high. For the whole 1986–2007 period, it is estimated that it reached an average of 3.25% per year. However, there were variations through time: There was an expansionary phase, 1986–1990/91; a phase with a somewhat lower growth (1990–1998: 2.7%), influenced by the 1993 crisis; and a new phase with a higher growth (1999–2007: 3.7%). These rates have been clearly above those of the Euro area (specifically, 1.5% points during the period 1999–2007).[4] The above, together with a relatively modest population growth (below 1% on a yearly average during 1986–2006), explains the important convergence process of Spain and its regions to the European average in terms of GDP per head.

In 1988, Spain had a GDP per head index of 74 compared to the EU-15 GDP p.c. average (expressed in PPP terms), while 10 years later, that index was of 81, and in 2005, the Spanish average already overcame the European average, with a value of 103, although this result is not only due to the differential growth of the Spanish economy, but also to the accession of the new State Members from Central and Eastern Europe into the EU. Really, although the data differ according to the source used, in 2007, Spain recorded a GDP per head index of 95 in comparison with the EU-15.

The important fact to highlight is that during this period *all the Spanish autonomous regions recorded progress towards the European average*, although at different paces. Thus, a clear convergence process of Spanish regions towards the EU has taken place. Currently, the average European (EU-27) income per head is exceeded by Madrid (value 133), Navarre, the Basque Country, the Balearic Islands, Catalonia, La Rioja, and Aragón. On its part, Cantabria reaches the value 100, while regions, such as Extremadura (index 70), Andalusia (80), and Galicia (82) show still lower values, although they have progressed, both as a result of their own growth and because of the "statistical effect" resulted from the European Union expansion to the East.

---

[4] Figures estimated by the Bank of Spain.

13.3.2 But ... Very Limited Regional Convergence "Within" the Country and With Factors That Slowdown the Process

From the internal point of view, disparities among the Spanish regions show a considerable resistance to change. The GDP per head is, obviously, related to population changes. That is why some autonomous regions, which have had a small increase in their number of inhabitants have progressed faster (for instance, the Basque Country) than others which received important immigration flows (for instance, the Balearic Islands). A final result of this has been that some regions have lost the preminent position which they had in 2000.

But there are other issues, which must be borne equally in mind, as the fact that the good results of the most developed regions (La Rioja, the Basque Country, Navarre, Catalonia, and Madrid) has meant that the distances between the most and least developed regions stayed the same at first, and that they tend to be larger since 1996. Thus, in 2007, income per head in the wealthiest regions was almost 60% higher than that in the regions with the lowest levels. Something which practically has not changed in 20 years is a fact which does not constitute good news for regional policy. Actually, the estimate of the σ-convergence only shows a very small improvement during the last 5 years of the period 1986–2007.

The *conclusion,* that perhaps no *lesson, which can be drawn from the above* is that the convergence process of all Spanish regions towards the European average did not mean also the internal convergence. Notwithstanding the above, a more positive result is that if regions are grouped together according to their income, in 2007, the dispersion *within* each of those groups (that is, intragroup) is very small. The above implies that the dispersion among the groups is what explains most of the existing deviation. Figure 5.4 showed the regions with a convergent behavior towards 100 for Spain. Regions which have most converged have been those starting with high GDP p.c. values (the Balearic Islands and La Rioja) and three which had values below the average (Extremadura, Galicia, and Cantabria). A slightly divergent path due to their relative improvement has been followed by Aragón, Madrid, Catalonia, Navarre, the Basque Country, among the wealthy, and by Murcia and the Valencian Community among those which appeared below the Spanish average.

As was pointed out before, the explanation of these changes is linked to the improvements in productivity at regional level (which have been positive, although low) in opposition to the bad behavior of employment. *A lesson which had already been highlighted in the above paragraph.* Since 1986, the most advanced regions have leaded, in general, the growth process (in production and in unemployment reduction), which is behind the halt of the reduction in the imbalances among the regions.

At the same time, this process has produced *a higher concentration of the population, the production, and the employment at regional level.* A concentration which is particularly remarkable in output terms: four regions (Cataluña, Madrid, Andalusia, and the Valencian Community) were, and still are, those with the highest weight in the generation of total product (60% of total Spanish GDP in 2006), and each of them separately increased its relative share during the last 20 years. Employment concentration has also increased, always in favor of some of the wealthiest and largest regions.[5]

From the analysis of the β-convergence, it is possible to see the existence of obstacles (conditions or factors impending their progress) which are not only related to the production structure of each region, but also to their deficiencies in infrastructures, human capital, availability of some resources, and others (see Chap. 4). The above opens a number of possibilities for economic policy actions, which must tend to eliminate those obstacles or limitations, something which is not shown by the nonconditioned economic convergence. This is, without a doubt, *a lesson which can also be drawn from the case studied*, but which surely can be generalized to many countries.

13.3.3 Progresses and Inequalities in Terms of Well-Being and Intraregional Income Distribution

The improvements in terms of income per head cannot be limited to examine whether there has been or not a convergence among the regions of a country, or whether among those regions and the set of countries to which that country belongs (in our case, the EU). It is important to analyze also whether there have been positive changes in terms of social well-being and an improvement in the *income distribution within each region*. The above can show a different view from that based on the conventional analysis of regional convergence, and that is why Chap. 11 supplies the results of a research using different data and methods.

The first of the results obtained is that in Spain, with data for 2006 and applying the Gini coefficient, it is necessary to make reference to two large categories of autonomous regions: those which show internal inequalities relatively less important, and those in which internal inequalities are high. Although there are significant differences in their respective situations, in the first category are Navarre, the Basque Country, La Rioja, Aragón, and the Balearic Islands. All of them show inequality levels significantly lower than Spain as a whole. In the second category are included Andalusia, the Canary Islands, Murcia, and Madrid, where the internal distributive process has entailed inequality levels, which are above the national average. From these results, it can be inferred that *there is no close link between the average income level and the degree in which it is distributed*. Actually, in both categories, it is possible to find regions whose average income per head is high and others which are clearly below the Spanish average. However, using other indicators,[6] it is possible to see that regions which showed the highest inequality some years ago continue doing so now, and that actually, the ranking is rather stable.

---

[5] The immigration arrived in the last 8 years (which represents almost 10% of the Spanish population, when in 2002 it represented less than 5%) is at the base of the explanation of this fact.
[6] See Chap. 11.

The evolution of the relative differences with respect to the Spanish average for different years (1973, 1980, 1990, 2000, and 2006) shows that there are a number of regions which have historically maintained more equitable distributive processes. This is the case of La Rioja, the Basque Country (with the exception of the 1980s, when the industrial reorganization took place), Asturias (which is heavily dependent on Social Security transfers), Navarre, the Balearic Islands, and the Valencia Community. On the contrary, in other regions *inequality seems to be more deeply entrenched* (the Canary Islands), or *it can even be surprising* (Madrid), although the atypical employment, the changes in the household composition, the impact of immigration, and tensions resulting from the social and economic changes can explain it.

The analysis in terms of social well-being by regions is complex, but it can be approached through the construction of some types of indexes. Again, when doing so, several regions having an average income above the Spanish average show inequality indexes which are below that average (Navarre, the Basque Country, Asturias, the Balearic Islands, Catalonia, and the Valencia Community), while Madrid, with the highest average income, records a higher inequality than the Spanish average. Heterogeneity is higher in the lowest income regions, regardless that their inequality positions are below or above Spain as a whole.

From these approximations, and from others which are not commented here, it is possible to draw *a lesson from the Spanish experience*: income differences between regions and their trend towards converging or not, *do not take into account some questions which are, and should be, very significant*. Regional inequalities do not say anything, or very little, about the differences within the regions and their evolution through time. There is no direct relationship between the average income level of a region and its evolution through time or about how/where such region is placed in terms of inequality and well-being when comparing it with the Spanish average. Both in this area and in that regarding the well-being levels, Spain shows a rather high degree of permanence of many regions in the same relative positions. This leads to the need of having available mechanisms for correcting inequalities within the regions themselves, as it is necessary to continue reinforcing the tools for correcting the differences among regions at national level.

13.4 The Investment in Infrastructures, Its Contribution to Convergence and the Spillover Effects

Spain has carried out, during the last few decades, a significant investment effort in infrastructures (for transportation, water works, urban facilities, and services) by the different levels of Spanish Administration, including also those made by some large state-owned enterprises, by State agencies, and by the enterprises which have a State license for operating turnpike highways. Those investments were already very important during the period of the Development Plans (1964–1975), declined as a result of the oil crisis (since 1975–1976 until practically 1987), and have increased again since then. In part, thanks to the support of the EU structural funds to which Spain has been able to draw, although the country always contributed its share to the joint financing. On average (1964–2004), the investment in infrastructures meant 2.35% of the Spanish gross value added (GVA) and 12.7% of the total nonresidential investment. Has this contributed to a reduction in regional imbalances? Have been spillovers towards other regions?

13.4.1 The Investment in Infrastructures and Its Contribution to the Reduction in Regional Imbalances

The total amount of the investments mentioned above has been distributed in a rather unequal way among regions. Those which were more favored have been Aragón, La Rioja, and Asturias, while the less favored were Murcia, the Balearic Islands, and Andalusia. On average, total investment has tended to be higher in the regions which were wealthier at the start, but the population growth experienced by some of them, together with the halt in their population expansion experienced by others, result in the first having lost positions in terms of infrastructure facilities per head, the opposite of that which happened in the poorer ones. As a whole, the data show that there has been a trend to make the same regional investment in infrastructures per head, although some regions, and not the most dynamic ones, recorded levels well above the average.

A really interesting aspect is that of knowing whether the investments in infrastructure have contributed to increasing GDP and employment and, in our case, which regions have benefited the most from it. From the analysis made, it is possible to draw *some lessons from the Spanish experience*:

(1) The first is that, effectively, those investments have promoted the GDP and the employment of the country as a whole, although with very large fluctuations. During the first half of the period analyzed (1965–1980 approximately), the estimated effect shows a decreasing trend, which can be attributed both to the decline of public investment and to the existence of decreasing returns (reduction in the profitability of successive investments). However, since the beginning of the 1980s, this trend begins to be reversed, especially as a result of the recovery of the investment in infrastructures, which must be linked to the priority given to them, both as part of regional policy and as the State additional investments outside it. On average, during the period analyzed (1965–2004), the investment in infrastructures contributed 0.47% points per year to the increase of national income, and 0.23% points to the increase of employment.[7] By regions, the estimated effects vary between 0.35% and 0.55% points, those of Castile and León and Canarias, respectively, differences which, at a lower level, are also reflected in employment.

---

[7] This amounts, respectively, to a 14.6% increase in total income and a 24.9% increase in employment (See Chap. 8).

(2) The *second lesson* which the experience offers regards the *redistributive impact which the public investment may have generated*. The estimates made taking into account whether there was or not population changes (see Chap. 8) show that the effect of the investment in infrastructure becomes diluted in the regions with highest income due to the population increases (both internal and through migration flows), which does not happen in the remaining regions. The result is that β-convergence in income per head, with a constant population or with a changing population (Fig. 8.9) shows the significant redistributive impact which infrastructures had since the 1970s until the middle of the 1990s, followed by a gradual reduction during the final years of the period.
(3) A *third lesson* which can be drawn from the analysis is that the *devolution process lived by Spain*, thanks to the existence of the autonomous regions coincides with the gradual adoption of a clearly redistributive model of investment in infrastructures, which has contributed to reducing the income differences among regions (or at least to limit the increase in such differences provoked by other factors). The promotion given to infrastructures since the accession to the EU provoked a further investment in the poorest regions ("Objective 1" regions in the EU regional policy), which has played a significant role in the reduction of regional differences. This redistributive bias was already clear before the Spanish accession to the EU, but it begun to be reversed in the middle of the 1990s, when EU aid was at its highest level. This would show that some change in the investment policy followed by the Spanish Administration took place, which prevails even over the markedly redistributive bias of the European aid.
(4) Finally, it must be pointed out that the assessment of the redistributive effects which appears linked to the investment in infrastructures *might have had, and probably had, a high opportunity cost* in terms of the country's aggregate growth, because the profitability of investment in infrastructures tends to be – in Spain and in almost any other country – lower in those regions with the lowest income. This leads, at the end, to the well-known and ever present dilemma between equity and efficiency.

13.4.2 The Effects of Public Capital and the Spillovers at Regional Level

The analysis of growth accounting (see Chap. 6) leads to the breakdown of the low growth of the productivity in the contribution made by the different factors, among which the infrastructures appears. As it has been pointed out, the investment in infrastructures shows an unequal distribution by regions.[8] The issue dealt with in Chap. 9 is the study of the answer given by Spanish regions to the impact which the State investment had, and the existence of spillover effects. From the analysis, as

---
[8] See also: Mas et al. (2007).

well as from other works which have been included in this volume, it is possible to draw several *interesting results or lessons*:[9]

1. It is clearly established the economic relevance which the stock of public capital has, both directly (as a result of its location in the territory) and indirectly (as a result of the spillover effects which this stock has towards economically interrelated territories). The real impact of public investment must take into account both effects.
2. The *direct effects* show a notable territorial heterogeneity. But, in the Spanish case, this does not contradict that the amount of the State capital which exists in the different regions is highly correlated with the direct impact over the private output, employment, and capital.
3. The autonomous regions with *relatively less State capital* show more sensibility of the output and employment with regard to State investment and even a higher complementarity with the stock of private capital. In the regions with a relatively higher stock of State capital, these relations take place in the opposite direction; the investments have clearly lower direct effects.
4. The *indirect or spillover effects of the infrastructures* are significant in all the autonomous regions, and are little affected by the geographical location or by the relative stock of capital which the regions might have. Those spillover effects are, in any case, a stimulus for the economies which are more directly linked among them.
5. What the analysis shows too is that *the investment in public capital is not equally efficient in all the autonomous regions*. It is more productive in those regions whose capital stock in terms of GDP, employment, and private capital is smaller. Contrary to this, when the stock of public capital is already high, the effects are smaller, which can be seen in the cases of La Rioja, Extremadura or Aragón, among others.
6. Finally, a lesson which confirms that drawn by many studies over this issue is that public investment *cannot be unrelated to economic activity*. By itself, this investment promotes the economic activity, but its best results are achieved when it effectively satisfies a high and/or growing demand, and not when this must still be generated.

13.5 The Strong Promotion to Human Capital Generation and the Historical Resistance of the Existing Differences

The changes experienced by the Spanish society during the last few decades, and especially, since the second half of the 1970s, have been important from many points of view: political, economic, coverage of social well-being, etc. and, of

---

[9]The results of the analysis coincide with many of the studies of this kind made for other cases and countries.

course, the education field. Obviously, the advances recorded in this last case have been the joint result of the decisions and efforts of the families, together with the educational extension policies followed by the different governments, both at State and regional level.

There is no doubt that the *Human capital accumulation and its growing use* constitute one of the most significant features in Spain's evolution during the last few years. This factor has become also in one of the keys of the regions' growth, and the administration has invested a large amount of funds and efforts towards its achievement, with the support also of the regional policy applied since the last 1980s.

The synthetic indicator of the average number of years studied by the population, distinguishing between the population of working age, those in the labor force, unemployed and in employment (Fig. 10.1) clearly shows that the improvements in the education of the Spaniards during the period 1977–2007 have been significant in all categories, and they have taken place practically in a constant manner. In any case, special mention must be made to the fact that the analysis shows a higher qualification of the labor force against the population of working age, a fact ratified by many studies, which show that the disposition of the persons to participate in the labor market is higher as the amount of human capital (education) increases. It is also ratified that, the more education the persons have, the higher are their opportunities of finding a job and of being in employment.

In the Spanish case, special mention must be made to the increase in the percentage of persons with tertiary education (at the end of the period mentioned it was 3.3 times higher than at the start). A very large increase was also recorded by those with nonuniversity noncompulsory education (there are 2.6 times more of them than in 1977). Illiteracy has been eradicated, with the exception of very marginal social groups.

Of course, such a positive evolution is compatible with the existence of regional differences in the stock of human capital. For Spain as a whole, the average number of years in school in the population of working age (16+ years of age) are 10.2, but Madrid (11.2), the Basque Country (11) and Navarre (10.9) record higher levels, while in Castile-La Mancha (9.4) and Extremadura (9.5 average years), respectively, occupy the lowest positions, together with the city of Ceuta (9). This situation is very much like the one which already existed in 1977, when the same regions were in the highest and lowest places, although with an average number of years in school significantly much lower and a reduction in the differences among regions.

The first lesson which can be drawn from the analysis of the Spanish case is that, *despite the fact that the efforts made and the resources used have promoted the educative level of the total population and by regions, there are still differences which already existed three decades ago*, although the variation coefficient and the relative range of variation when comparing the regional data have significantly decreased. Really, there has been a σ-convergence in human capital by regions during the period 1977–2007, although during the last few years (2003–2007), the estimate shows an upturn in regional inequality. The gradual reduction in the differences in education among the regions is mostly due to the advances recorded by those regions with the less qualified population. Thus, it can be stated that a catching-up process has been taking place by the more backward regions with respect of those wealthier and with more schooling. The latter record a somewhat slowed progress in education; this is in part due to the high level which they had already achieved, and also to the effects of the immigration flows received. Madrid constitutes a good example of this trend.

13.5.1 To What Extent the Human Capital of the Regions is Used? Where?

These two questions are related to the idea that the availability of more and better human capital *does not guarantee that this is employed at its source or that it is adequately used by the enterprises or entities in which it provides its services.* When this is the case, the human capital available cannot contribute to the production of more goods and services, nor does it improve the productivity, nor contributes to economic growth, as it should in theory. Thus, it is possible to estimate a rate of nonused, or badly used, human capital. The estimate made shows that in Spain as a whole, the rate of occupation of the human capital in 1986 was lower than in 1977, which basically was due to the unemployment rate, which the country was suffering since the start of the so-called oil crisis. This situation improved during latter years, so that in 2007, it is estimated that Spain used 62% of its potential human capital, the highest level reached up to this date.

But the analysis of the Spanish case allows drawing *an important lesson or result*. Although trends at national level are reproduced at regional level, the differences among the regions are very large. In 2007, the activity rates of human capital varied between 71.8% in the Balearic Islands to 59.2% in Asturias. The most developed regions (for instance, Catalonia, Madrid, Navarre) appear in the first places according to the activity rate of human capital. Moreover, the inequality indicators through time show that there has been a slight increase. The regions with more human capital per capita are the same which record the highest use of this human capital, while the opposite happens among those which have the least human capital. This fact is somehow contributing to generating regional inequality in income per head.

Another *lesson which can be drawn from the Spanish case* is that *the improvement of human capital can also take place with an inefficient use of it.* In the Spanish labor market, it is possible to see the "over-qualification" phenomenon (a person employed in a job which requires a lower qualification than that which that person has) and also, although to a lesser extent, the inadequacy of the training content in relation with the social needs and the demands of the production system.

The final conclusion is that the improvements in the stock of human capital and in their level of use, together with the efficiency in its use have been key factors in the growth of Spanish regions. But differences in these three fields are also significant, and one of the features which continues to be present in regional inequality.

All in all, it is not just a question of accumulating more and more human capital (something which, without any doubt, Spain needs to do), but of using a higher percentage of it and in an efficient manner, all of which must progress at the same time in order to reduce regional differences.

13.6 Is it Possible to Talk of Regional "Competitiveness"? Why is it Important?

A long time ago, the European Commission included the concept of competitiveness among the possibilities which the regions have for growing and generating employment.[10] This idea has been often repeated in many documents and reports, and it has been even included into the objectives of the EU regional policy. Actually, the EU regional and cohesion policy designed for the period 2007–2013 also makes an express reference to this concept as a priority objective, linking it to the Renewed Lisbon Strategy. To sum it up, regions must seek to improve their competitiveness, both themselves and their enterprises.

The competitiveness concept is relatively easily applied to the case of the enterprises. But to translate it from this level to the regions or countries level, constitutes a change of scale which, as is mentioned in Chap. 12, raises important analytical difficulties. Actually, there is no shortage of authors who reject that such a translation is feasible, or at least convenient.[11] However, there is a growing acceptance of the use of the competitiveness concept applied to the terms and conditions making possible that the characteristics of a specific territory can be a plus of competitiveness to the enterprises located on that territory, and making also more attractive the set up of new enterprises or the location of others from abroad. This is the reason why it seemed important to include, in a book like this, a work on the competitiveness of the Spanish regions.

For measuring the competitiveness of a region, it is possible to make use of two sets of indicators: one is referred to as "indicators of results," while the other as the "indicators of causal factors." The first seeks to show the situation of an economy in terms of competitiveness through some of the variables which can be associated to the results achieved. The most direct of all of them is the GDP, and a way for explaining the differences in GDP per capita among regions consists in the

---

[10] In its *6th Economic Report on the Social and Economic Situation and Development of the Regions in the European Union* (1999), the European Commission defined competitiveness as "the ability of companies, industries, regions, nations and supra-national regions to generate, while being exposed to international competition, relatively high income and employment levels."

[11] Krugman qualified as a dangerous obsession the tendency to adopt the criterion of competitive rivalry, which is characteristic of the enterprises, to the international trade relations field. (Krugman, 1994).

breakdown of this variable into its multiplicative factors: labor productivity, the proportion of persons in employment relative to the labor force, global activity rate, and the weight of the population of working age with regard to total population. The second set of indicators points in a quite different direction: it seeks to make an inventory of the items and factors which can positively influence on the competitiveness capacity of a territory. Thus, the starting point is the idea that there exist factors which exert an influence on the production and which are "located" on the territory, or which are relatively immobile, as happens with infrastructures, corporate culture, social capital, the stock of human capital (at least in part), and others which contribute to the creation of a "more or less favorable environment" for capital and labor performance, or for attracting them towards those territories.

The analysis made in Chap. 12 defines the methodology and indicators to be used, and estimates them for the case of the Spanish regions. The results reached are, without a doubt, of outmost interest for locating each region in a certain position in competitiveness terms and as an explanation for regional growth and for its future possibilities. From all of this, it is possible *to draw also some lessons, or perhaps better, some orientations for regional policy*. Among them, it is possible to highlight the following points:

1. The regions can develop a set of factors which *promote improvements in the enterprises' productivity and efficiency,* so that the territory offers especially favorable conditions for attracting the mobile production factors, and thus, to promote its production system.
2. Since regions do not have some of the adjustment mechanisms (exchange rate, adjustment wages/productivity, ...), *the differences of costs and productivity in absolute terms* are especially important for explaining interregional trade flows.
3. The research made in the Spanish case has opted for making competitiveness indicators based on a *macroeconomic approach*, taking labor productivity as the basic reference. The first step consisted in the breakdown of the GDP per capita into a series of multiplicative factors. Then, a large number of partial indicators were estimated in order to build four aggregated indicators: infrastructures and accessibility, human resources, technological innovation, and productive environment.
4. The regional ranking obtained from the breakdown of the GDP shows quite a few coincidences with that explained by the more localized and environmental factors. *Technological innovation and the availability of a favorable productive environment* mark more intensively the differences among those regions which appear as more competitive (Madrid, the Basque Country, Navarre and Catalonia) and those which are less competitive.
5. The characteristics of labor markets are also very influential for assessing the territorial competitiveness. In the Spanish case, the regions which appear in the best positions of the competitiveness ranking are also those which in 2007 recorded the highest activity rates and, in general, the lowest unemployment rates.

13.7 Facing a New Economic Scenario, with Many More Uncertainties than Certainties

It is not possible to close this chapter without making a reference to the serious economic crisis, which has been taking place during the last months, whose effects have extended practically allover the world. We are facing a really different scenario from the one which we had enjoyed till the second half of 2007. A scenario in which the problems of an almost strictly financial nature appear more and more intertwined with the evolution of the real economy, promoting unemployment, business closures, the halt of investments in productive capital and, in general, the generation of an economic environment of generalized uncertainty.

All this is activating again the reappearance of some criteria and ideas which seemed rather outdated, as the protectionist approaches, State interventionism and nationalizations, the search of solutions for the largest industries (the automobile industry and some basic industries). At the same time, the States are resorting more and more to indebtedness and budgetary deficits, both for trying to save the financial industry and for halting the sinking of a number of manufacturing industries. All this will entail serious adjustment problems in the near future.

From the regional view, the crisis raises, and will raise, problems which can be significant. In no country, the effects of the crisis will be uniformly spread. Besides, the general economic situation might have the result that, as it happened during the crisis of the 1970s and early 1980s, the "regional" problems be relegated to a second or third plane, since the most urgent issues are those of a macroeconomic or sectorial nature.

Possibly, the EU Regional and Cohesion Policy will not be very directly affected, as the programming was already set and was approved for the period 2007–2013. It is necessary to remember that the criteria and objectives which inspire the objectives to be reached in that phase are not incoherent, but quite the opposite, with that which seems must be done in the future, both in the EU as a whole, and at the regional and national levels.

But the crisis is going to bring quite a few problems related to the territory, which in many aspects are going to have a rather different profile in each country. In the case of Spain, the impact can be very strong. It must be borne in mind that the Spanish economy has been already in recession for the last few months (with a fall of the GDP of more than 3% points in 2009 and an unemployment rate which has already reached the 15% mark, and which might soon reach 18% or more). The effects which this and the sectorial crisis will have at national level will doubtless vary according to the region, although all regions will be affected.

It must be taken into account that, in the case of Spain, the crisis has two very clear focal points, which must be distinguished from each other: one of a domestic nature, linked to the excesses accumulated during the expansionary phase; and another external, the result of the shocks in the international finances which began in July 2007. Regarding the domestic dimension of the crisis, some facts appear as crucial factors: the easy credit due to the very favorable conditions at the time (low interest and availability of resources), which provoked very positive expectations about the future by households and enterprises. The turn experienced by the situation has provoked not only the fall of the investment decisions, but also of consumption. The result is a dramatic fall of the real estate industry and, with it, of residential construction (which for some years had been suffering from overcapacity and was the object of a large speculative bubble), and a decline in the expense in consumption by individuals and households, which affects both common consumption and that of capital goods. All this has had a negative impact on many productive activities (manufacturing and services), to insolvency situations, closures, or employment and production adjustments.

Regarding the external dimension of the crisis (which is not either entirely external, of course), linked to the financial questions, the large current-account deficit, which Spain has been experiencing during the last few years cannot any longer be financed, and the indebtedness of the domestic financial institutions with abroad is also taking its toll, forcing adjustments in the financial institutions, with serious cuts in the amounts of the loans granted and more stringent terms and conditions applied to them. To this must be added that, although the Spanish financial system seems to be in better conditions than that of other countries, the difficulties which some financial institutions are going through, as their portfolio is closely linked to the real estate and construction industries.

It would be inadequate to enter in details about the expected effects at regional level. In the case of Spain, it is clear that the convergence towards the EU is going to be halted, or that it will come into reverse for some time, that unemployment will show (as it is already doing) larger differences among regions than it did in the past, and that the demands for support are going to increase, not only from the most backward regions, but also from those which are regarded now as wealthy and more dynamic. The positive note perhaps will be that, if no new approach is adopted, the EU Regional and Cohesion Policy can operate as a fallback for absorbing the impact of the crisis in some regions. Especially in the case of those which currently are included within the "Convergence" regions (generally qualified as Objective 1 regions, in the past of the regional policy) for 2007–2013, which is the group of European regions to which most of the structural funds are earmarked for (Mancha and Garrido, 2008). But, in the Spanish case, the total amount which the structural funds will provide during the current programming period is going to be rather much lower to the amount received by the country in the past.

References

Alcaide, J., Cuadrado-Roura, J. R., & Fuentes Quintana, E. (1990). El desarrollo económico español y la España desigual de las autonomías. *Papeles de Economía Española, 45*, 2–61.

Cuadrado-Roura, J. R. (1988). Tendencias económico-regionales antes y después de la crisis. *Papeles de Economía Española, 34*, 17–61.

Cuadrado-Roura, J. R. (1991). Structural Changes in the Spanish Economy: their Regional Effects. In L. Rodwin and H. Sazanami (Eds.), *Industrial Change and Regional Economic Transformation* (pp. 168–201). London: HarperCollins Academic

Cuadrado-Roura, J. R. (2002). Incorporación y desarrollo de los temas regionales en el análisis económico. In E. Fuentes Quintana (Ed.), *Economía y Economistas españoles,* vol. 7, (pp. 747–808). Madrid: Galaxia Gutenberg.

Krugman, P. (1994). Competitiveness: a dangerous obsession. *Foreign Affairs, 73*(2), 28–44.

Mancha, T., & Garrido, R. (2008). Regional Policy in the EU: The Cohesion-Competitiveness Dilemma. In: *Regional Science Policy and Practice in Regional Science, 1,* 1:47–66.

Mancha, T., & Garrido, R. (2009). Regional Policy in the European Union. The Cohesion-competitiveness dilemma. *Regional Science, Policy and Practice, 1,* 1.

Maroto, A., & Cuadrado-Roura, J. R. (2006). *La productividad en la economía española* (350 p). Madrid: Instituto de Estudios Económicos.

Mas, M., Quesada, J., & Robredo, J. C. (2007). In E. Reig (dir.) *Competitividad, Crecimiento y Capitalización en las regiones españolas* (371 p). Madrid-Bilbao: Fund. BBVA.